DISCARD

LORENZO DA PONTE

OTHER BOOKS BY THE SAME AUTHOR

History Play

THE LIBRETTIST OF VENICE

THE REMARKABLE LIFE OF LORENZO DA PONTE

Mozart's Poet, Casanova's Friend, and
Italian Opera's Impresario in America

Rodney Bolt

BLOOMSBURY

Published by Bloomsbury Publishing, New York and London
Distributed to the trade by Holtzbrinck Publishers

All papers used by Bloomsbury Publishing are natural, recyclable products made from wood grown in well-managed forests. The manufacturing processes conform to the environmental regulations of the country of origin.

Library of Congress Cataloging-in-Publication Data

Bolt, Rodney.
The librettist of Venice : the remarkable life of Lorenzo Da Ponte, Mozart's poet, Casanova's friend, and Italian opera's impresario in America / Rodney Bolt.
p. cm.
ISBN-10 1-59691-118-2
ISBN-13 978-1-59691-118-5
1. Da Ponte, Lorenzo, 1749–1838. 2. Casanova, Giacomo, 1725–1798—Friends and associates. 3. Librettists—Biography. 4. Impresarios—Biography. I. Title.

ML423.D15B65 2006
782.1092—dc22
2006005713

First U.S. Edition 2006

1 3 5 7 9 10 8 6 4 2

Typeset by Hewer Text UK Limited, Edinburgh
Printed in the United States of America by Quebecor World Fairfield

For those who
shine in small corners

Chi crede a' sogni è matto; e chi non crede, che cos'è?

He who believes in his dreams is mad;
and he who does not believe in them – what is he?

Lorenzo Da Ponte

Contents

PART III LONDON
Pigmies on Parnassus

PART IV AMERICA
Mozart's Grocer

Acknowledgements

I am most grateful to the Authors' Foundation for a grant that contributed considerably towards the travel costs involved in researching this book.

My thanks, too, to my agent David Miller and editor Bill Swainson for their enthusiasm and support, and to Emily Sweet for her careful eye. Especial thanks go to Chris Chambers, who introduced me to Da Ponte, and to Philip Balma, whose work on the trickier translations, particularly with Da Ponte's letters and verse, has been invaluable. To those who helped untie me – often at a moment's notice – when I was bound up in further linguistic knots, a huge *grazie*, as well as a *vielen Dank*: to Lorenza Bacino, Sandra Ponzanesi, Liliana Pestman, Nele Ysebaert and Shaun Whiteside. Anya Schiffrin and Joe Stiglitz offered warm and unstinting hospitality in New York, which was hugely appreciated, as was Bob Bomersbach's spontaneous and energetic help with research. Lorna Marshall's advice was, as ever, a gem.

I owe a debt to earlier biographers Joseph Louis Russo, April FitzLyon, Sheila Hodges, and Aleramo Lanapoppi, and in particular to Andrew Steptoe, whose book *The Mozart–Da Ponte Operas* (Oxford University Press, 1988) did much to guide my thinking on the social context of opera in Vienna. References to Da Ponte's letters were sourced from *Lorenzo Da Ponte, Lettere*, edited by Giampaolo Zagonel (Dario De Bastiani, 1955), and I am most grateful for his permission to do this. I would also like to thank the Rare Book and Manuscript Library,

Butler Library, Columbia University and Luciano Rebay for permission
to publish his translation of Da Ponte's 'Sad Farewell' to his books.
Quotations from David Coward's translation of Beaumarchais in *The
Figaro Trilogy* (2003), and from Gozzi's *Useless Memoirs* (edited by P.
Horne, 1962), are used by permission of Oxford University Press.
Translations of Mozart's letters are from *Mozart's Letters, Mozart's Life:
Selected Letters*, edited by Robert Spaethling, translated by Robert
Spaethling, copyright 2000 by Robert Spaethling and used by permission
of W.W. Norton & Company Inc. Extracts from the shareholders'
agreement of the New York Italian Opera Association (BV Italian
Opera) are quoted courtesy of the New-York Historical Society.

Staff at the British Library and in the libraries of Cambridge University
and Columbia University, the New-York Historical Society and the
Northumberland County Historical Society were invariably helpful,
interested and prepared to cope with the odd difficult request. Sandra
Stelts and her associates in the Rare Books and Manuscripts Library at
Pennsylvania State University, especially, went out of their way to assist
me. I am grateful, too, to Ines Griesser and the Vienna Tourist Board for
their assistance, and to Reinhard Eisendle of the Da Ponte Institute.

Truly heartfelt thanks go, once again, to Hans Nicolaï, Gerard van
Vuuren, Andrew May and Anna Arthur. Without their tolerance of my
foibles, stalwart support, and practical help, such tasks as this would
simply never be completed.

Picture Credits

Letter to Don Pietro Bortoluzzi. A.D.V.V., Seminario, b.2, fascicolo X, n. 119, Archivio Diocesano di Vittorio Veneto.

Giacomo Casanova in Dux 1796. Oil. Portrait by Francesco Casanova, his brother. Copy from the original by H. Schuddebeurs. Museum Duchcov. Photo: Marco Leeflang.

Lorenzo Da Ponte in his youth. Reproduced by kind permission of Giampaolo Zagonel.

Portrait of Wolfgang Mozart by Johann Nepomunk. © Internationale Stiftung Mozarteum (ISM).

Portrait of Nancy Storace by von Bettelini. Austrian National Library, picture archives, Vienna (Anna Selina Storace, v. Bettelini 1788, NB 512.468-B).

Emperor Joseph II at the clavier. Kunsthistorisches Museum, Wien.

Portrait of Michael Kelly by John Neagle. National Portrait Gallery, London.

The Michaelerplatz, Vienna. Copyright Wienmuseum.

Interior of the Burgtheater. From H. C. Robbins Landon's *Mozart: The Golden Years*.

Portrait of Wolfgang Mozart by Johann Georg Edlinger. bpk/ Gemäldegalerie, SMB/Photo: J. P. Anders.

Portrait of Antonio Salieri by Heinrich Eduard von Wintter. Austrian National Library, picture archives, Vienna (Antonio Salieri, Stich v., Winter 1815, 106.803-C).

Costumes from Salieri's *Axur, re d'Ormus*. Gabinet Rycin Biblioteki Uniwersyteckiej w Warszawie.

1791 cartoon satirizing the London opera battles. V&A images/Victoria and Albert Museum, London.

Anna Celestina Ernestina 'Nancy' Grahl. Collection of The New-York Historical Society (negative #78494d).

Ticket for the premiere of *Le nozze di Figaro*. Austrian National Library, picture archives, Vienna (Theaterzettel: Le Nozze di Figaro 1786, NB 606.783-C).

Five Points, New York. Collection of The New-York Historical Society (negative #44668).

The Italian Opera House, New York. From Henry Krehbiel's *Chapters of Opera* (New York, 1908).

Interior of the Park Theatre, New York. Collection of The New-York Historical Society (accession #1875.3).

Professor Da Ponte at Columbia College, New York. Unidentified artist: Portrait of Lorenzo Da Ponte, Columbia University in the City of New York.

Portrait of Lorenzo Da Ponte by a Venetian painter of the nineteenth century, from a miniature by Nathaniel Rogers (1788–1844), oil on canvas, 630 × 550mm. Museo del Cenedese, Vittorio Veneto, Treviso, Italy (photo from Museo del Cenedese, Treviso, Italy).

View of New York from Brooklyn Heights. Collection of The New-York Historical Society (negative #74719).

Preface

I N T H E 1958 Lerner–Loewe musical *Gigi*, the characters played by
Maurice Chevalier and Hermione Gingold recall a love affair of
long ago. They met at nine, he recollects; at eight, she dryly corrects
him. He was on time, the old man reminisces; no, late, says she. But, oh
yes, he remembers it well – they dined with friends. Alone. As he recalls,
a tenor sang. It was a baritone. But, of course, he remembers it all.
Families recounting old anecdotes stumble down a similar 'It was on a
Thursday', 'No, a Wednesday' path. Nor are the writers of memoirs
exempt from what may be called the *Gigi* effect. Biographers are
frequently faced with sincerely held, yet fundamentally conflicting,
versions of the same event from different sources. Then, there are the
lies outright – as writers of autobiographies exercise their prerogative to
display themselves in the brightest possible plumage.

Lorenzo Da Ponte's memoirs abound with errors, both unintended
and deliberate, and are infused with romance – as the writer takes his cue
from the works of his good friend Casanova. The *Memorie* further cloud
the truth in that they were written when Da Ponte was in his eighties,
and bitter with life. In his old age he makes sour sense of events that he,
and others, viewed more positively at the time. Accounts by contem-
poraries help in sifting out the facts. Letters written as events were
happening also throw sharper light on the truth – though letters are, as
Virginia Woolf once noted, partly a reflection of the other person. Da
Ponte writing to his father puts down what he thinks his father wants to

hear; in complaining to Casanova he exaggerates those aspects of his tale likely to elicit Casanova's sympathy.

The following pages present a portrait of Lorenzo Da Ponte, in the manner in which a painter might portray a subject. The biographer, like the painter, is a presence in the finished product (though in this instance I would hope to be more of a Gainsborough than a Francis Bacon). I have not made anything up, but have on occasions confined the necessary bickering of biographers to the endnotes in order to portray more clearly the shape of the man that, after examining all the evidence, I believe to have been Da Ponte.

Why Da Ponte? He lived in four cities – Venice, Vienna, London and New York – at fascinating moments in their histories, and in a sense he experiences four very different eras. Venice, in its splendid last throes, looked back on a thousand years of glory; Vienna was at a peak of eighteenth-century social experiment, and London the height of con-temporary fashion; while New York surged into a post-Enlightenment, democratic, industrialized world. Da Ponte's arrival in America as a penniless Italian immigrant trying to reinvent himself and make good is mirrored in countless nineteenth- and even twentieth-century stories.

In this tale of four eras and four cities, Da Ponte is never the hero – yet nor is he entirely left out in the wings. He was, in his own words, 'if not the protagonist of the tragicomedy, at least one of the leading players'. Following his progress, one gets an intriguing glimpse of the period and is offered something of a history of opera from the inside.

This book does not offer a detailed musical analysis of Mozart's operas. That is left to writers infinitely more adept than I am at edging forward the boundaries of Mozart scholarship. Instead, it takes a closer look at how the operas were made, in that complex (and for the eighteenth century extraordinarily egalitarian) co-operation of artists and artisans the genre demands. More particularly, the book examines the relationship between composer and librettist. It is curious that in the world of the musical, lyricist and composer receive equal billing – we speak of Rodgers and Hammerstein, Lerner and Loewe, Rice and Lloyd Webber. Yet in opera, the writer is all but ignored. This sidelining of the librettist is often justified by the sorry quality of the libretto, but at his best, Da

Ponte warrants praise and attention. Even the most careful commentators will talk of *Mozart's* characterization when referring not to the delicious complexity his music gives but to what characters say, and how they interact dramatically. Writers not infrequently quote *words* from *Don Giovanni*, *Figaro* or *Così fan tutte*, and attribute them to 'Mozart'.

Da Ponte railed against such unfairness. I hope this book goes some way towards redressing the balance.

Rodney Bolt
Amsterdam, 2006

PART ONE

VENICE

An Abbé Errant

Chapter One

BOYS OF FOURTEEN are frequently in conflict with their fathers, and young Lorenzo Da Ponte had reason for rancour. He was about to acquire a stepmother young enough to be his sister; his father had whisked the family away from their old home in the ghetto, and Lorenzo was forbidden the company of his boyhood friends. His name was not even Lorenzo Da Ponte. Or at least it had not been until a few minutes earlier.

Emanuele Conegliano was the name he had grown up with, the one he had just lost for ever. His father, a Jewish leatherworker, had pitched his small family into a new religion. No sooner were the *buricche* of Emanuele's bar mitzvah feast cold than the boy had Christian wafers on his tongue. His father, Geremia, would now be known as Gaspare; Emanuele would have to learn to call his brothers 'Girolamo' and 'Luigi' instead of Baruch and Anania. As custom dictated, they would all take the surname of the bishop who had baptized them and, as the eldest son, Emanuele would take the prelate's first name, too. The four processed behind Monsignor Lorenzo Da Ponte, after a lavish cathedral ceremony, out into the blinding light of the *piazza maggiore* in Ceneda.

Ceneda, a 'small but not obscure city in the State of Venice', was squeezed between the Dolomites and the limpid, icy River Meschio. The mountains began abruptly, hoisting up the western edge of town as if it were the corner of a carpet. Snow gripped the peaks well into springtime, and in winter the drinking fountains froze. But summer

brought a hissing heat. Geckoes flicked between the stones of garden
walls; sunlight glinted on the white gravel in the streets. Silkworms that
had been feeding themselves fat all spring curled into cocoons, ready for
the plucking fingers of the townsfolk. All year round, along the river,
waterwheels chopped and churned, operating spinning- and paper-mills;
further downstream tanners treated stinking hides, and descendants of
the Marsoni family forged their celebrated sword blades. Beyond that –
though never more than a few minutes' walk from Ceneda's streets and
squares – lay vineyards, fertile farmland and forests. Emanuele Conegliano could run wild in the countryside, or cavort in the streets with his
friends. Even in the ghetto, in the west of town, he woke on fine
mornings to the sound of doves and woodland chirruping, to the
crowing of cockerels and asthmatic hee-haw of farm donkeys.

Some fifty Jews lived in Ceneda's ghetto, many of them descended
from one Israel da Conegliano, who had been invited to the town in
1597 by the then bishop, Marcantonio Mocenigo, to open a pawn-
brokers (a profession forbidden to Christians under usury laws). The
Coneglianos, originally Ashkenazi Jews who had settled in the town of
that name, were moneylenders throughout the region. Many of them
were rich, and in the seventeenth century the family had provided
Venice with some of its most distinguished doctors, but Emanuele's
father Geremia, who was born in Ceneda in 1719, was of a withered
branch of the clan, a leatherworker of modest means who made belts and
bridles. Geremia married another Cenedese, Rachele Pincherle, who
does not appear to have brought much money to the match – though the
Pincherles, too, were a prominent family in the area. In Gorizia, near
Trieste, the Hapsburg rulers had granted the family the title of *Hofjuden*,
or Jews of the court, allowing them special privileges.

Emanuele was born on 10 March 1749, followed by brothers Baruch
in 1752 and Anania in 1754. Rachele died when Emanuele was five years
old, probably in giving birth to Anania. '*Ahi che la morte avea / colta la
madre ai miei primi vagiti!* [Alas, that death had / taken my mother upon
my first cries!]' her firstborn wrote, remembering, decades later, the
anguish of the wrench, the sense of abandonment. After Rachele's death,
Geremia paid little heed to his boys; he certainly did not bother himself

much about their education. Until he was ten, Emanuele could barely read and write. Yet he was a lively lad, quick, insatiably curious, always ready with a dancing answer, and with bright eyes that grasped what people were saying before they had finished saying it. Eventually, it occurred to his father to give him an education – which in those days meant Latin – and he did a deal with the self-made son of a local peasant to come and knock a few elements of the language into the ten-year-old's head. It was a commission the tutor took literally, belabouring the boy's forehead with his calloused knuckles 'like Steropes or Brontes beating the anvil'. Daily, little Emanuele fought back his tears. And learned nothing. Concerned that his investment in lessons was bearing so little fruit, Geremia one day climbed the stairs and stood quietly in the doorway to observe. What he witnessed was one of Steropes' rages. Within minutes, Geremia had grabbed the tutor by the hair, dragged him to the door, and thrown him down the stairs – followed by inkwell, pens, and the sole copy of Alavro's grammar. There was no more talk of Latin.

Once again, Emanuele was left adrift – bright, but burning with inner shame at his lack of learning. Other boys laughed, and branded him *lo Spiritoso ignorante* (the ignorant genius). Then, one day while poking about in the garret where his father stored unwanted papers, Emanuele discovered the remains of the Conegliano family library. One by one, he took up the old books and brushed off the dust: *Buovo d'Antono*, a French *roman de geste*; a sixteenth-century collection of stories by Tomaso Costo; *Guerin Meschino*, a chivalrous romance; *Cassandra, Bertoldo*, medieval tales, and books of poems – enough to keep him occupied for months. Emanuele was transported. He devoured the books. Day after day he read each in turn, but the ones he came back to, the only ones he read twice, were the few stray volumes by the imperial laureate of Austria, the Italian poet Metastasio, whose dramas drawn from classical mythology were considered the absolute apotheosis of Italian opera libretti. Even the contemporary English critic Thomas Wilkes, not usually an enthusiast of the genre, praised Metastasio as doing Italy 'as much honour as Corneille does to France, or, almost, as Shakespeare to England', as in his delicate, free-flowing verse he 'neither enslave[d] himself to rhime nor to equal measure'. For young Emanuele, Metastasio's poetry 'produced in [his] soul the very sensation of music itself'.

While Emanuele hid himself away and read, Geremia Conegliano was coming to the decision that would change the direction of the boy's life. Jews in Ceneda endured similar restrictions to those living elsewhere in the Venetian Republic. In public, they had to wear red headgear (hats for men, scarves for women); they could not work for Christians, and only certain trades and professions were permitted them; some religious rites were restricted, and although Jews were allowed anywhere in the city during the day, they were shut away in a ghetto at night.

The original Ghetto had been set up in Venice in 1516, deriving its name from the old public foundry (*geto* in Venetian dialect) formerly sited on the island where Jews were forced to live. Over the next two centuries, encouraged by anti-Semitic papal bulls, other Italian cities followed suit in confining Jewish residents. In the earlier years, traditions of a freer existence were still strong but as time wore on, life in the ghettoes became more restricted, more impoverished, and more dreary. In a report to the central government of Venice in 1752, the mayor of Rovigo (a town about sixty miles south of Ceneda) painted a picture of conditions characteristic of other ghettoes in Italy:

> The shopkeepers among those of this nation number fourteen. There are only two general shops, badly provided. All the rest are reduced to dealing in miserable rags, with the exception of two which sell food, but of little or no significance. The rest of this people have to live by the most restricted occupations, which provide (though badly) for only a few of them, so that the rest are reduced to being a burden on the community, which supports them by alms.

The new thinkers of the Enlightenment – at least at the beginning of the period – did little to ease matters. Leading *philosophes*, Voltaire among them, were notably anti-Semitic, and though the Hapsburg Emperor Joseph II would introduce reforms in 1781, his mother and predecessor the Empress Maria Theresa, a zealous Catholic, expressed strong antipathy to Jews. Just five years before Emanuele was born, she had attempted to banish all Jews from Prague, and her feelings of dislike at times amounted to expressions of physical aversion.

In Ceneda, following precepts set by the liberal bishop Marcantonio Mocenigo (he who had invited Israel da Conegliano to town), conditions were not as repressive as elsewhere, yet prospects for Geremia Conegliano and his family in the early 1760s were dismal. The economic decay that was undermining the Venetian Republic had led to a credit crisis among Jewish moneylenders, who found themselves holding huge debts that their creditors found impossible to service. This caused a souring of relations between the Jewish community in Venice and the State, a revival of prejudices about Jewish perfidy which sent ripples through the entire Republic. In 1751, Jews were forbidden to enter St Mark's Square, and throughout the 1760s, Andrea Tron – known as *il Paron* ('the Boss' in local dialect) – was consolidating his influence among a group of ultra-conservative Venetian nobles, until he wielded more real power than the Doge himself. Tron hated Jews, and in the following decade would put through savage anti-Semitic legislation, which reduced an already depleted community to little more than rag-and-bone merchants. Between 1700 and 1766, the city of Venice lost more than half its Jewish population, either to emigration or conversion to Christianity.

Geremia Conegliano and his sons were not the first Jews from the Ceneda ghetto to convert. They were not even the first members of the Conegliano family to do so. In 1690, one Dolceta Conegliano had been baptized by Bishop Pietro Leoni, and in October 1724 the daughter of Salvatore Conegliano, Sara (an 'aunt' to Emanuele), ran away from home to hide in the local monastery, and went on to take the veil as Sister Francesca Maria in the convent of San Pietro di Feltre near by. More recently – on 5 June 1762 – a friend of the family named Baruch Scaramatta (or Scaramella), a teacher who in all likelihood had given rudimentary lessons to Emanuele and his brothers, had been baptized.

In the spring or early summer of 1763, Geremia moved his family up the mountainside behind the ghetto, into the ancient stone castle of San Martino, residence of Monsignor Lorenzo Da Ponte, Bishop of Ceneda, where the bishop's assistant, Canon Gerolamo Ziborghi, began to instruct them in the Christian faith. Bishop Da Ponte's delight at the Conegliano family's imminent conversion was warm and genuine. In his report the following year to the council of bishops on the state of the diocese, he seems profoundly moved by the event. It is not clear whether that sincerity was matched by the purity of Geremia's motives.

Plucked from his books in the attic, young Emanuele Conegliano was suddenly also severed from his friends. Social contact between Jews and Christians was severely proscribed, and the strictures applied especially to recent converts. A stone tablet still visible in the Ghetto in Venice forbids 'any Jewish man or woman having been made a Christian to visit or work under any pretext whatsoever in the Ghettos of this city', threatening transgressors with 'rope, prison, galley, whip, pillory . . .' Already bereft of his mother, Emanuele had no choice but to follow his father up the hill, losing home and playmates as well. Yet he still had his brothers for company – and he could throw away the humiliating red beret he had been forced to wear ever since he had turned thirteen. As the weeks went by, a further overwhelming advantage of his new situation became clear. It occurred to him that he could now get a real education. And after a run-down house in the ghetto, to be staying in the castle high on a spur of Monte Altare was the stuff of dreams.

That heady luxury, though, could last only for the duration of their religious instruction. After their baptism, the family would need a new house and Geremia another location for his business, as they could no longer return to the ghetto. A solution to their problem presented itself in the form of Orsola Pasqua Paietta.

Orsola Pasqua was the daughter of Andrea Paietta, one of the poorest men in town. Her sisters Maddalena and Giovanna had already been granted alms – in 1754, 1756, and 1760. Andrea was seriously ill (he died a few months later, on 19 September 1763), and wanted to secure a future for his daughters. Giovanna had married in 1761, and it seems that Maddalena was betrothed (she married two months after her father's death), but eighteen-year-old Orsola Pasqua had no husband in prospect. Her marriage to Geremia Conegliano – once he had been baptized – would solve a number of the good bishop's pastoral concerns in one swoop. It meant Andrea Paietta could die in the knowledge that all his daughters would be looked after, that the neo-converts could move out of the episcopal palace, and that Geremia would have both a house and an inroad to the Christian community. Geremia jumped at the chance of an eighteen-year-old bride. Young Emanuele was not at all pleased with the prospect of a stepmother just four years his senior. He could see that, for him, the consequence of this '*matrimonio sì disuguale*' (imbalanced marriage) meant further paternal neglect. He decided to take matters into his own hands, and to 'obtain from the charity of others what I could not hope to gain from fatherly solicitude'. If his father wouldn't do anything about his education, he would have to arrange things himself.

Bishop Da Ponte had rather taken to the clever, bright-eyed young Emanuele. Bravely – and with quite some cheek – the boy asked for an audience, and begged the bishop to find places for himself and his brother Baruch at the local seminary. Monsignor Da Ponte was 'a man of renowned piety and charitable religion', a Venetian patrician who spent most of his money on rebuilding the cathedral in Ceneda, in providing relief for the sick and the poor, and in making his seminary one of the most learned in the region. If he was taken aback by the young lad's impudence, he did not show it. He not only secured the two boys places in the seminary but agreed to pay for their tuition.

In converting his family to Christianity, Geremia may, like his kinswoman Sara, have been following true religious conviction; or he may simply have been making a desperate attempt for a better life. Although his eldest son might resent the upheaval his father had caused in his life, whatever his attitude to his lost friends and old faith, he too could appreciate the benefits that were in store. On 14 July, young Emanuele, still stumbling over his bad Italian grammar, penned a letter to Don Pietro Bortoluzzi, the chancellor of the diocese, who was assisting Girolamo Ziborghi in the family's religious instruction. It is the only surviving letter signed with his old name. Written in an untidy, cramped hand, with the odd trace of an inky fingerprint, it oozes with ingratiating piety.

Every day, the more I discover the truth of the Christian faith, I lament the blindness of the poor Jews with bitter grief, and I don't have words

to thank God, who took me from the claws of the Pharaoh. What a
wonderful grace the Lord bestowed on me! I would never tire of
speaking of it!

These may be the sincere exaltations of a fervent new convert, but they
carry more of the wide-eyed wiliness of a fourteen-year-old who has
realized on which side his bread is lavishly being buttered.

At two o'clock in the afternoon on 29 August 1763, after all of
Ceneda's church bells had been ringing and cannon had been firing off
salvoes over the town at regular intervals – for four days – a company of
halberdiers began beating their drums and His Excellency the Bishop of
Ceneda emerged from the Castello San Martino in full regalia, preceded
by his household and a grand host of clerics, accompanied by the lustre of
the city's great and good, and a blaze of local aristocrats. Silks shimmered,
buckles and buttons glinted in the sunlight, the breeze puffed gently over
newly powdered wigs. People flocked into town from far and wide –
they had been promised festivities and spectacular fireworks in the piazza
– and the cathedral was adorned with banners and flowers. In the midst
of it all walked the Conegliano family, to baptism and their first
communion. Young Emanuele Conegliano, the outcast, *lo Spiritoso
ignorante*, was for a moment the focus of public adulation. He emerged
from the cathedral that afternoon as Lorenzo Da Ponte, to a very
different life. We know about the celebrations from a document in
the Ceneda seminary archives. In his *Memoirs*, Lorenzo Da Ponte does
not once mention his Jewish origins.

Gaspare Da Ponte married Orsola Pasqua Paietta on 10 September,
twelve days after the baptism ceremony, at the parish church of San
Martino di Colle, just outside Ceneda. She would bear him ten children.
Lorenzo Da Ponte developed a deep affection for his new brothers and
sisters, creating an idyllic image of their warmth and support, but he
regarded his freshly stamped stepmother with acrimony. In all of the rest
of his life he did not write one caring word about the pauper girl who
took over his mother's place. He fails, even, to remark on her death in
1790.

Conversion and marriage did not immediately ease Gaspare Da Ponte's financial difficulties. The family moved into a small house overlooking the town square, where he set up a shop. In 1770 – admittedly a bad year – he declared an income of just thirty ducats, barely sufficient to support his growing brood. For Lorenzo, privations at home and antipathy to Orsola Pasqua faded like damask in the sunlight in view of his admission to the seminary. He and Girolamo (Baruch) were enrolled as boarders in 1764, and pitched immediately into a foreign world. Not only was the language of the seminary Latin, but one of the leading Latin scholars of the era, Egidio Forcelloni, the 'Prince of Lexicographers', had been rector there between 1724 and 1731, and his ardent disciple Giambattista Modolini was the Da Ponte boys' demanding tutor. Strict he may have been, but Modolini's methods succeeded where the calloused knuckles of the peasant Steropes had singularly failed. In under two years, Lorenzo was 'capable of composing in half a day a long oration and perhaps fifty not inelegant verses in Latin'. His native Italian, on the other hand, had stalled at the point where he could not write a letter of even a few lines without making ten mistakes. All that changed with the arrival of a revolutionary young scholar, Gianandrea Cagliari, fresh from the famous University of Padua and 'full of fire and poetic valour'. Abbé Cagliari brought with him the astonishing idea that Dante and Petrarch were as worthy of study as Virgil and Horace. He broke through the ivy-hug of Latin, and introduced his charges to the gentler embrace of the Tuscan tongue. He instilled good taste, and awoke an awareness of the beauty of Italian poetry and prose – or in Lorenzo Da Ponte's case a rekindling of the delight he had felt at reading the books he had found years before in his father's attic.

The twin stars of Cagliari's innovative classes were Girolamo Perucchini and Michele Colombo – both captivating, witty young men capable of writing graceful verse. At nineteen, Michele Colombo was just two years older than Lorenzo but inspired the younger man's complete awe. Colombo read his poems to his idolizer, and encouraged him to try his own hand at the art. Lorenzo's first attempt was a sonnet to his father – begging for a little money. He had barely finished it when he was startled by a guffaw from behind. Colombo had been reading the rather tramping verses over his shoulder, and began chanting them in the drone that blind street beggars used, pretending to strum a lute. Once again *lo Spiritoso ignorante* burned with shame. For three days, he did not look at Colombo or speak to him – but his years in the ghetto had taught him tenacity. Lorenzo set himself to studying Italian poetry with such ferocity that he barely stopped to eat, and within six months he knew Dante's *Inferno* by heart, as well as most of Petrarch's sonnets, and the choicest passages from Tasso and Ariosto. Then he secretly composed, and burned, more than 2,000 verses, imitating styles, practising metre, echoing phrases he found beautiful, until he felt ready – on the occasion of the rector's farewell celebrations – to present a sonnet in public. No one believed it was his. But either his energy or the poem (an infinitely more elegant achievement than his first attempt) had endeared him to both Perucchini and Colombo, and the three became passionate friends.

The poetic fervour had added fuel to another passion: Lorenzo's love of books. It had begun among the dusty tomes in the ghetto garret, and he had already built up a small Latin library, but it was Italian works he desired, and books were expensive. He already had an eye for a good bargain. There was in Ceneda 'a bookseller who, though an ignorant and stupid man, kept, as a pure whim, a shop of excellent books', and Lorenzo coveted some beautiful Elzevir editions which, even at the ignorant bookseller's prices, way exceeded his means. The bookseller's son was a shoemaker in need of fine leather for fashionable shoes – a little too expensive for *his* means. The old man suggested a swap: books for coloured leather and calfskin from Lorenzo's father's shop. Lorenzo sneaked into the storeroom, selected three fine hides and stuffed them up the back of his coat. He had hardly left the building when he saw Orsola Pasqua gossiping in the street. As he crossed the road to avoid her, he heard one of her friends remark, 'What a pity about that poor hunch-backed boy!' – just at the moment that the bundle of calfskins descended from their hiding place on to the cobbles. With a gale of women's laughter behind him, Lorenzo did not dally to discover the conse-quences. Orsola Pasqua lost no time in reporting the incident to her husband. Lorenzo's father arrived at the seminary in a fury, creating a public scene. Word reached the bishop, and Lorenzo was summoned to the palace – but the prelate couldn't help laughing at the young man's version of story. He gave him the money to buy the books. Lorenzo Da Ponte had the beginnings of an Italian library, and was learning the value of charm.

Lorenzo's friendship with Girolamo Perucchini and Michele Colombo, meanwhile, was blooming. Michele Colombo became the soul mate Lorenzo had so lacked in the ghetto, cracking through the carapace of *lo Spiritoso ignorante*, releasing all the ardour that the motherless boy had been damming up for years. The two tore about the seminary – talented, irresistible and gloriously disruptive. 'Never was a friend dearer to me,' Colombo wrote, years later, in a letter to the librarian at the University of Padua. 'He belonged to me and I to him, two crazy heads of the first rank. Nobody could believe the wild things we did in that place . . .' They improvised sonnets; they fell distractedly in love with the same girl; they secretly passed notes to each other in class, composing line-by-line poems that others could not discern as being the work of two hands. They caused such rumpus that they were expelled – but then readmitted because, Colombo says, 'crazy as we were, we were – even so – better than others who were wiser than we'. Their behaviour reached the point where the authorities decided that they would have to be separated. The calamitous events of 1768 made that unavoidable.

The year 1768 saw Lorenzo succumb to 'a terrible illness' that brought him near to death, keeping him from his studies for six months and forcing him to drop back a class. To make matters worse, his father – financially unsound at the best of times, and already the begetter of four more mouths to feed – became involved in 'various domestic difficulties' that reduced him to poverty. Most upsetting of all was the death, in July, of Bishop Da Ponte. Not only had the bishop been patron to all three Da Ponte boys at the seminary (Luigi had joined his siblings there in 1767), but he had also helped Gaspare financially. The brothers' future as boarders was in jeopardy, and their father could not afford to take them back into the fold. One by one Lorenzo sold the precious volumes he had bought from the bookseller in Ceneda to raise money to support the family. Once again his hopes for an education had been garrotted.

Canon Gerolamo Ziborghi, the man who had first given the family religious instruction, stepped in with a solution. He and Gaspare Da Ponte decided that the boys would become priests. That meant transferring them to a seminary at Portogruaro, where La Pia Casa dei Catecumeni, a Venetian charitable foundation that specialized in re-educating converts, would pay for their upkeep. For Lorenzo, it meant separation from Michele Colombo, and following a course from which he recoiled. He had already taken minor orders, in 1765. The tonsure and black garb were alien enough to him, but the act had pleased the bishop and, for once, Lorenzo had blended in with his peers. Taking minor orders was not uncommon for boys educated in a seminary – it meant little more than the monkish garb and a promise not to duel or dance. They were not seen as very different from lay boys. Major orders, on the other hand, he saw as 'wholly contrary to my temperament, my character, my principles, and my studies'. He had, also, to 'renounce the hand of a noble and entrancing girl whom I loved tenderly'. If this was Pierina Raccanelli, the Cenedese Aphrodite to whom he and Michele Colombo had fired off adoring sonnets, she would also be denied the hand of the rival for her affection, as Colombo, too, eventually became a priest. In any event, the 'noble and entrancing girl' slips by almost unnoticed in comparison with the fervour of Lorenzo's feelings for his friend.

Entry into the priesthood was a gainsaying of all that the newly minted Lorenzo Da Ponte perceived as his make-up and imagined as his destiny. Yet there was no question of compromise. For a poor boy in desperate pursuit of learning there was simply no other way. At the end of October 1769, a lovelorn Lorenzo together with his brothers Girolamo and Luigi, wrapped up against icy winds blowing down from the mountains, set off across the Venetian plain, floundering through pitfalls in the road and traversing deep bogs on the way to Portogruaro.

Midway between Venice and Trieste, on the banks of the River Lemene near where it fed into the Càorle lagoon, Portogruaro was a busy town, and a rich one. For centuries the river port had been filling its coffers with profits of trade between the Republic and the surrounding Austrian territories – and spending freely. Lacy Gothic façades stood alongside stolid medieval stonework; fine Renaissance frescoes decorated the outer walls of its *palazzi*; long arcades with looping arches shaded the fronts of well-stocked shops. Through the heart of town the river flowed – swift, cold and erupting over waterwheels in the same bravura performance as the Meschio gave in Ceneda; the one familiar sight and sound to the Da Ponte boys as their cart trundled across the cobbles to the seminary.

The Portogruaro seminary was relatively new, dating from the beginning of the century. Groups of young men paced the sober porticoes around its grassy courtyard, reciting their rosaries. One or two wore iron collars – the punishment for having lapsed from Latin into speaking Italian. Strict rules and a rigorous routine governed their daily lives; pious exercises prepared them for becoming good servants of the Church. Three nights a week, they met to discuss classical poets. After three years, the best students were allowed to learn Greek and Hebrew (in which Lorenzo had a head start) – but there was no revolutionary Abbé Cagliari here, as there had been at Ceneda. Anyone who wanted to study Italian writers did so in secret. Science and mathematics were very much part of the syllabus, but other lessons shielded the would-be clerics from philosophical attack. Just four years earlier, a further ten volumes had been published of the *Encyclopédie*, the massive dictionary of knowledge and thought begun in the 1750s and edited by the philosopher Denis Diderot. The articles it contained attacked superstition and Christian credulity and were becoming widely read, helping to spread the ideas of the French Enlightenment throughout Europe (the original financial backers of the *Encyclopédie* earned a profit of 300 per cent on their investment). It would not do for such ideas to find foothold in the seminary.

Girolamo took to the regime with ease (he would later become a dedicated priest). Lorenzo surreptitiously read Italian pastoral dramas while the proctor explained Euclid, Galileo and Newton; he threw himself into furious secret discussions with the 'wild followers' of Aristarco, the controversial intellectual who wanted to promote a new Italian literature. Despite their diverging paths, the brothers stuck together – firm friends as well as siblings – and at every opportunity he had, Lorenzo wrote to Michele Colombo: sending poems, enquiring after colleagues, complaining of toothache, making fruitless plans to meet, patching up quarrels, arguing about literature, showering his friend with kisses. Gaps in correspondence wrought anguish and evoked outpourings of adoration:

> Not because I have spent more than three months without writing to you, and without receiving your letters: nor for my not having any news of you in such a long time, have I ever been able to love you less than I love you, or have I let a single day pass without remembering you, and I hold this constancy of mine very dear, since, if it were otherwise, I would repent myself to the Heavens, knowing that in that case I would love you a lot less than I owe; because even at present, even though I love you as much as I know, and can, yet I love you less than you deserve, and for the love that you have for me, and for that extraordinary privilege, that makes you most lovable.

Lorenzo found some consolation on a trip to nearby Venice. At the height of the Carnival in January and February of 1771, all three Da Ponte brothers were sent there to recover from 'a terrible fever' and 'fierce convulsions'. Lorenzo prissily claims, in a letter to Michele Colombo, that as Carnival is a time when clerics are better indoors than out, he is staying at home to converse with his Muses. (Had the pious poet at this time shown any inclination towards an enjoyment of music, he may well have attended a concert given by a brilliant young visitor to the 1771 Carnival, a fifteen-year-old who also had a somewhat complicated relationship with his father: Wolfgang Amadeus Mozart.) The letter would most certainly have been subject to the censoring – and censorious – eyes of senior priests at the Ceneda seminary. Off the page, Lorenzo appears, nevertheless, to have enjoyed revels and wild rumpus – and to have fallen in love with Angela Tiepolo.

An impoverished member of one of Venice's leading families, and just a year younger than Lorenzo, Angela Tiepolo was 'petite, delicate, genteel – white as snow, with soft, languorous eyes, and two charming dimples that adorned cheeks which were pure roses'. Teeny and fragile she may have appeared, but petite Angela was possessed of an impetuous temper that blew swiftly into ungovernable rage. She was also married.

Having recovered from their fever, the brothers returned to Portogruaro and their studies. Lorenzo kept his new love secret. In his letters to Colombo, he bewails the fact that his enforced concentration on philosophy leaves him no time to write poetry, and fears that – vexed by neglect – his Muses have turned against him. Perhaps his friend can effect a reconciliation. At times, he cannot resist a little boast – for it is clear that the young Da Ponte burned bright among his fellow students, and that he had dazzled both the rector and the local bishop. In September 1771, just a year after the brothers arrived at the seminary, the rector appointed Lorenzo as an instructor. A year later, the young man's recitation of a poem he had written – in Italian – in praise of Saint Louis earned a 'Bravo!' from a local aristocrat, and led to the bishop's instantly offering him the chair of rhetoric. In the spring of 1772, again after special intervention by his champions, he was made a vice-rector at an annual salary of forty ducats. For a moment he had hesitated – if his Muses had been vexed earlier, they would be furious at the amount of work he now had to take on. There would be little time for poetry at all, but at twenty-three Lorenzo knew his remaining days as a charity student were being counted out. He made his bid for independence, accepted the post, and immediately began sending remittances home to support his new brothers and sisters (who by now numbered six).

Vice-rector Da Ponte's duties were to teach Italian to fifty-two of the best students, to see to discipline, and to write the inaugural speech for the beginning of the academic year, as well as poems for the final *accademia* – the prestigious public ceremony in the presence of all the city notables that brought studies to a close. 'What do you think of that?' he enthused to Michele Colombo. 'None of the other vice-rectors has so much to do, but the generosity of Monsignor and the rector, and their good opinion of me, made them decide to give me these duties. In short, vice-rector here is the same as rector in Ceneda.' He had every right to be pleased with himself, but the son of a poor leatherworker was becoming just a little self-important, in an age when, although the old order was being given a shaking, it was by no means dead. Deference and attention to decorum were still important, and one had to be circumspect with dangerous ideas about rank. Ignoring that could get the young vice-rector into trouble.

Lorenzo Da Ponte was beginning to breed devils of envy among his older colleagues. The mutterings in the corridors of the seminary at Portogruaro were no longer just recitations of the rosary. When detractors tried to strike at his weak spot, taunting the *arriviste* with not having studied physics and calling him 'nothing but a wind-bag, a rhymester without science', Lorenzo responded by declaring the theme of the 1772 *accademia* to be *la fisica particolare*, and delivering a dithyramb on odours that caused 'praises and caresses [to be] heaped upon me by the literati in that city, by the pupils in my school, and by the Bishop himself'. That, of course, soured his relationship with his colleagues even further. For another year he endured the bitter jibes, ignored the pricks and whispering. He was scourged all the while by a 'very violent passion' for Angela, and began slipping away from the seminary to meet her. On 27 March 1773, he was ordained, laconically dismissing the event in a single sentence in a letter to Michele Colombo, giving equal weight to his hope to see his friend again: 'God willing, I will be ordained at Mass on the Saturday before Passion Week, and perhaps will have the pleasure of seeing you there and embracing you.' Technically, his priest's vows put Angela beyond reach, but starved of tenderness for much of his life, Lorenzo Da Ponte was headlong and reckless in his devotion when love came to him. 'Greet Baliana for me,' he noted in a postscript to a letter to Colombo in July, referring to a lovelorn friend in the Ceneda seminary, and tell him, *that I suffer for his pain*. Because Love truly is a sad mess.' In November 1773 Angela gave birth to her second child, a boy named Niccolò Maria. Her husband, Giulio Maria Soderini (who was much older than she) refused to recognize the boy, and left her – to become a priest.

In the autumn of 1773, before the child was born, Da Ponte pocketed what was left of his forty-ducat salary, abruptly resigned from the seminary and left for Venice.

Chapter Two

GOSSIP ALONG THE Canal Grande told of how at a ball given by the celebrated Foscarini family, as Caterina Querini was dancing with the King of Denmark, a thread gave way, sending the pearls with which her gown was spangled cascading to the floor. Smiling and quite unconcerned, she carried on dancing until the music ended, while her jewels rolled away. The gracious *contessa* makes a fitting metaphor for Venice in the eighteenth century, as her home town, rich but no longer powerful, frittered away its wealth in a glorious final fling. One hundred years later, the poet Robert Browning would write:

> As for Venice and her people, merely born to bloom and drop,
> Here on earth they bore their fruitage, mirth and folly were the
>   crop:
> What of soul was left I wonder, when the kissing had to stop?

Browning's contemporary, the French historian Philippe Monnier, hinted more darkly at the 'coffin under a heap of flowers'. Yet as the Most Serene Republic – which had lasted for over a thousand years – went into decline, its citizens ostentatiously kept up the dance. The party would go on right up until Napoleon stopped the music.

By the 1770s, the city that was once the unchallenged mistress of the Mediterranean, that had created a small empire and done fierce battle with the Turk, could barely control the approaches to her own lagoon.

The exotic cargoes that once packed her warehouses had given way to olive oil, salt and raisins – but the money still flowed in. Fat-pursed foreigners flocked to the pleasure capital of Europe. Buoyed additionally by vigorous local trade, and after more than half a century of peace, Venice was spending its gains on music and revelry. Its Carnival was the longest and most abandoned anywhere, lasting nearly half the year. Masks – the *moretta* that covered only the eyes, or the hooded *bauta* – were de rigueur from October to Lent; behind them rank disappeared, rules could be broken, gossip, audacity and intrigue flourished. Anyone in a mask could enter the Ridotto, the famous gaming-house in San Moisè, or could attend the beginning of the Doge's banquet on the Feast of the Ascension. Friends gathered in *casini* – private pleasure salons – for elaborate dinners, or slipped in separately for scandalous trysts. Hester Lynch Piozzi (formerly Thrale, née Salusbury), erstwhile intimate of Dr Johnson, having shocked her friends by marrying an Italian musician and setting off on a Grand Tour, exclaimed that Venice was:

> . . . adorned with every excellence of human art, and pregnant with pleasure, expressed by intelligent countenances sparkling with every grace of nature; the sea washing its walls, the moonbeams dancing on its subjugated waves, sport and laughter resounding from the coffee-houses, girls with guitars skipping about the square, masks and merry-makers singing as they pass you . . . whoever is led suddenly I say to this scene of seemingly perennial gaiety, will be apt to cry out of Venice, as Eve says of Adam in Milton,
> With thee conversing I *forget all time*
> All *seasons*, and their *change* – all please alike.

Charles Burney, the eminent musical historian who published his journal of a tour through Italy in the year that Lorenzo arrived in Venice, noted that the first music he heard in the city was in the street: a band of 'two fiddles, a violoncello and a voice' that would have merited applause throughout Europe. Venetian dramatist Carlo Gozzi remarked a half-naked urchin moving through the streets 'all harmony like a nightingale'; his rival Carlo Goldoni writes that squares, streets and canals were 'all full of singing; tradesmen sing as they dispose of their goods, workmen sing as they leave their tasks, gondoliers sing as they await their customers'. The Irish tenor Michael Kelly, who was performing in Venice around this time, was enthralled by 'the gondoliers singing barcarolles, or the verses of Tasso and Ariosto to Venetian airs; barges full of musicians on the Grand Canale serenading their enamoratas'. In the orphanages for female foundlings – the Pietà, the Incurabili, the Mendicanti and the Ospeda- letto – the young charges entranced with their musical prowess. At the height of the Carnival, seven opera houses and four playhouses squeezed in audiences to the sweaty seams, there not merely for the shows, but for the raillery, repartee and flirting that went on during the performance. Favourites were pampered, liaisons flourished, and the courtesans of Venice had the reputation as the loveliest, most elegant and most skilful anywhere. 'Venice! dear beautiful Venice! scene of harmony and love!' recalled Michael Kelly, somewhat disingenuously. 'Venice was the paradise of women, and the Venetian women worthy of a paradise at least of Mahomet's. They were the perfect *houri*; and the Venetian dialect, spoken by a lovely woman is the softest and the most delicious music in the world to him whom she favours.' William Beckford noted, in the brightly lit casino of a most distinguished family, 'a great many ladies negligently dressed, their hair falling very freely about them, and innumerable adventures written in their eyes'.

The mistress of the Mediterranean had become a spirited *madame* – ancient, decaying, but full-bent on giving her devotees the time of their lives.

The Venetian philanderer and adventurer Giacomo Casanova wrote of the eyes of a famous courtesan that they were 'illuminated by an eerie iridescence that nature rarely grants, and only to youth, and which normally disappears around age forty, after having worked miracles. The late King of Prussia kept it until his death.' Lorenzo Da Ponte had such eyes, and like the King of Prussia's, they would keep that seductive iridescence until the end. Charm and a ready wit were part of the secret of their light. The corners of his lips seemed constantly dappled by a smile; his speech was softened by a lisp. A strong jaw, fine cheekbones, and a noble aquiline nose made him a fitting match for the beautiful Angela – if he could weather her tirades.

As he made his way along the coast to Venice, Lorenzo had no need to disguise his tonsure or cloak his clerical garb. His liaison, though illicit, was not without precedent among his fellow clergy. A priest might quite acceptably become a *cicisbeo* or *cavaliere servente*, a supposedly Platonic devotee of a married woman, who 'attend[ed] on [her] with as much attention and respect as if they were lovers', visiting her before she rose, gossiping during her morning toilette, taking her on his arm to the theatre, holding her gloves, planting her beauty spot with a moist fingertip (the *coquette* above the lip, the *appassionata* in the corner of the eye), hearing her secrets, carrying her lapdog, passing a hand beneath her bodice to thrust down the fold of her chemise.

Venetians had long stopped seeing priests as models of high moral behaviour, and had themselves grown God-shirking and hedonistic. Casanova (who had also taken minor orders) and the Abbé de Bernis once shared the love of a beautiful nun from the island of Murano. Some years before, two abbesses had fought a duel with knives for the favours of the companionable Abbé Pompone, and caused a scandal only because they did so outside the convent walls. The French astronomer and geographer Jérôme Lalande noted in 1765 that: 'The people [of Venice] are attached to their religion as in the rest of Italy, but that has little influence on their behaviour. The people give way to their passions quite naturally, then go to confession and begin all over again.' An anonymous English traveller writes of them as:

> . . . grave, yet trifling; zealous yet untrue,
> And even in penance planning sins anew.

The Venetians themselves summed up their way of life with the saying: *'La mattina una messeta, l'apodisnar una basseta, e la sera una donneta* [In the morning a little mass, in the afternoon a bit of a flutter, and a little lady in the evening]' and called their city 'a paradise for friars and whores'.

The Abbé Da Ponte, as he crossed the lagoon from the mainland, would have been less concerned with the social delicacy and theological intricacies of his position than with where he would live and how he would make money. In leaving the seminary, he had joined the growing breed of men who — as the strictures of rank began to loosen and the structures of economies became more diverse — found they had to live on their wits. For some, long-standing props of patronage or family money had been knocked away; others, like himself, had set off on paths that took them beyond what might once have been seen as their station in life, and they had to improvise as they went along. At the core of this agile band were such adventurers as Casanova and 'Count Cagliostro' (the alluring charlatan Giuseppe Balsamo), men who were quick on the scent of financial gain: 'They baptize themselves, give themselves titles, recreate themselves as often as they please, and as the matter in hand requires,' wrote one well-born observer. 'What they cannot pull off as a simple nobleman they attempt as Marquis or Abbé or officer . . . With admirable adroitness, with a *savoir-vivre* that better men might learn from them with advantage, they obtain things which honest and capable men have not the courage to desire.' Around the edges of the pack were those 'honest and capable men' who did have the courage to desire, and who were having to fare for themselves in resourceful ways. Alongside the many labels that can be applied to the period is that of the 'Age of Reinvention'.

On visits to Venice with his brothers, Lorenzo had lodged with La Pia Casa dei Catecumeni, the foundation that had paid for their education. That was now out of the question. He had decided it was unwise to stay with Angela, even though her husband had left her. Despite the lax moral atmosphere in Venice, people — patricians in particular — were strict about the surface rules and customs of matrimony (though one of the aspects of Venetian life that most shocked visitors was the ease and frequency with which marriages were annulled). Despite its eminence, Venice was a small town, of only some 160,000 people, crowded on to a few islands and notorious for their gossip.

If fortune favoured him, Lorenzo might be able to afford the style of accommodation the Irish tenor Michael Kelly enjoyed towards the end of the decade, with 'a good bed-room, the use of a large drawing-room in common with other boarders, with breakfast, dinner, coffee, supper, and as much of the wine of the country as I chose every day'; if not, he would be reduced to lodgings situated down one of the city's dank alleys or beside a stinking slip of canal, in surrounds similar to those that greeted the playwright Carlo Gozzi as he climbed the stairs of his family's decaying ancestral home in the Calle della Regina: 'The stone floors were worn into holes and fissures, which spread in all directions like a cancer. The broken window panes let blasts from every point of the compass play freely to and fro within the draughty chambers. The hangings on the walls were ragged, smirched with smoke and dust, fluttering in tatters.'

Driven by his passion for Angela Tiepolo, the young priest in the gondola nearing the islands of Venice was taking his chances with fortune. Hester Lynch Piozzi wrote that on leaving the mainland, she left her cares and her coach behind her, 'superfluous as they both are, in a city that admits of neither'. Lorenzo Da Ponte carried his cares with him, but he cannot have helped being swept up by the verve and romance that greeted all new arrivals to the 'seat of enchantment! head-quarters of pleasure':

> . . . an azure expanse of sea opened to our view, the domes and the towers of Venice rising from its bosom . . . We were now drawing very near the city and a confused hum began to interrupt the evening stillness; gondolas were continually passing and re-passing, and the entrance of the Canal Reggio, with all its stir and bustle, lay before us. Our gondoliers turned with much address through a crowd of boats and barges that blocked up the way, and rode smoothly by the side of a broad pavement, covered with people of all dresses and all nations.

The dashing young abbé was soon enveloped not just in the embrace of his mistress, but in the even firmer clasp of the city itself.

Lorenzo Da Ponte's clerical status would not have held much sway with potential landlords, but it was of help in securing him a position as tutor to two sons of a local patrician family. Lessons were squeezed into gaps between pleasure. Angela whirled the 24-year-old Lorenzo into a life which began after dark. 'These dear Venetians have no notion of sleep being necessary to their existence,' a worn-out Hester Piozzi complained. 'The earliest Casino belonging to your soberest friends has not a candle lighted in it till past midnight.' After sunset, wrote William Beckford, 'a thoughtless giddy transport prevailed . . . anything like restraint seem[ed] perfectly out of the question . . . [the town] grows gayer and gayer as the day declines'. The opera went on until two o'clock in the morning, and people sauntered the streets through sunrise until the heat of the day drove them home. Exhausted gondoliers slept in their boats or on stairways, awaiting their master's or lady's call; gondola lanterns blinked like fireflies through the night. It was a life of long hours spent drinking champagne in *casini*; of candied citrons and Neapolitan bonbons, hothouse pineapples and luscious peaches (bought at the fruit market at dawn, on the way home to bed); of sipping chocolate for breakfast (whatever the hour), downing quantities of coffee to keep awake, and eating ice cream (the era's supreme culinary invention) at the end of long siestas.

Gambling, the opera, and theatre were the torches around which these night-moths fluttered. The Tiepolo family had provided financial backing for 'S. Benedetto', one of the leading theatres in the city, and among the first in Europe to have a decorated curtain lowered between acts. Here baked apples and *dosa* – a spicy punch – were sold on the stairs, and the foyer opened into a rowdy taverna, where the audience munched happily on fried fish and polenta during the intervals. In the absence of a court, Venice had produced the first public opera house, to which one had to pay for admission. Money, more than rank, determined who could attend. Stately court operas gave way to those that combined high drama and bawdy farce, and which boasted spectacular stage effects. Venice also introduced tiers of boxes into the auditorium – a door behind leading into a private 'withdrawing' room, curtains or shutters in front to turn the box into the architectural equivalent of a mask. Night after night Lorenzo and Angela joined the comings and goings, as box doors slammed and people gossiped throughout the performance, as high-spirited patricians projected food and candle-stubs (as well as insults and spittle) at the actors and singers. Not content with mere applause they would whistle and miaow their delight, or, if they disapproved, hiss, hoot and shout such advice as, 'Get off, you goat!' Opera came in for burlier treatment than the sensuous ballet interludes between acts. Casanova remarked, 'The insolent noise one hears in Italy during the singing is truly scandalous, and one cannot help but laugh to note the silence that follows, when the dancing begins.' One traveller wrote in astonishment of a gentleman, transported by a singer's beautiful voice, threatening to throw himself from his box, with an *'Ah! Cara! Mi butto, mi butto!* [Ah! Darling! I'll jump, I'll jump!]' Other visitors to Venice, including Montesquieu and Rousseau, were appalled at the noise and disorder; Goethe on his visit related in a letter to Charlotte von Stein: 'The public enjoy themselves like children, coming to yell, to applaud and make a racket.' When the shows were over, Lorenzo and Angela would join the flow of the audience – gondoliers fighting for position, gondolas bashing and crashing, jamming the narrower canals – to the inns and coffee-houses: L'Aurora and La Venezia Trionfante (later known as 'Florian') on Piazza San Marco, where women went despite a law forbidding them entry; to a *malvasìa* (busy public bar, serving mainly malmsey wine to people of all ranks); or even to a *bastion* (a low-life bar for cheap, bad wine and cheap, bad company).

That year, 1773, in Vienna, a sensuous new dance was sweeping through the ballrooms. It was called the waltz. Across the Atlantic in Boston, a group of citizens – some dressed as Native Americans – boarded three British boats in the harbour and dumped the cargo into the water in protest against the royal parliament's tax on tea, a significant signpost of defiance on the road to the American Revolution. In Parisian salons, conversation turned on events in America, and the works of radical thinkers – but it was news of the waltz that sparked conversation in the *casini* of Venice. Though for centuries the city's tolerance and humanism had set it apart (of all the states in Catholic Europe, Venice alone had never burned a heretic), now in an Age of Reason, when the rest of Europe was enthusiastically adopting the values for which the Republic had always stood, Venice itself no longer cared for philosophy. The guest list for a ball was more important than Voltaire; gossip about a mistress more intriguing than Rousseau. Many key cultural figures fled the city for more stimulating climes: the playwright Carlo Goldoni had gone to live in Paris in 1762; Aristarco (Giuseppe Baretti) left for London after the authorities banned his controversial literary journal *Frusta letteraria*.

Young Lorenzo Da Ponte, 'at youth's boiling point', was 'swept away into a life of voluptuousness and diversion, forgetting or neglecting literature and my studies entirely'. Angela's allure was not intellectual. 'She had no great cultivation of mind, but she was graced with such charm of manner, and with such vivacity in conversation, that not only did she slip her way into one's soul, but fairly bewitched everyone.' If only it were not for the tempers. Crippled by love for Angela, Lorenzo became ever more entangled by her tyranny, slave to her fire-eyed rages. Guilty about his neglected muse, he tried to ensure that he read for an hour each night, but even this resolution melted away as Angela lured him into further 'feasting, carousal and debauchery'. Tantrums followed his visits to bookshops (where, as Goethe noted, anyone connected with literature dropped in for long conversations), and jealous tirades met his attempts to spend time in the '*Caffè de' letterati*' – the Caffè Menegazzo halfway down the Merceria, where what remained of Venice's intellectual set gathered, and where revolutionary ideas were beginning to seep in.

The café was the meeting place of the *Accademia Granellesca* – a lively, mocking, literary society ('*granellesca*' can mean both 'testicles' and 'simpleton'), which had also a serious remit, one close to Lorenzo's heart: the rehabilitation of Italian as a literary language. At the heart of this crazy *accademia* was Carlo Gozzi, a noble from a family of dwindled fortune who had realized that the world he was born to was decaying, and had set about earning money with his pen. His play *L'amore delle tre melarance* (The Love of Three Oranges) had been an enormous success, and the fairy-tale style of the dramas that followed fascinated Lorenzo. Gozzi railed against the 'false, emphatic, metaphorical, and figured fashions, which had been introduced like plague-germs' by the *Secentisti* (seventeenth-century authors with an affected, extravagant style) and by some blustering eighteenth-century writers who followed in their wake. He stood for purity of diction, and appropriateness of style. The

Granellesca indulged in noisy antics – the 'Arch-big-simpleton' reading gibberish dissertations from his 'throne' on an outsize antique armchair – but, writes Gozzi:

> When we had amused ourselves enough . . . [we] drew from our portfolios compositions in prose and verse, serious or facetious as the theme might be, but sensible, judicious, elegant in phrase, varied in style, and correct in diction . . . This serio-comic Academy had for its object to promote the study of our best authors, the simplicity and harmony of chastened style, and above all the purity of the Italian tongue. It drew together a very large number of young men emulous of these things; and few foreigners of culture came to Venice without seeking to be admitted to its sessions.

At the edge of this hubbub sat Lorenzo Da Ponte, unproductive but absorbent – until Angela Tiepolo sent someone to drag him away.

Even more dangerous to Lorenzo's poetic muse than Angela's tyranny was the presence in the household of her twin brother Girolamo. Vicious, imperious and wild, Girolamo Tiepolo was one of the *barnabotti* – impoverished nobles, too uneducated or lacking in influence to occupy any but the most paltry administrative positions, yet precluded by their rank from doing any useful work. They were a discontented lot, often dissolute and corrupt, embittered against more powerful members of their class. Girolamo was every bit of their ilk – as obsessive gambler on the scrounge for money whenever his luck was low; louche, lascivious and possessed of a shattering disdain for those lower on the social scale.

Attitudes towards the nobility were changing, and the Venetian aristocracy was diminishing, hobbled by the practice of families that, in an attempt to retain riches and position, allowed only one son to marry and channelled all their wealth into a single line of male heirs. The numbers of poor *barnabotti* grew. Charitable hand-outs helped them preserve their position in society, and propped up the status quo. Behind masks in Venice all ranks mingled, but in reality a tiny group of ruling families fiercely resisted any attempt to loosen their hold on power, and became defensive about decorum, obsessive about rules. Poverty had forced Girolamo Tiepolo to give up his gondola, but he was still required by law to wear silk, and kept tight hold on his aristocratic mien. Precedence, heredity, posturing and contempt for inferiors became hallmarks of an aristocracy desperate to assert its status. Venice had always been an odd mix of republic and autocracy, its government (Hester Lynch Piozzi noted) being 'rich and consolatory like its treacle . . . compounded nicely of all the other forms: a grain of monarchy, a scruple of democracy, a dram of oligarchy, and an ounce of aristocracy'. The Republic was by no means egalitarian – a wide gulf still existed between people and patricians.

Becoming a priest had edged Lorenzo Da Ponte into a higher social sphere, but he hovered far below the Tiepolo realm. Angela and Girolamo made a fearsome patrician pair that the former poor boy from Ceneda, the would-be dandy and gallant buck, found impossible to oppose. He wagged his tail at Angela's whim, and bounded along at Girolamo's beck and call. But along the way he learned how to behave like an aristocrat, to pick a path past the pitfalls that surrounded social status, to learn the manners that marked out a new territory. Slowly, he pushed Ceneda further behind, and acquired the skills that would equip him for survival in another world.

From time to time he would try to break the spell that Angela had cast over him and escape Girolamo's malign influence. His account of these attempts has the hue of fantasy, the boisterous palette of an opera-buffa plot. One late autumn evening, he tells us, a few months after he had arrived in Venice, while he was sitting in the *Caffè de' letterati*, a gondolier in a *moretta* came in, looked about the room, and silently beckoned him to follow (the *moretta* mask was often kept in place by a button held between the teeth, so prevented speech). On many previous occasions Angela had thus had him summoned from his dull haunt, and he obediently left the café. Beyond the reach of light cast from the windows, past the patch made by a solitary street lamp, a gondola bumped gently against the canal wall, its black wood and dark curtains barely distinguishable from the night. When Lorenzo climbed in and the gondolier dropped the curtain, he could see nothing at all. The hand he grasped to kiss was rather more plump than Angela's. A hurried

conversation ensued, Lorenzo in his soft, lisping Venetian dialect, and a
startled woman's clipped Tuscan. There had been some mistake. She
tried to withdraw her hand, Lorenzo held tight. Could he see her to her
door? Could he at least offer her some dainties from the café? She
demurred, but the gondolier was despatched after she had elicited
Lorenzo's promise to leave the gondola immediately they had finished
refreshments, and not to press her with any questions. For a while there
was nothing but the rustle of silk, the whisper of the water; then the
gondolier returned bearing not only cakes and candies, but with a
lantern. The light revealed an exceptional beauty of around seventeen,
clearly a noble, dressed with taste and with an air of quiet charm. The
handsome couple sat in silence, gazing at each other. With all the grace
he could muster, all his newly wrought show of good breeding and every
sign of respect for her station, Lorenzo again pressed his suit to take her
home. His efforts clearly impressed. In a while she replied: 'The strange
circumstances in which I find myself forbid me to acquiesce to your
desire. It could be that they will change, in which case we may meet
again – that much I promise you! If you must know more, I may tell you
frankly that I too wish for such a happy outcome and shall use every
means to bring it to pass.' Her sparkling-eyed suitor stepped back ashore,
promising to return to the same spot, at the same hour, every night until
he saw her again. He did not even know her name.

Night after night he returned, but the gondola was never there.
Dreams that a new love might set him free from Angela's hold crumbled
into vain hopes. In a moment of panic, he suddenly pulled back. He left
Venice, thinking distance would cure his obsession with his fierce
mistress, only to discover that his desire increased and, as it did so,
the power to resist weakened. He returned after a week – and moved in
with her. In the *Caffè de' letterati* he learned that a gondolier had been
looking for him, and had been told that he had left the city. Then one
day, in the bustle on the Piazza San Marco – among the ballad singers and
mountebanks, the stalls selling books by weight and fortune-tellers
imparting secrets to the ears of the curious through long speaking-
trumpets – he felt a twitch at his coat sleeve. It was the *incognita*'s
boatman.

'I am glad you have come back,' whispered the gondolier. 'I will take the good news to my mistress. Farewell till this evening, sir!'

That night, the gondola was waiting near the *Caffè de' letterati*. Lorenzo was taken to the young woman's home, and shown to an elegant salon. From an alcove she emerged, 'sumptuously but simply gowned', and began her story.

Matilda was her name, the daughter of a Neapolitan duke. Her mother died when Matilda was a child, and after ten years her father married a younger wife, a grocer's daughter who gained despotic dominion over him and succeeded in snuffing all fatherly affection. At the age of eleven, Matilda had been placed in a convent in Pisa, and didn't see her family for another six years. She resisted all attempts by the nuns to make her take the veil, until her stepmother came to visit with an ultimatum: either she become a nun or get married to an ugly old man (Matilda calls him a 'monster' and a 'fetid corpse') that her stepmother had chosen for her.

'I hated the convent, the nuns, and my association with them,' Matilda told Lorenzo. 'After six years of prison, I was yearning for my liberty.'

With a purse of gold and casket of jewels that had once belonged to her mother, Matilda began a frantic flight, barely stopping to sleep, through Rome and Florence to Padua, then dressed as a man to Venice, where she reasoned life would be safer as everyone went masked. A young gallant of the illustrious Mocenigo family (the current Doge was a Mocenigo) had seen through her male disguise and, sympathetic to her plight, found her the house in which she was now sitting, confiding to Lorenzo. She had begun to fall in love with the young Mocenigo – it was he she had been waiting to meet in the gondola outside the *Caffè de' letterati*. Mocenigo had hinted at marriage, but had begun to borrow money from her. He was, like so many Venetian nobles, addicted to gambling and hopelessly in debt. Emboldened by her encounter with Lorenzo, Matilda had broken off relations with the young cavalier.

'If your heart is free,' she could now tell Lorenzo, 'if you have the courage to leave your native land, if the beautiful things you said to me the first time we met are true, I make a gift to you of myself, and of all I possess – which I judge quite sufficient to permit us to live decorously in any part of the world.'

Suddenly offered all he had hoped for, Lorenzo found he did not have the courage to accept, and asked for three days in which to decide. Angela seems immediately to have suspected something was amiss. Lorenzo arrived home to 'a little battle of jealousy', and spent the rest of the night dissolved in contemplation.

On the one hand was vivacious but explosive Angela and a life of pleasure, on the other the tall, dark-eyed Matilda, whose beauties 'were animated by the charms of a cultivated mind, a purse of doubloons and a casket of diamonds'. Heart pleaded for Angela; good sense argued for Matilda. Eight days passed. Yet another outburst from Angela tipped the balance. Lorenzo had been visiting Matilda and had returned home a little too late for easy explanation. Angela was waiting with a stiletto. In the fight that followed, Lorenzo managed to disarm her and break the blade. Without stopping to pack, he set off back to Matilda, resolved to leave Venice. It was around two in the morning. He beat and kicked at Matilda's door. At last her old maid came downstairs, weeping, to tell him that just after he had left, a sergeant of the Inquisitors of State had arrived with several guards, routed the girl from bed, seized all her possessions, and carried her off to a gondola.

That was chilling news. The three Inquisitors of State were a sinister offshoot of the Council of Ten, the secretive executive branch of government that was ruling with growing disregard for the assembly of patricians, the Great Council. They worked swiftly and violently, without having to answer to anyone beyond their number. Their network of spies had once given every keyhole an eye, wrought terror with the creak of a floorboard, and brought danger to every shadow. Although, by the eighteenth century, the spy network was much diminished, and the Inquisitors were not feared as much as they had been a hundred years earlier, their name could still unnerve – particularly if one mixed with the *barnabotti*, who formed the most active resistance to the increasing authoritarianism of the Council of Ten. Even the supremely nonchalant Casanova found, when arrested by the Inquisitors, that he urinated involuntarily every fifteen minutes for a full four hours.

Lorenzo froze. He felt that he had in some way 'been the cause of [Matilda's] misfortune by [his] unjustifiable irresolution', yet while this 'doubled [his] sorrow and remorse', he was powerless against the insidious brutality of the Inquisitors: 'The mystery in which that diabolical tribunal cloaked its barbarous and despotic sentences, and the terror its awful judgements inspired generally in Venice, caused me not only to despair of being able to aid her in any way, but even of ever discovering what had become of her.' Instead, he 'shed a few tears over the cruel fate of that most beautiful girl', and slunk back to Angela.

As autumn gave way to winter, Angela and Girolamo strengthened their hold over him. Under Girolamo's influence, Lorenzo became addicted to gambling. The disease riddled much of Europe, but nowhere were the stakes higher, the betting more fevered, than in Venice. Gaming laid ruin to swathes of the aristocracy, and by the early 1770s was quite out of control. The Ridotto, the public gaming-house in San Moisè, was open through the long Carnival, and anyone of any rank could enter, providing they were masked. Faro was the game of the moment, a tricky gamble that involved one banker (in the Ridotto always a noble, unmasked) and an unlimited number of players who staked bets on the dealer turning over particular combinations of cards. Odds were hugely in favour of the bank (second only to those in roulette), and this contributed to feelings of resentment against a ruling elite, who alone were permitted to open a faro table. Every night the three would head to the Ridotto and return in the early hours, their purses usually empty, 'cursing cards and the man who invented them'. They borrowed, they pawned, they sold, they stripped their wardrobes bare to feed the habit.

On the occasions that he won, Lorenzo could be generous, and his munificence was sometimes returned. One night just before Christmas, he and Angela, sullen and cleaned out after a bad run at the Ridotto, were being taken home by a gondolier whom Lorenzo had often liberally tipped. Noting their sour moods, the boatman guessed the cause and flippantly asked if they needed any money. Lorenzo joked back that he could do with fifty sequins – an enormous sum, nearly the annual earnings of a Venetian labourer. After mysteriously leaving the gondola for a moment, the gondolier returned with the money and said, 'Go, play your cards, and learn something about your Venetian boatmen!'

Back at the Ridotto, their luck turned and they won enough not only to repay and reward the gondolier, but to return home with a pile of gold. Lorenzo had just poured the winnings out on to the table when Girolamo came into the room. Lorenzo's account of their exchange encapsulates the relationship between the young *arriviste* and the overbearing patrician:

'You won this money at cards?'

'Yes, *Eccellenza* [Excellency].'

'Have you counted it?'

'No, *Eccellenza!*'

'Would you like to double it?'

'Yes, *Eccellenza!*'

'I am going to open a bank at the Ridotto – and don't you go doubting the result!'

'No, *Eccellenza!*'

This 'no' was not altogether clear; so he added, gritting his teeth, which were of enormous size:

' "Yes, *Eccellenza!* No, *Eccellenza!*" – Do you want to or do you not?'

'Yes, *Eccellenza!* Yes, *Eccellenza!*

Of what use could a 'no' of mine have been?

'Very well then, take my sister with you and follow me.'

'Yes, *Eccellenza!*'

'Don't dally!'

'No, *Eccellenza!*'

This said, he was off down the stairs, and I followed after with his sister, scratching my head and cursing His Yes-*Eccellenza*, the Golden Book [the exclusive list of Venice's aristocratic families], and the whole quarter of San Barnabà [home to most *barnabotti*].

Girolamo, as one might have predicted, lost the lot.

Angela and her brother went home. Lorenzo, despondent (and perhaps a little worse for wear), retired to the Chamber of Sighs –

the room at the Ridotto where luckless gamblers shared their woes and dozed. He fell asleep in a chair, and the following morning was approached by a man in a mask who asked for two soldi (barely enough to buy a cup of hot chocolate for breakfast). To Lorenzo's surprise, he found on feeling in his pocket that he had, wedged under a handkerchief, some gold coins that had escaped his notice and Girolamo's grasp the previous evening. Having nothing smaller, he offered the man a sequin. The man accepted, with the proviso (writing his address on a playing card) that Lorenzo come later to his home to be repaid. Lorenzo rushed back to tell Angela about his new-found stash of gold. As he approached their door, he saw her gesturing from a window that he should not come in, but instead wait for her in a nearby café. Two hours later she came, in a storm of tears, to tell him that Girolamo had evicted him from the house, banned him from seeing her again, and had even pawned his bed – for six sequins, which he had taken to gamble. Lorenzo revealed his new treasure, which amounted to the equivalent of over one hundred sequins. Together, the pair conjured up a plot to reclaim Girolamo's goodwill by telling him that Lorenzo had been given the secret of making gold – an idea not as outlandish as it may sound, as many Venetian nobles believed in alchemy (Casanova had once exploited such beliefs to some gain). Lorenzo went to the gaming-house Girolamo frequented, left the odd sequin lying on the table in an offhand way, and was soon back in the patrician's favour – lending him gold, and hinting at its magical secret source. For a while the scheme worked, as all three had a run of good luck that meant the original supply of gold was not depleted.

During this time, Lorenzo paid a visit to the old man who had left his address on a playing card in the Chamber of Sighs. His account of what followed rivals the story of Matilda in romance. The old man, he says, revealed himself to be a beggar king. For some time he had been observing Lorenzo from his daily post on the Ponte San Giorgio, and was moved by Lorenzo's frequently giving him alms, despite evidently not having much money himself. Born in Livorno, he had lost a large inheritance through generosity and imprudent ventures, had come to Venice, where he had picked up a wasting fever, and so – friendless and without support – had taken to begging. Over the course of nearly half a century he had amassed a fortune in this way. He had married a poor widow's daughter, who, though she later died, had left him with a child. The beautiful young Annetta he now offered as a wife to Lorenzo, with a 5,000-sequin dowry and the promise of another 4,000 sequins' inheritance. Lorenzo was clearly no longer dressing as a priest.

Passion for Angela was a hard bit in his mouth, but his clerical status put an even greater restraint on any idea of marriage to an unsuspecting Annetta (something that does not appear to have troubled his reasoning when he decided to elope with Matilda). The old man's generosity deserved a frank response: 'I feel, sir, to the very depths of my soul, the weight of the treature you offter me: but it would not please God were I to be the possessor of it. Since I can return your kindness in no other way, I shall at least repay it with a sincere confession which cannot offend you. I must tell you straightforwardly that I am not in a position to marry.' Possessed of a little more honour than after the Matilda affair, Lorenzo made his way home – again having stayed out later than he should.

This time Angela was waiting 'in the clutches of a thousand furies', with not a stiletto but a bottle of ink, which she launched at him the moment he appeared at the door of her room. It shattered on the arm he put up to protect himself, and his hand was so lacerated by shards of glass that he could not use it for a month. Angela appeared calmed by the outburst, but the lull was deceptive. That night, as Lorenzo slept, she stealthily cut off his hair. Her ploy, he says, was to stop him going outdoors. At the time, wigs were widely worn among men in the upper strata of society – human hair if funds permitted, otherwise horse or goat hair, powdered white with rice-meal or wheat-flour and liberally greased so the powder would stick. If Lorenzo had one, Angela must also have made off with that, or (as he admits), '*Vedi se Amor m'avea tolto il cervello!* [See how Love has removed my brain!]' – his passion had not only resulted in the loss of his hair, but had removed his brain. He stayed in the house.

Through all these wild months in Venice, Lorenzo had somehow managed to continue giving lessons to the two patrician boys he had begun to teach on his arrival. When he did not turn up for a number of days in a row, their mother, who had become friendly with the young tutor and was concerned that something was amiss, came personally to call on him. Shocked at the dissolute company she discovered him to be keeping, she sacked him the following morning. That left Lorenzo without any income, yet Angela – who allowed him out only at night, and exclusively in her company – continued to whirl him through theatres and public spectacles (the big attraction that year was Rousseau's *Pygmalion*, now seen as the world's first melodrama), to faro games and society dinners.

Soon he was desperate for money. To aggravate matters, Girolamo had come to the end of his winning streak, and accosted Lorenzo in his room, demanding a hundred sequins. When Lorenzo said he had none, the patrician said menacingly; 'Make it, then! I know very well, milord Lorenzo, that you know how to make gold, and I demand – and I think I have the right to demand – that you give me the secret.' Cowed, and frightened, Lorenzo promised him something within four or five days. He tried frantically to find more employment, and was desperate enough to sell some books, which was always for him a painful last resort. On 19 January 1774 he wrote to his old friend Michele Colombo (in one of only two letters still extant from his time in Venice), saying that he would be sending on a bundle of books worth seventy-five lire, and that Colombo should get thirty-five lire for them from one Durigon (perhaps the 'ignorant and stupid' bookseller from Ceneda) – the other forty lire being required to pay off a debt. Lorenzo begged for the money in advance. He had been sick for a fortnight, was penniless, and though an intermediary had found him work, he was having to pay up front for the favour. 'If you do not have the money yourself, find it somehow, but do not leave me without this help,' he entreated his friend. 'Remember that any delay is the same as denying me help, and that to deny me help will mean my ruin.' For a moment the poor boy from Ceneda resurfaced, desperate not to lose the approval of the father who for most of his childhood had shown him no real affection, nor of the society that had scorned *lo Spiritoso ignorante* but accepted the clever abbé: 'Say nothing of this to my father, nor to anyone in the world.'

★　　★　　★

As 1774 progressed and Lorenzo sunk further into the morass, the sole
hope of rescue centred on his own brother Girolamo, an 'angelic youth'
who had followed him to Venice from Portogruaro. Since their earliest
days in the ghetto, the boys had been inseparable. 'I was tied [to him]
with bonds,' Lorenzo wrote, 'I know not whether more of friendship or
of nature . . . [He was] comrade, counsellor, and friend – qualities, as a
rule, so rare and so difficult to find in a brother.' Modest, already wise,
and affectionate, Girolamo was on the way to becoming a respected
priest and scholar. For weeks he tried to pull his older sibling back from
the dual grasp of Angela and gambling. Girolamo was also in intermittent
contact with Michele Colombo. Just a few days after Lorenzo wrote
begging money in January, Girolamo sent a letter fraught with concern
for his brother.

> You ask me what is happening with Lorenzo, and I would rather not
> be in this world than tell you anything about it. The wretched man has
> brought so many disgraces upon himself that I could not describe them
> to you, nor could you imagine a worse state. He is no longer able to
> clothe himself, he has no money, no friends, and what matters most is
> that he has no more credit or fame [i.e. has lost his good name]. I
> would not suffer so much in this respect if I did not see him so very
> unconcerned about remedying his own catastrophes; discouraged, and
> abandoned by all, scornful of my frequent admonishments, in posses-
> sion of an amorous passion that blinds him completely. His only
> amusement is enjoying nights at the theatre, in the Ridotto, and
> sleeping through the day. He does not look for work because he has
> lost all hope of finding any, accusing me of urging him to out of my
> own interest and ambitions.

Lorenzo's behaviour was indeed affecting Girolamo's own reputation in
Venice, yet he was racked by guilt at even thinking about this.
Eventually, even the angelic younger brother seems on the verge of
giving up, with a 'Basta! May God provide for us, because now I'm not
going to torment myself any further.'

Not just Lorenzo but the whole city seemed to be hurtling ever faster in its hedonism. In 1773, the authorities had tried to apply the brakes. The Greater Council passed a law prohibiting the sale of alcohol to men under thirty in the city's forty-eight *osterie* and *locande* – inns notorious for their rowdiness – and exhorted moderation and decency among theatre audiences, threatening with fines those who insulted actors. As if in sympathy, the S. Benedetto theatre (the one that had been built with Tiepolo family money), one of the most infamous for audience bad behaviour, burned to the ground. The following year, the government would close the Ridotto.

In February, and again in March of 1774, Girolamo implored Colombo to help him in trying to rescue his brother; night after night he tried to talk Lorenzo out of his downward spiral. Yet although Lorenzo admitted he could see the logic in Girolamo's arguments, he could not summon the strength to resist. Gradually, though, Girolamo won him over. Through the auspices of a priest at the church of San Maurizio, the pair were given positions as teachers at the seminary in Treviso. Angela's response to the news is unrecorded.

Lorenzo gives a note of drama to his decision to leave, saying that one night a fellow wayward priest from the Portogruaro seminary visited him at home, and on the way out stole his cloak, which he pawned at the shop next door for gambling money. Seeing that someone could sink to such depths provided the impulse he needed, Lorenzo says, and he wrote to his brother:

> Girolamo:
>
> No more gambling, no more women, no more Venice! I would leave tonight if I had any money. But I swear not to stay here three days longer. Let us thank God and the poor thief! I will see you in the morning!

Girolamo, Lorenzo relates, arrived that night with enough money for their departure. It is more likely to have been debt and fear of Angela's brother than such an epiphany that impelled Lorenzo's exit from Venice. A letter of 8 October 1774, from Lorenzo to Michele Colombo, shows that he had been offered the position in Treviso before he left, and

Girolamo's letters to Colombo become less panicked after April – but whether or not the flight was sudden, there is no doubt that young Girolamo Da Ponte provided the leg-up.

The brothers' problems were not over. They were sacked before they had even arrived in Treviso. A priest from Ceneda had been blackening Lorenzo's name with vile slanders about his behaviour (not a feat that required much imagination), including the accusation that he had been dismissed from the seminary at Portogruaro because he had run away with a woman from Ceneda. The Bishop of Treviso, Monsignor Paolo Francesco Giustiniani, had believed the charges and retracted his offer. Lorenzo's October letter to Michele Colombo was an urgent plea for his intervention; Colombo knew the priest in question: 'You are my only ray of hope, since you still love me, and this priest loves you greatly.' Colombo evidently had some influence. The Da Pontes were reinstated. At the beginning of the 1774–75 academic year at Treviso, after a ten-day holiday in Ceneda, Lorenzo took up the post of master of humanities (meaning Latin literature), and Girolamo became a teacher of grammar. Lorenzo was to be paid a yearly salary of 217 Venetian lire – the equivalent of just over 27 ducats – substantially less than he received as a vice-rector at Portogruaro and a fraction of the money he had frittered at the Ridotto. Girolamo – who had given up a lucrative and prestigious position as secretary to a patrician family in order to keep an eye on his brother – earned just 155 lire, under 20 ducats.

Angela Tiepolo took another lover the moment they left town, but she was not yet finished with Lorenzo Da Ponte.

Chapter Three

T REVISO OFFERED SOME respite from the wiles and seduc-
tions of Venice, though not a complete escape. Rich Venetians
migrated there to evade clammy summers on the lagoon, and
those travellers who did not approach Venice by river from Padua
generally passed through Treviso on the way to Mestre, the chief mainland
departure point for gondolas, just two and a half hours' journey away. The
itinerant voluptuary William Beckford stopped in Treviso to dine before
completing a jolting chaise-ride to the boats, admiring, as he bumped
along, the 'grand villas and gardens peopled with statues'. Michael Kelly,
on the lookout for singing engagements, was similarly 'delighted by the
appearance of the elegant villas which surround [Treviso], belonging to
noble Venetians, who, during the theatrical season, pass their *vendemmias*
[grape harvest] there, and have what they call their *cuganas* (i.e. revelries)'.
He happily joined the beau monde in their rounds of concerts and parties,
noting that 'the theatre was crowded every night, and the opera, as well as
the ballets, gave great satisfaction'.

At the kernel of the decorative husk of country mansions was a compact,
colourful town, famed for its outdoor frescoes and ringed by canals and a
sturdy city wall. The Da Ponte brothers entered its shelter. With Girolamo
to keep an eye on him, in the sobering atmosphere of the seminary and
without Angela Tiepolo as a social pander, Lorenzo was able to detach
himself from what giddy '*cuganas*' there were in Treviso and rebuild
something of the life he had once foreseen for himself. The cool climate,

pure air and gentle landscape of Treviso were an inspiration to poets, and in addition to the dizzy dance of Venetian summer exiles, a brilliant society of literati flourished. 'Thus my liberated soul began anew to wander among the sweet and delightful fields of the Muses,' he wrote. The clatter of the Ridotto gave way to the repose of a 'beautiful and copious library'; expensive scents and fragrant pomades to the milder aromas of paper and vellum. Once again there were minds to engage him, books that held him in awe. Lorenzo set about cataloguing the library, and adding new volumes to the shelves. He found his pupils 'full of vivacity and talent', and Bishop Giustiniani wise and devoted to the school. When lessons were over and the library work done, he spent all his time with his brother Girolamo and Giulio Trento, an eminent scholar from a local noble family. Good-looking, of agile mind and irresistible charm, the regenerate young Abbé Da Ponte in turn made an impact on his students and the bishop. Angelo Marchesan, who held the same post as Da Ponte 120 years later, records something of the energetic master's reputation:

> . . . [Da Ponte was] full of life, of passion, of poetry, extremely clever, with a lively imagination, quick of tongue, and very learned. All their lives his young pupils remembered their teacher, who not only fired them with the joy of studying literature but showed them such genuine affection and influenced them so greatly through his teaching, by this very influence making the tedium of the seminary walls seem less oppressive and the schoolroom benches less hard . . .

Lorenzo was happy, appreciated, productive and fulfilled – but Angela Tiepolo was not going to let go so easily. Daily, despite having a new lover, she sent letters 'omitting . . . neither artifice nor phrases calculated to convince me of her tenderness and constancy', until, late on New Year's Day of 1775, a startling missive arrived:

> Lorenzo:
>   If you love my honour and my life, come to Venice at once. About ten o'clock in the evening you will find me at my cousin's.
> Your faithful love.

It was an icy night, with a frost *che gela fin ai pensieri* ('which freezes even one's fancy' as a local saying went), yet Lorenzo – wrapped in a heavy cloak and armed against whatever dangers he might encounter – set out immediately by carriage for Venice. The wintry conditions slowed his journey, and it was almost midnight by the time a gondolier dropped him on the *riva* of Angela's cousin's *palazzo*. As his hand reached for the door knocker, another grabbed at it, pulled him violently away and dragged him into the dark cover of a nearby bridge. A hoarse voice whispered, 'For Heaven's sake, boss, don't go in there!' Lorenzo recognized the croaking tones of an old servant from Angela's household. The letter was a ploy, it turned out, by Angela's new lover, one Michele Dondirologi – 'One of the most arrogant and dangerous bullies in Venice,' said the servant – to lure Lorenzo to the house and beat him up. Evidently Angela had met her match when it came to jealous furies. Now in a rage himself and heedless of the old man's pleas, Lorenzo hammered on the door. It clicked open, as someone pulled on the cord that drew back its bolt, and he cautiously climbed the stairs (the old servant quaking behind him), past a single flickering lantern, to find Angela emerging, in dishabille, from a bedroom. She was alone. Luckily for Lorenzo he was hours late – he had been expected at around ten o'clock and an impatient Dondirologi had gone off gambling. Angela sidled into Lorenzo's arms, giving a little cry of delight. That act of brazenness, he recalled, more than anything else, propelled him to breaking point: 'At that moment I rushed headlong down the stairs, like a man escaping from a great danger, rushed to the nearest landing, took a gondola, returned to Mestre and thence to Treviso, with the firmest resolve never to see or hear of that woman again. It was as if at that point a ray of heavenly light had descended on my mind to illuminate my reason and cure me entirely.'

Back in Treviso, to Girolamo's undoubted relief, now that Lorenzo had finally severed ties with Angela Tiepolo he steered with clear focus along his new course. A year after arriving at the seminary he was promoted to the chair of rhetoric, which meant he could once again teach the Italian literature he loved so much; Girolamo stepped up to occupy the post he had vacated. Older colleagues smarted at the brothers' rapid elevation. Wagging tongues were sharpened, as they had been in Portogruaro, by Lorenzo's airy arrogance – his attitude that 'though not completely lacking in erudition and scholarship, [the other teaching staff] were entirely devoid of the talent and good taste which are the soul of letters' (which he, of course, had in abundance).

Lorenzo took to his new task with all the zeal instilled in him by the innovative Abbé Cagliari a decade earlier in Ceneda, helping to establish Italian literature as a discipline worthy of serious study in the seminary. His own muse responded accordingly. With Giulio Trento as an erudite and penetrating critic, Lorenzo began to write poetry again, fired by his new friend to greater literary heights than he had ever achieved. At an *accademia* of literati in the city in March 1776, he recited *Il Cechino*, a charming pastoral poem that displays a delightful delicacy of touch. It was a resounding success. 'There was such applause,' he wrote to Michele Colombo, 'that some fifteen or twenty copies were printed in eight days.' Riding high on his new poetic fame and the bishop's good opinion, Lorenzo set about the most prestigious duty of his post as professor of literature: composing the poems for select students to recite at the public *accademia*, at the end of the academic year in August 1776.

During the Da Ponte brothers' first year at the Treviso seminary, on 19 April in far-distant America, near a town called Concord some twenty miles out of Boston, a force of insurgent militia (the 'embattled farmers' later celebrated in a poem by Ralph Waldo Emerson) had 'fired the shot heard round the world' against an expedition of British infantry sent to challenge them. The War of the American Revolution had begun. Just over a year later, on 4 July 1776, Congress voted its approval of the document lucidly penned by Thomas Jefferson, a declaration of independence with a preamble that included the assertion:

We hold these truths to be self-evident, that all men are created equal, that they are endowed by their Creator with certain inalienable Rights, that among these are Life, Liberty and the pursuit of Happiness. That to secure these rights, Governments are instituted among Men, deriving their just powers from the consent of the governed . . .

News of that declaration would not have reached Treviso by the time Lorenzo was writing the poems for the August *accademia*; and, besides, America was a very different world, far away, with no resident king or local aristocrats, no established church or feudal system of land tenure. Yet the sentiments the declaration expressed had an echo in an Old World whose social order was based on hierarchy and on the commands of a church that preached that the pursuit of earthly happiness was a delusion, and the only true reward was to be found in heaven. Jefferson's words encapsulated thoughts that had been darting around many men's minds in both America and Europe for some decades, thoughts that were also finding direction in France – the phrase about 'inalienable Rights' might easily have been a quotation from a work by Rousseau. They were ideas that might not have had much currency in Venice, among an elite determined to preserve power, or with those who were simply dancing while the pearls dropped off, but they did find hold in the literary minds of Treviso, and in that of the young man from Ceneda who was so certain of his own worth, yet aware of his lowly rank. He had clearly been reading or discussing Rousseau. For the 1776 *accademia*, Lorenzo Da Ponte chose the theme: 'Whether Mankind had attained happiness by uniting in a social system, or could be considered happier in the simple state of nature.' In his *Discours sur les sciences et les arts*, an essay on a subject proposed by the Academy of Dijon in 1749, Rousseau had argued that far from elevating human behaviour, the spread of knowledge and culture had been a corrupting force leading to inequality, idleness and luxury. The idea would have appealed to the reformed young man shedding the likes of Angela Tiepolo, and extricating himself from the corrupted slime of Venice.

Poems in an *accademia* were presented in a *pro et contra* manner, so that the event took the form of a debate that enabled students to show off their skills at declamation. The Abbé Da Ponte had written four Latin and eleven Italian poems, introduced by a prose preface. As form dictated, he presented both sides of the argument, but his *contra* compositions were daring, dissenting, quite astonishing in their temerity. His preface struck the first challenging note. After a conventional admission that man, though longing for happiness, has on earth to settle for an approximate version of the ideal – and an acknowledgement that laws improve the chances of happiness by protecting order and property and punishing crime – he raised the provocative question of whether this happiness, based on fear, really was superior to that of the Golden Age, when love was the only law. The poems that followed took differing angles of approach to an answer.

The first, a Latin elegy entitled 'The American in Europe', proposed that by increasing both fears and hopes, laws had driven man further from happiness. The second, a long Italian composition in blank verse, argued that man could only wish for happiness in life, and that since that desire existed in men in both a social and a natural state, laws could not contribute to happiness. So they went on, through an *anacreontic* that developed the theme that laws prevent man from reaching happiness by following the impulses of his heart – and which challenged the power of a father to refuse his daughter the right to marry the man she loved, and questioned the right of a state to compel military service – to a gloomy *canzone* based on the assumption that man's approximate happiness is but a state of mind, apt to be wrong, so laws neither afford nor deny the means of reaching it. Even the *pro* arguments seemed to take a dangerous tilt. One by one, the young seminarists came to the podium to declaim: a Latin ode treating the argument that happiness is related to wealth, and that as the laws of society distribute wealth unevenly, they make happiness more easily obtainable for some than others; a *sermone* that violently attacked privileged classes for claiming rights not accorded them by nature, and maintained humanity had enslaved itself by submitting to laws; a sonnet that deplored the fact that poverty prevented the education of so many gifted minds – all the way to a harmless pastoral dialogue of general thanks, and an *anacreontic* expressing gratitude to the bishop, who presided over the *accademia*.

The young professor's audacity may well have provoked a sharp intake of breath among the dignitaries present, but in the refined literary and academic atmosphere of Treviso his poems, though startling, were not damnable. As was the custom, they were published subsequent to the ceremony. The problems began when the poems reached the sharp eyes and sensitive ears of Venice. It did not take long. Within weeks,

Inquisitor Padre Giuseppe Frassen had denounced them to the *Riformatori*, the body of three patricians that held control over education and
publication in the Venetian territories, men, Da Ponte sniffed, 'who had
more need of being reformed than morals and sense to reform with'. The
Riformatori submitted a report to the Senate, who twice summoned the
rector of the seminary for questioning. The situation was beginning to
look serious. Throughout the process, the culprit remained teaching in
Treviso, apparently unconcerned. Girolamo, Giulio Trento, and eventually Bishop Giustiniani himself urged him to go to Venice to build up a
defence. Finally, in October, he demurred and set off once more for
Mestre.

The Venice life Da Ponte returned to was very different from the one
he had left behind two years earlier – the city continued on its merry
dance, but he began to mix with people of a markedly more refined
calibre than Angela and her ilk. The Giustiniani family was an old and
influential one, with a doge among their ancestors. The bishop, it would
seem, had had a few quiet words in selected family ears. Within days of
arriving back, Da Ponte met Bernardo Memmo, scion of an even
grander family than the bishop's – his brother Andrea was later to
become Procurator of St Mark, the second highest office in the Republic. Both brothers had been close friends of Goldoni's before the
playwright fled Venice for the more stimulating intellectual atmosphere
of Paris. Some twenty years older than Da Ponte, Memmo had himself
once been a state senator, and was a man of erudition and talent. Da
Ponte also renewed contact with Pietro Antonio Zaguri, with whom he
and his brother Girolamo had once dined. Zaguri was the genial and
influential head of an important family and, though very much at the
centre of Venice's pleasure-seeking society, was also a protector of such
men of letters as the incorrigible Casanova.

Memmo was able to procure the support of Gasparo Gozzi – a fine
poet, one of Italy's foremost literary critics, and a man with some
influence with the *Riformatori*. Urged on by Memmo, Da Ponte sent
a copy of the offending poems to Gozzi, with a flattering verse letter
beginning:

Gozzi, se un cor gentil giammai non seppe
Negar soccorso a un infelice oppresso
Da fortuna crudel, il favor vostro
Non indarno a sperar certo mi tragge
Un ardito pensiero: io so che sempre
Gentilezza, e pietate il proprio loco
Ebber nel vostro seno . . .

[Gozzi, if a kind heart was never able
To deny assistance to an unhappy man
Oppressed by cruel fortune, your favour
Does not bring me to think
An audacious thought in vain: I know that kindness
And compassion always had their place
In your heart . . .]

Gozzi responded by declaring, 'This young man has talent, and ought to be encouraged.' This elicited the rejoinder from the *Riformatori*: 'So much the worse; we must deprive him of the means of becoming dangerous.'

Gozzi's younger brother Carlo provided much of the energy behind the *Accademia Granellesca*, the literary society that made the *Caffè de' letterati* its headquarters and the purity of the Italian language its aim. During his earlier time in the city, on the nights that he had escaped Angela Tiepolo's net, Da Ponte had fluttered unnoticed at the edge of this company of Venice's intelligentsia; now he was at its core – and he discovered that he was a celebrity. His case was causing quite a stir among those Venetians whose gaze reached beyond the faro table. Zaguri, Memmo and Giovanni Da Lezze (Girolamo's erstwhile employer) drew up a petition to the Council of Ten, to whom Gozzi also made a number of appeals. Despite this, the Senate decided to bring the matter to trial, setting a date for 14 December. The cocksure Abbé Da Ponte, enjoying his fame and confident of the influence of his supporters, or simply unable to take the situation seriously, deigned not to attend. None of his new-found friends chose to speak publicly in his defence. There is a note of hurt in his memoirs as he tries to excuse the fact that they 'did not judge it prudent or necessary to speak.'

Michael Kelly tells of a hearing before the Inquisition (admittedly renowned for its unconventional practices) where the entire room was draped in black, and part of the proceedings involved a curtain being suddenly drawn aside to reveal a strangled corpse; Goethe describes a buffo-like trial in the Palazzo Ducale, before a semicircle of judges on a raised dais, in which a short, fat advocate had each booming interjection timed by a clerk with an hourglass, and elicited roars of laughter from an admiring public with his facetious remarks. Da Ponte's trial displayed the full pomp of state authority, with the senators in crimson robes and similarly dazzling prosecutors who denounced the poet with sharp invective, and orated the offending works to a tumult of hisses and jeers. The chief prosecutor, Francesco Morosini, a forceful orator whom Da Ponte branded 'the hunchback', received surprise assistance from Pietro Barbarigo ('the cripple'), who was ostensibly there as defence for the censors who had failed to stop the publication of Da Ponte's poems, yet joined in the onslaught, reading out 'in stentorian tones' not only 'The American in Europe', which was in Latin, but also the more publicly accessible Italian *sermone*, which attacked the privileged classes. Here matters took a dangerous turn, when a line ridiculing lords with '*corna aurate*' (golden horns) was taken to refer to the little horn on the Doge's cap — such sedition was serious.

Da Ponte was declared guilty. Memmo, who was at the hearing, came running with the news, and everyone urged Da Ponte to flee before sentence was passed. 'But I laughed at them and at their fears,' he recalled. 'I could not believe that [the Senate] would proceed with severe punishments after having beaten so many drums to make an effect. Venetian policy never barked when it intended to bite.' His nonchalance carried through to his appearance before the Senate to receive sentence — which could quite easily have been banishment, or death. Instead, he was forbidden to teach at any school, college, seminary or university throughout the Republic. 'I bowed my head,' he continues, 'pressed my hand and my handkerchief to my lips to keep from laughing, and went out.' Memmo and Girolamo were on the steps of the Palazzo

Ducale to meet him, and the remainder of the day was spent in carousal and feasting.

If Da Ponte did not (or could not) take the affair seriously, the Senate certainly did. Every copy of the poems that could be found was destroyed; Bishop Giustiniani was severely rebuked (even though, unbeknown to Da Ponte, he had sent the Senate a letter claiming that the young teacher had without consultation changed the theme for the *accademia* from the approved one at the last minute); and an investigation was announced into education not just in Treviso, but at every school in the Republic.

Though he may well have pressed his handkerchief to his lips and laughed at his sentence, Lorenzo Da Ponte at the age of twenty-seven was once again without a means of income, or anywhere to live. Bernardo Memmo opened his home, and his purse. Ever faithful, Girolamo returned to Venice, and resumed as tutor to the sons of Giovanni Da Lezze, the position he had abandoned to accompany Lorenzo to Treviso. The brothers were back in the lap of the wizened *madame* of the Adriatic.

The chatter in the *casini* over chicken and champagne, the gossip over breakfast chocolate, the talk behind newspapers in the coffee-houses, was full of Da Ponte's trial and his poetic ability. The boy who had been *lo Spiritoso ignorante* had become a man fêted by Venice intelligentsia, called on to recite his poems in society – and he discovered a new talent. He could speak verse after just a minute or two of preparation. He and Girolamo became known as 'The Improvisers of Ceneda'. The English writer Tobias Smollett, on his travels through Italy, witnessed a performance such as they might have given:

> One of the great curiosities you meet with in Italy, is the *improvvisatore*; such is the name given to certain individuals, who have the surprising talent of reciting verses extempore on any subject you propose. Mr Corvesi, my landlord, has a son, a Franciscan friar, who is a great genius in this way. When the subject is given, his brother tunes his violin to accompany him, and he begins to rehearse in recitative, with a wonderful fluency and precision. Thus, he will, at a minute's warning, recite two or three hundred verses, well turned, and well adapted, and generally mingled with an elegant compliment to the company. The

Italians are so fond of poetry, that many of them have the best part of Ariosto, Tasso and Petrarch by heart; and these are the great sources from which the *improvvisatori* draw their rhymes, cadence, and turns of expression.

Poetry improvised to violin, guitar or harpsichord music was the jazz of eighteenth-century Italy. Carlo and Gasparo Gozzi were also good at it; Da Ponte's hero Metastasio had as a boy improvised eighty stanzas in one session, and ruined his health with similar exhausting performances. The most famous *improvvisatore* – Perfetti, who started slowly to quiet harpsichord music, then built to a resounding crescendo that left him utterly limp after each performance; and the cross-eyed Maria Maddalena Morelli, known as Corilla Olimpica – both received Rome's highest literary accolade, the Crown of the Capitol (though La Corilla's notoriety was such that the ceremony had to take place at night). Many disagreed with official plaudits for such a populist art. Carlo Gozzi, despite his own prowess, was reserved about state honours being accorded extemporizers and wrote: 'If a painter sought to depict foolhardiness or imposture wearing the mask of poetry, I could recommend nothing better than the portrait of an *improvvisatore*, with goggle-eyes and arms in the air, and a multitude staring up at him in dumb amazement,' but admits that when the art was well done 'the immense crowds of people hanging with open mouths upon the lips of an *improvvisatore* only prove that, in spite of the contempt into which poetry has fallen, it still possesses that power over the minds and brains of men which their tongues deny it.' For Da Ponte (goggle-eyed, arms in the air, or not), improvising helped channel the huge surge of poetry he had committed to memory during his early days in the seminary at Ceneda, the rhymes and rhythms that still washed in his head, into a facility for skilful, easy recitative. Memmo's house thronged with admiring visitors. Da Ponte remembers: 'At this juncture, I was loved of women, esteemed of men, cosseted by patrons, and full of the brightest hope.' Such felicity was not to last.

Exactly what happened between Da Ponte and Memmo's live-in mistress, Teresa Zerbin, is unclear. Da Ponte says Teresa resented his

influence over Memmo, who was nearly fifty and infatuated with the
young woman, and that she did her best to drive him from the house;
Teresa claimed that Da Ponte tried to seduce her; Memmo maintained a
gentlemanly silence. Whether a touchy Da Ponte stormed out of the
house in an impetuous fit at Teresa's rudeness, or whether Memmo had
quietly given him his marching orders, the result was he found himself
early in 1777 homeless, penniless, and on the road to Padua. His younger
brother Luigi was a student at the university there, and might provide
some refuge.

Dr Charles Burney, who had visited Padua just a few years earlier,
found the city 'very disagreeable, the streets being dark, narrow, and very
ill-paved with great rambling stones of different sizes', and thought the
porticoes that lined the roadsides 'low and clumsy' even if they did
provide shade and shelter from wet weather. Young Joseph Spence,
travelling earlier in the century, wrote home to his mother that he had
expected the famous university town to be like Oxford, but found
instead 'the ghost of a great city', where 'the grass gets the better of them
in several of the streets for want of feet enough to tread it down'. Michael
Kelly complained of the hordes of beggars. Yet Gozzi wrote of its
temperate air – a remark which may also be read metaphorically, as
Padua was less decadent than Venice, and moved at a gentler pace.

Having paid for a stagecoach for part of the way, and walked the rest,
Da Ponte arrived in Padua with little more than his priest's cassock and
just fifty lire – to find Luigi 'more in need of receiving help than of giving
it', and unable to house him. Instead, he found the cheapest inn in town,
and worked out that he could scrape by on one lire (twenty Venetian
soldi) a day – eight soldi for a bed, five for a coffee, and seven for a diet of
bread and salty black olives, which would make him drink large
quantities of water to fill his stomach. Memmo sent on his clothes: 'I
was therefore able to present myself decently in the cafés and public
resorts of that city,' he wrote, 'where every day I showed myself
scrupulously groomed, and beautifully attired.' He had learned to keep
his poverty hidden.

Da Ponte's abysmal financial predicament did little to suppress his taste
for gambling, and he began to bolster his purse a little by playing draughts

and *ombre* (a card game) against students innocent of his Venetian sophistication. After forty-two days of his bread-and-black-olive existence, he earned enough in one evening of *ombre* for a good meal, and the fare back to Venice. Caterino Mazzolà, an acquaintance from the glittering parties of a few months earlier, and himself a poet of note, effected a reconciliation with Memmo. Mazzolà was everything Da Ponte might have been, had poverty not forced him into the priesthood and teaching; and love for Angela Tiepolo not veered him so drastically off course. The son of a rich furnace-owning family from Murano – the island where Venetian glass is made – Mazzolà had never had to worry about money, and had devoted his full energies to writing. He had already caused a ripple of approval, when he was just twenty-six, with an *opera seria, Ruggiero*. The great Metastasio had used parts of the libretto as the basis for his own *Ruggiero* in Milan in 1771. For the 1777–78 season in Venice, Mazzolà was working on an opera buffa, *Il marito indolente*, which the following year would catch the eye of a visitor to the city, the composer Antonio Salieri, and result in a commission for an opera that became an enormous success: *La scuola dei gelosi*. If Da Ponte felt any twinge of envy at Mazzolà's easy path to poetic glory, he did not allow it vent, and the two men became good friends.

Bernardo Memmo welcomed Da Ponte back into his orbit, but the errant abbé did not return to live in Memmo's house. Instead, he took lodgings with a working-class family in the San Luca quarter, where he officiated in the local church. His other patron, Pietro Antonio Zaguri, took him on as his secretary. There was something preternatural about Da Ponte's charm. No matter the scurrilities of which he might be suspect, in spite of his impetuousness, petty arrogance and at times infuriating manner, person after person melted to his allure – from the bishops of Ceneda, Portogruaro and Treviso, to Memmo, Zaguri, and even his brother Girolamo and Michele Colombo. Yet there was a hollowness to his position. His new patrician patrons were not his friends. There were strict limits to their protection and a distance to their goodwill. They may have drawn up a petition during his trouble with the *Riformatori*, but no one would speak up for him before the Senate. And while they had the leisure to lead a life of genteel study and conversation, Da Ponte had to earn his living. He may have shone in their company, but he was still an employee – not always joining them at the dinner table, but copying their letters, teaching their offspring. Many of his new milieu remained '*Eccellenza*', while he was mere 'Abbé'.

Behind Da Ponte's back, Zaguri could be condescending and scathing, once describing his secretary as, 'A strange man; known for a scoundrel of mediocre calibre, but gifted with great talents for literature, and with physical attractions which win love for him!' and later, 'Da Ponte is a madman in every sense,' and, 'There can hardly be a worse individual than Da Ponte.' Yet on the surface relations were cordial, and at Zaguri's house Lorenzo once again mingled with the likes of Bernardo Memmo and Gasparo Gozzi. He also met the wayward man of letters Giacomo Casanova, who had returned to Venice after many years of exile, and the politically radical Giorgio Pisani.

Casanova had been a close friend of the Memmo brothers – especially Andrea – in the 1750s. Together they led a life of merry riot, drinking cheap malmsey in a *malvasìa* and arguing loud and late in coffee-houses, in boisterous support of plays by their friend Goldoni. Mother Memmo was not best pleased by the corrupting influence of the man she saw as a dangerous atheist and dissolute on her impressionable boys, and she had used family contacts to speed Casanova's arrest by the Inquisitors in 1755. (The Inquisitors' spies had already built up a fat and damning dossier on this wild son of two theatre folk.) Casanova was imprisoned beneath the lead roofs of the Palazzo Ducale, a dismally secure gaol known as 'the Leads'. His spectacular escape and flight the following year became the talk of society, as was his prowess at seduction – both reputations skilfully fanned by the man himself. Not everyone succumbed to his charm. 'He has gained admittance, I don't know how, to the best Parisian society,' wrote an unimpressed Giustiniana Wynne in 1758 from France, to Andrea Memmo, her long-time secret lover. 'He is quite full of himself and stupidly pompous. In a word, he is unbearable. Except when he speaks of his escape, which he recounts admirably.'

Finally allowed back to his homeland in 1774, the self-styled Chevalier de Seingalt was down on his luck. Though a dextrous writer, and of impressive intelligence, he had experienced a run of literary mishaps, and his latest effort – a translation of the *Iliad* – was faltering for lack of subscribers. He had sunk to working as an occasional spy for the Inquisitors. Once tall and broad-shouldered (his friend the Count de Ligne had dubbed him 'Hercules'), with burnished skin, flaring nostrils, and an awe-inspiring nose, Casanova had, at fifty-two, grown disturbingly and prematurely old, in his person and attitudes – or so Henriette, perhaps the greatest love of his life, had told him. He had become bitterly critical of Voltaire, with whom he had once skilfully bantered and so admired as to describe their meeting as 'the happiest moment of my life', and he seemed puzzled by a world that was moving on while he remained stuck. A life of self-invention and adventure had propelled him through the capitals of Europe in the company of kings, philosophers and some of the glitterati of the age; yet his currency of urbanity and genteel wit was being slowly devalued by changing times. And he had offended too many former friends, crossed with powerful enemies, taken that step too far once too often. All across the continent, doors had closed against him. The rash, clever, young Abbé Da Ponte, with his edge of arrogance and ready charm, must have seemed an echo from one of the old rake's former lives. The pair embarked on a prickly friendship.

Giorgio Pisani brought more than a whiff of danger to the circle. Like Angela and Girolamo Tiepolo, Pisani was of the ranks of *barnabotti* – embittered patricians deprived of family wealth, and thus of political influence. Unlike them, he was doing something about it. Since the beginning of the decade he had been campaigning fiercely against corruption, the criminal mismanagement of government by the Council of Ten, and the excessive powers of the Inquisitors. The most vocal spokesman of the *barnabotti*, he was de facto leader of the movement for political reform. He pitted himself volubly and vehemently against the particularly nasty and manipulative arch-conservative Andrea Tron, '*il Paron*'. 'The Boss' had just that year forced through his savage legislation barring Jews from manufacturing, owning property and employing Christians – an humiliation that could not have failed to make an impact on the convert from Ceneda, who may well have had relatives in the Ghetto. Da Ponte's status as a *convertito* was known in Venice. Patricians such as Memmo and Zaguri, who felt the weight of responsibility of long family histories, might entertain radical thinkers and discuss enlightened ideas, but they remained observers when it came to challenging the State, pressured by the past and their present connections to stand fast and, if necessary, go down with the ship. Many were simply content with the good life. Pisani, on the other hand, in almost daily speeches, ripped at the gaudy curtain of Venetian luxury and abandon, to reveal the cold, hard steel of a police state. To a Jew in a cassock, an outsider forced by his quest for independence into a role he despised, a poet who had already made his sympathies public, Pisani and his cause held inevitable allure.

The family with whom Da Ponte lodged in the San Luca district was named Bellaudi. The household comprised Widow Bellaudi, her twenty-year-old son Carlo, her daughter Caterina, aged nineteen, and Carlo's wife Angela, who was eighteen and from Florence. Angela, whose name Venetian dialect softened to Anzola, or Anzoletta, was four months pregnant when Da Ponte arrived as a lodger. Caterina was also married, to one Gabriele Doria, but he appears to have continued living with his father who worked as a butler in the *palazzo* of the fiercely conservative Pietro Barbarigo, 'the cripple' who had greatly aided the prosecution at Da Ponte's trial, and who was a tireless enemy of Giorgio Pisani. Venice was a small town.

All the Bellaudis busied themselves with making plumes for fashionable head-dresses. Ostrich-feather ornamentation, especially, was fashionable and kept the Bellaudi fingers busy. Not so their tongues. Not long after Da Ponte had moved in, Caterina reported to her brother (and then to the whole family) that she had seen Anzola and Lorenzo, while the two were sitting at the same table – he writing, she working on her plumes – caressing each other in turn under their clothing. Abbé Da Ponte swore with a flourish – 'May God strike me dead with a thunderbolt while I am celebrating Mass!' – that the story was not true, and was grudgingly believed. A month later, the Widow Bellaudi weighed in with the accusation that, coming home unexpectedly one day, she had found the priest parading naked (or in his underwear – the word '*nudo*' at this time could be taken both ways) in his bedroom with the door open, and Anzola looking on from the room opposite. These testimonies were made much later, as part of a venomous deposition against Da Ponte, but Anzoletta's proclivities appear confirmed by the report of a friend of hers, one Zecchini, who claimed that Anzoletta once told her that years before she married Carlo Bellaudi, she and a young man who lived opposite had shown themselves off to each other and pleasured themselves on their respective balconies. She appears also to have had other affairs since being married. Anzoletta, claimed irate mother-in-law Bellaudi, had always been somewhat prudent with her modesty, and 'when the Priest took a fancy to her, he found it was readily reciprocated'. He might not have chosen the most salubrious of mates, but Lorenzo Da Ponte had once again fallen in love.

Initially, Carlo Bellaudi did not seem much to mind – he had married Anzoletta when she was pregnant, at the age of fifteen, and he in turn was secretly having an affair with a neighbour, Franca Bertoti. Franca looked after children (including Anzoletta's) during the day, when their mothers and fathers were working. Her parents were suspicious of the relationship with Carlo, and had even gone so far as to prevent her going on a perfectly innocent Sunday outing with the Bellaudis, but the pair kept up a secret correspondence. It was one such letter that caused the problem. In it, just days before Anzoletta's baby was due, Carlo is supposed to have written: 'The woman whom I hate will soon be a mother. I will deliver her myself and our troubles will be over. If this is not enough, I will send her to sleep.' Franca and Carlo said the letter was a forgery (and indeed it is grammatically more adept than Carlo's other efforts, and no one was able to produce the original, only a copy); Lorenzo and Anzoletta said she had found it in the lining of Carlo's clothing. All agree that Anzoletta fled the house on 31 August, as soon as labour pains began – though whether it was in terror of her life or to a pre-arranged plan was a matter of hot dispute. She took a gondola to Zaguri's *palazzo* (witnesses agree to that), where Da Ponte was working, but he was not there. Refusing to go in, she lay down in the street outside. She waited for four hours, as the pains grew sharper and closer together, as window shutters edged open and closed again. When Lorenzo finally arrived, he took her to the house of a cousin – another convert, named Pietro Mariani, who was living with a woman (who was

also pregnant) in the Santa Margherita quarter. The baby, a girl, was born
that night.

Venetian society tolerated all manner of titillating gossip, but frowned
on scandal. Though *cicisbei* were allowed tremendous licence with their
stray kisses and roving fingers, and the walls of *casini* all around town
enclosed a myriad illicit sighs and groans, blatant adultery was taboo – the
Republic upheld strict laws against it, and the 'rape of an honest woman'
meant not mere scandal but infamy. Anzoletta's flight into his arms
presented Da Ponte with a problem. He had to protect himself against
any dangerous accusations. The Bellaudis would not let him back in to
the house, so he went to their priest and gave him the secret letter that he
said Anzoletta had intercepted between Carlo and Franca. As the scandal
broke, Zaguri, far from offering assistance, dismissed him with the words:
'Too many incidents, Abbé, too many incidents!'

Two or three days after the birth, a party set out from the house in
Santa Margherita – comprising Pietro Mariani and his mistress, the
midwife, and the baby girl (some say discreetly accompanied by Da
Ponte) – to present the child at her father's house. They were turned
away. Anzoletta's baby was taken, as were so many other unwanted and
illegitimate children of the day, to the Pietà orphanage on the Riva degli
Schiavoni, the home for female foundlings that was renowned for its girl
orchestra. For a while, Anzoletta stayed on at Pietro Mariani's house. Da
Ponte continued to officiate at the church in San Luca, while Giorgio
Pisani – defiant towards social scandal, and showing a contempt for the
Senate that had banned Da Ponte from teaching in schools – offered him
the position of tutor to his two sons. Lorenzo responded with loyalty,
and public support for Pisani's cause. When Pisani's bid for election as
Avogador di Comun (an important councillor of state) failed due to
machinations by conservatives, Da Ponte responded with a long poem
– doubly dangerous because it was in Venetian dialect, the language of
the people – in his support. Pisani, trumpeted the poem, would certainly
have been elected had he been an impostor, bully, thief or whore-
monger, if he had – as did milords – a hundred tarts, a hundred sluts;
instead he lost because he upheld the constitution, because he could not
bear oppression, because he spoke his mind to Excellencies, and told the

Great Council just what he thought of Andrea Tron. As ever, Lorenzo Da Ponte was as rash as he was loyal.

For nearly two years after Anzelotta had run away, she and Lorenzo braved the gossips of Venice. His situation was impossible – though a tutor in the Pisani household, he was a priest and still celebrated mass in the church at San Luca. They could not live together publicly, and his thin purse suffered badly in fattening separate landlords. At first Lorenzo took a room near the Rialto, and Anzoletta stayed on with the Marianis. A witness testified that she never saw anyone visit but the priest, and that Anzoletta left only to go to special masses. But Pietro Mariani and his wife (they had married) lived in just one room, and when their baby was born Anzoletta had to go. From place to place she and Lorenzo moved, sometimes singly, sometimes in tandem (though to separate rooms), staying in one place until the looks grew too knowing, or silence fell when they entered shops; until greetings were countered by closed lips and raised eyebrows; until they caught the stinging tail of an insult as conversation slipped suddenly away from neighbours clustered at the side of a bridge, or where an alley met a canal. Often Lorenzo passed Anzoletta off as his sister, but few people believed him, and she became known as 'the priest's whore'. In August 1778, Anzoletta was boarding with two sisters named Beccari in the parish of Santa Sofia, and gave birth to Lorenzo's child – the baby was immediately taken to the Pietà. At the Beccaris, a friend of Anzoletta's reported, the couple were not allowed to close the door when Lorenzo visited, and they had to 'operate standing up' as she dropped her skirt over him, and he closed his cassock around her. By Christmas she had to leave there, too. Da Ponte found her room in the San Luigi inn, near his lodgings in the Rialto. It was Carnival, and he visited her masked, but despite that the innkeeper recognized 'the teacher from Ca' Pisani'. A small place, Venice.

At the San Luigi inn, Orsola Pasqua – of all people – came to visit. Lorenzo's stepmother, now in her thirties, brought one of her young children with her, and stayed for a month. Then Anzoletta, who was pregnant again, went back with them to spend a week in Ceneda and meet the rest of the family. Anzoletta and her priest were married in all but name. Lorenzo's brother Luigi – the one who had not been able to offer shelter in Padua – passed on his good wishes to an 'Angioletta', quite probably Anzoletta Bellaudi, through a letter to Colombo in Ceneda on 12 September. In the letter he despaired of his older brother ever growing up and acting with adult restraint. 'God willing,' wrote Lorenzo's younger sibling, 'may time make him more mature, and render him more circumspect in his actions.' He laments that Lorenzo is 'quite exhausted, and far from that calmness of spirit that he has never known,' saying that he is capable of commanding 'love, even adoration', if only he would control his frenetic excess.

Anzoletta's room at the San Luigi was separated from that of the innkeeper's daughter by a thin wooden partition, and the girl was able to report that she heard Anzoletta inviting Da Ponte to feel her swelling belly, an invitation followed by 'squeals of the most advanced sexual nature'. She had to leave that inn, too.

Da Ponte was by this time living in Pisani's house, and in April 1779 installed Anzoletta in his room near the Rialto, which he had kept on. In January of that year, a new doge had been elected. Paolo Renier had a reputation for sharp practice, and was rumoured to have bought the dogeship by bribing 300 members of the Great Council. Though corrupt, he was terribly timid, and could hardly be heard at his election address at San Marco. Shouts from the crowd to speak up made his legs shake so that he could barely climb into the *pozzo* for his circuit of the piazza. His one flash of colour was that he had married a Greek tightrope-walker, whom he had met in Constantinople, but she was shunned by Venetian society, and his niece had to be his consort at official ceremonies. With such a limp hand on the helm, Venice began to drift towards becoming ungovernable. Opposition by the *barnabotti* surged, and Pisani was aiming at election as Procurator of San Marco – one of the most powerful offices in the Republic. In response, the iron fist of the Establishment clenched even tighter.

Towards the end of May an anonymous denunciation was thrown into the mouth of the stone lion at San Moisè, accusing Da Ponte of scandalous crimes. The *bocche dei leoni* were placed at strategic points around town, and a letter placed in the mouth was assured of direct passage to the Council of Ten or the Doge. Each lion served for a different nature of denunciation – for thieves, spies and traitors, even one for people who tipped rubbish into the canals – though by the eighteenth century they were hardly ever used: both Dr Burney and Giuseppe Baretti noted that the lions' mouths at San Marco were full of cobwebs. This rather antiquated method of denouncing Da Ponte accused him of *mala vita*, a ragbag of scandalous crimes ranging from being a converted Jew who brought the Christian faith into bad repute to seducing another man's wife and fathering children by her. The foul handwriting and bad grammar of the note pointed to its author being Carlo Bellaudi, a fact he later acknowledged. Nearly two years after Anzoletta had left him, he appeared to be doing something about it.

The *Esecutori contro la bestemmia*, a body set up some three centuries earlier to keep an eye on public morals, acted swiftly. Witnesses were called in – neighbours and gossips, innkeepers and priests, friends, relations, and above all the irate Widow Bellaudi. Testimonies poured forth. It was like lancing a pox pustule. The Abbé Da Ponte combed his hair too fashionably and eyed women in church; he went straight from his adulterous sheets to celebrate mass, he had played the violin at dances in a house of ill repute, while dressed in his cassock! For three and a half months the *Esecutori* gathered a thick wad of outraged, outrageous and often conflicting reports. Some are patently false – such as the statement that Da Ponte was expelled from the seminary at Treviso for immoral behaviour; others have a ring of truth, and dirt flung at Da Ponte stuck easily. Yet though he is accused of all manner of wickedness, the figure that emerges through all the fug is that of Anzoletta. Here was no Don Giovanni, but a man devoted to one woman alone, who was forbidden to have her, and who went to extraordinary lengths to hold on to her.

Asked why he had taken so long to complain about Anzoletta's seduction, Carlo Bellaudi replied, 'I didn't have the means to maintain her in a convent' (adulterous women were often sent for a period of seclusion to a nunnery, at their husband's expense), and then, more tellingly, 'I have a great fear of Father Lorenzo, both for his resolute spirit and for the significant protection he enjoys, being tutor to the sons of the nobleman Giorgio Pisani, where he currently lives; and he also spent time in the House of Zaguri.' His linking the names of Da Ponte and

Pisani, and implying danger, hints at a weightier motive for discrediting Da Ponte. By May 1779, it was clear that Pisani was in the ascendant, and that he was set on constitutional reform. The Inquisitors had him, and his circle, under close surveillance. Stirring up an attack on Da Ponte had the advantage of blackening Pisani's name among the people by revealing that he allowed such a dissolute to teach his children, while at the same time ridding the Republic of the potentially troublesome poet. Da Ponte always believed his poem about Pisani to be the true reason for the antagonism of the Venetian authorities, and that Bellaudi had been egged on to denounce him by Caterina Bellaudi's husband – the shadowy Gabriele Doria, who lived in the *palazzo* of Da Ponte's arch-enemy, 'the cripple' Pietro Barbarigo.

News of the investigation spread quickly, as witness after witness was called before the *Esecutori*. The situation for Da Ponte began to look dangerous. When word reached the ear of the ecclesiastical authorities, he was called before the priest of San Maurizio – the same one who had found him the position at Treviso – but was only mildly rebuked for 'consorting with a pregnant young woman' (such behaviour was, after all, not rare among the clergy). The priest was later able to report to the *Esecutori* that Lorenzo had promised that he would 'make the young woman leave', and that he would 'no longer visit the said young woman', and that he was satisfied the promises would be kept – but the *Esecutori* seemed intent on their pursuit.

Still the rumours about the investigation spread, as ever-increasing numbers of witnesses were called in. Lorenzo and Anzoletta were not permitted by law to present any evidence at this stage of the proceedings, so were helpless. Though he had once laughed off the threat of a trial by the Senate, Da Ponte seemed to realize that this time dangerous forces were being mobilized against him. At the end of July, a few weeks after his interview with the priest of San Maurizio, he fled the Pisani household for Padua, where his brother Girolamo's employer, the nobleman Giovanni Da Lezze, offered him shelter in a country house. Anzoletta, left alone in Venice, gave birth to their second child on 24 August, a few days before the final session of the inquiry. That baby, too, was taken to the Pietà. Anzoletta then went to join Lorenzo in hiding in

Padua (despite what he had promised the Church), but it was clear by then that he was in danger of his life, or at very least his liberty. He decided to flee the country and before the month ended, he had left.

By 13 September the *Esecutori* reached the conclusion that the evidence was serious enough for Da Ponte to be brought to trial, and a summons was issued ordering him to appear before the Council of Ten within three days. When he could not be found, a warrant for his arrest was sent to Padua. He still did not appear, and on 17 December 1779 sentence was pronounced in his absence. The priest Lorenzo Da Ponte was banished from Venice and from all other cities, land and sea dominions of the Serene Republic, as well as from any ships in the Serenissima's control, for a period of fifteen years. If he was found contravening this banishment, he would be thrown into a cell without light for seven years.

Anzoletta did not follow her lover into exile. A note in the margin of the document bearing Da Ponte's sentence records that 'the woman returned from Padua and was reunited with her husband'. Early in 1780, Giorgio Pisani was successful in his bid to be elected as Procurator of St Mark, but on 31 May he was arrested in his house on San Moisé, and imprisoned. By then, Lorenzo Da Ponte had long found refuge across the Austrian border, in Gorizia.

PART TWO

VIENNA

That True Phoenix

Chapter Four

TOWARDS THE END of August 1779, Lorenzo Da Ponte slipped out of the Venetian state without the necessary papers or (even more important in the eighteenth century) any letters of introduction. He followed back-roads from Padua, heading east over fertile flatland, crossing shallow, shaly rivers, then turned north towards the mountains. If Casanova's flight from the Leads offers a parallel, Da Ponte walked rather than took a carriage, kept to fields and forest paths, scrounged food from farmhouses, and with feet swollen and shoes in tatters found his way out of the country, avoiding border posts. Under his arm he carried a small bundle containing part of a new suit of clothes, a few undergarments, and — always his most treasured possessions — a small clutch of books: the tiniest and most portable copy of Horace he could find, a Dante scribbled with his own notes, and a buffed and battered old Petrarch.

As he trudged, each footfall measured not a step forward, but yet one more away — from country, family and Anzoletta. He was on his own, and knew not a soul in the land he was going to — for once even Girolamo was staying behind. For the fourth time in his adult life, Lorenzo was homeless and without an income, forced to move and invent himself anew; though this time it would be with German rather than his beloved Italian in his ears, in a land bound by the laws of a fervently religious Empress Maria Theresa.

Gorizia was just beyond the Austrian frontier, on the edge of Alpine foothills north of Trieste. Exhausted and starving at the end of his clandestine journey, Da Ponte went up to the first inn he saw. A bedraggled figure with one small bundle, he could not have presented a very encouraging prospect as a customer but, even dishevelled and unshaven, the abbé had allure. The young mistress of the inn greeted him with an '*occhiantina espressiva*', a most expressive glance. After his hard days on the road, she appeared to him as a vision – 'pretty, fresh and vivacious beyond all belief'. Lorenzo's eye flicked from her German-style lace cap to her plump, alabaster-white neck – noting a necklace of fine-linked gold, which encircled her throat about thirty times before descending (his eyes followed its path) in ever-widening coils over an ample breast, which it only partly hid from view. Her soft, rounded form fitted snugly in a well-shaped bodice, and silk stockings 'ended in two rose-coloured slippers [that] drew the adoring eye to the exquisite shape of a tiny foot'. Lorenzo Da Ponte could not live for long without being in love. But more mundane appetites clamoured for precedence. He was starving – so hungry, he said, that he 'could have devoured pebbles'. Unfortunately, the well-fed vision in pink slippers could not understand Italian. Lorenzo pointed to his open mouth – a gesture, it appears, the nymph entirely misunderstood. Luckily for him, a maid came past bearing some fried chicken, intended for another guest, and he leapt on it with feline agility, devouring a leg and thigh within seconds and making his immediate needs abundantly clear.

The comely hostess sat with Da Ponte as the maids served him a delicious meal in his room. Unable to speak to each other, they communicated with little glances and gestures. When the fruit came, she picked out a pear, produced from her pocket a little silver-bladed knife, peeled the fruit, cut it in half, gave one part to him, and ate the other herself. Then she handed him the knife and encouraged him to do the same. She filled two glasses with cool new wine, taught him to toast with '*Gesundheit*', giggled when he could not pronounce it correctly, refilled the glasses and repeated the lesson – until they were both quite flushed, and 'in her eyes burned the flames of voluptuousness'. From time to time, she would rise from her seat, stretch, gaze at him, sigh, and sit down again. Then she called for a dictionary, dismissed the maids, and spelt out, '*Ich liebe Sie*'. Lorenzo garnered the meaning of the phrase from the Italian-German section of the book, and returned with, '*Und ich liebe Sie*' – and so the conversation continued, growing somewhat franker, for the next hour and a half, until the sound of carriages outside heralded more guests and demanded the hostess's presence.

Lorenzo was astonished, and a little afraid. Stories abounded in pleasure-seeking Venice of moral strictures across the border. Whereas Venetians maintained a careful gap between legislation against adultery and the carryings-on in *casini*, Maria Theresa made sure her severe laws against promiscuity were upheld to the letter. Spies entitled 'commissioners of chastity' locked up even innocent women presumed to be walking suspiciously in the street, and some unscrupulous girls earned money on the side by acting as agents provocateurs, luring men into the commissioners' ambushes. Da Ponte knew all about the Empress and the rigour of her penal codes – 'things which I had heard spoken of as one speaks of the Holy Inquisition of Spain' – so when his German nymph returned with her two handmaidens, bearing ices and sweets, to sing to him, he picked up the dictionary and – tiredness vying with desire and trepidation – pointed to the word for 'sleep'. He was put to bed immediately, but in the days that followed was surprised not only by his hostess's forwardness, but by visits from pretty pedlars, who 'under pretext of selling pins, needles, handkerchiefs, necklaces, ribbons, and similar trifles, [found it easy] to sell things not to be found in baskets'. Double standards were not unique to Venice, only a little more dangerous.

Da Ponte stayed on at the inn for another ten or twelve days, dictionary in hand, 'building up some little vocabulary . . . composed almost wholly of words and phrases of love', and reconciling himself to exile in the comforting cushion of the innkeeper's embrace. She helped repair his damaged soul and ease a troubled heart, and Da Ponte remembered her with deepest affection to the end of his life, as 'beyond doubt one of the best women' he had ever known. She even left a little purse of coins tucked under his pillow when she realized he was short of money, but unlike his friend Casanova, Lorenzo had 'never mastered the craft of decimating the purses of women'. He refused the offer and looked for cheaper accommodation. Lorenzo continued to see his pretty innkeeper after he moved, and implies that he may well have loved her for ever, had not death snatched her seven months later, at the age of twenty-two.

On arriving at the inn, Da Ponte had been required, by law, solemnly to swear to his name and surname, birthplace, where he had come from, and his purpose in being there. He had to be careful. Although he was now perfectly safe from the authorities, rumours of a scandal in Venice – which, after all, was not very far away – could instantly ruin any standing he might acquire in Maria Theresa's severe and conservative land. Italian cities to the south of the Republic, though still mostly under Austrian domination, might have offered Lorenzo a more familiar milieu, but Gorizia was popular as a refuge for those at political odds with Venice, a place to wait quietly in the wings until the wicked rulers left the stage. At this point the rebel Pisani was still at liberty, rising in political influence, and might one day be in a position to support Da Ponte's return. Lorenzo's mother's family, the Pincherles, had a prominent presence in Gorizia, so he may well have known the town from childhood. Small, and surrounded by vineyards and rich farmland set against a backdrop of mountains, Gorizia had something of the atmosphere of his home town, Ceneda, but the overwhelming argument for going there was a strong hint at the prospect of work. His prompt in this direction would have been his friend Casanova, who had spent the autumn and part of the winter in Gorizia in 1773 as he, too, bided his time waiting for the Venetian authorities to revoke his banishment. Casanova noted in his memoirs that he had made the decision because in Gorizia one could live in liberty, that the town had a pleasing social ambience, and that it offered all manner of opportunity for staving off indigence. Lorenzo's former patron Pietro Zaguri was well known there, and his friend Caterino Mazzolà was just about to marry a girl of Gorizianese stock. But it was Casanova, especially, who had gossip and advice on Gorizia's leading families – the prime source of patronage for a jobbing poet. Casanova considered Count Guidobaldo Cobenzl, one of Gorizia's most powerful politicians, to be wise, erudite . . . and generous.

Although German was the language of the people in Gorizia, Italian was widely spoken among the aristocracy, and seen as a language of culture and intellectual pleasure. An Italian poet carried with him a touch of high fashion. As soon as he had moved out of the inn and found himself modest quarters in a grain-merchant's house, Da Ponte made a wily bid for Cobenzl's patronage. The old count's son, Johann Philippe, was a comet in Austrian government, the right-hand man of Chancellor Kaunitz and a chief negotiator of the Treaty of Teschen, which had ended the War of the Bavarian Succession with Prussia just a few months earlier. Da Ponte astutely wrote an ode in celebration of the event. Entitled *La gara degli uccelli* (The Contest of the Birds – making reference to respective eagles on the coats of arms of both Maria Theresa and Frederick of Prussia), it lavished praise not only on the Empress but on the young Cobenzl too. It was not a very good ode, but it warmed a proud father's heart. Da Ponte presented it personally to the count, who at his own expense had numerous copies made and distributed among his noble friends. This was just the break Lorenzo needed. As he had done in Venice, the handsome poet leapt directly from the forsaken fringes of society to its glittering centre. Invitations, favours and largesse flowed from the Attemses and the Tuns, from the Strasoldos and Lanthieris, the Coroninis and Torrianis.

Cunningly, Da Ponte had fired off *La gara degli uccelli* as a double-headed arrow. Although he had presented it to Count Cobenzl, and praised the young Johann Philippe, he dedicated the poem to Count Rodolfo Coronini, another of Gorizia's foremost citizens. Count Coronini had a mission in life. He had spent years unravelling and constructing the genealogies and histories of the leading families of the city to produce, in three volumes, in Latin, and in verse, *Fastorum Goritiensium* (The Splendour of Gorizia). Casanova, with his usual sting of malice, maintained: 'Nobody actually read [Coronini's] works; they preferred to grant him the title of scholar on trust rather than going to the trouble of seeing whether he merited it.' At heart the old pedant must have known this, so when the bright young abbé swooped on Gorizia with *La gara degli uccelli*, he knew he had found just the man to translate his work into Italian and give it wider appeal. It was a long task, and a lucrative one. Da

Ponte had landed himself employment for a good few months, but with
it he unwittingly stirred a hornets' nest.

Happily ignorant of what lay in store for him, Lorenzo moved from
the grain-merchant's house to quarters more comfortable (and possibly
more stimulating to his muse) with the printer and publisher Valerio De
Valeri. He graced salons and animated parties, composing new poems
and digging a few old ones from the bag, including the pastoral *Il
Cechino*, which had so charmed the literati of Treviso. When a company
of actors came to town in the early spring of 1780, the wife of one of his
patrons – some say the Countess Cobenzl ('as beautiful as a star'
according to Casanova), others Aloisia Lanthieri (whose husband described her as having 'no temperament, but . . . the most beautiful
behind he had ever seen') – commissioned a play, the first he had
attempted. The drama was a translation of a German tragedy, and was a
dismal failure – perhaps not surprisingly, as just a few months earlier Da
Ponte had been battling over '*Ich liebe Sie*' with a German-Italian
dictionary. Girolamo was visiting him at the time, and together the
brothers made amends with a translation from the French of the play *Le
Comte de Warwick*, by Jean-François de la Harpe, a protégé of Voltaire.
This second essay into theatre met with greater success.

When Girolamo returned to Venice at the end of March, he was able
to report in a letter to Michele Colombo that he had found Lorenzo 'in
good health, and not at all badly set up'. Lorenzo's present condition was
balmy, and the horizon was beginning to clear. On 8 March, Giorgio
Pisani had finally succeeded in being elected Procurator of St Mark,
second in power only to the Doge, and the prospect of Lorenzo's being
allowed to return home – something he longed for – was looking a little
better. The poet-abbé, meanwhile, with what seemed to be becoming a
peculiar knack at upsetting a happily trundling apple cart, had ridden into
a spot of bother.

Count Coronini had long been involved in a feud of bickering and
acid remarks against the Attems family. They had spread word that the
count plagiarized work by their own heraldic scholar (who died in 1758),
and he in turn put out the rumour that one of the Attems offspring had
admitted to him that the family portraits had been bought at an auction

in Rome, and had new coats of arms superimposed on them. By accepting the commission to work on the translation of *Fastorum Goritiensium*, Da Ponte found himself to have unknowingly taken sides in the spat – and having an adept poet in his employ gave Coronini an idea for a quick malevolent thrust at the Attemses. Da Ponte was also at the time working on *La gratitudine*, a poem in praise of women, and Coronini leant on him to insert some extra lines, which, behind a thin veil of allusion, veered off into wicked satire of the Attemses, their ambition and shaky antecedents. *La gratitudine* had barely left Valeri's presses when the counts Antonio and Niccolò Attems were pounding on the printer's door, 'armed with stick and sword to look for the Abbé Da Ponte'. Antonio threatened to shoot the priest, Niccolò to kill Count Coronini, in retaliation to the insult. The old count was so panicked by this reaction that he applied to the imperial authorities for protection – which is how we come to know about the incident. Da Ponte glides past it in his memoirs without a glance – though when *Fastorum Goritiensium* was published (as *Fasti Goriziani*) late in 1780, he dedicated his translation to Count Alessandro Attems, the head of the family, and sent Attems a grovelling letter saying that Coronini had given absolute encouragement for him to do so.

The printer Valeri was spared any further such disruption of his home life. Shortly after the incident, Da Ponte moved out to stay with Count Luigi Torriani, by all reports a violent and scurrilous man, one who revelled in dispute, to whom, appropriately as it turned out, Da Ponte had dedicated *La gratitudine*. Casanova had stayed with Torriani in 1773, and loathed the man. He found the count's hospitality abysmally deficient, and was shocked at the vicious way he had one day beaten up a priest for beginning mass without him. He describes Torriani's face as being of sinister aspect, one on which one could read 'cruelty, disloyalty, treason, pride, sensual brutality, hate and jealousy'. A one-time mistress remarked that, when with Torriani, women soon learned to suppress their ecstasy, lest they be strangled, so jealous was he of other people's pleasure. Count Zinzendorf, erstwhile Governor of Trieste, noted in his diary after a visit that: 'The Countess Torriani is a lovely woman, but her husband is an animal.' Torriani would die insane a few years later. But Lorenzo Da Ponte had seen lower life, and appears to have survived the count's hospitality for a good many months.

Some time in September, Caterino Mazzolà passed through Gorizia on his way to Dresden, where he had been invited as poet to the opera. He brought the devastating news that, shortly after a triumphal procession through Venice, Giorgio Pisani had been arrested, imprisoned, and was unlikely ever to be released. Da Ponte took the news as a 'tremendous catastrophe', not just for Venice and Pisani, but because it shrivelled all hope he had of returning home. This happened just as his Gorizian satin was beginning to lose its sheen. The contretemps with the Attemses had given Lorenzo a taste of the pettiness of provincial society; and now that he had finished translating *Fastorum Goritiensium*, life was looking a little less plush, as Gorizian purses were unlikely again to sustain a commission quite so easy and lucrative. There was also the torrid Torriani to contend with. The time was coming to move on, and the idea of a big city renowned for its culture and glittering social life appealed immensely. Da Ponte begged Mazzolà to try and find him a position in the Elector's court. He began to dream of a shining future – and in the weeks following Mazzolà's departure, let drop the odd remark that he might be leaving for Dresden. One of the men he mentioned his ambitions to was Giuseppe Colletti.

Colletti was the moving spirit behind Gorizia's *Colonia Arcadica Romano-Sonziaca*. The first such 'Arcadian Colony' had been founded in Rome in 1690, and had gradually sprouted offshoots all over Italy as more people became drawn to the aims of upholding the purity of Italian as a literary language. In Austrian territory, where Vienna was trying to keep a firm lid on the influence of Italian language and culture, the colonies had added piquancy. Colletti set up Gorizia's colony (named after the River Isonzo which flowed past the town) in August 1780 – when Da Ponte was embroiled in the Attems affair. He persuaded Da Ponte's first patron, Count Cobenzl, to become president, and Count Torriani to assume the (for him) highly inappropriate role of censor. Most of Gorizia's leading families were represented among the founders. Da Ponte was only admitted a month later, on 8 September 1780. As was the custom, he took on a classical nom de plume: Lesbonico Pegasio – an apt one, given his love of women and susceptibility to flights of fancy. He would use the name for many years, as belonging to an Arcadian colony carried some status in the literary world. In establishing a colony in Gorizia, Coletti had notched up a significant advantage over the other non-aristocratic Italian poet of note in town.

Coletti was a bad poet, but a serious rival. The pair were in direct competition for patronage and social favour. Also a newcomer (having arrived in Gorizia some ten years earlier), he had a similar history of reinvention and adventure. Educated by the Jesuits, he had, when the order was abolished, enlisted as a musketeer, later giving up soldiering to become a printer and publisher. He was a middling sort of scholar, producing mainly school books and religious texts, but he had considerable business acumen. On arriving in Gorizia, he had worked as an assistant for the ailing Tommasini press – the family firm of Mazzolà's wife, and competitors to Valeri. Coletti had managed to turn around the business so dramatically that in 1778 it received imperial authorization to print school books and official publications, and four years later opened a branch in Trieste. He was a tireless and canny promoter of Italian literature in Gorizia; the establishment of the Arcadian colony was, in the long run, good for trade.

Valeri was not at all pleased with this burst of energy from his competitors the Tommasinis. The moment he heard there was a new poet in town, he pounced. He fervently courted the *arriviste*, and his bringing Da Ponte to live with him had been something of a social and commercial coup. Tommasini had published *La gara degli uccelli*, Da Ponte's debut in Gorizia, but after Valeri invited Lorenzo into his household, he brought out all the works Da Ponte wrote over the ensuing months. The rival publishing houses brandished their bards at each other, and set rumours scuttling to stir up sales. As the presses creaked and thumped downstairs, Valeri took Da Ponte aside, constantly thorning him against the rival poet Coletti, saying that, behind his back, Coletti was deriding his talent. Lorenzo was (to borrow a phrase from Michael Kelly) as touchy as gunpowder, and could sense attack in quite innocent remarks. Valeri goaded him into retaliation, and Da Ponte succumbed with a savage little satire of Coletti entitled *Il capriccio*, which

Valeri gleefully published. As landlord and publisher, Valeri did hold some power of obligation over Da Ponte, but even so, the poet capitulated rather too quickly to his will. Either the young poet was naively unaware of the prick of his pen, or he was developing a facility for intrigue and malice.

Coletti seems to have taken Da Ponte's spite in good grace, pretending not to realise *Il capriccio* was about him, and refraining from responding in kind – unless he was behind the delay in Da Ponte's admission to the Arcadian colony. The two continued the round of salons and picnics, concerts and readings – cuckoos in the nobles' nests by dint of their art and the slow thaw in the social climate. Publicly, Coletti offered Da Ponte every cordiality, and promoted the abbé's work, but, spurred on by Valeri, Da Ponte continued to believe the worst of his rival, and was convinced of Coletti's deep animosity. Da Ponte's mentioning to Coletti, after Mazzolà's visit, of his plans to depart for the glories of Dresden perhaps had the tinge of a boast. And Coletti, quiet for so long, and an intimate of Mazzolà's in-laws, perhaps saw his chance for a little harmless revenge.

The potential for antagonism between the two men adds a touch of mystery to an episode that changed the course of Da Ponte's life.

In November 1780, Da Ponte says, he received a letter from Dresden, in Mazzolà's handwriting and with his name signed to it, instructing him to leave Gorizia immediately and come to take up a distinguished post in the Elector's court. Da Ponte lost no time in reading the letter to all who would listen, and within weeks he was on the road again, this time very much enriched by his patrons' generosity, and bearing those crucial letters of introduction. In the eighteenth century, a letter of introduction made the difference between languishing in obscurity and that all-important entrée to court. One of the letters that Da Ponte carried was from Count Cobenzl to his son Johann Philippe, Chancellor Kaunitz's right-hand man in Vienna.

The route Da Ponte took, like many other travellers of the time, avoided the terrors of mountain passes by skirting the highest of the Alps, going from Gorizia through Graz, and on to the Austrian capital, then northwards to Dresden. Hester Piozzi, travelling in spring, deemed such an approach to Vienna 'eminently fine'. On his way from Gorizia to Graz, Michael Kelly (journeying as Da Ponte did, in winter) 'suffered greatly from the cold . . . the roads were hilly and heavy, the cattle miserable, and the post-boys incorrigible'. He found the springless chaise 'a complete bone-setter', and what was worse:

> While undergoing its [the chaise's] operations, nothing could have so ably aided its torments as the unconquerable phlegm of the postilion; whatever one suffers, whatever ones says, there he sits, lord of your time; you may complain, but it is useless; his horses and his pipe are his objects, and his passengers are but lumber.

Da Ponte's journey was slow and uncomfortable, and he arrived in Vienna to find the entire city in mourning – the Empress Maria Theresa had died a few days earlier, on 29 November. Ever the jobbing poet, he composed a rather stolid sonnet, *Per la morte di Sua Maestà l'Imperatrice Maria Teresa*, which he managed to have printed as a flyer by the publisher Thomas von Trattner before leaving. He also presented his letter of introduction to Johann Philippe Cobenzl, who 'graciously received' him, then sent him on his way with the gift of a travel diary with a 100-florin note 'for travel expenses' pinned to its frontispiece.

North of Vienna, the going grew worse. German roads were notoriously awful – even, in bad weather, the major highway of the Hapsburg dominions from Vienna to Prague (Da Ponte's route to Dresden). Accidents were common and the jolting of the chaise relentless. One traveller, all 'shook to a jelly, and half dead', found himself on roads barely wide enough for a single vehicle, where 'one wheel sometimes would slip into a great hole, and almost overturn the chaise, which made me funk my soul out'. Da Ponte's 100-florin windfall might have effected a step up from a chaise to a speedier diligence, but this resulted in little increase in comfort. Four decades later, the Scottish lawyer John Russell would still find the experience appalling:

The breath of life is insipid to a German without the breath of his pipe;
the insides [passengers] puff most genially right into each others' faces.
With such an addition to the ordinary mail-coach miseries of a low
roof, a perpendicular back, legs suffering like a martyr's in the boots,
and scandalously scanty airholes, the Diligence becomes a very Black
Hole. Half-a-day's travelling in one of these vehicles is enough to
make a man loathe them all his lifetime.

When the snow grew too heavy, passengers had to get out and walk, or
transfer to sledges; and if the roads and carriages were bad, the inns were
even worse. Night after night Da Ponte found himself bedding down in
communal rooms on a pile of straw – and that 'very often stinking,
because there is no fresh to be had'. But he pressed on, Mazzolà's letter
burning in his pocket with its promise of a life of ease and glory in the
Dresden court. As soon as he arrived, he went to see his friend, and nearly
half a century later could still recall the encounter:

> When he saw me entering his room, he exclaimed in the greatest
> astonishment:
> 　'Da Ponte in Dresden!'
> 　It is not difficult to imagine my astonishment at this welcome. He
> ran to embrace me, but I hardly had the strength to open my mouth,
> let alone respond to his gesture. Noting my silence, he cried:
> 　'Can it be that you have been named poet to the theatre at St
> Petersburg?'
> 　'I came to Dresden,' I then responded, 'to see my friend Mazzolà,
> and to profit, if possible by his friendship.'
> 　I made this reply mechanically, hardly aware of what I was saying.
> 　'Bravo!' he replied. 'You may have arrived just at the right time!'

Mazzolà took Da Ponte across the way to a tavern, where it became clear
not only that had he not written the letter that had brought Lorenzo to
Dresden but that he had sent one Da Ponte had not received, telling him
that no opening had as yet presented itself. Da Ponte was too proud to
admit the true cause of his journey. There was just a glimmer of hope

(the reason Mazzolà had said Da Ponte had arrived 'just at the right time'), in that Prince Anthony, the Elector's brother, was currently looking for a secretary. Mazzolà would see what he could do.

Back in his room, Lorenzo examined more closely the letter he had received in Gorizia. While the outer sheet bearing the address was clearly in Mazzolà's hand, he now saw that the inner one was of different quality paper, and that there were discrepancies in the writing style. What was more, he discovered this second sheet bore the watermark of a stationer in Gorizia. Da Ponte immediately blamed Coletti for the trick, and indeed Coletti had both motive, and possibly also the means – as an employee of Mazzolà's wife's family – of gaining access to samples of the playwright's handwriting and signature. But exactly how Da Ponte was catapulted from Gorizia remains a riddle.

He had left town with such swagger and display, laden with such generous gifts from his former patrons, that return would be impossibly humiliating. The wave of high hope that had carried him to Dresden had cast him suddenly upon the shale, and had sucked back into the sea, leaving him stranded and uncertain. Outside his tavern window, sedan chairs edged and dipped on wide, paved streets; the city was clean, bright and well ordered (crowds crossing the bridge over the River Elbe, remarkably it seems, stayed on one side while walking in one direction and took the other coming back); the buildings were magnificently ornamented; blue and green porcelain tiles glinted on the church spires. Dresden was Lutheran, but tolerant; the court had a reputation for culture and ease; and the local Saxons were 'well-bred, airy and agreeable', if a little forced in their gaiety. It was an attractive city, Da Ponte had a well-connected friend there, and there seemed ripe opportunity for employment. Waiting in the hope that Mazzolà would be able to secure him the secretaryship was Da Ponte's only really viable option.

Mazzolà's petition did not succeed. The playwright generously shared some of his own work with his friend, paying him to help with translation, with writing the odd aria, a duet, occasionally a scene or two. Da Ponte scorned writers of Italian opera at the time, apart from his childhood hero Metastasio, Mazzolà himself, and one or two others, all of whom had left Italy. It was not a career he had even considered – he thought the standard of poetry poor, and believed Italian impresarios to be mean and exploitative. Librettists came low on the payroll in an art where singers had become supreme. Now, after his tentative venture into drama in Gorizia, he worked with Mazzolà at ground level, picking up day by day 'those numberless rules, laws and tricks of the trade which are essential for constructing a good piece of theatre'. The Italian opera company was a strong one, much improved under the skilful and daring impresario Pasquale Bondini from the sorry troupe which seven years before had caused Count Podewils to write to a friend in Berlin that 'the Italians only keep going by issuing subscriptions of two florins a month to officers of any rank'. In the ten months that Da Ponte stayed in Dresden, the company produced around fifteen Italian operas, by some of the most fashionable composers in the genre, including Paisiello, Cimarosa and Antonio Salieri, court composer at Vienna and one of the leading musicians of the day.

Mazzolà introduced Da Ponte to his circle, praising his abilities as an extempore versifier (the fad was just beginning to become popular in Germany), though, perhaps understandably, less eager to promote his career as an independent poet. Da Ponte, 'neither blind, nor unjust, nor ungrateful', accepted the role as assistant and improviser, but one of Mazzolà's friends inspired him to create something more considered. Father Michael Jerome Huber, an ex-Jesuit, was a cultivated man who had translated Metastasio into German, and who held 'a sort of holy veneration' for the poems of Bernardo Tasso. Da Ponte warmed to Huber immensely, and decided to write for him some psalms in the style of Tasso – a genre that would not threaten Mazzolà as operatic poet. Whether it was through Tasso's hovering spirit, Father Huber's calm profundity, or because Da Ponte for the first time in many years was surrounded by true hearts rather than patrons and nobles in the guise of friends, he produced some of the most beautiful, meditative poetry he would ever write. The first psalm, particularly, is infused with a quite uncharacteristic sense of religious repentance, a regret at past follies and frivolity, and a lingering note of sadness.

Signor, di fragil terra
formasti il corpo mio,
a cui fa sempre guerra
crudo nemico e rio,
che nutre il fier desio
del pianto de' mortali;
e danni a danni aggiugne e mali a mali . . .

[Lord, with fragile dust
you formed my body,
against which a crude and guilty
enemy always wages war,
one who is fed by the proud desire
for the cries of mortals
and adds damage to damage
and evil to evil . . .]

The rhythm is delicate and exquisitely poised, rhymes curl softly into each other; it is a poem that cries out to be sung.

Father Huber, who was rich and well connected, handed the poems to the Prime Minister and to the Elector himself. Da Ponte says, quite believably, that his psalms were later praised by the great Italian poet and tragedian Ugo Foscolo – but his immediate reward was more tangible, in the form of much-needed coin.

Lorenzo Da Ponte left Dresden with an abruptness that was becoming something of a hallmark. In painting and music particularly, Dresden had close ties with Italy and the city was home to an active Italian community. Da Ponte met up with Giovanni Alvise Casanova – Giacomo's brother – who had been born in Dresden when their mother, a renowned Italian actress, was living there. Giovanni Alvise had returned to Dresden to teach in the academy of fine arts, where the teachers included a Venetian, one Giuseppe Camerata. Da Ponte, in an episode in his memoirs that has more than a pinch of the spice of a Casanova story, claims not only that he fell madly in love with Camerata's two daughters (whose names he disguises as Rosina and Camilla) but that he carried on a provocative flirtation with

Camerata's wife. One can only imagine that, in this Lutheran town, Da Ponte had again abandoned his priest's garb. He writes that the situation became so fraught that the girls were taken away on a journey, and that Madame Camerata ordered him to make his choice – a preference, given his clerical orders, which would have been quite irrelevant. Whatever the truth of the affair, he takes the opportunity in his memoirs to open his heart a little and reveal just how Lorenzo Da Ponte fell in love, not as a seducer, but as a sincere, serial romantic:

> At that time I was not more than thirty years of age and, people said, of a pleasing appearance – with some little wit, a poetic and Italian soul, and not ignorant of the ways of love. It was no marvel that I found few great obstacles between me and the tender hearts of the two girls. I must protest, however, that I never abused these advantages; and from the time I first began to love, which was at the age of eighteen (up to the forty-second year of my life when I took a companion for all the remainder of it), I never once said to a woman: 'I love you,' without knowing that I could love her without any future loss of honour or respect. Often my attentions, my glances, and even my expressions of ordinary politeness, were taken for declarations of love; but my lips never sinned, nor, without the consent of heart and mind, did I ever seek out of vanity or caprice to inspire in any credulous or innocent breast a passion which would inevitably have terminated in tears and remorse.

As Lorenzo himself sat in tears and remorse, wondering how to escape the tangle, Mazzolà came into his room carrying a letter from Ceneda, with the news that his younger brother Luigi – the medical student with whom Lorenzo had once sought refuge in Padua – was dead. With what seems to have been a rather ham-fisted attempt to cheer Lorenzo up, Mazzolà added the news that he had received a letter from a mutual friend in Venice bearing the preposterous warning that 'Da Ponte has gone to Dresden to do you out of your post as poet at court there. My dear fellow – be on your guard.' The ever-touchy Lorenzo was convinced that Mazzolà was not joking at all, and that he took the warning seriously. This insult to his integrity, he writes, compounded by his grief, and the Camerata tangle, exploded in a decision to leave Dresden immediately. He wrote a note to Father Huber, and another to Madam Camerata, telling them he would be on the diligence for Vienna at ten o'clock the next morning. Like his flight six years earlier from Venice to Treviso, it may well be that this departure was less spontaneous than Da Ponte makes out – there is a likelihood that he had an introduction from Casanova to friends in Vienna who might offer him work, though such assurances probably only added impetus to his decision to go.

In Da Ponte's version of the story, Father Huber was waiting next morning with a basket containing coffee, chocolate and travelling biscuits, as well as several bottles of delicious liqueur. It was a cold October day, and Huber also made Da Ponte a gift of a fur coat, a travelling cape, and his very own muff – which had inside it a secret pocket secured with silver buttons (always a boon at the pawn shop). The pocket bulged, but Lorenzo had to promise not to open it until he was well on his way. Wrapped in his new furs, he ran to tell Mazzolà he was leaving. Mazzolà seemed upset and astonished at the news, but Da Ponte turned on his heel and hurried away. Just as the diligence was departing, Mazzolà suddenly appeared with a letter, which he pressed on his friend.

Jolting out along the dreadful road to Vienna, Da Ponte examined the contents of the bulging secret pocket, and discovered a tiny copy of Boethius's *Consolations*, the *Imitations* of Thomas à Kempis, and a purse containing twelve gold pieces, each worth 100 florins. The note from Mazzolà was a letter of introduction – to a man who admired Mazzolà's libretti, and with whom he had recently worked. 'My beloved Da Ponte will hand you these few lines,' it read. 'Do for him everything that you would do for me. His heart and his talents deserve everything.' The letter was directed to 'My dear Salieri'.

Chapter Five

TRAVELLERS ARRIVING IN Vienna were often taken aback by the dust. That, and the silence. 'The Viennese are very quiet in public streets,' wrote Johann Pezzl, an indefatigable observer of life in the capital in the 1780s. 'Even when a hundred people are crossing a square, almost all you will hear is the sound of their footsteps.' The composer Joseph Haydn sorely missed Vienna's stillness when he moved to rowdy London, but to Da Ponte, who yearned for the singing and scaramouching in the Piazza San Marco, the nightingale urchins and serenading gondoliers, the city must have appeared still to be in mourning.

Dust hit you first, and then diarrhoea (an inevitable visitation on foreigners for at least a month, according to Pezzl, as innocent guts adjusted to the city's unsavoury water supply), but it was the dust that created the most discomfort. A plague of dried-out chalk and gravel, it was a common cause of 'wounded lungs', a doctor from Ragusa told Hester Piozzi when she complained of having to sleep in rooms with double windows and no chimneys. It was thickest of all on balmy Sunday evenings, when carriages pressed back through every gate as all who had been out in the country, in the suburbs, in the Prater and Augarten, came thundering home.

Vienna had a curious layout. Around a densely packed inner city was a glacis of green, a consequence of the Turkish siege a century earlier, during which everything outside the city wall had been razed. New dwellings were rebuilt at a distance, leaving a wide verdant Esplanade (freshly planted with horse chestnuts the year Da Ponte arrived) between the old town and the suburbs. Beyond the suburbs lay the public parks of the Augarten and the Prater (the latter with wilder spaces, too), and the deep, clear Danube, which flowed so fast that boats built upstream to carry goods to Vienna couldn't manage the return journey, and were broken up for firewood. Maps depicting the odd city topography were often printed on ladies' fans, presenting, Pezzl thought, 'the best opportunity, when one was in the carriage with one's lady, trotting out in the direction of Nußdorf, Laxenburg or Dornbach, to teach her the rudiments of geography'. (One can only imagine the delight with which young ladies of Vienna must have greeted the news that Herr Pezzl was to be a passenger in their carriage for the long, hot drive to a summer resort.)

The Dresden diligence rattled its way through the suburbs, across the Esplanade – where boars and stags roamed free – and on into the dust clouds of the city. Lorenzo Da Ponte, homesick for the canals of Venice and spoiled by the ordered boulevards of Dresden, could not have viewed his new home town with much joy. 'The streets of Vienna are not pretty at all; God knows,' complained Hester Piozzi, 'so narrow, so ill built, so crowded, many wares placed upon the ground where there is a little opening . . . the people cutting wood in the street makes one half wild when walking.' Another English traveller was displeased that every 'street, almost every house, and every hour has its own appropriate, peculiar and by no means enviable smell. The pavements, with a few exceptions, are of the most nobbly and excruciating kind,' adding that it was all too easy to break one's neck or bones, 'put out an eye, or tear off a cheek'.

Of course, Vienna was not all dust, diarrhoea and dangerous paving. As capital of the Hapsburg Empire it attracted a cosmopolitan milieu, for Lorenzo an echo of Venice: 'a feast for the eyes' of Hungarians in fur-lined dolmans and close-fitting trousers, Serbians with twisted moustaches, Armenians, Wallachians and Moldavians in half-Oriental costumes, Poles with monkish haircuts and flowing sleeves, Muslims with broad knives in their belts, Greeks smoking long pipes. German mingled with French and Italian in the streets; Hungarian, Turkish and Flemish burbled in the coffee-houses, and blended with Latin, Illyrian, Wendic and Romany. For a few pieces of gold, Da Ponte could find 'anything he desire[d] to satisfy his senses, his comfort and his humour. Chocolate made in Milan; pheasant raised in Bohemia; oysters fished in Istria; wine from the cellars of Tokay . . . Works of art and music from Italy, France's fashions, Germany's books, [might appear] at his command, as if by rubbing Aladdin's lamp'. The cooks were renowned as among the best in Europe; one Robert Townson, travelling in 1793, noted that among 'the Vienna people, who are noted for being addicted *à la gourmandise* . . . a deficiency in livers of geese and small birds might cause a revolution, or be considered sufficient cause of delivering up the city if besieged'. Dressed-up dolls, sent post-haste from Paris, brought the latest styles within days for seamstresses to get busy with. Ladies in the wide, sideways-hooped skirts that were still the rage glided through salons and parks, across squares and into ballrooms, like ambulant high altars (or herring-barrels, harrumphed Pezzl, who thought the skirts a 'monstrous contrivance', far preferring the softer lines of servants' wear).

Society glittered in a manner that Lorenzo had not encountered since Venice, not even in Dresden, and though Vienna was not the absolute vortex of the music world it would become in the following century, it was well on its way to being so. Public and private concerts abounded, as did balls, masquerades and grand dinners. 'All ranks of society were doatingly fond of music,' remembered Michael Kelly, who arrived a year or so after Da Ponte, 'and most of them perfectly understood the science. Indeed, Vienna then was a place where pleasure was the order of the day and night.' Yet unlike the night-moths of Venice, the people of Vienna were early abed, the streets empty and silent after eleven o'clock, just the occasional carriage rumbling by after midnight, returning from supper in one of the grand palaces. And unlike the old Mistress of the Adriatic, Vienna was not whirling in a manic death-dance of the *ancien régime*. Conversation in the coffee-houses delighted in controversial and en-lightened topics; the Emperor Joseph II, having assumed full reins of state on the death of his mother Maria Theresa, was introducing extraordi-narily liberal reforms to almost every walk of life. Vienna combined the serious and the frivolous in an exhilarating way. John Moore, tutor to the young Duke of Hamilton, who had accompanied his wilful young charge on a Grand Tour in the mid-1770s, wrote:

I have never passed my time more agreeably than since I came to Vienna. There is not such a constant round of amusements as to fill up a man's time without any plan or occupation of his own; and yet there is enough to satisfy any mind not perfectly vacant and dependent on external objects.

In this congenial atmosphere, Lorenzo Da Ponte found himself yet again without home or work, but (for all Vienna's dust and silence) in a more familiar milieu than any town his exile had yet afforded.

Da Ponte (if he followed the usual course of new arrivals) booked into an inn for two to three days, while he sent out his letters of introduction and awaited results. In the meantime, he looked for lodgings, walking the streets to read the handwritten notices posted on house doors. The advertisements abounded, and it seemed as if the entire town had its furniture in moving-carts – the fortnight after Michaelmas was one of the two most popular times of year to change apartment. Lorenzo was less lucky in finding work. His store of social entrées was a meagre one: he might be able to count on another favourable reception from Johann Philippe Cobenzl; and he had Mazzolà's letter to the energetic Antonio Salieri, who although a year younger than Da Ponte was already court composer, and was sure to have some influence. He appears, too, much in the same way as he did in Gorizia, to have followed up on a Casanova connection, though perhaps not with a direct letter of introduction, as the pair had fallen out some years earlier – bickering over 'some trifling point of Latin prosody' claimed Da Ponte. Late in 1781, Da Ponte published a pastoral poem, *Filemone e Bauci*, which at the suggestion of a visiting cleric, the Abbé Eusebio Della Lena, he dedicated to a rich local merchant, Johann Baptist von Puthon, on the occasion of Von Puthon's moving into a new home. Both these men were intimates of Casanova.

It was Della Lena who introduced Da Ponte to Metastasio. Ever since the young Emanuele Conegliano had discovered a stash of books in his father's attic in Ceneda and begun avidly to read, Pietro Metastasio had been his literary hero. Metastasio's works were the only volumes from the find that the boy had read twice, and they had unfolded in him a love for the Italian language, a love that slowly grew into his own desire to write. Metastasio's libretti were among the few that Da Ponte did not scoff at as trivial and unworthy of the name of poetry. The ancient Italian – he was now eighty-four – had been imperial poet at the Viennese court since 1730, and was a leading writer of *opera seria*, an ornamented, formal style of 'serious' opera, generally on a classical theme.

Part of Metastasio's success lay in his perception that in opera the poet must humble himself, that the composer was doing much of his work for him – he even went so far as to set every one of his arias to music himself, though he showed his music to no one. This attitude held especially for the arias and duets. The blank-verse recitative that carried the narrative forward was more the bard's domain, but in *opera seria* it was the arias, and hence the singers (especially the castrati), that ruled. *Opera seria*, with its complicated and formulaic conventions, had become little more than a costumed concert, and was beginning to fade from fashion in the work of modern musicians, such as the court composer Salieri. Indeed, Metastasio's peak of production had been in the years immediately following his arrival in Vienna, and since the 1740s he had written little, but lived off a pension from the Empress Maria Theresa and the proceeds of numerous new editions of his work.

The mild old man – Dr Burney described him as 'innocuous'; Casanova said that he was so modest that it did not seem natural – was an impeccable craftsman, who laughed at the idea of poetic inspiration and (according to Dr Burney) 'made a poem as another would make a watch, at what time he pleased, and without any other occasion than the want of it'. His life, too, went like clockwork, 'ranged with such methodical exactness,' Hester Piozzi relates, 'that he rose, studied, chatted, slept, and dined at the same hours for fifty years together . . .' Sweetly urbane, though a fearful hypochondriac, Metastasio had lodged in the home of the Spanish Neapolitan merchant Nicolo Martinez for over half a century, seldom going out except to mass, and never learning German. 'I have been a bird of court, almost *immemoriabilie,*' he wrote of himself when he was just forty-four, 'not one in the woods, but used to ease, comfort and repose; and unable to fly here and there at a venture, exposed to all the severities of the season. So that to be safe conducted, I must be transported in my cage, with my water-glass and keeper to supply my wants.'

In his last years he kept up a chatty correspondence with his dear friend Farinelli, the great castrato singer once so fashionable as to have inspired the exclamation that there was 'one God, one Farinelli'. The aging poet doted on his 'adopted twin', and enjoyed the gifts that Farinelli sent him – such as succulent Ferrarese peaches and sweet liqueur, some fruit already eaten and the flask breached so that Metastasio could imagine the pair were relishing the feast together. In reality, he ate entirely alone, always, even his nearest intimates seldom seeing him take more than a single biscuit with his lemonade. His pleasures comprised solely music, poetry and conversation. At home, Metastasio was pampered by the young Misses Martinez, who themselves set his poetry, played and sang. An Italian abbé told Hester Piozzi: 'Oh! he [Metastasio] looked like a man in a state of beatification always when Mademoiselle de Martinas [*sic*] accompanied his verses with her fine voice and brilliant finger.' The aged poet presided, splendidly old-fashioned (he had not changed the style of his wig, nor the cut nor colour of his coat, for decades), over these salons at the house on Kohlmarkt Gasse. It was to one such gathering, on an evening early in April 1782, that the Abbé Della Lena took the Abbé Da Ponte.

Della Lena had already shown the imperial poet a copy of Da Ponte's *Filemone e Bauci,* and told him something of the young man. Metastasio warmed to the new arrival. The two men had similar backgrounds. Born Pietro Trapassi, the son of Felice Trapassi, a grocer in Rome, Metastasio displayed early brilliance as an *improvvisatore.* Giovanni Vincenzo Gravina, a distinguished Roman jurist and Arcadian, had taken up the youthful prodigy, hellenized his surname, and later formally adopted him. Felice Trapassi relinquished his first-born to the prospect of a good education and an introduction to society. Metastasio took minor orders, and as a young abbé renowned for his charm, beauty and talent (and later with a considerable inheritance from Gravina), he edged into higher social spheres – although, because of his plebeian birth, especially in mid-eighteenth-century Vienna, he was always an outsider in the aristocratic milieu through which he moved. Lorenzo Da Ponte carried (as he had done for Casanova) an echo of the older man's youth.

While the guests sipped wines and sampled sweetmeats, the great poet himself (no doubt having nibbled on his single biscuit) started to read from *Filemone e Bauci*. '*Era Bauci una ninfa, a cui non nacque*,' Metastasio began, '*altra pari in bellezza a'tempi suoi . . .*' The poem – an elegant though conservative pastoral about the love of the nymph Baucis and shepherd Philemon lasting into old age, their hospitality for the gods Zeus and Hermes, and their transformation after death into intertwining trees – pleased the old man, but although (in Da Ponte's words) Metastasio 'retained in his extreme age all the freshness and vivacity of youth and all his pristine vigour as a fertile and hardy genius', after twenty or so lines he had not the energy to go on, and asked Da Ponte himself to continue the reading. The imperial poet's praise rippled out into general approbation among the literati of Vienna – though that was all the help that Metastasio could give Da Ponte. A few days later, on 12 April 1782, the gentle bird of court finally flew its gilded cage.

Lorenzo Da Ponte, on the other hand, surged along like a boat coming down the Danube, buoyed by the small fortune Father Huber had given him, and with the strong wind of public praise at his back. He became a popular (if not always fully comprehended) feature at local parties, as he noted in a verse letter to his friend Count Zaguri in Venice:

> I'm a poet, and improvise in odes
> and see now that everyone seeks me out, longs for me,
> Everyone competes to get to listen to me;
> To lunch this one, and to dinner the other one calls me,
> I say what I can, and that which I please,
> And these good people praise me
> To show that they understand what I sing.
>
> Because if I have to confess the truth to you,
> I think that among such a great crowd who would hear me,

Not a single dog understands an entire line of verse;
Just as I myself would not understand it:
One day a thought crossed my mind,
To sing the Hail Mary in Hebrew
And it was the source of an argument between a Friar and a
    Dwarf;
And they thought I was singing in Italian.

Unfortunately, little of this goodwill converted itself into good gold. Vienna was musically vibrant, but the other arts fared less prosperously and music was not Da Ponte's forte. 'Music is the only thing for which the nobility show a taste,' wrote Baron Johann Kaspar Riesbeck, a contemporary traveller through Germany. Pezzl believed that a 'painter, a sculptor, an engraver, a musician, etc., possesses a certain cachet in society, where he is respected and welcomed, especially in the great houses. A simple scholar, an author, a man of letters, is accepted only with some equivocation, and his title is seldom mentioned without a hint of scorn . . . Spending two ducats on taking a drive is less shocking to the Viennese than paying thirty kreuzer for a book'. Apart from *Filemone e Bauci*, and a sonnet written to commemorate a visit by the Pope around the time that Metastasio read his poem, Da Ponte did not publish anything for over a year. Without noble patronage or family money, a writer struggled to survive by his pen alone. There was no resident Italian opera in Vienna, so the sort of jobbing work Da Ponte had done for Mazzolà in Dresden was not available; and Salieri had failed to respond to Mazzolà's letter of introduction with any concrete proposal. Other lines of employment for Da Ponte were limited. Despite having lived for nearly three years in Austrian territory, and those first '*Ich liebe Sie*' efforts notwithstanding, Lorenzo barely spoke German. It was a language, he said, he would have to learn, even though it was one that would frighten St Francis:

> *Voglio mo dir che parlano il tedesco,*
> *Lingua da far paura a San Francesco.*

There was a sizeable Italian contingent in the inner councils of the Emperor and among the court bureaucracy, so secretarial work might be possible, but the leading families and rich merchants were German-speaking, and his lack of facility with the language narrowed the scope for work as a tutor, his usual fall-back for income.

Yet Lorenzo was living grandly, in the fashionable inner city. The green glacis beyond the city wall created more than a topographical gap between the old town and the suburbs. The nobility and court officials all had palaces in the centre; the craftsmen that served their needs joined them, and the middling sort of burghers were cast out beyond the walls. Da Ponte saw that to carry any social weight whatsoever, one had to reside within the city walls; and for a poet hoping to meet patrons, there was simply no alternative. Lorenzo had learned the value of appearances – even at his poorest in Padua, he had taken care to present himself 'scrupulously groomed and beautifully attired'. He clearly did not skimp. His windfall from Father Huber – twelve gold pieces worth 100 florins each – was enough to live on, fairly comfortably, for two years. Pezzl estimated the annual expenditure for a single man, who did not gamble or have a mistress – something that caused complications and required 'a certain type of wardrobe' – to be 464 gulden (a gulden was the equivalent of one florin). Moving in higher social circles cost consider-ably more. The court actor Joseph Lange took home the handsome stipend of 1,400 gulden, supplemented by private appearances, and leading actor of the time Johann Müller received 1,600 gulden – both considerably more than the average musician or middling merchant. Da Ponte projected himself into this realm, and after less than a year, without any supplementary income, his money was running out.

Retrenchment meant moving. Even within the city walls, Lorenzo could, if lucky, find a cell of a room 'containing a bed, a chest of drawers, a rickety table and a pair of old chairs' with the only view 'into an airless courtyard or narrow street' for around forty gulden. Instead of taking meals at taverns, he could slip unobserved into a *traiteur* for a set dinner at a low price, to Zur Blauen Flasche on Stock-im-Eisen-Platz, where hundreds of people crowded into two rooms: clerks and minor officials for the ten-kreuzer meal; mainly liveried servants for the eight-kreuzer meal, the latter calling each other not by their real names but by the names of their masters, so that 'Cobenzl!', 'Kaunitz!', 'Zinzendorf!' – the very men Lorenzo needed to be dining with – would have echoed about his head as he ate. But Da Ponte's purse had grown too thin even for eight-kreuzer dinners or a cell-like city-centre room, so thin that he feared a return to the dreadful days of black olives and *l'acqua di Brenta* he had suffered in Padua. Some time after the spring of 1782, he took the socially debilitating step of moving to the suburbs, to board with a tailor in Wieden, where not a single street was paved and few houses were more than three storeys high – but where, to his good luck, he met 'an erudite and cultured youth, a great lover of Italian letters, who, though not rich, was so generous as to supply me, with noble bounty, with enough to keep me from neediness over many months'. Penniless, in a foreign country, and with just a single friend to count on in Vienna, Lorenzo began to slide into artistic oblivion.

Meanwhile, back across the Esplanade, in a house called '*Zum Roten Säbel*' (the Red Sabre) on the Hohe Brücke, a small domestic drama was playing to its climax.

Wolfgang Amadé Mozart (he preferred the French over the Latin version of his second name, or the German 'Gottlieb' with which he had been christened) had, in March of the previous year, been summoned to perform in Vienna by his employer the Archbishop of Salzburg, who was there on an extended visit. Seven years younger than Da Ponte, Wolfgang Mozart was 'a remarkably small man, very thin and pale, with a profusion of fine fair hair, of which he was rather vain'. His head seemed rather too large for his body, though perhaps that was just as well, as he had inherited his mother's fulsome nose. Most people first noticed not the pale proboscis, but his wide, intense blue eyes – sometimes melancholy, but usually gleaming with a boisterous, merry wit, an occasional flash of sarcasm. He had fleshy hands. Young Mozart dreaded returning to Salzburg and was determined to stay in a city he found infinitely more stimulating, and which he maintained held better prospects for him – a notion that brought him into conflict with both the Archbishop and Leopold Mozart, his controlling father back home. To make matters worse, by the summer of 1782, Wolfgang was careering towards marriage with Constanze Weber, sparking another clash with his father and without his blessing.

Some years earlier, Wolfgang had been in love with Constanze's elder sister, the queenly, fine-voiced Aloysia – but she had later spurned him. The girls' mother, Cäcilia Weber, was a schemer and an old soak – Mozart had to admit this in a letter to his father, though he was adamant he had never seen her really *besoffen* ('sozzled'). When her husband died in 1779, Widow Weber had moved her marriageable brood into a house named '*Auge Gottes*' (the Eye of God) on Petersplatz, and let out rooms to eligible young men. Aloysia was the first of the four sisters to ensnare a husband, not a lodger but the well-to-do court actor Joseph Lange, who was obliged to pay his mother-in-law 700 gulden a year for life for the privilege. Mozart was next. He was a lodger – in the early summer of 1781, he had moved in with the Webers in the course of a bitter (and as it turned out final) row with his patron, the Archbishop. After a footman had told him to leave his lodgings at the house of the Teutonic Order, where he stayed with rest of the Archbishop's staff, he wrote to his father: 'Madame Weber was kind enough to offer me her home – where I now have a pretty room and am among helpful people who lend a hand with things one might need in a hurry, the sort of thing one doesn't have when one lives alone.'

Mother Weber did more than just lend a hand. The availability of the pretty room was enhanced by the presence of a reasonably pretty daughter. (A painting of Constanze done by her brother-in-law Joseph Lange in 1782 depicts her as pert and rather sulky, but shows well the 'two little black eyes' which Mozart said together with a good figure comprised her 'whole beauty'.) Wolfgang fell in love with Constanze – for her part, she later said she was 'perhaps more attracted by his talents than his person' – and an imbroglio worthy of a comic opera ensued. Madame Weber disingenuously sanctioned Mozart's continuing to live in the house. As soon as the couple were sufficiently compromised by gossip, she colluded with the girl's guardian, Johann Thorwart – a factotum of Count Rosenberg, the director of court theatre – to exact from Mozart a contract of good intent. Wolfgang, who had already moved out of his pretty room to new lodgings on the Graben, signed a letter promising to marry Constanze within three years, or pay her 300 gulden per annum if he changed his mind. Constanze dramatically tore up the contract, saying she trusted Wolfgang; when her mother began to make life difficult for her, she left home and went to live with one of Mozart's protectors, the Baroness von Waldstätten (herself, alas, of not sufficiently impeccable reputation to staunch the gossip).

All the while, a furious correspondence was zigzagging between Wolfgang in Vienna and Leopold Mozart in Salzburg. Leopold was horrified at the suggestion of marriage, writing that Mother Weber had opened her house to Mozart in order to entrap him, and that she and Thorwart 'should be put in chains, made to sweep streets and have boards hung round their necks with the words "seducers of youth" '. He went on to say he had been reliably informed that Constanze was little better than a slut; when that didn't work he fell to threats and self-pitying demands (a pattern in his relationship with his son) designed to wheedle his will through guilt. Wolfgang was twenty-five years old, but a callow twenty-five. As a child prodigy he had for years been dominated by his father as they toured the courts of Europe, and his rebellion against the Archbishop of Salzburg, his determination to make a life for himself in Vienna, and now his decision to marry were all part of a brave and shaky bid for independence. Events were gathering their own momentum, and propelled him down the final straight.

Around the time Lorenzo Da Ponte slunk out to live in the suburbs, Wolfgang Mozart heard that Madame Weber was about to call the police to remove her daughter from the home of the Baroness von Waldstätten. The ensuing scandal would be intolerable. A quick marriage was the only solution, and the couple were wed on 4 August 1782 – the day before the letter with Leopold's grudging consent arrived. Constanze joined Wolfgang in his chambers at Zum Roten Säbel, but a few months later the couple moved to more suitable accommodation further along the Hohe Brücke.

Mozart's professional life had also erupted in drama. The newly married musician was in a predicament that he shared with other young men of his rank and time, who were trying to make money from their

art, including the destitute Lorenzo Da Ponte, languishing above a
tailor's shop in Wieden. In the weeks after Wolfgang had moved in with
the Webers, in the early summer of 1781, he had finally broken with the
Archbishop of Salzburg, and been left to his own devices. A few months
before his wedding, Mozart had written to his father:

> There is nothing more disagreeable than to be obliged to live in
> uncertainty . . . Well, I want to give you my opinion as to my
> prospects of a small permanent income. I have my eye on three
> sources. The first [composing for Prince Alois Joseph Liechtenstein's
> proposed wind band] is not certain, and, even if it were, would
> probably not be much; the second [a position with Emperor Joseph II]
> would be the best, but God knows when it will ever come to pass; and
> the third [an appointment with Archduke Maximilian] is not to be
> despised, but the pity is that it concerns the future and not the present
> . . . It is indeed a pity that these great gentlemen refuse to make
> arrangements beforehand . . . Dearest, most beloved father! If I could
> have it in writing from God Almighty that I shall keep in good health
> and not get ill, ah! then I would marry my dear faithful girl this very
> day. I have three pupils now, which brings me in eighteen ducats; for I
> no longer charge for twelve lessons, but monthly. I learned to my cost
> that my pupils often dropped out for weeks at a time; so now, whether
> they learn or not, each of them must pay me six ducats. I shall get
> several more on these terms, but I really need only one more, because
> four pupils are quite enough. With four I should have twenty-four
> ducats, or 102 gulden 24 kreuzer. With this sum a man and his wife can
> manage in Vienna if they live quietly and in the retired way which we
> desire; but, of course, if I were to fall ill, we should not make a farthing.
> I can write, it is true, at least one opera a year, give a concert annually
> and have some things engraved and published by subscription. There
> are other concerts too where one can make money . . .

Mozart had to be something of an artistic entrepreneur. It was a question
of scraping together the coins – a concert here, a pupil there, an opera, a
sonata, a little from publishing – all the while keeping an eye open for a

possible patron. The uncertainty, the scrabble for money, the catastrophe of cancelled arrangements and the threat of ill health scuppering earnings, are all features of what, a century later, would be termed a freelance career. Men like Mozart and Da Ponte were caught up in the swell as the arts moved away from the court and went public; as opera ceased to be a court spectacle, and moved to theatres where people had to pay to get in (but where anyone could attend); as literacy rates rose, as novels reached a popular readership, and writers moved to publish work in a burgeoning number of newspapers and periodicals. This was not an entirely new phenomenon: audiences had paid to see Shakespeare's plays at the Globe; Mozart and Da Ponte had forerunners in such men as the poet Alexander Pope in England, one of the first to make a good living from his art (particularly from translation). The composer and impresario George Frederick Handel made a fortune from the paying public, and Voltaire had for a while lived comfortably off the proceeds of his epic poem *Henriade* – but the late eighteenth century saw an expansion in the scale and scope of the commercialization of culture. Not that this made it very much easier to earn a living from art. The model for literary activity still favoured gentleman writers, who rather frowned on making money from their labours. Booksellers rather than authors owned works once an initial purchase fee had been settled. The concept of copyright had its nascence in a British law of 1709, but the idea spread slowly and it wasn't until the end of the century that even English writers began to receive royalties. Journalism flourished, particularly in England, France and Italy, but was looked down upon by many genteel men of letters. Periodicals and newspapers created new roles and new avenues of employment, but were on the whole owned by booksellers who kept their writers in poverty.

Yet as sources of income grew more varied, and art diffused out of court, there was a concomitant change in focus by its practitioners. Metastasio had been content to be a bird of court, even though his social status was lowly. Mozart and Da Ponte still had to keep an eye out for noble patrons, but the shift in earning potential contributed to a feeling of independence – and independence meant greater self-respect and a little more Enlightened dignity, even if life could be a struggle. Part of

Mozart's conflict with the Archbishop of Salzburg had been his resistance to the indignity of being treated as a servant. A nobleman's musicians took their place alongside his other lackeys. Joseph Haydn – for years attached to the Esterházy family – always wore the white hose and powdered wig of his master's livery when performing. Some musicians even doubled up on their role: when the violinist and composer Karl Ditters entered the service of the Bishop of Grosswardein in 1765, one of the members of the orchestra was the bishop's confectioner, another a valet, and one of the singers was a cook.

In a sense, Mozart's was a special case. As a child prodigy he had been cosseted by countesses, kissed by queens, so as an adult he found a servant's role distasteful. On 17 March 1781, having just arrived to join the Archbishop of Salzburg's suite in Vienna, he wrote sarcastically to his father, in a letter which clearly shows he feels above the company he is forced to keep:

> We lunch about twelve o'clock, unfortunately somewhat too early for me. Our party consists of the two valets, that is the body and soul attendants of His Worship, the *contrôleur*, Herr Zetti, the confectioner, the two cooks, Ceccarelli, Brunetti and – my insignificant self. By the way, the two valets sit at the top of the table, but at least I have the honour of being placed above the cooks . . . A good deal of silly, coarse joking goes on at table, but no one cracks jokes with me, for I never say a word, or, *if I have to speak*, I always do so with the utmost gravity, and as soon as I have finished my lunch, I get up and go off.

Mozart's disdain was not simply the result of a childhood that had given him an idea of himself that was above his station, nor was it exclusive to him. His past experience simply sharpened a perception that was beginning to be shared by others in creative professions who identified with the aspirations of the rising middle classes, and whose sources of income were becoming more diverse. The security a patron offered continued to be a very attractive prospect – Mozart still wanted to introduce himself to the Emperor 'in some becoming way, for I am absolutely determined that he shall *get to know me*' – but patronage restricted independence. Quite as strong as his objection to a servile role in the Archbishop's retinue was Mozart's belief that the strictures the Archbishop placed upon him – by the constant requirement that he play on demand – thwarted his ambitions as a musician. With emancipation from patronage came the freedom to carve out an autonomous artistic (and social) existence – but for the small matter of having to scrape together a living. The notion of the solitary, unconventional artist starving in a garret, largely a product of the Romantic era, was just around the corner. In some ways, both Da Ponte and Mozart had already taken a step in that direction.

The *ancien régime* had, quite literally, booted Wolfgang Mozart in the backside. Count Arco, the Archbishop's chief steward, had simultaneously put an end to the young musician's dispute with his master and terminated his employment with a kick to the buttocks that sent him from the room. Mozart raged at such 'insolence and rudeness', and fantasized in his letters about repaying the gesture in kind – but the truth was that whatever he may have considered his own worth, an assault on a nobleman was a serious offence. Instead, he had to set about putting together a new life from the gainful pieces he had at his disposal. Lorenzo Da Ponte was not so lucky, and might be excused a mood of gloom and bitterness. But in the spring of 1783 something occurred that would transform Da Ponte's life, and lead to some of the most sublime music Mozart would ever compose.

The Emperor Joseph II established an Italian opera company in Vienna.

Chapter Six

GOSSIP WAS THE oxygen of eighteenth-century society. It fuelled the chat of fine ladies who paused at each others' sides in public parks, hooped silks rustling; it brought life to conversation at salon soirées, and fed the murmur in theatre boxes. It emanated from coffee-houses (where newspapers, too expensive for many to buy, were available for all to read) and found a tangible form in the pamphlets that flitted about market-places and through the streets. It moved from an ear in court to lips that whispered on the soft pillow of a mistress. It coloured Metastasio's gentle banter with the Misses Martinez, and gave relish to Casanova's letters. It toted praise of the Abbé Da Ponte's poetry, and ferried the latest scandal from Widow Weber's house. It brought word of an extraordinary clavier contest at the palace between Wolfgang Mozart and the celebrated Muzio Clementi (the Emperor was still talking about that a year later). It was the swiftest channel for the spread of news, a bobbing barque for carrying ideas, a free and tireless entertainment.

The talk as the winter of 1782 drew in was of how the Emperor had dismissed a company of French comedians performing at the palace, through the insolence of one of the players. His Majesty had been passing the hall where they were dining, when an actor jumped up, followed him and complained that the wine they were given was vile, that it could hardly even be termed Burgundy. Now Joseph II was an easygoing man, for an emperor. 'He was an enemy to pomp and parade,' wrote Michael

Kelly. He usually dressed in simple military uniform, without medals or decorations, at his own meals drank plain water or just one glass of Tokay wine, and 'almost always dined on one dish – boiled bacon, which the people, from his partiality to it, called *caizer flush* [*sic*]'. Lord Stormont, the British Ambassador in Vienna, reported:

> He . . . has the truest & most unaffected Simplicity of manners. He often runs about [i.e. in a carriage] with a single Servant behind Him; likes to converse with all ranks, puts those He talks to, quite at their Ease; loves easy, familiar Conversation, as much as he hates to talk in a Circle . . .

The monarch himself admitted, one evening at the Countess Waldstein's:

> It would be hard indeed, if, because I have the ill fortune to be an Emperor, I should be deprived of the pleasures of social life, which are so much to my taste. All the grimace and parade to which people are accustomed from their cradle, have not made me so vain, as to imagine that I am in any essential quality superior to other men; and if I had any tendency to such an opinion, the surest way to get rid of it, is the method I take, of mixing in society, where I have daily occasions of finding myself inferior in talents to those I meet with.

This was in astonishing contrast to the behaviour of other monarchs of the time – most notoriously that of Joseph's sister, Marie Antoinette, but even that of King George III in a more informal English court, where, as a close attendant of the Queen, Fanny Burney felt constrained to choke rather than cough, to grind her teeth and break a blood vessel, but never sneeze. Yet a lowly actor running up behind the ruler of the Holy Roman Empire and complaining that the wine he had been given gratis was vile, was too familiar even for such a reforming monarch as Joseph II. His Majesty, the gossip went, with gracious composure, tasted the glass that was proffered him, and said, 'I think it is excellent, at least quite good enough for *me*, though, perhaps, not sufficiently high-flavoured for *you*

and your companions; in France I dare say you will get much better.'
The French comedians were sent home.

In their place, people said, Joseph had decided to establish an Italian
opera company. Noisome French actors aside, this was probably a step he
had been considering for some time. Joseph's grandfather, Charles VI
(Emperor from 1711 to 1740), maintained a lavish court theatre, staging
pompous spectacles and opera in a grand baroque playhouse. These
occasions – held to celebrate name days, weddings and other important
events – were a significant part of court ritual, proclaiming the regal state
of the monarch as well as being a display of wealth. Joseph's mother,
Maria Theresa, whose reign got off to a shaky start (Charles VI had left
no male heir, leading to the eight-year-long War of the Austrian
Succession) was forced to economize in scale. She turned the old
playhouse (comprising two separate theatres) into ballrooms, the Redoutensaal, and commissioned a new, much smaller theatre to be built in
a converted indoor tennis-court behind the palace. This Burgtheater
(condensed from 'Hofburgtheater' – court theatre) was leased out to a
manager who, although contracted to stage some operas for the court,
was obliged to make most of his money by opening to the public. Opera
detached itself from the realms of court ritual – the people who attended
now came voluntarily, and the middle classes who might previously
never have made it to court were admitted into the audience.

At the same time, popular theatre stepped up on to the respectable
stage. Until the first part of the eighteenth century, there had been a
distinct division in German-speaking cities between shows (often largely
improvised) presented by travelling players on temporary stages, and the
more sumptuous, scripted goings-on in court. The itinerant troupes
tended to perform in German, while the court companies were usually
French or Italian. Vienna was one of the first towns to give travelling
players a permanent theatre, the Kärntnertortheater, built at public
expense near the city wall (probably in 1710) – though still under court
control. Under Joseph II, these two strands – of vernacular entertainment
and court theatre – began to intertwine.

Early in 1776, Joseph had proclaimed the *Schauspielfreiheit* ('liberty for
theatre'). Part of this proclamation ended court monopoly over theatre,

offering the Kärntnertortheater gratis to all comers (including sets and costumes), and allowing other entertainments to sprout all over town – but it was in the Burgtheater that Joseph most exercised his reforming zeal. Here he took control back from the manager-lessee, and elevated the theatre to the status of a 'National Theatre', moving away from a predominantly French repertory to present German-language plays, comprehendible by the general public. This was in part for nationalistic reasons, but largely because Joseph saw the theatre as an instrument for spreading Enlightenment principles – in the words of one of his censors, 'a school of manners and taste'. Spoken drama in German was also easier on the royal pocket than Italian opera or French ballet.

This purity did not last long. By June 1776, Italian opera was back; and by July, so was French ballet. Although the Burgtheater had been detached from the rituals of court, it was not free of the diktats of society, and fashion declared for music, or at least music-based entertainments. In 1778, bending his earlier aims slightly, Joseph established a 'National *Singspiel*' in the Burgtheater – a German musical theatre, with spoken dialogue between the sung parts. For a while, society approved. The young court composer, Antonio Salieri, returning from a leave-of-absence in April 1780, shrewdly noted the new penchant for *Singspiel*, and wrote one for the Burgtheater. *Der Rauchfangkehrer* featured his mistress, the soprano Caterina Cavalieri, in the leading role, and was a great success. A year later a new arrival in town, Wolfgang Amadé Mozart, was also caught up by the growing taste for *Singspiel*. In the final stages of his fight with the Archbishop of Salzburg, he was on the lookout for new employment and secured a commission from Count Rosenberg that resulted in *Die Entführung aus dem Serail* (The Abduction from the Seraglio). When *Die Entführung* opened the following summer, it, too, proved enormously popular – becoming Mozart's first stage work to achieve wide public renown. Once again Caterina Cavalieri took the lead, playing the part of Constanze, the namesake of Mozart's inamorata. Wolfgang was at the height of his imbroglio with the Webers. His friends began jokingly to refer to *Die Entführung aus dem Serail* as '*Die Entführung aus dem Auge Gottes*'.

If Lorenzo Da Ponte had at this point any inclination to continue the sort of jobbing work he had done with Mazzolà in Dresden – or even to attempt a libretto himself – he must have viewed the triumph of the *Singspiel* with gloom. He was not alone. Italian singers, composers and musicians still working at the Burgtheater were beginning to form a cabal – Mozart was sure they were behind a claque paid to hiss and disrupt the first two performances of *Die Entführung*. The wagging tongues of Vienna let out that the Italians had the Emperor's ear. Franz Xaver Niemetschek – clearly not of the Italian camp – wrote, in 1798:

> [*Entführung*] created a stir; and the cunning Italians soon realized that such a man might pose a threat to their childish tinkling. Jealousy now reared its head with typical Italian venom. The monarch, who at heart was charmed by this deeply stirring music, said to Mozart nevertheless: 'Too beautiful for our ears and an extraordinary number of notes, dear Mozart.' 'Just as many, Your Majesty, as are necessary,' he replied with that noble dignity and frankness which so often go with great genius. He realized that this was not a personal opinion, but just the repetition of somebody else's words . . .

In any event, society's taste for *Singspiel* was short-lived. The influential aristocratic audience at the Burgtheater considered Italian opera to be more sophisticated, and as the available performers were essentially singers anyway, rather than actors able to sing, *Singspiel* began to lose its supremacy. When Joseph II officially installed an Italian opera company at the Burgtheater in the spring of 1783, *Singspiel* slipped off to the Kärntnertortheater and the suburbs, where increasingly it came to be seen as a poor bourgeois cousin to a more cultured Italian counterpart. The Burgtheater became home, on Mondays, Wednesdays and Fridays, to Italian opera and on other days of the week to straight German drama.

Months before the curtain rose on the new company's first production, the word was out backstage in theatres across Europe. As audiences left for home and the capstans were turned to lower guttering chandeliers into silent auditoria; as the little oil lamps that lit orchestras were doused and the candles along the sides of scenery flats were snuffed; as singers and dancers changed out of their stage clothes, and wandered off into the night for a little post-performance flirtation or champagne, the conversation turned to the news that the Emperor of Austria was going to establish an opera company in Vienna. Everyone knew of the Viennese taste for music, and an opera company at the heart of the Hapsburg Empire was likely to be one of the richest and most prestigious in the world. There was work to be had, and well-paid work at that (though not for castrati, as this was to be a modern company). Pleading letters were written, favours called in, elderly lovers nagged and influential connections carefully courted. From Vienna, the Emperor's chamberlain Count Franz Orsini-Rosenberg, in his role as director of court theatre, sent letters to ambassadors abroad, instructing them to find artists of the first order, sparing no expense. Count Rosenberg worked closely on the selection of singers with the Emperor himself. The new company was to perform opera buffa – not the rule-bound, old-fashioned *opera seria* that had been the domain of virtuoso singers and at which Metastasio had so excelled as a writer, but a humorous, less formal opera that relied more on dramatic effect than the vocal acrobatics of castrati. In most other major cities, opera buffa (which had grown out of lighter interludes between the acts of opera proper) was relegated to minor theatres while *opera seria* dominated the major house, but the Burgtheater was to break with this pattern and move to the forefront of a change in public taste – largely because Joseph II himself disliked *opera seria*.

Stefano Mandini and Francesco Benucci, two of the best buffo singers in Europe, were called to Vienna. The Emperor had heard Benucci sing in Rome, and instructed Count Rosenberg to engage him whatever the cost (though he was later to quibble). In Florence, the soprano Nancy Storace had caused a sensation at the Teatro Pergola – and been sacked. The dark-eyed daughter of a Neapolitan father and English mother so skilfully parodied Luigi Marchesi's vocal trickery that the great castrato refused to remain in the same company with her. '*L'inglesina*' was just eighteen when she, too, received an invitation to Vienna. From Venice came the tenor Michael Kelly, with a healthy batch of letters of introduction and a very favourable contract, offering not just a princely 1,640 gulden a year, but also free accommodation, and four large (and expensive) wax candles. Kelly was delighted to find that Nancy Storace was part of the company. The two had been firm friends ever since, some years earlier in Livorno, she had mistaken the pretty young man (with his great quantity of floating fair hair) for a girl in boy's clothes, and commented on him to her brother Stephen in English, not realizing Kelly could understand. Kelly had replied, 'You are mistaken, Miss; I am a very proper *he* animal, and quite at your service!' – though, on his part, their ensuing friendship was untrammelled by any hint of an amorous advance. As an opera soubrette, Nancy was appreciated not only for her voice, but for her voluptuous figure and winning ways. Gossip had her down at different moments as the mistress of Benucci, Mozart, Prince Dietrichstein, and even of the Emperor himself, though not all men were so enamoured – Johan Pezzl thought her 'a small, dumpy creature, without a single feminine grace, except for a pair of large – though not very compelling – eyes'. Nevertheless, Kelly revelled in her company. He put up at the White Ox inn, sent out his letters as soon as he arrived, and was conducted to his apartments ('an excellent first and second floor, elegantly furnished, in the most delightful part of Vienna') by court composer Salieri in person – 'a little man,' Kelly noted, 'with an expressive countenance, and his eyes . . . full of genius'. (Nancy's mother, who accompanied her daughter as a somewhat ineffectual chaperone, thought Salieri looked like the young Garrick.)

From far and wide they came, some of the very best that the opera world had to offer, converging on Vienna. That made it all the more curious when the position of poet to the court theatre was given to a complete unknown. A Jew turned Christian, or so the gossip went, who passed himself off as an abbé.

Lorenzo Da Ponte may have retreated to the suburbs in 1782, but he had not given up hope. Pezzl's description of life beyond the green glacis could have been written for the fallen abbe:

> For 12 gulden p.a. [a man] can find a little room in the suburbs. A cook-shop will furnish him lunch for 2 groschen, a second-hand clothes shop will provide his needs for a pittance. Meanwhile, clad in

his greatcoat, he visits the magnificent palaces and pretty gardens, and walks alongside generals, ministers and princesses, whose countenances the wealthiest provincial citizen looks for in vain.

Lorenzo joined the promenade in the Prater and Augarten, where finely bedecked ladies paused to swap news, moving off with a slightly quicker step; where gentleman in tricorn hats and silk stockings exchanged the odd word with courtiers; where he might even see the 'truest & most unaffected' Emperor out for a ride with his single servant, or sitting in a carriage with a friend. The Prater was, Kelly thought, 'the finest promenade in Europe, far surpassing in variety [London's] beautiful Hyde Park'. Hundreds of carriages passed down avenues shaded by chestnuts, deer grazed and gazed at passers-by, there were pheasants aplenty and wild boars which might disturb one's picnic (one once put Kelly and Salieri to flight). Along the way were coffee-houses, taverns, summer pavilions, bowling alleys and a merry-go-round. Pezzl notes that 'under the trees are tables with roast chicken and bottles of wine; all around there are games, music, the cries of children, the sound of happy laughing people . . . some wandering in the shade, some playing dice, some lying on the ground, some further away, friends or lovers strolling arm-in-arm amid the shrubbery . . .' In the evenings there were fireworks, and (Kelly noted in wonderment) 'innumerable cabarets, frequented by people of all ranks . . . who *immediately after dinner* proceed thither to regale themselves with their favourite dish, fried chickens, cold ham and sausages; white beer and Hofner wines, by way of dessert; and stay there until a late hour; dancing, music and every description of merriment prevail.'

The fireworks, with a twenty-kreuzer entrance fee, would have been beyond Lorenzo's means, as were top-up suppers of sausages and cold ham – but much of the enjoyment was open to all for the price of a cup of coffee, and promenading was for free. Perhaps to compensate for his decline in circumstances, Da Ponte adopted a strut of grandeur – 'a remarkably awkward gait,' wrote Michael Kelly, 'a habit of throwing himself (as he thought) into a graceful attitude by putting his stick behind his back and leaning on it'. He posed in the parks, he lingered in coffee-houses, he sauntered through squares in the more fashionable parts of town, snaring society where he might. Always meticulous in his dress, he had Father Huber's fur coat to carry him through the winter, and no doubt managed at other times to show himself 'decently' and 'scrupulously groomed and beautifully attired', as he had done in similarly straitened circumstances in Padua. He had certainly not lost any of his near-magical charm. That, he turned on the court composer Antonio Salieri.

Da Ponte had never written a libretto in his life. Any help he had given to Mazzolà for the Italian opera at Dresden had been marginal and unofficial; his sole foray into spoken theatre (in Gorizia) was purely as a translator and was by and large a disaster – yet he managed to persuade Salieri, whom he found 'a most cultured and intelligent man', to put in a good word with Count Rosenberg and secure an audience with the Emperor, with a view to becoming poet to the new opera company. It was even more impetuous a deed than the young Emanuele Conegliano asking the Bishop of Ceneda to pay for his education, an arrow set off at a target beyond any plausible range. Mazzolà's letter of introduction to Salieri, which Da Ponte had delivered as soon as he had arrived in Vienna, must have helped; as, surely, did talk of Metastasio's endorsement of his talent; but neither can fully account for how this quaint outsider in his costume of carefully preserved cast-offs was able to enchant his way to the post which – apart from that of imperial poet – was the highest to which any poet in the empire could aspire, and one for which he was almost entirely unqualified. Yet the arrow reached its mark with ease:

Salieri managed the matter so deftly, that I went to Caesar for my first audience not to beg a favour, but to offer gratitude for one granted. I had never before spoken to a monarch. Everyone told me that Joseph was the most humane and affable prince in the world, yet I could not appear before him without the greatest apprehension and timidity. But the cheery expression of his face, the soft sound of his voice, and above all the utter simplicity of his manner and his dress, nothing of which I had ever imagined in a king, not only gave me good heart, but left me scarcely aware that I was standing before an Emperor.

Emperor and poet appear genuinely to have warmed to each other. Joseph would stand by Da Ponte through all manner of court intrigues. For his part, Da Ponte was always rich in his praise for the monarch. Joseph II is one of the very few to survive Da Ponte's memoirs entirely unscathed by the poet's pen, alongside the bishops of Ceneda, Porto-gruaro and Treviso – all men who offered Lorenzo the affection, example and support that his father so singularly failed to provide.

The Emperor asked Da Ponte various questions relating to Italy, his studies, and why he had come to Vienna:

> Finally, he asked me how many plays I had written, to which I responded frankly:
> 'None, Sire.'
> 'Good! Good!' he rejoined smiling. 'We shall have a virgin Muse!'

The virgin Muse had to take rapid and pragmatic steps to acquire some substitute for experience. Vienna's new theatre poet 'searched out the sources of all the [libretti] that had previously been written and per-formed in the city to get an idea of the kind of composition they were and, if it were possible, to learn something'. A certain Giuseppe Varesi, he was told, had a magnificent collection of near three hundred opera scripts. Varesi had tried his own hand at the odd opera buffa, and, given the chance (Michael Kelly observed), 'was particularly fond of singing in a tremendous voice, accompanied by extraordinary gestures and a shake of the head'. He was also a notorious miser, pilfering fruit and sweetmeats from parties to make up his meals back home, and barely spending a groschen on 'the common necessaries of life'.

Da Ponte's reception was unpromising. When he asked to borrow a few volumes, Varesi laughed in his face, saying that the collection had cost him a fortune, that they were jewels, treasures; that he would rather lose an ear or all his teeth than relinquish a single one of them. Begrudgingly, he agreed that Da Ponte might peruse them in his presence. Lorenzo was allowed to skim twenty or so libretti, with the mean old man glowering fixedly at his hands – just in case they pocketed one of the precious tomes. He was shocked by what he found.

Poor Italy, what poor stuff! No plots, no characters, no tension, no
sense of scene, no grace of language or style! . . . There was not a line
in those miserable pastiches that contained a flourish, an oddity, any
elegant wit – nothing that by these sorry means could inspire a laugh.
So many heaps of insipid ideas, idiocies, buffoonery! Such were the
jewels of Signor Varese [sic], such the burlesque operas of Italy!

Writing libretti would be as easy as making a punch. All he needed were
the ingredients, and a little more flair than was evident in the limp efforts
he had seen in Varesi's library. And that presented no difficulty at all – he
would not be able to 'compose things so wretched as those [he] had
read', even if he tried. Brimming with impulsive enthusiasm, Da Ponte
set about finding an 'amusing subject, capable of supplying interesting
character and fertile in incident'. He presented Salieri with a list of
enticing proposals, but his eyes lost a deal of their shine when the
composer chose the one Da Ponte thought least promising: an adaptation
of Giovanni Bertati's *Il ricco d'un giorno*, the story of two brothers, one a
miser and one prodigal, who come unexpectedly into an inheritance,
and are in love with the same girl. Undaunted, Da Ponte set to work.

Dreams and dynamic fervour can take one just so far. Alone with his
quill and paper, Da Ponte soon ground up against the very real difficulties
of writing a libretto: 'My dialogue felt dry, my arias laboured, my
sentiments trivial, the action languid, the scenes cold. In short, it seemed
to me as though I had never known how to write, or rhyme, or
colour, that I had undertaken to wield the club of Hercules with the
hand of a child.' It wasn't just that he was, for the first time, trying to
construct a drama, but that he had a composer and a set of conventions to
bear in mind, and nowhere was that combination more impossibly
demanding than in the finale, which had to be a miniature drama in itself,
which had to 'glow with the genius of the *maestro di cappella*' and produce
on stage every singer of the cast, 'be there three hundred of them . . . in
solos, duets, terzets, tenets, sixtyets', belting forth in every form 'the
adagio, the allegro, the andante, the sweet, the harmonious, and then –
racket, forte-racket and racketatissimo; for the finale almost always closes
in an uproar'. Into this tumult the composer would want to insert the

clash of tambourines (*tamburino*), banging of hammers (*martelli*), the ding-dinging of bells (*campanelli*), the rumble of wheels, millstones, frogs, cicadas, voices on high:

> Or il canto degli augelli,
> Or il corso de' ruscelli,
> Or il batter de' martelli
> E il dindin de' campanelli,
> E la ruota, e il tamburino,
> E la macina, e il mulino,
> E la rana, e la cicala,
> E il pian pian, e il cresci, e cala.

If the plot of the drama did not permit this, the hapless poet 'must find a way to make it permit, in the face of reason, common sense, and all Aristotles in the world; and if then the finale happens to go badly, so much the worse for him!'

Da Ponte wanted to resign. Ten times, he says, he was on the verge of throwing it all in, and just as often wanted to burn everything he had written. Once, he locked the scarred and blotted pages in his wardrobe for a fortnight, so that he might read them again with an unclouded mind. He squinted, scratched his head, bit his nails, invoked the saints and the midwives of Pindus, and finally – some months later, with 'ears laid back' – presented the finished work to Salieri. The court composer bade him wait while he read it. Then, tactful and cautious, said that while there were songs and scenes he liked very much, some few changes would have to be made here and there – more for musical effect than anything else. Lorenzo was 'as cocky as a paladin'. He was yet to discover just what labours these 'few changes' involved.

Fortunately for all concerned, Da Ponte's debut as a librettist was not to be the first opera the new company performed. It had long been settled that this would be Salieri's *La scuola dei gelosi*, the opera he had created with Lorenzo's friend Mazzolà, after being so impressed by the librettist's work during the 1777–78 Venice carnival. This was not straight opera buffa, but a *dramma giocoso* (literally a jesting, or playful, drama) – a form in which serious and comic elements mingle. It was a popular choice. Haydn had already twice staged *La scuola dei gelosi* at the Esterházy summer palace south of the city, and it had been the talk of the salons. Salieri freshened the piece up with new music composed especially for Nancy Storace, adding further complexity to the character of a countess torn between impulsivity and caution, as she decides whether to try to make her errant husband jealous by means of a fake love letter.

La scuola dei gelosi opened on Tuesday 22 April 1783. 'A blaze of beauty and fashion' crowded the theatre, Kelly remembered. The Emperor attended, accompanied by his brother Maximilian and the Archbishop of Cologne. Da Ponte does not mention the event in his memoirs, but surely was there. Carriages rolled across the Michaelerplatz, depositing ambassadors and duchesses, princes and counts in a rustle of silk, a glint of diamonds and gold. The Burgtheater stood at one end of the square, across the way from the austere Michaelerkirche and next door to the Spanish Riding School – a baroque extravaganza topped by a dome, and carvings of an imperial eagle, angels, warriors' torsos and decorative urns; an appropriately exuberant backdrop to the glitterati milling below. Beyond the riding school was a wing of the imperial buildings containing the Redoutensaal ballrooms (the home of the waltz), and then a little archway that led to a road skirting the palace, along which further carriages arrived. The façade that the theatre presented to the square was modest – an airy, delicate classicist design by the French architect Jean Nicholas Jadot, done for Maria Theresa when she first renovated the building. This was the rear wall – the crowd on the Michaelerplatz filed off to an entrance that, from the square, appeared to be behind the building, but was more convenient for the palace.

Inside, Jadot's restrained hand continued, with white lacquered frontages to the boxes, a plain painted ceiling, red baize upholstery, and just a touch of classical ornament. It was an intimate theatre, though the murmurings were that it was too small and uncomfortable to be a worthy home for the court opera. Three tiers of boxes were arranged in a U-shape that gave the occupants a better view of each other than of the stage, but a good look at who was with whom and what they were dressed in was as much a reason for coming as the music. Lustres burned throughout the performance, as was the custom, and though no eating was permitted and audiences were far better behaved than in Venice, conversation seldom dwindled to silence, nor did comings and goings ever completely stop. That, too, was customary as nobles dined at around four in the afternoon, and came on to the opera, which started at seven, whenever they felt ready. (Joseph very magnanimously gave permission for operas to begin without him if he was late, which was not always the case with monarchs in other countries.)

La scuola dei gelosi was a dazzling success. Count Zinzendorf, a keen observer of the theatre both in Vienna and on his postings abroad, thought Nancy Storace had a '*jolie figure voluptueuse*'. He rather admired her voice, too, saying she sang like an angel. Benucci was '*tres [sic] bon*' (though Bussani less so), and the audience '*fort content*'. He returned to see the opera three times.

The season continued with *L'Italiana in Londra*, *Fra i due litiganti* ('a charming opera', thought Zinzendorf), and on through *Il curioso indescreto*, *Il falegname*, and Paisiello's *Il barbiere di Siviglia* – twelve productions in all – but not *Il ricco d'un giorno*. Da Ponte struggled with his libretto well into the spring of 1784. He was kept frantically busy, though, as part of his duties as theatre poet were to tailor others' libretti to suit the demands of the singers, to prepare the libretti for publication (he earned extra income from the sale of the books at performances), and to play a part in co-ordinating singers, musicians, costume-makers and scene-builders. 'We have a certain Abate da Ponte here as text poet,' wrote a young man who met him one evening at Baron Wetzlar's house. 'He has an incredible number of revisions to do at the theatre – he also has to do *per obligo* a whole new libretto for Salieri – which he won't be able to finish for two months.' That young man was Wolfgang Mozart. Though *Die Entführung* had been enormously successful, Mozart was perfectly aware that *Singspiel* was no longer the way to go if he wanted lucrative commissions. He was keen to compose an opera buffa, and hoped that Da Ponte would agree to writing the libretto – though he had his doubts. The Burgtheater seethed with intrigue. Mozart was certain that Salieri was trying to block his path. The new theatre poet, he wrote to his father, had promised to write him a libretto, but in addition to the fact that Da Ponte was so busy, 'who knows whether he will keep his word – or even wants to! – You know, these Italian gentlemen, they are very nice to your face! – enough we know all about them! – and if he is in league with Salieri, I'll never get a text from him – and I would love to show here what I can really do with Italian opera.'

Da Ponte was a novice at the game of intrigue, as with so much else his new post entailed, although he had tried his hand at it during the spat between his patron in Gòrizia, Count Coronini, and the Attems family. In Vienna, the game was played in deadly earnest. Stakes were high, gossip was vicious, and the skills of even an arch-Machiavellian barely sufficed for survival. People spoke quite starkly of their 'enemies'. The Italian faction at the Burgtheater had been given a tremendous boost by the creation of the opera company, and the arrival of new blood; now it was the turn of the German artistes of the original troupe to connive. Rivalry between Aloysia Lange (Constanze's sister and Mozart's erst-while love) and the *arriviste* soprano Nancy Storace was instant. In June, Mozart composed two arias for Aloysia Lange, to be inserted into Pasquale Anfossi's *Il curioso indiscreto* – the first time a German singer was appearing with the new company. She came to her brother-in-law's new apartment on the Judenplatz to rehearse. (Her lungs would have had to compete with those of her two-week-old nephew, as Constanze had just given birth to Raimund Leopold, 'a fine sturdy boy, as round as a ball', according to his proud father.) Aloysia was bridling with gossip. 'Mad.^{me} Lange was here trying out her 2 arias,' Mozart wrote. 'We also discussed how we could outshine our enemies, for I have plenty of them, and Mad.^{me} Lange, too, has had enough of Storaci [*sic*], the *New Singer*.' After the first night he gloated: '[The opera] was a complete failure, except for the 2 arias I had contributed; – in fact, my 2nd one, a bravura aria, had to be repeated. – Now I must tell you that my enemies were malicious enough to start a rumour beforehand, saying that *Mozart wants to improve on the opera by Anfoßi*.' Incensed, Mozart had sent a message to Count Rosenberg threatening to withdraw his aria if the rumour were not scotched. In the libretto that went on sale at the theatre Da Ponte had Mozart's notice printed in both Italian and German, stressing that the new arias were composed to please Signora Lange, and to suit the qualities of her voice, rather than as an affront to Anfossi. Whether intentionally, through naivety, or simply by default, Da Ponte had joined the fray.

Chapter Seven

LORENZO DA PONTE'S new position as theatre poet hoisted his fortunes from the abyss. His official annual salary was 600 gulden. This comfortably topped the 350 gulden earned by most orchestra members annually, though was nowhere near Nancy Storace's 3,240 gulden, or Kelly's handsome earnings – and theirs were the circles in which he needed to move. Da Ponte did have further sources of funds. In addition to his basic salary, the opera poet received an income from the libretto booklets sold at the theatre, one-off payments for the individual libretti he wrote, as well as the takings from the third performance of any opera by his own hand. All together he might have been able to reckon on something over 1,000 gulden a year. At first the money came in slowly – and Da Ponte had debts to settle, higher rent to pay (he had moved from the room at the tailor's shop, back into the city centre), and a more expensive image to maintain as he edged up to join the sparkling opera set. Nevertheless, he was the richest he had ever been in his life, and could begin to restore his sheen.

Distressingly for Lorenzo, in August of 1783, Girolamo Da Ponte died – ironically just at the moment when Lorenzo was able to turn back to the younger brother who had so often rescued him and kept him afloat through the turbulent years in Venice, and claim some sort of triumph over life's tempests. The death of the 'comrade, counsellor and friend' to whom Lorenzo had felt 'so closely bound' tore at the fibre of his new-found felicity. 'I have never ceased to mourn his irreparable loss,' Da

Ponte wrote as an old man. 'I shall never mourn it enough.' Girolamo's passing also proved a financial drain, as Lorenzo took over from him the responsibility of helping to support their father and a large brood of half-siblings. (Orsola Pasqua had her tenth child that year, a son named Enrico Lorenzo, perhaps in acknowledgement of Da Ponte's new role as family benefactor.) However little succour he had gained from his family as a child, Lorenzo continued to fret about his father's approval and retained a loyalty to brothers and sisters he hardly knew, creating in his need to belong something of an idyll of his family (apart from Orsola Pasqua) in tender, sentimental poems he wrote throughout his life. In one verse letter to his father he dreams up an ideal of this family, supported by his gold, playing and celebrating, in the shade in July, beside the fire in March – his 'Heaven', he writes, to which he will one day return.

Despite the misfortune of Girolamo's death and the added financial load, Lorenzo began to build up a new life for himself as 'a son of feather and fashion'. He expanded his hotchpotch wardrobe, indulging his taste for fancy clothing. Dress, traditionally a marker of status, no longer signalled rank quite so clearly, as grand apparel had become cheaper to reproduce. 'Vienna swarms with literati,' wrote Baron Riesbeck in the early 1780s. 'When a man accosts you, whom you do not know by his dirty hands for a painter, smith or shoemaker, or by his finery for a footman, or by his fine clothes for a man of consequence, you may be assured that you see either a man of letters or a tailor; for between these two classes I have not yet learned to distinguish.' There is some excuse, then, for Da Ponte's extravagant clothing and ostentatious gait. How one presented oneself influenced how one got on in this new society. Mozart was even more obsessed with finery than Da Ponte. Leopold Mozart wrote unabashedly of he and his son 'producing themselves' for concerts. Wolfgang had a fine blue coat trimmed with fur for winter; he dressed himself in silks and satins to perform, and on at least one occasion entirely in shining white. He once wrote to the Baroness von Waldstätten with a blush-makingly clumsy hint:

As for the beautiful red jacket that is tickling my heart so mercilessly, please let me know *where it can be bought and how expensive it is*, for I completely forgot to check how much it was; my attention was totally drawn to its beauty and not to its price. – I simply must have such a jacket so it will be worth my effort to get those buttons, which I can't get out of my mind. – I saw them some time ago in the Brandau Button Shop opposite the Milano at the Kohlmarkt when I bought some other buttons for a suit. They are made of mother-of-pearl with several white stones around the edge and a beautiful yellow stone in the middle. – I would like to have all things that are good, genuine, and beautiful! – I wonder why it is that those who cannot afford it would like to spend all they have for this sort of thing and those who could afford it, don't?

Wolfgang got his jacket. The Abbé Da Ponte's penchant for fancy clothing caught Michael Kelly's eye: 'He had . . . a very peculiar, rather dandyish way of dressing; for in sooth, the abbé stood mighty well with himself and had the character of a consummate coxcomb.' *Lo Spiritoso ignorante* of Ceneda, having preserved a measure of the affection he had picked up in Venice, was becoming something akin to the 'bowing, smirking, smart abbé' of William Cowper's satire of the Grand Tour. His youthful cockiness began to acquire a harder edge of vanity, his confidence in his own talent puffing up like one of the gorgeously coloured Montgolfier balloons which that year carried a man aloft for the very first time. Salieri would soon effectively prick the bubble, unwittingly aided by two new arrivals in town.

Yet in the summer of 1783 Lorenzo Da Ponte was in full flight. Once again he shone as a guest in the very best houses – not as he had done from Venice to Dresden, as tutor, secretary, protégé or paid friend – but now with status in his own right, as poet to the court theatre, at a time when ranks outside the nobility were beginning to count. Vienna was letting out a great sigh of relaxation, as the stays of the old regime were eased. Joseph II had ruled in conjunction with his mother Maria Theresa from 1765, but it was only after her death in 1780 that he let loose his more radical reforms. He suppressed rich monasteries, and in his *Toleranzpatent* of 1781 abolished discrimination against Protestants and softened anti-Jewish laws (moves that brought a hurried visit from the

Pope, whom he skilfully snubbed); he eased the lot of peasants, did away with many aspects of censorship, and curtailed the more excessive punishments meted out by courts. This was not done in an instant – though there was something of the crack of a whip about the reforms. Joseph could, paradoxically, be peremptory and despotic about implementing his liberal will.

In some quarters the Emperor's new edicts met with cold resistance, and many would eventually be repealed. Despite Joseph's moves towards a more egalitarian society, a gulf far wider than the green glacis still separated the aristocracy from other mortals. The former saw themselves almost as a race apart, quite entitled to social privilege, political advantage, differential treatment and deferential manners – but a new nobility had been created by the sale of titles and rewards to loyal civil servants, and its members tended to mix more with the merchant ranks from which they derived than did the hereditary aristocrats. 'People of different ranks now do business together with ease,' commented John Moore when in Vienna with his aristocratic charge, the young Duke of Hamilton, late in Maria Theresa's reign; yet he noted that the niceties of rank still led to tensions: 'The higher, or ancient families, keep themselves as distinct from the inferior, or newly created nobility, as do these from the citizens; so that it is very difficult for the inferior classes to be in society.' Talent was a passport to acceptance. In the midst of despotism, wrote the editor of the literary survey *L'Histoire de la République des Lettres en France* in 1780, 'there exists a certain realm which holds sway over the mind . . . that we honour with the name Republic [of Letters], because it preserves a measure of independence, and because it is almost its essence to be free. It is the realm of talent and thought.' In Vienna, an unpompous monarch and a concentration of the new nobility created a free-thinking social climate in which men like Da Ponte and Mozart could flourish, despite the frostiness of the old guard. By the 1780s the new counts and barons mingled with an urban intelligentsia to create a vigorous, enlightened circle of society that was pitched at an antagonistic angle to the traditional aristocracy. It was among this new nobility that Lorenzo Da Ponte now moved, and from them that Wolfgang Mozart drew most of his income.

Soirées in these fashionable houses moved the focus of intellectual activity away from court. Coffee-houses, with their masses of free newspapers, offered an even more public forum for fertile conversation. Vienna was one of the first cities in Europe to start serving the energizing brew, and by the time Da Ponte came to live there, over seventy coffee-houses catered to all ranks, served food as well as coffee, and were open most hours of the day. Lorenzo could take his breakfast chocolate at the Taroni, with a little crescent roll (later known as a croissant), or have a dinner of Danube carp at Kramer's; he could join the 'dandies, dawdlers and strollers' who planted themselves with their spyglasses outside the Milano (opposite Mozart's favourite button shop) to ogle ladies coming back from mass; he could sit at Dukati to read the *Gazzetta di Vienna*, or the *Gazzetta Toscana* from Florence, and argue the afternoon away.

The talk that autumn was of America, of how a citizen army had overthrown the mighty British. In September, the war between America and Britain had officially ended, and the independence of the United States was confirmed − creating a new nation, and a republic with a written constitution at that. For some time in Vienna it had been fashionable to learn English, in order to follow the latest events in the English-language press. Even Mozart (who paid scant attention to events in America) was taking lessons − he ends his red-jacket letter to the Baroness von Waldstätten with a slightly ungrammatical salutation in English. Devouring English newspapers led to a fascination with the culture and its fashions, as described by Johann Pezzl:

> The results of this anglomania are to be seen in people reading and speaking English, round hats, large greatcoats of rough material, full neckerchiefs, dark frock-coats with high collars, boots and spurs at all times. A slovenly, heavy gait, large branch-like clubs instead of walking sticks, a kind of rusticity in attitude and manners, cadogans [knots of hair at the back of the head], punch [Mozart's favourite drink], jockeys, whisky, racing, etc.

This simple, nonchalant *mode à l'anglaise* had a parallel in the popular blue frock-coat, yellow waistcoat and boots, known in German as *Werther-*

tracht (Werther-wear) as it was the dress of the hero of Goethe's *Die Leiden des jungen Werther* (The Sorrows of Young Werther). The novel about a sensitive young artist, at odds with society and unrequited in love, who eventually commits suicide, caused a sensation throughout Europe for years after its 1774 publication. Werther's combination of *Weltschmerz* (ill-ease with the world) and *Ichschmerz* (dissatisfaction with self) — his search for personal happiness, the emphasis on passion and imagination rather than the hard reason of the Enlightenment — were major tributaries of a stream of Romanticism that would flow with gathering strength well into the next century. Two years after the novel was published, at the time the War of American Revolution began, Friedrich Klinger wrote a play set partly on the American continent entitled *Wirrwarr* (Confusion), later renamed *Sturm und Drang* (Storm and Stress). The play gave its name to a literary movement of angry young men (which included Goethe) who, inspired by Rousseau's idealism, revolted against literary convention, upheld the cult of genius, and advocated a return to nature. It was around this time that Lorenzo Da Ponte wrote his elegy 'The American in Europe' — the poem that got him into so much trouble in Treviso. But stylistically Da Ponte's work had remained very much in the classical mould, and in Vienna, Lorenzo — courtly, rather than rustic, with his very un-gnarled walking stick, his affected gait, and dandyish manner of dress — aligned himself with the old school. While starving in his room above a tailor's shop in Wieden he had had something about him of an artist in young Werther's image. As poet to the court theatre, he had taken a firm step back to an earlier style. Like Mozart — continually courting patrons while also scrabbling for a freelance living — Da Ponte was poised over the cusp between two worlds, alighting sometimes on the one side, sometimes on the other.

As the autumn of 1783 turned to winter, Da Ponte was still busy with *Il ricco d'un giorno*. The 'little changes here and there' that Salieri said he required turned out to consist of:

> . . . mutilating or stretching out most of the scenes; of introducing new duets, terzets, quartets; of changing meters half way through arias; of mixing in choruses to be sung by Germans! In cutting almost all the

recitatives, and thus all the plot, all the dramatic tension of the opera, if any there were. In this way, when the drama went on the stage, I doubt whether there remained a hundred verses of my original.

The drama was not to go on stage quite yet. At the beginning of 1784, with *Il ricco d'un giorno* still unfinished, Salieri went to Paris, where his *Les danaïdes* was scheduled for production at the Opéra. Da Ponte's pride was somewhat deflated. While Salieri was away, two men arrived in Vienna who brought Lorenzo even more roughly down to earth. They were the composer Giovanni Paisiello and another adventuring poet-abbé, Giambattista Casti. They came to the city scenting lucrative work. Both enjoyed a considerable measure of fame – or, in Casti's case, notoriety.

The Abbé Casti could barely talk when he arrived in Vienna. His throat and palate were ravaged by syphilis, and (Da Ponte delights in recounting) he had to communicate by an odd gargling through the nose. A portrait from the time depicts him with thin, unkempt hair, skin that appears pickled rather than wrinkled, and hard, small eyes that glint beneath a crumpled brow. A scholar who met him some years later in Paris said his face was the perfect image of a satyr's. Some twenty-five years older than Da Ponte, Casti shared a similar background with the new theatre poet. Of modest origins, he was seminary-educated and had followed a career that took him through the courts and grand houses of Europe, eventually to become (in 1766 or 1767) court poet to Joseph II's younger brother, Grand Duke Leopold, in Tuscany. Over the decades he had charmed Joseph II with his conversation, been a favourite of Catherine II in St Petersburg, and a travelling companion for the younger Kaunitz, son to the all-powerful Viennese Chancellor. He was also a close friend of Count Rosenberg. Unlike Da Ponte, who had a peculiar facility for turning friends to enemies, Casti left a wake of influential people who were only too delighted to see him again.

Casti's chief reputation was for writing witty, salacious satires, as a sort of obscene, Italian Voltaire. Casanova had been keen to meet him because of 'certain very blasphemous little poems of which he is author', and he did so when Casti accompanied Count Rosenberg to Trieste in

1773. But the wayward abbé (whose name, ironically, means 'chaste') was too dissolute even for the irascible Casanova, who called him 'a shameless libertine, an ignorant and immodest rhymester'. Yet Casti is also described as 'full of fire', and it is clear from his other friendships that he had a penetrating mind and (in the words of one of his early English translators) 'great learning, sound judgement, and an inexhaustible invention and humour'. Like Da Ponte, he had scant experience at writing opera libretti; nevertheless it is curious that Casti did not conspire with his friend Count Rosenberg (who, it will be remembered, was director of court theatre and responsible for setting up the Italian opera company) to secure the position of poet to the theatre for himself – but Casti had his sights set even higher. He wanted to pick up Metastasio's recently relinquished lyre as imperial poet. In the meantime there was good money to be made from writing one-off libretti for the opera, and here his friend the count was only too willing – and more than able – to help.

If the Abbé Casti posed a threat to Da Ponte, Giovanni Paisiello shook the renowned Salieri's pedestal. Paisiello, considered one of the great composers of the moment, came to Vienna from an eight-year residency at the court of Catherine II, on his way to another appointment in Naples. Two years earlier in St Petersburg, his *Il barbiere di Siviglia* had met with extraordinary success; it had also taken Vienna by storm during the opening season of the Italian opera, running to twelve performances. Joseph II was a great admirer of Paisiello's music, and requested the composer together with Casti be presented to him at his levee. Kelly relates that the Emperor declared he had before him two of the greatest geniuses alive, and that he would dearly like to see an opera that was a collaboration of their talents.

The word whirled about backstage at the Burgtheater. The singers were elated. A new opera by Paisiello just for them! And a libretto by the wickedly skilful Abbé Casti! 'There was no talk of anyone but Casti,' wrote Da Ponte dejectedly. 'Imagine the expectations of the singers, of Count Rosenberg, of the not very chaste friends of Casti, in fact of the whole city, which resonated to the heights with his chaste name.' On returning from Paris to a climate of such bristling expectancy, Salieri decided not to risk exposing himself to the public with a new opera by an inept novice, and *Il ricco d'un giorno* was, for a while at least, 'put to sleep'.

The opera Paisiello and Casti settled on was entitled *Il re Teodoro in Venezia*, for which Casti drew heavily on a chapter from Voltaire's *Candide*. The pretty 21-year-old Michael Kelly landed himself the pivotal role of the ancient major-domo Gaforio, when he impressed Casti with his 'monkey anticks' in sending up the old miser Varesi (he who had so meanly refused to lend Da Ponte any libretti) at a soirée at his house – an evening, incidentally, that included a performance by a composers' string quartet with Haydn on first violin, Karl Dittersdorf on second violin, Johann Vanhall on violoncello and Mozart on viola.

As it was Da Ponte's task to arrange for the printing of libretti for sale at the theatre, he was one of the first to receive a copy of *Teodoro*. As soon as he had it in his hands he hurried to a coffee-house and settled down to read. He read it from beginning to end. Twice. He had to admit that 'it was not lacking in purity of language, nor vague in style, nor deficient in grace and music of its verse, nor in its wit, elegance and brio', and that the lyrics were beautiful, the ensembles delightful, the finale a masterpiece – but he thought its qualities as a drama were, on the whole, 'monstrous'. The defects of *Teodoro* threw a sharper light on the shortcomings of *Il ricco d'un giorno*. 'I realized it was not sufficient to be a great poet (since, in truth, such was Casti) to write a good play, but that it was necessary to learn all manner of tricks.' He resolved to watch more drama and opera, to note others' mistakes, and to work out how a part must be carefully fashioned to give it shape on stage. He could not, though, let drop a word of criticism. 'Casti,' he wrote, 'was more infallible in Vienna than the Pope in Rome.' And, he might have added, Paisiello was almost divine.

The opera had its premiere on 23 August, and was a triumph – an 'astonishing success', admitted Da Ponte; 'overflowing houses', enthused Kelly; 'superb music', wrote Count Zinzendorf. Kelly's depiction of the ancient major-domo went down enormously well – so much so that the Emperor immediately gave him a raise, and wherever he went people called him 'Old Gaforio'. Mozart, who was also at the premiere, during the performance broke out in a sweat that drenched his clothes, and was ill with colic and vomiting (at precisely the same hour daily) for four days. Varesi's reaction is not recorded, though there were no doubt any number of wags who were willing to pay for his ticket.

Il ricco d'un giorno, which finally opened on 6 December 1784, was by contrast a dismal failure. Nancy Storace fell ill and withdrew from the performance; the other singers said things about the opera 'that would make one shudder', and wondered how they had ever been able to recite such wretched words, or how the maestro was able to set them to music. Zinzendorf observed that the composer had done so by 'stealing from everywhere' – though he did like the scenery, especially an illuminated gondolier. A librettist named Gaetano Brunati, perhaps with his own eye on the position of theatre poet, published a scathing lampoon on Da Ponte, which was sold at the theatre. A spat of satirical sonnet-writing broke out, with Lorenzo adding his fair share to the ruckus. Casti damned with faint praise, saying that of course Da Ponte was competent, and did it make a difference that a man of such merit did not know how to write an opera? Shrugs, shakings of heads and clickings of tongues rippled through salons and coffee-houses. As for Salieri, he said publicly that he would rather cut off his fingers than set another verse of Da Ponte's to music. He was to keep his promise for another four years.

Amidst all this, Lorenzo was not without allies. Walking one morning on the Graben he spotted a familiar figure, of Herculean height and bowsprit nose: his old friend Casanova. The two had argued before Da Ponte left Venice ('as to some trifling point of Latin prosody . . . that strange man could never admit he was in the wrong!') and had had scant contact since then. They embraced joyfully, the niceties of poetic metre forgotten. Casanova had once again been expelled from Venice – this time after writing a scurrilous pamphlet – and in his old age (he was now nearly sixty) was having to re-fire the ingenuity that had enabled him to survive as a young man, wandering Europe trying to scratch out a living. In Vienna he had found some secretarial work for the Venetian Ambassador, though Lorenzo was never quite sure what he did, or how he made a living. A year or so later, he would slip away to Dux, near Prague, into semi-retirement as librarian to Count Waldstein, and write his memoirs. In Vienna in the meantime, the two old friends saw each other daily, trawled the coffee-houses, paraded in the Prater, enjoyed Da Ponte's new-found affluence, and got up to such adventures as can only be imagined.

Da Ponte discovered that he also enjoyed the support of a more powerful figure. When Count Rosenberg – with Casti present in the Emperor's box during the abysmal first night of *Il ricco d'un giorno* – said pointedly to the monarch, 'We shall have to have a new poet,' Joseph replied, 'First I would like to see something else by Da Ponte.' And to the poet himself, the Emperor later said, 'You know, Da Ponte, your opera, after all, isn't half so bad as they would like to have us think. You must take courage and give us another one!'

In Venice, Lorenzo's former patron Pietro Zaguri, usually so nasty about him behind his back, nominated him to a literary academy on the strength of his new opera. And in faraway Trieste, Giuseppe Coletti – the rival in Gorizia that Lorenzo suspected of forging the letter that took him to Dresden – now that Da Ponte was safely distant, published some of his verses in the newspaper he was editing and prefaced them, apparently without irony, with these words:

> After the applause obtained in Vienna by the comic opera *Il ricco d'un giorno* of Signor Abate Lorenzo Da Ponte, member of the Arcadian Academy of Rome and Gorizia, and Poet to the Imperial Theatres in Vienna, the said author has published a *Canzonetta* dedicated to the Fair Sex as an apology for his way of writing against the same and proof of the respect which he professes to have towards it.

And what of that 'Fair Sex'? What of the heart of the Abbé Da Ponte, for whom love was more necessary 'than the bread I eat, than the air I breathe'? Given his penchant for women who could hold their own, Lorenzo was in his element in Vienna. Nathaniel Wraxall, on a tour that took him through the courts of northern Europe, declared that 'Vienna abounds with beautiful women' and commended them especially for their conversation, which 'if not improving, is rarely deficient in spirit, vivacity and anima-tion'. Michael Kelly admired their fine complexions and beautiful figures, and was particularly taken by the serving maids who seemed continually anxious to show off their feet ('which are universally handsome').

Yet for once, Lorenzo Da Ponte is silent about love . . . or at least he was not in a liaison that he was prepared to admit to. Centuries later, some nifty detective work by Da Ponte scholar Giampaolo Zagonel revealed that Lorenzo and a woman named Annetta had an illegitimate son, whom they called Felice, some time late in 1783 or 1784. Felice and his mother slip silently and mysteriously from view – Da Ponte does not even hint at their existence at this point in his memoirs – though Felice will suddenly resurface at the age of thirteen, when he steals a necklace and runs away from the care of his uncle Agostino Da Ponte in Venice, to join the French Army. Although Lorenzo makes no direct mention of Felice in Vienna, he does relate an event (he has to, given the very visible impress it left) that may be connected with the scandal of Annetta's pregnancy.

Da Ponte was, he writes, at the time of this 'strange and cruel misadventure' boarding in a household that included at least two beautiful young women. An Italian surgeon named Doriguti – a wretch of a man, 'neither handsome, nor amiable, nor young, nor rich' – had fallen desperately in love with one of them; Lorenzo (who at the time considered himself fairly well possessed of all of the aforementioned qualities) was somewhat enamoured of the other. It was a house filled with flirtatious glances, banter in the corridors, and who knows what else, given what Da Ponte had got up to when doors were left ajar in Widow Bellaudi's home, back in the San Luca district in Venice.

Doriguti eventually declared his heart, and was spurned, his inamorata giving as her reasons: 'First, because you are uglier than the devil; second, because I am in love with Da Ponte.' At which point she launched into a panegyric of Lorenzo's charms, even though (he indignantly points out) he had not spoken to her over six times, and she knew his heart lay rather with their housemate. Doriguti appeared to take the brush-off in his stride, though secretly he seethed with a bestial jealousy. Lorenzo was ignorant of the encounter. He had other matters on his mind – a painful abscess had grown on his gum after a tooth had been pulled, and he sat downcast in a coffee-house, contemplating an imminent lancing. In walked surgeon Doriguti, apparently brimming with good nature, with the offer of a supremely effective cure. It came in the form of a bottle of a powerful liqueur that Da Ponte should dab on the growth with a cloth. After a week the abscess had disappeared – and after another, so had sixteen of Lorenzo's teeth. The liqueur turned out to be *aqua fortis* (nitric acid), which not only denuded Da Ponte's gums, but – in this city of fat pheasants and fleshy artichokes – totally destroyed his appetite for over a year. The lisp that had always hissed through his strong Venetian accent became even more sibilant.

This adventure would have taken place at the time Annetta was pregnant with Felice. It takes just one turn of the spyglass lens to sharpen focus on the reason for Doriguti's jealousy, or to transform it into the fury of a brother or cousin at the loss of Annetta's honour. But posterity must be content with the bare facts – the invisible (for the time being) Felice, and Da Ponte's sunken lip-line.

Scrawny, toothless, his one opera a debacle, Da Ponte was swept along towards 1785 with his small moment of triumph in becoming theatre poet already a husk. He began to sniff out conspiracies, to refer to Casti and Rosenberg as his 'enemies', to talk of the 'malice of my persecutors'. Later, he saw this moment as the start of a battle he would fight out 'over many and many a year'. Da Ponte had felt conspired against before: by wagging tongues at the seminary in Portogruaro; by older colleagues envious of his success in Treviso; by the subterfuge and betrayals that had him banished from Venice; by Coletti and his allies in Gorizia. But now he began to sense intrigue everywhere. There was a root of hurt and anger in him that reached deep into the past, to *lo Spiritoso ignorante*, mocked by other boys in the ghetto in Ceneda. When the forces ranged against him let loose their arrows, those that wounded the most were the ones that struck at his early lack of learning – such as the accusation in Portogruaro that he was 'nothing but a wind-bag, a rhymester without science' – or the lines he singles out from the literary ruction that followed the premiere of *Il ricco d'un giorno*: '*Asino tu nascesti, ad asino morrai.* [An ass you were born; an ass you will die.]' Da Ponte had made up for his fragile grounding, but remained sensitive to reminders of these intellectually impoverished beginnings – and to attacks on another facet of his past. For the first – and only – time in his writings, he referred to his Jewish origins in a verse letter to Pietro Zaguri, written in 1785:

Questo diè il colmo a l'ira ed al dispetto;
Crucifigatur ciaschedun dicea,
Soggiungeva talon si ficchi in ghetto,
Donde sortì la sua prosapia rea . . .

[This brought the ire and the spite to a head;
Crucifigatur [Let him be crucified] each one would say,
One would add let's thrust him in the ghetto,
Whence his guilty stock came . . .]

In Joseph II's tolerant Vienna, anti-Semitism should in theory not have been a weapon Da Ponte's enemies could use – but the Emperor's edicts were often in advance of the thinking of his subjects. That Da Ponte mentions the insults makes clear, if nothing else, the vindictiveness with which parts of Viennese society made him feel an outsider. Lorenzo fared well when he felt appreciated – he wrote that Joseph II's approbation gave him 'the strength to endure everything' he encountered working at the Viennese opera, that it was 'of greater help to me than all the precepts and the rules of Aristotle'; it was 'the soul of my inspiration, the guide of my pen'. Since childhood he had craved affection. His need for acceptance in Viennese society caught him up in a self-defeating circle. In effect, he desperately wanted to be liked by people he saw as his enemies, so overreacted to any rebuff with hate and suspicion, thus making himself unlikeable.

Lorenzo had always been quick to spark, easily taking offence. He could give a bad turn to quite innocent remarks, perceive slights and detect plots on the flimsiest of evidence – yet though he may have embellished schemes against him, and even in some instances imagined persecution, there was a core of truth to his claims. Da Ponte had to survive in a culture of intrigue. Pezzl noted a darker side to the attractive picture of Viennese life: 'Excesses, intrigues, frauds, hypocrisies and depravities exist cheek by jowl with wisdom, generosity and bonhomie.' Scheming and conniving characterized cliques both in court life and in the Burgtheater. For those who had to make a living by acquiring favour and seizing chances, it was not sufficient simply to move forward; one had to block the paths of rivals. Influential allies were the currency of power, and personal advancement could be facilitated by destruction of the reputations of others. Intrigue was the nasty razor edge of gossip. Da Ponte was not alone in suspecting plots and persecutors – both Leopold and Wolfgang Mozart complained of Italian cabals (and especially of Salieri) thwarting their ambitions; Joseph Haydn wrote of 'various rumours' about him in Vienna, designed to crush his talents, and again of Italian conspiracies in the London music world.

Lorenzo did not shrink under attack; on the contrary, he gleefully joined in the snide humour and spiteful remarks, and became quite adept at creating turmoil. The dung of vilification and deceit that underlay the Viennese opera world fertilized an unpleasant, scheming side of his character. This is not to say that he lost his ability to enchant, but there had always been a flip side to Lorenzo's charm. People succumbed to it, while feeling secretly riled, and then not only turned on him, but united with each other to do so. He could be seductive, and irresistible, but there was something about Lorenzo Da Ponte that encouraged people to kick him when he was down.

Rescue arrived in 1785 in the form of a Spanish composer, Vincente Martín y Soler, who washed up on the banks of the Danube as part of the continuing flow of artists to Vienna hoping for employment with the new opera. That year's flotsam also included Nancy Storace's brother Stephen, a composer of some note. Gossip had it that the pretty, pert Nancy – whose white throat, beautiful eyes, fresh mouth and clear skin Count Zinzendorf could not restrain himself from praising – had, with her angel's voice and the 'naïveté and petulance of a child', quite won the heart of the Emperor. Da Ponte suggests that Martín's champion, the Spanish Ambassador's wife, also enjoyed Joseph II's extraordinary favours. Vienna's cliques, Lorenzo maintained, got down to work. Backstage at the Burgtheater there were 'various connivings and secret comings and goings' involving the singers and Abbé Casti. The abbé encouraged Gaetano Brunati (the rival who had penned a lampoon against Da Ponte) to collaborate with Storace. Voices whispered in Martín's ear of the dreadful risk to his reputation of working with Da Ponte; and to be doubly sure of scuppering any collaboration between

the two, told Da Ponte that though Martín was an excellent instru-
mentalist, as for the vocal: 'God protect us!'

The Emperor cut through the knot. Good to his word that Da Ponte
should take courage and write another opera, Joseph commissioned him
to work together with Martín. Once he had heard Martín's music, Da
Ponte realized he wrote 'sweet melodies . . . which one feels deep in the
soul, but which few know how to imitate'. Kelly, too, thought 'his was a
soul of melody . . . the rarest gift a composer can possess'. (Both Kelly
and Nancy Storace knew Martín from Venice, where Nancy had
enjoyed great success with an opera of his some years before.) Martín
y Soler, six years younger than Da Ponte, shared Lorenzo's delight in the
company of pretty women. He looks out from a contemporary portrait
with benign good humour, a glint in his eye, the beginnings of a teasing
smile dimpling the upper corners of his lips. Composer and librettist were
soon firm friends. Together they produced *un succès fou*.

For months Da Ponte had been studying, adapting and preparing for
publication the libretti that came into the Burgtheater – striding, with his
haughty gait and walking-cane, manuscript under arm, through the stage
door between the Burgtheater and Spanish Riding School, braving the
Michaelerplatz as carriages criss-crossed it from the Herrengasse, the
Kohlmarkt, and two other directions at once, to find refuge in a coffee-
house and read. In the work of his friend Mazzolà and of his rival Casti, in
the libretto of *La villanella rapita* by fellow Venetian Giovanni Bertati,
which was in his hands in the autumn of 1785, Da Ponte began to pick
up traces of a change that was infiltrating opera buffa. Serious elements
entered these comedies, often in a parody of aloof *opera seria* characters.
'Serious', Da Ponte realized, need not necessarily mean 'solemn'. He saw
the potential of weaving a reflective strand through the comic frivolity –
a strand of more profound characterization, of more thought-provoking
material than was usual in opera buffa. Bertati's script, especially, was a
thunderclap, a libretto of revolutionary social criticism that worked
precisely because of its buffo costume, making points which, had they
appeared nakedly in a pamphlet, would have spelled serious trouble for
the author. Amidst pipe-haze and coffee smells, with newspapers rustling
around him and young men arguing politics, the bony abbé devoured

the new writing; and, true to his resolution, in the evenings attended opera after opera. Da Ponte was piece by piece constructing the technique with which he would give a turn to opera buffa that would lead to his being acknowledged as one of the greatest librettists the world has known.

For his new friend Martín y Soler, Da Ponte chose to adapt Goldoni's play *Le bourru bienfaisant*, which had been written in French for the marriage celebrations of Marie Antoinette and the Dauphin (later Louis XVI). He called his version *Il burbero di buon cuore* (The Gruff Man of Good Heart). Such plundering was perfectly acceptable and commonplace in the absence of copyright laws. To Lorenzo, Goldoni brought a whiff of Venice – the dramatist had been a close friend of one of his Venetian patrons, Bernardo Memmo. Although Goldoni had left Venice some years before Lorenzo went to live there, his plays were still often performed at the time, and he remained the talk of the town – certainly of the *Caffè de' letterati*, where Carlo Gozzi argued spiritedly against his style. Both playwrights had ripped the masks off the old Italian *commedia dell'arte*, and rejigged its traditions, but they moved in different directions. Gozzi gave refined literary expression to the deceptively simplistic elements of folklore in *commedia*; Goldoni favoured narrative plays that drew on the characters and conventions of the genre to examine human dilemmas that hovered over matters of love, sex, and money. Both approaches appealed to Da Ponte. From Gozzi he derived an ironic, whimsical style, the mixture of humour and gravity that characterized the doings of the *Accademia Granellesca*. Goldoni gave him themes of erotic confusion and social and financial advancement; and introduced him to the possibilities of deeper characterization within comedy – particularly in giving servants a fuller dramatic role. There was a flash of the social rebel in Da Ponte yet, of the man who had outraged the authorities with his radical *accademia* in Treviso, who had written a fiery sonnet in support of Giorgio Pisani in Venice. Goldoni himself denigrated opera buffa – as Da Ponte had done on reading the libretti in Varesi's library – and wrote that he only ever composed comic-opera libretti 'from motives of complaisance or interest' rather than 'from taste or choice', yet paradoxically his stage plays fuelled Da Ponte's awakening awareness of the scope for profundity within comic bounds.

Il burbero di buon cuore, with its gruff yet good-natured central character, was a modest first step in this direction. Though Lorenzo appears to have worked closely with both Nancy Storace and Benucci as he developed the piece, he had still to contend with intrigue and malicious gossip. Casti put it about that Da Ponte had made a sorry choice, and that this was no subject for a comic opera.

'Da Ponte, your friend Casti claims that *Burbero* will not make anyone laugh,' said the Emperor to his theatre poet one day.

'Your Majesty,' replied Da Ponte, 'we shall need patience. I shall be satisfied if it makes *him* weep.'

The Abbé Casti may well have shed a quiet tear of envy. *Il burbero di buon cuore* was a conquest. At its premiere on 4 January 1786, it was applauded from beginning to end – even the recitatives. As the Emperor left the theatre, he passed Da Ponte in the corridor leading from his box and whispered, '*Abbiamo vinto!* [We have won!]' – two words, Da Ponte said, that were worth more to him than 'a hundred volumes of praises'.

But two words of praise are never enough. Elated, yet desperate for a sign of approval, Da Ponte called next morning on Count Rosenberg. Casti was already in the count's chambers. The atmosphere was grim. Da Ponte's heart sank as the two greeted him with the barest acceptable measure of cordiality.

'What can I do for the *signor poeta*?' the director of court theatres asked dryly.

'I have come to hear my sentence from the *signor direttore degli spettacoli!*' responded Da Ponte, with a half-flourish at humour.

'The *signor poeta* has already heard his sentence from our kind-hearted public! How just a one, I am not in a position to say.'

With that, protector and protégé smiled wanly, and turned their backs on the theatre poet.

Lorenzo realized he was up against a pair of enemies so determined and (in Rosenberg's case) so powerful that not even royal favour could protect him. Rosenberg was not only the Emperor's chamberlain, but one of his most intimate and long-standing confidantes. Nor could Da Ponte expect any support from court composer Salieri, who having had his fingers burned was by no means willing to sacrifice them again. Exposed to the depth of Rosenberg's animosity, Lorenzo decided resignation would be preferable to the ignominy of an inevitable sacking. Impulsive as ever, he went directly to the palace.

Joseph II was jubilant over *Burbero*. He would brook no talk of resignation, pooh-poohed Rosenberg's comment as 'just Casti speaking', and suggested an immediate new collaboration with Martín y Soler. Da Ponte left buoyed by the monarch's support. In the face of both public and royal approbation, Rosenberg and Casti kept up a surreptitious campaign of polite nit-picking, backhand half-compliments, and semi-veiled criticism of Da Ponte's ability with language. But the librettist himself found that the warmth of the Emperor's approval 'created new spirit in me, redoubled my enthusiasm for the labours I had undertaken, and gave me courage not only to meet the attacks of my enemies, but to look upon all their manoeuvres with disdain'. He finished the opera he was busy with – *Il finto cieco*, for the Veronese composer Giuseppe Gazzaniga (which received three performances before disappearing from view) – and then leapt forward, not as the Emperor had suggested to a new opera for Martín (though one was soon to come), but with a piece he had recently been working on with a young man to whom he had promised a libretto some years before, the dazzling composer who wanted to break into opera buffa, whom he had met at Baron Wetzlar's house: Wolfgang Amadé Mozart.

Chapter Eight

WOLFGANG MOZART AND Lorenzo Da Ponte had much in common. Across the room at Baron Wetzlar's palace, that spring day back in 1783, the two dandies had rustled in mutual finery. Both knew the benefit of stylish self-presentation among the rich, influential and intelligent beings who sipped coffee and nibbled dainties at the baron's home; yet both would also no doubt have agreed (to borrow a definition from Samuel Johnson's *Dictionary of the English Language*) that a patron was 'commonly a wretch who supports with insolence and is paid with flattery'. Both had a leg in the old world, yet were gingerly reaching with the other to find foothold in a new territory that offered dignity and independence, but was perilous with pitfalls and threatened poverty and disaster. Da Ponte, especially, had experienced the privation that could result from a false step. Both men were sensitive to slights, 'as touchy as gunpowder'. Mozart already suspected that Salieri and various cabals were ranged against him; Da Ponte was in 1783 not yet embroiled in Burgtheater intrigue, but would soon be even more convinced of enemies working for his downfall than was the young composer.

It is said that people on entering the company of strangers are drawn to those individuals in the group who have a similar emotional background to themselves. If that is so, Mozart and Da Ponte may well have sensed in each other the ache of the loss of a mother, and the tug of a distant father, from whom each craved affection. Da

Ponte's longing was unfulfilled, though patrons sometimes stepped into the role that pater had not much bothered about. Mozart, who as a child would keep asking people if they loved him, and burst into tears if they teasingly denied it, as an adult entered into a subtle and complex conflict with his father – Wolfgang simultaneously rebellious yet dependent on his father's approval; Leopold proud of his son's music, yet self-absorbed, manipulative and a skilled practitioner of emotional blackmail.

To the brilliant clavier player, whose reputation as a composer was burgeoning, Baron Raimund Wetzlar von Plankenstern was patron, landlord, and soon to be godfather to his first child. To the foppish, recently appointed theatre poet (yet to experience the disaster of his debut opera), Wetzlar was just the sort of new friend he desired to cultivate. Perhaps, as Wetzlar was part of a circle of ennobled Jewish converts, Da Ponte felt a little more at ease in the baron's home than in wider Viennese society, where Joseph II's liberal laws did not silence sharp tongues nor entirely stifle prejudice. Baron Wetzlar took respite from his highly successful business ventures in musical soirées, where he might sometimes be heard playing the guitar (an instrument then coming back into fashion, largely because of its popularity in England and America). The astute baron's skills appear not to have been confined to property speculation and plucking out Spanish tunes. In introducing his tenant and protégé to the new theatre poet he would seem to have been possessed of extraordinary insight, for of all the pair had in common, the attribute that most uniquely linked Wolfgang Mozart and the Abbé Da Ponte was one they had yet to discover. Together they would find a way of transmuting potentially warring elements of words, music and drama (often with the added vitriol of performers' temperament) into operatic gold.

For decades the figure of Metastasio had reigned over Italian opera, with composers doing battle to set his words to music. Now that he was dead, musicians were beginning to claim supremacy. Mozart had already expressed his views on the matter. In a letter to his father on 13 October 1781, he had written:

. . . I should say that in an opera the poetry must be altogether the obedient daughter to the music. Why do Italian comic operas please everywhere – in spite of their miserable libretti . . .? Just because there the music reigns supreme and when one listens to it all else is forgotten. Why, an opera is sure of success when the plot is well worked out, the words written solely for the music and not shoved in here and there to suit some miserable rhyme . . . I mean, words or even entire verses which ruin the composer's whole idea. Verses are indeed the most indispensable element for music – but rhymes – solely for the sake of rhyming – the most detrimental . . . The best thing of all is when a good composer, who understands the stage and is talented enough to make sound suggestions, meets an able poet, that true phoenix; in that case no fears need be entertained as to the applause even of the ignorant.

Mozart had found his phoenix. One of Da Ponte's skills as a poet was a delicacy of touch with rhyme (no mean feat in Italian), and his recent verses were 'easy, harmonious and almost singing of themselves'. His love for the language and its finest flowers wound from his first discovery of Metastasio in his father's attic, to Abbé Cagliari's lessons at the seminary in Ceneda and evenings with the *Accademia Granellesca* in Venice, and on through trenchant advice given by the young nobleman Giulio Trento in Treviso and Father Huber in Dresden. As a poet he stood on firm ground. Yet, as has been seen, he was soon to discover that being a good poet was not enough. The disaster of *Il ricco d'un giorno* would shake him into realizing that 'no end of tricks had to be learned' to understand the stage, and that great flexibility was required to write workable libretti. And flexibility would indeed be needed with Mozart. Writing in later years on the role of a librettist, Da Ponte took a stance almost exactly antithetical to that in Wolfgang's letter:

. . . if the words of a dramatic poet are nothing *but a vehicle to the notes, and an opportunity to the action,* what is the reason that a composer of music does not take at once a doctor's recipes, a bookseller's catalogue, or even a spelling book, instead of the verses of a poet, and make them

a vehicle to his notes, just as an ass is that of a bag of corn? . . . Mozart
knew very well that the success of an opera depends, FIRST OF ALL,
ON THE POET: that without a good poem an *entertainment cannot be
perfectly dramatic* . . . I think that poetry is the door to music, which can
be very handsome, and much admired for its exterior, but no body can
see its internal beauties, if the door is wanting.

That first conversation between composer and librettist must have been
lively. Yet behind the partisan bluster lies a knowledge that the process of
creating an opera was one of forging links, of give and take. It was a
process at which the two men were to prove adept. Their position
within Viennese society was a strong catalyst to collaboration – to getting
the job done, and done quickly. Mozart and Da Ponte were not writing
for posterity, but for survival: to earn a fee, to meet a deadline, to fill a slot
at the Burgtheater, to flatter specific voices and make use of certain
musicians, for the success that ensured the next commission. It is a mark
of their genius that these conditions did not produce banality, but three
of the most sublime operas ever composed.

   In Vienna, young Mozart had an acclaimed *Singspiel* behind him, and
a number of highly praised concerts – including the much talked-about
clavier competition with maestro Clementi. He was already making his
mark on the musical life of the city, but had an inexpressible longing 'to
show here what I can really do with Italian opera'. Like Da Ponte
discovering 'poor stuff' in the miser Varesi's library, Mozart had already
'looked through at least a hundred libretti' and found not a single one
that he thought worthwhile. He realized that the best way forward was
'a completely new text'. Seven years his senior, the 34-year-old poet to
the court theatre was a figure of some obscurity, yet in his new position
could be just the person to realize Mozart's desires – that is (Wolfgang
wrote to his father) if he wasn't 'in league with Salieri'. Wolfgang did
some fast talking that spring day at Baron Wetzlar's in 1783, and
emerged with the promise of a libretto, but also with the doubt, given
his mistrust of 'these Italian gentlemen', that the promise would be
fulfilled.

   At first, Mozart's suspicions appeared justified as Da Ponte was not forthcoming – largely because tasks as theatre poet kept him so busy, and also as he was struggling with the long and defeating task of trying to write *Il ricco d'un giorno* for Salieri. So Wolfgang approached two other Italian librettists. In desperation he sought out Giambattista Varesco, the poet he had had such a difficult time with on an earlier opera, *Idomeneo*; the second was an unknown poet, fished out (it would appear) of the steady stream of hopefuls flowing to Vienna, attracted by the feeding possibilities around the new Italian opera. While Da Ponte was tussling with Salieri's 'little changes here and there', and Vienna gossip was fizzing with news of the collaboration between the recently arrived Paisiello and the syphilitic Abbé Casti, Mozart worked on Varesco's *L'oca del Cairo* (The Goose of Cairo), and then on *Lo sposo deluso* (The Deceived Bridegroom). Both he abandoned.

As 1784 drew to a close, and Da Ponte (devouring new Burgtheater libretti in his coffee-house corner) was beginning to ponder the possibilities of introducing more serious elements into opera buffa, Mozart appears to have been moving along a similar course. After seeing Paisiello and Casti's *Il re Teodoro in Venezia*, in which the tragicomic libretto was populated by far more complex characters than the jealous maids, faithless shepherds, furious sultans and mechanical geese that had been his sorry lot to set to music thus far, Mozart had been ill for four days – his frequent response to moments of stress and challenge. In November, he also surely saw the revolutionary *La villanella rapita*, in which Bertati's libretto dressed up social criticism in buffo costume, as a trio and quartet of his were interpolated into the first performance. To an even greater extent than *Teodoro*, *La villanella rapita* indicated a new direction for opera.

In *La finta giardiniera*, a comic opera written ten years earlier in Munich, Mozart had already included two *seria* parts – though in a way that relied more on convention and on the categories to which the singers who took the parts belonged than on any intrinsic tragic qualities in the character of the role. In a letter of 1781, he seems keen to keep styles distinct: 'In an *opera seria* there should be as little frivolity and as much seriousness and solidity, as in an opera buffa there should be little seriousness and all the more frivolity and gaiety . . . in Vienna they make the proper distinction on this point.' Mozart was astutely aware of the tastes of the audience for whom he was composing, but by the time he met Da Ponte (and was sending instructions to Varesco) he was of the opinion that though 'the whole story should be really *comic*', at least one of the female parts should be '*seria*' and be given significant weight and excellence.

Varesco's attempts had been hopeless. For a moment it seemed that Da Ponte would not be much better, as Vienna gossiped about his abysmal debut in the December of 1784. In the cut-throat world of Viennese opera, people fled from the slightest whiff of failure, and Mozart was perhaps not quite so keen to court Da Ponte after the debacle of *Il ricco d'un giorno*. The year that followed was as grand for Mozart as it was humbling for Da Ponte: 1785 was the pinnacle of Mozart's performing career, with no fewer than fifteen public appearances documented. His concerts filled to overflowing, publishers were glad to issue his works (even bringing out juvenilia) – and his father was there to witness his success. Leopold Mozart arrived for a two-month visit in February, and found Wolfgang and Constanze living in lavish style, paying a resounding 480 gulden rent. They bought a carriage, a horse, a new fortepiano and enormous billiard table for Wolfgang ('He loved playing billiards passionately', wrote his biographer Niemetschek), and of course the most expensive and fashionable of clothes. Success (as it had done to Da Ponte) led to a great, gaudy balloon of vanity, pretensions to higher status, and the attendant anxieties.

Yet Mozart still desperately wanted a librettist for an Italian opera, and he may well have taken some encouragement from reports that Salieri would no longer have anything to do with the theatre poet. He and Da Ponte were developing enemies in common. For most of 1785, as Da Ponte's standing gradually recovered, the two men circled warily, like dogs about to settle in the same basket. It appears that they collaborated on a cantata, '*Davidde Penitente*', and on part of another for Nancy Storace, to celebrate her return to the stage in September after a long illness. (The soubrette's voice had suddenly failed during the performance of an opera by her brother Stephen at the beginning of June, though the duration of her absence is more likely to be related to pregnancy; her baby later died of neglect in a foundling home.) Finally, in November – with Da Ponte already hard at work on *Burbero*, and Casti scoffing at it as too serious for an opera buffa – Mozart suggested to the theatre poet an adaptation of *Le Mariage de Figaro* by the French playwright and erstwhile gunrunner to insurgents of the American Revolution, Pierre Augustin Caron de Beaumarchais.

Selecting the second play from Beaumarchais's *Figaro* trilogy was both a clever and a daring move. It was astute in that *Il barbiere di Siviglia*, Paisello's operatic version of the first play, had been far and away the highlight of the Italian opera's opening season in Vienna, and audiences would be sure to be attracted to *Le nozze di Figaro* as a sequel. Mozart's audacity in suggesting Beaumarchais's second play lay in the fact that Joseph II had just a few months earlier objected to its performance in Vienna in a German version. On 31 January 1785, the Emperor had written to one of his ministers, Count Pergen: 'I hear that the well-known comedy *Le Mariage de Figaro* is said to have been proposed for the Kärntnertortheater in a German translation; since this piece contains much that is objectionable, I therefore expect that the Censor shall either reject it altogether, or at any rate have such alterations made in it that he shall be responsible for the performance of this play and for the impression it may make.' The censor had opted for a complete ban.

Le Mariage de Figaro was notorious. The play had originally been banned in France – even a private performance at the house of the Count d'Artois was prohibited – but it continued to circulate among a frivolous nobility who appeared to delight in the birching it gave them, until there was such talk about it that public performance became inevitable. On the opening night at the Comédie-Française in Paris in 1784, the play had caused a near riot. Embedded in the story of the valet Figaro and his fiancée Suzanne's machinations to avoid their employer Count Alma-viva's exercising his feudal *jus primae noctis* – in effect his right to rape Suzanne on her wedding night – are trenchant passages of social criticism. The most pointed is in Figaro's long monologue in Act V, scene iii, in which he lashes out at the absent count in a way that most certainly would have had resonance with both Mozart's and Da Ponte's positions in life:

No Count, you won't have her, you shall not have her! You think that because you are a great lord you are a great genius! Nobility, wealth, rank, high position, such things make a man proud. But what did you ever do to earn them? Chose your parents carefully, that's all. Take that away and what have you got? A very average man. Whereas I, by God, was a face in the crowd. I've had to show more skill and brainpower just to stay alive than it's taken to rule all the provinces of Spain for the last hundred years. And you dare cross swords with me!

Three years before the Paris premiere of the play, Mozart, having been summarily booted from his patron's employ by Count Arco, wrote to his father lines that could quite easily have come from Figaro's mouth:

It is the heart that ennobles a man; and though I am no count, yet I have probably more honour in me than many a count. Whether a man be count or valet, the moment he insults me, he is a scoundrel.

How he must have enjoyed setting to music Figaro's aria '*Se vuol ballare/ Signor Contino/Il chitarrino/Le suonerò* [If, my dear little Count, you feel like dancing, it is I who will call the tune]'.

Mozart, who had once been hostile to Enlightenment ideas (on hearing of Voltaire's death he had cooed '. . . that godless arch-rascal Voltaire has pegged out like a dog, like a beast!') was feeling the influence of the free-thinking milieu in which he mingled in Joseph II's tolerant Vienna, and also moving closer to an espousal of rationalist beliefs.

The tumult on the first night of *Le Mariage de Figaro* in Paris engendered even greater publicity for the play than gossip among aristocratic circles had done, and it became the success of the season, running to a further sixty-eight performances. King Louis XVI on first reading the script had exclaimed, '*Cela est detestable, cela ne sera jamais joué!*', yet in the end even the royal couple had somewhat injudiciously appeared at the theatre. But Joseph II proceeded from a rather different standpoint to that of his sister Marie Antoinette and her husband. It will be remembered that the Emperor regarded the theatre as an instrument for spreading Enlightenment principles, 'a school of manners and taste', so censorship of the theatre became (initially at least) less a device of suppression than an instrument to further Enlightenment ideas. Joseph's letter to Pergen had not demanded an outright ban, but had allowed the censor the option of excising 'objectionable' elements and taking responsibility for the performance and 'the impression it may make'. Though the Emperor entertained an animus against the old aristocracy, his political reforms were by no means aimed at universal equality. It would not do to present so scathing a view of the nobility in such an accessible form as a play to the citizen audience at the Kärntnertortheater. A book was a different matter. Emanuel Schikaneder, the impresario of the Kärntnertortheater, learned of the Emperor's directive three days before his show was due to open, from placards announcing that the play was 'approved for publication but not for performance'. The text was published immediately, with a bitter dedication by the translator Johann Rautenstrauch, 'to the memory of 200 ducats' – the fee he had had to forfeit because of the cancellation of the performance.

If Joseph had permitted *Le Mariage de Figaro* to appear in German in book form, there was every likelihood that he would allow an Italian opera of *Le nozze di Figaro* at the Burgtheater, where the audience was from the upper ranks – unlike the impressionable and corruptible folk at the town theatre. He might even actively approve of an opera that, like *La villanella rapita*, held a satirical mirror up to the aristocracy crowding the boxes – and, of course, the opera could tone the play down a little: Da Ponte could excise some of the speeches Joseph objected to. Lighting on *Figaro* for a new opera was politically daring, but Mozart and Da Ponte were hardly seething with revolutionary fervour. Though both might object to the arrogance and prerogative of the *ancien régime*, neither was averse to the benefits of the status accorded them by the new nobility – in a way, this nobility afforded them a guarantee of that status. The counts and barons with whom Mozart and Da Ponte mingled had, by and large, as merchants and court officials achieved their rank through their own hard work, and they afforded the young men personal dignity based on recognition of their talent, rather than their origins. For their part, Wolfgang and Lorenzo both very much relished the trappings of the

privileged realm into which they had clambered. The angry young Da
Ponte who had gone on trial for his disruptive *accademia* in Treviso, and
penned a revolutionary sonnet in support of Giorgio Pisani, appears to
have been growing a little more muted in his opposition to authority.
Mozart may well have borne – in, as it were, his mind's buttock – the
imprint of Count Arco's boot, but in his letters he is seemingly
indifferent to politics. Nevertheless, the pair had strong sympathies with
Beaumarchais's central tenet of self-esteem as a product of personal
morality or worth, rather than as a consequence of high birth – and the
controversy surrounding his play's premiere, together with public
perception of an operatic adaptation being a sequel to *Il barbiere di
Siviglia* (and in the same tradition as *La villanella rapita*, which had also
been popular), spoke strongly for a collaboration on *Le nozze de Figaro*.

Together they decided to work on the opera in secret, and present it as
a fait accompli to Rosenberg or the Emperor when a favourable
opportunity arose, as they would then stand a greater chance of getting
permission to stage it. Writing an entire opera without a solid commission was an extraordinary move, perhaps also indicating that Mozart and
Da Ponte were already fuelling each other's suspicions of the intrigues
forming around them. The generous Baron Wetzlar was willing to
support the two artists he had brought together by purchasing the
libretto and trying to have the opera staged in London or Paris if
attempts to have it put on at the Burgtheater failed, but Da Ponte
writes that he refused the baron's offer and (casting himself as hero in his
version of events) took on the responsibility of approaching the director
of theatres or the Emperor himself. He and Mozart set to work. 'As soon
as I wrote the words,' Da Ponte recalls, 'Mozart set them to music.'
There was no time for tortuous soul-searching (that facility so highly
developed by Romantic-era artists): men without commissions must
needs work rapidly.

Both Mozart and Da Ponte were living near the Stephansplatz at the
time, neighbours in one of Vienna's most fashionable quarters. For the
next six weeks there was a constant back-and-forth between Da Ponte's
modest chambers and the Mozarts' grand new apartment. Neither has
left posterity details of how they worked, but they clearly found a

happier modus operandi than the constant disputing with which the one usually kept his librettists on the hop, and the frustrating '*Qùi cangiar vuol metro, o rima/E porre A dove U v'è prima* [And here wants to change metre, or rhyme/and put an A where a U was before]' which the other complained to be the usual method of composers. Along the way, Da Ponte would appear to have edged Mozart further from the view that 'the whole story should be really *comic*' and convinced him of the viability of the fluctuations in mood his text contained. Here was a librettist who offered shades in his characterization that a composer could enhance and swell with the extra layers of meaning that music can imbue, the gut responses it can excite, to raise the piece to a transcendent level. Nor did Mozart find words in Da Ponte's adaptation 'shoved in here and there to suit some miserable rhyme'; indeed, Da Ponte could dance a rhyme through an aria in a way that quite overcame Mozart's antagonism to a poet's obsession that could 'ruin the composer's whole idea'. Both had developed a sharp sense of theatricality, an awareness of the chops and changes made to shape an opera for the stage. Pride in their craftsmanship meant collaborating in a way that acknowledged the completed work as more important than their individual contributions to it. One can imagine the plotting and planning that took place beside Mozart's fortepiano, as arias were written with specific Burgtheater singers in mind: the alluring, coquettish Nancy Storace to play Susanna, master of comic acting Francesco Benucci as Figaro, Michael Kelly doubling as Basilio and Don Curzio, the twelve-year-old wonder Anna Gottlieb as Barbarina.

As Da Ponte moulded and cut the original play to shape it into an opera, one eye was certainly on political expedience (out went Figaro's inflammatory speech), yet his hand was governed by theatrical pragmatism. Beaumarchais's drama was too cumbersome for an opera buffa, too discursive, with too many diversions. Da Ponte honed and telescoped the action, drawing the teeth from some of its political bite in the process, but at the same time creating a streamlined plot that would work as opera. Skimming off subplots and topical allusions had the consequence of softening the point, but the essential thrust of the central social criticism remained.

Like the play, *Le nozze di Figaro* revolves around the intrigues of Figaro's and Susanna's attempts to ensure that Count Almaviva does not seduce Susanna; and the long-suffering Countess, married to a man who is simultaneously jealous and neglectful, becoming embroiled in a ruse aimed at teaching the Count a lesson, involving the page Cherubino (a sort of pubescent Don Giovanni, in love with almost any woman he encounters). In both, Marcellina and Bartolo plot to blackmail Figaro into marrying Marcellina, but instead turn out to be his parents.

Da Ponte's characters emerged as less complex than Beaumarchais's, closer to large-writ buffo stereotypes – the Count coarser, motivated almost entirely by aristocratic pride and lust, with little of the self-awareness of Almaviva in the drama; the Countess less equivocal in her attitude to Cherubino (his advances do make her rather wistful in the play), though with two interpolated arias that give her qualities of pensiveness and melancholy not present in the original; Figaro more a buffo schemer than a vehicle of scathing social critique, his fiery monologue reduced to the standard cuckold's diatribe on the fickleness of women (a transformation certain to appeal to the Emperor, whose ambivalent attitude to women bordered on misogyny). But Da Ponte left in the edge of social conflict, the egalitarian exchanges between Figaro and the Count, and between Susanna and the Countess in particular, who are more friends than mistress and maid. This social equality is given greater impact by being seen from the bottom up; the aristocrats are still deluded about what really matters. The Count reveals his hand in the aria '*Vedrò mentr'io sospiro*' as he rages, 'Must I see a serf of mine happy', furious that his desire is thwarted by a servant, that one of low birth can have something that he cannot. The Countess, too, feels doubly humiliated in that the Count's behaviour forces her to seek help from a servant – as Mozart's music with delicious irony reaches a tragic climax on her lines, '*Fammi or cercar da una mia serva aita!* [[My cruel husband] now forces me to seek help from my servant!]' All this had resonance for the aristocratic audience at the Burgtheater. The central image of the Count's abuse of power and of Figaro's and Susanna's disruptive opposition would be set before an audience in contemporary dress, an unclouded reflection of their own milieu. But – even though

Napoleon later said of Beaumarchais's play that it was the first stone thrown in the French Revolution – both it and the opera that Mozart and Da Ponte were constructing were not revolutionary convulsions of aristocracy versus bourgeoisie, but tales of a more conservative, personal conflict between master and servant. The German author Christoph Martin Wieland, writing in 1793, gave a definition of equality that would probably have sat well not only with Mozart's and Da Ponte's views, but with that of their sovereign: 'By equality I do not understand the right of absolute equality, which overthrows all distinctions in civil society between classes and estates, between rich and poor, educated and raw; but only that every citizen of the state shall be without exception equal before the law.'

We do not know the full extent of that back-and-forth across the Stephansplatz, of how much composer and librettist argued, of whose ideas shaped what, but it is clear that as Da Ponte delivered page after page of prose drama transfigured into poetry that sang in itself, and a form that would be effective as opera, Mozart was able to take the pragmatically simplified plot and re-endow the characters with subtlety, providing an audible commentary, one moment sarcastic, the next touching, then deliciously witty. And so the simple conversation between Susanna and the Countess, as they compose a letter to entrap the Count, became a duet of extraordinary sweetness and intimacy; Susanna's aria '*Deh vieni*', when pretending to be waiting for a tryst with the Count, intertwined her aim to teach Figaro a lesson for doubting her with a heartfelt expression of desire – a genuine hymn to love in a stock scene of buffo deception. The music infused the characters that the words had conjured up with the contradictions, doubts, ironies and warmth of richer humanity.

Mozart and Da Ponte worked like the autumn wind that whipped about the spire of the Stephanskirche. They were not averse to taking short cuts – as composers and librettists of the time so often did. Cherubino's aria '*Voi che sapete*' shows marks of being derived from Lisetta's song '*O giovinette innamorate*', from the pen of Da Ponte's arch-rival Casti, in *Il re Teodoro*; the magnificent finale in Act II has direct ancestors in those from Act I and Act II of Haydn's *La fedeltà premiata*, performed the previous December. The pair battled with the length of the piece, and with 'other considerations of prudence, of costume, place and public' to create (Da Ponte penned in a preface to the libretto) not a 'translation of that excellent comedy [the Beaumarchais original] but rather an imitation, or let us say an extract'. Together they took a step away from traditional opera buffa 'to paint faithfully and in full colour the divers passions that are aroused [in the characters], and to realize our special purpose, which was to offer a new type of spectacle'. They called their new type of spectacle a '*Commedia per musica*', using the word '*commedia*' in the sense Dante had, the purpose of which was 'to remove those living in this life from the state of misery and lead them to the state of bliss' – though in this case bliss was not to be found in heaven, but in happy marriage on earth.

Before Christmas they had their dainty dish to set before the king . . . and awaited the 'favourable opportunity' to present it to him. Their occasion arose after Da Ponte's success with *Il burbero di buon cuore* in January, when by good chance a slot became vacant in the Burgtheater programming. Lorenzo was shining in royal favour. The Emperor's '*Abbiamo vinto!*' still rang in his ears – rather like Susanna's triumphant aside to Figaro: '*Hai già vinto la causa!* [We've won our case!]' Joseph's support created 'new spirit' in Da Ponte and upended any thought of his resigning. The time had come to unveil the secret.

In his memoirs, Da Ponte writes that he bypassed Count Rosenberg and went directly to offer *Figaro* to the Emperor. He recalls the monarch's response:

'What?' he said. 'Don't you know that Mozart, though a wonder at instrumental music, has written only one opera, and nothing remarkable at that?'

'Quite so,' I replied quietly, 'but were it not for Your Majesty's clemency I would have written but one drama in Vienna!'

'That is true,' he answered, 'but this *Mariage de Figaro* – I have just forbidden the German troupe to perform it!'

'Yes,' I rejoined, 'but I have written a *dramma per musica*, and not a comedy. I had to omit many scenes and to cut others quite considerably. I have omitted or cut anything that might offend good taste or public decency at a performance over which the Sovereign Majesty might preside. The music, I may add, as far as I may judge of it, seems to me to be marvellously beautiful.'

Joseph sent for Mozart, commanding him to come to the palace, bring his score, and play through parts of the opera. Mozart surely chose those parts he knew would particularly appeal to his sovereign, such as Figaro's warning about the wiles of women, '*Aprite un po' quegl'occhi, uomini incauti e sciocchi* [Open your eyes a little, you incautious silly men]', which was to be followed by a solo for French horns – in Italian *corni*, which also means horns on the head (the symbol of a cuckold), an allusion that would not have escaped the multilingual, musically literate and rather misogynistic ruler. The Emperor, Da Ponte writes, was '*piacquegli maravigliosamente* [*sic*] [most marvellously pleased]', if not astounded, and immediately gave the go-ahead for the opera to be staged. *Le nozze di Figaro* was scheduled for the Burgtheater by royal command. Count Rosenberg, Casti, and Salieri were not best pleased, but there was little they could do – or so Da Ponte thought.

On 7 February 1786, to celebrate the visit of his sister Maria Christina, imperial regent in the Austrian Netherlands, the Emperor gave a fête at his summer palace of Schönbrunn, 'for the ladies of Vienna'. Count Rosenberg, as director of spectacles, was in charge of commissioning the entertainment. Together with a company of nobles, an additional forty gentlemen of the court were invited, each accompanied by a lady of his choice. Two-by-two, in barouches and closed carriages, the glittering party set forth (according to a report next day in the *Wiener Zeitung*), 'at three o'clock from the Hofburg of this town [i.e. the city palace] for Schönbrunn, and there all alighted at the Orangerie. This was arranged for luncheon in the most magnificent and elegant manner for the reception of these guests. The banqueting table under the trees of the Orangerie was decked in the most agreeable fashion with native and exotic flowers, blossoms and fruits.' Joseph II had even-handedly had the long Orangerie built with a stage at either end, one for German *Singspiel*, the other for Italian opera. After their midwinter banquet in a summer setting, the company were entertained by two performances that toyed wittily with the world of theatre – first, at one end of the glasshouse, a comedy with music by Mozart entitled *Der Schauspieldirektor;* then (over coffee, once night had fallen) with a short Italian opera at the other end of the hall, *Prima la musica e poi le parole* (First the Music and Then the Words) by Salieri, with a libretto not by the theatre poet (Salieri still wanted his fingers) but by Casti. In *Der Schauspieldirektor* two Burgtheater prima donnas, Salieri's mistress Caterina Cavalieri and Mozart's sister-in-law and former love Aloysia Lange, gamely portrayed a pair of vain, competing singers. Their colleague and rival Nancy Storace had her chance to shine in the Italian piece, which allowed her to air her famous imitation of the castrato Marchesi. *Prima la musica e poi le parole* dealt light-heartedly with the central problem in making an opera, opening with a duet between the Maestro and the Poet: an opera has been commissioned at short notice; the Poet says it cannot be done; the Maestro assures that it can, as the music has already been written, and points out that all the Poet has to do is fit words to the score. The Poet replies that this is like sewing a suit of clothes and then making a man to fit them. In the course of the ensuing rumpus librettist and composer, and later soubrette and soprano, all but come to blows.

In addition to Storace's mimicry, the highlight of *Prima la musica* for many was Casti's wicked satire, in the character of the librettist, of the Burgtheater's own theatre poet. 'My style of dress was adopted and the fashion in which I wore my hair,' wrote Da Ponte sourly. There was more to it than that. Casti's libretto poked fun at the fictional Poet's love for women of the stage (Lorenzo was clearly up to his old tricks) and (though Da Ponte does not admit this), given the scenario, no doubt also portrayed him as vain and touchy. Next day, Da Ponte circulated his own sonnet, '*Casti ier sera un'operetta fe*', huffing that everything Casti had portrayed applied more to himself, but the gossip was out. When the double bill was performed before the public later in February, there was a run on tickets. Da Ponte had to endure further humiliation some months on when Michael Kelly, famed for his mimicry and 'monkey antics', and clearly divining the bent of Burgtheater taste, based his interpretation of an amorous, eccentric philosopher in Righini's opera *Demogorgone, ossia Il filosofo confuso* on the theatre poet. The librettist for *Demogorgone* was Da Ponte himself. Kelly's description of the premiere provides a touching glimpse of Lorenzo, so proud of his new position and achievements, as his vanity is bruised:

> The first night of the performance, [Da Ponte] was seated in the boxes more conspicuously than was absolutely necessary, considering he was the author of the piece to be performed. As usual, on the first night of a new opera, the emperor was present, and a numerous auditory. When I made my *entrée* as the amorous poet [*sic*], dressed exactly like the abbé in the boxes, imitating his walk, leaning on my stick and aping his gestures and his lisp, there was a universal roar of laughter and applause; and after a buzz around the house, the eyes of the whole audience were turned to the place where he was seated. The emperor enjoyed the joke, laughed heartily and applauded frequently during the performance; the abbé was not at all affronted, but took my imitation of him in good part, and ever after we were on the best of terms.

It appears that, though he may have put up a brave face, the abbé was indeed affronted. Decades later he would write of Kelly with extreme rancour – but by then, he had all the more reason to do so.

According to Da Ponte, Count Rosenberg took advantage of the success of *Prima la musica* to put Casti forward for the position of imperial poet, and was rebuffed with: 'My dear Count, speaking for myself, I cannot use a poet; as for the Opera, we have Da Ponte.' In the way of court gossip, Da Ponte had the story that very day from Salieri, who had it from the Emperor – and later the sovereign himself repeated the story to Da Ponte. Yet Joseph's refusal had less to do with love for Da Ponte than with caution regarding Casti, who had been circulating politically inexpedient fragments of a ruthless satire on the court of Catherine II of Russia. The dividing lines of loyalties seldom appear clearly staked out in Vienna. Even as on one level antagonists fought cruelly for their interests, and often survival, on another they appear quite sincerely to show amity for

each other. Da Ponte took daily walks with Salieri in the park; he and
Casti quite genuinely praised each other's poetry (when their interests
were not in conflict). Da Ponte might scoff that Casti referred frequently
to a small encyclopaedia to make up for the poverty of his knowledge, but
when Casti made him a gift of the book, after Da Ponte had pulled him
up on a classical allusion, Lorenzo 'cherished it for more than twenty-five
years'. And though Da Ponte relished the belief that the Emperor
connived with him against Count Rosenberg, Joseph trusted his chamberlain implicitly, and Rosenberg was indisputably as near as the difference in rank would allow to being one of the Emperor's closest friends.

But Lorenzo could notch up a quiet triumph at the news that
Rosenberg's bid for Casti's elevation had failed, though he and the
count were to clash again before *Figaro* reached the stage. Indeed, the
entire Burgtheater was beset by an imbroglio of buffo proportions. As
ever, different versions of the reasons behind this abound. Da Ponte
blames Rosenberg's and Casti's antagonism to his success; Leopold
Mozart and Michael Kelly put it down to the manoeuvrings of Salieri's
cabal against Mozart; Niemetschek blames the singers, who he says
deliberately stumbled over their lines (no doubt complaining of the
fussiness of German music). The core of the problem would appear to
have been competition for the vacant spring slot in the Burgtheater's
programme, with new operas by Mozart, Salieri and Righini simultaneously available for production, and each composer wanting his work
to appear first. The flint-fire Mozart, according to Kelly, swore he would
burn his score if it did not have precedence. Righini, who at the time
enjoyed a considerable reputation, 'worked like a mole in the dark' to
ensure his *Demogorgone* prevailed. Salieri, 'a clever shrewd man, possessed
of what Bacon called crooked wisdom' stirred up a cabal that included
three of the principal performers (which might explain why certain
singers stumbled on their lines). 'The contest raised much discord, and
parties were formed,' wrote Kelly. 'Every one of the opera company
took part.' The Emperor's command that *Figaro* should fill the vacant slot
put an end to the immediate contest, but by no means quietened the fray.

Mozart began rehearsals almost immediately, first with individual
singers and then on stage at the Burgtheater. From ten o'clock in the

morning until two o'clock in the afternoon, the theatre seethed with intrigue. Battle was skilful and subtle, though cordiality and decorum reigned – theatre and court in Vienna were not forums for gladiatorial conflict, but the realm of secret sabotage, of the hidden thrust, the duplicitous smile. At some point during rehearsals, the bass, Francesco Bussani, reported to Rosenberg that *Figaro* contained a ballet, in apparent violation of the Emperor's prohibition of dance insertions into operas in the Burgtheater. Da Ponte was summoned before the count, and a dialogue ensued that – Da Ponte himself points out – was 'a fine counterpart' to the one he had had so many years before in Venice, with Angela Tiepolo's vile aristocratic twin brother. This time there was a note of defiance, and Da Ponte's 'Yes, *Eccellenza*. No, *Eccellenza*' contained as much barbed innuendo as his opponent's sarcastic '*signor poeta*':

'So, the *signor poeta* has introduced a ballet into *Figaro*?'
'Yes, *Eccellenza*.'
'The *signor poeta* does not know that the Emperor does not want dancing in his theatre?'
'No, *Eccellenza*.'
'In that case, *signor poeta*, I will tell you so now.'
'Yes, *Eccellenza*.'
'And I tell you further, *signor poeta*, that you will take it out.' [. . .]
'No, *Eccellenza*.'
'You have the libretto with you?'
'Yes, *Eccellenza*.'
'Where is the scene with the dance?'
'Here it is, *Eccellenza*.'
'This is the way we do it.'
Saying which, he took two sheets of my *dramma*, laid them carefully on the fire, and returned the libretto to me.
'You see, *signor poeta*, I can do anything!'

Da Ponte hurried to tell Mozart. The volatile Wolfgang (he once broke a shoe buckle stamping his feet during rehearsals) was all for confronting the count, giving Bussani a beating, appealing directly to the Emperor, withdrawing the entire opera – it took all Da Ponte's energies to calm him down. The dress rehearsal was in two days, and Da Ponte had a scheme of his own. He says he visited the Emperor to ask him to attend the rehearsal, though this was probably unnecessary, as Vienna society frequently wandered in on such occasions, even if in their eagerness for chat they didn't pay much attention to goings-on on stage. The first act went well, until the end, where instead of the planned ballet, the orchestra fell silent and Count Almaviva and Susanna began to panto-mime like puppets. Da Ponte reports the Emperor's reaction:

> 'What's all this?' exclaimed the Emperor to Casti, who was sitting behind him.
> 'You must ask the poet that!' replied the Abbé with a malicious little smile.

Da Ponte was summoned, but remained silent. Instead of answering the Emperor's question, he handed over his manuscript, with the ballet restored, so that the Emperor could see that it was not a gratuitous insertion, but a dramatically necessary part of the action. Given that this did not technically contradict his ban on unrelated ballet 'insertions', the sovereign asked why the dancers had not appeared. Again Da Ponte remained respectfully silent, thus hinting (he says) at intrigue. Rosenberg replied that the theatre had no dancers.

> 'But they have some at other theatres?'
> [Rosenberg] affirmed that there were.
> 'Very well, let Da Ponte have as many as he needs.'

The dancers were secured, but this is probably the reason that the opening night of Le nozze di Figaro was postponed from 28 April to 1 May.

Bussani's tattling to Rosenberg was not the only act of treachery among the singers. Niemetschek writes of their slanders, attempts to belittle the music and to sabotage the opera – but it would appear that along the way a different buzz among the cast began to grow, as it often does when performers in rehearsal realize they are tackling something new and quite extraordinary. Michael Kelly recollects the first rehearsal with full orchestra, admittedly in rosy retrospect, giving a perhaps slightly heightened version of the excitement that was slowly taking its grip. The dandy composer with his 'little animated countenance', which when lighted by inspiration was 'as impossible to describe as it would be to paint sun-beams' takes the stage:

> Mozart was on the stage with his crimson pelisse and gold-laced cocked hat, giving the time of the music to the orchestra. Figaro's song, '*Non più andrai, farfallone amoroso,*' Benucci gave with the greatest animation and power of voice.
>
> I was standing close to Mozart, who, *sotto voce*, was repeating, 'Bravo! Bravo! Benucci'; and when Benucci came to the fine passage, '*Cherubino, alla vittoria, alla gloria militar*', which he gave out with stentorian lungs, the effect was electricity itself, for the whole of the performers on the stage and those in the orchestra, as if actuated by one feeling of delight, vociferated, 'Bravo! Bravo! Maestro. Viva, viva, grande Mozart.' Those in the orchestra I thought would never have ceased applauding by beating bows of their violins against music desks. The little man acknowledged, by repeated obeisances, his thanks for the distinguished mark of enthusiastic applause bestowed on him.

Benucci's stentorian lungs were not his only asset; his fine comic acting was well suited to the part of Figaro. In a billet to Count Rosenberg, after seeing *Il barbiere di Siviglia* some years earlier, Joseph II had drawn special attention to the veracity of Benucci's performance, comparing him to the great actor Friedrich Schröder. Nancy Storace's comic ability and naturalistic style qualified her sublimely for the role of Susanna. In the same billet to Rosenberg, the Emperor wrote that Storace at times even surpassed Schröder's counterpart Maria Anna Adamberger in ability. Dorotea Bussani (who married the treacherous Francesco that year) made her debut as Cherubino, and must have been perfect for the part – years later a critic would still remark on her 'great vivacity and playful expression'. Some of the singers in the Italian opera were beginning to take a cue from performers in the German theatre company, which was cultivating a new school of acting. Vienna was comparatively advanced in this departure from the rigid formality of earlier operatic acting technique. The obsession with vocal display for its own sake (parodied by Storace's mimicry of Marchesi) was beginning to give way to greater involvement in character. Da Ponte and Mozart's 'new kind of spectacle' required this new approach to performing, though, as a contemporary critic pointed out: 'That which is called expression in song and penetration into the spirit of the characters, as represented by the composer, is extremely rare in all our opera houses.'

On the opening night, Niemetschek writes, some singers still seemed intent on sabotage, and 'out of hate, envy, and ill-will, tried to spoil the opera by making mistakes'. The initial reception was lukewarm. Count Zinzendorf in his box, distracted by his mistress Louise who was about to leave Vienna, gave *Figaro* scant attention, and was bored. Others in the audience did not quite know how to react to the novelty of Mozart and Da Ponte's 'new kind of spectacle', in which wit and melancholy intertwined. The innovations the performers had to tackle – or the weeks of intrigue and obstructionism – may well have meant that the opera was under-rehearsed. This, rather than the late addition of a ballet, was arguably the cause of the postponement of the premiere. Whatever the reason for its shaky start, *Figaro* soon righted itself, as a contemporary review, from the *Wiener Realzeitung* of 11 July, shows:

The *public* . . . (and this often happens to the public) did not really know on the first day where it stood. It heard many a *bravo* from unbiased connoisseurs, but obstreperous louts in the uppermost storey exerted their hired lungs with all their might to deafen singers and audience alike with their *St!* and *Pst!*; and consequently opinions were divided at the end of the piece.

Apart from that, it is true to say that the first performance was none of the best, owing to the difficulty of the composition.

But now after several performances, one would be subscribing either to the *cabal* or to *tastelessness* if one were to maintain that Herr Mozart's music is anything but a masterpiece of the Art.

It contains so many beauties, and such a wealth of ideas, as can be drawn only from the source of innate genius.

After the uneven reception at the premiere, the second night brought triumph – five numbers had to be repeated. At the third performance the encores rose to seven, with the duet '*Aprite presto*' being given three times. Audience enthusiasm so protracted the length of the opera that on 9 May Joseph II wrote to Count Rosenberg commanding him to issue a ban on encores for more than one voice. Three days later posters with notices to this effect were pinned up at the Burgtheater.

By the end of the year, *Figaro* would be received in Prague to even greater acclaim: 'Nothing is played, sung or whistled but "Figaro",' wrote Mozart on a visit to attend performances. 'No opera is drawing like "Figaro". Nothing, nothing, but "Figaro".' The pleasure-loving people of Prague had even arranged parts of the opera for dances, and 'flew about in sheer delight' to its tunes. At some performances, reported the *Prager Oberpostamtszeitung*, the theatre was so crowded that people could hardly move. But in Vienna *Figaro* was eclipsed in just a few months, by another opera with libretto by Da Ponte – his second collaboration with the Spanish composer, his friend Martín y Soler.

Chapter Nine

BEFORE WORKING AGAIN with Martín y Soler, the busy theatre poet had another libretto to finish. This was *Demogorgone, ossia Il filosofo confuso*, the Righini opera in which Michael Kelly would so cruelly poke fun at his gait, lisp and vanities. Da Ponte did not like Righini's music, saying that it drove every spark of inspiration from his head. He accepted the task only because Salieri especially asked him to, and he wanted to win back the court composer's favour. Tellingly, in his memoirs Da Ponte misremembers his subtitle to the opera as *Il filosofo punito*, and says a more appropriate title would have been 'The Composer and the Poet Punished Each in Turn'. *Demogorgone* premiered in July and, Kelly's popular mimicry notwithstanding, received only three further performances before dropping from the repertoire.

All Kelly's prancing and all the opera's failings could not dampen Da Ponte's fire, for shortly before *Demogorgone* opened, an event had occurred that 'roused [his] spirits greatly, restored [his] courage' and magicked away the obstacles that had so disturbed his peace of mind: the Abbé Casti left town. Casti had presented the Emperor with a beautifully bound copy of his satire on life in the Russian court, *Il poema tartaro*. Although Joseph had enjoyed earlier parts of the poem, which had been circulating since 1784, by 1786 he was looking to an alliance with Russia, and was shortly to visit Catherine II, so a vicious exposure of life at her court was hardly expedient – nor was the presence of its author under what amounted to imperial protection. Ever tactful, Joseph summoned Casti to his box at the opera, made him a substantial gift of 600 sequins, and said, 'These will serve for the expenses of your journey.' The syphilitic abbé was well enough versed in the ways of court to realize that he had been given his marching orders. Within a few weeks he was in Italy, and would not return to Vienna until after Joseph's death.

With *Demogorgone*, and Casti, out of the way, Da Ponte set to work for Martín in fine fettle. This time, he worked in secret. He had a plan to foil his detractors. Never, he wrote, had he composed verses 'with such celerity or with such delight', as he transformed *La luna de la sierra* by the seventeenth-century Spanish playwright Luis Vélez de Guevara into *Una cosa rara, o sia bellezza ed onestá* (A Rare Thing, or Beautiful and Virtuous). Once again Da Ponte's neat fingers tucked, cut and streamlined, yet allowed 'plenty of room to show off all the notable singers in our company to the best conceivable advantage'. He constructed a simple pastoral, in which an earthily virtuous village girl, Lilla, is supported by the Queen in her resistance to lustful advances by both the Mayor and the Prince. Dilemmas over love, sex and money (Prince and Mayor both offer gifts and social advancement that Lilla's shepherd suitor can't hope to match) lead to Goldoni-style confusion, then chaste, happy resolution – more conventional and less complex than *Figaro*, but not without subtle turns of character. Martín provided a tumble of whistlable, singable, danceable tunes, including a waltz – the first to be seen on stage, and reputedly the model for the fast Viennese style of the dance that would sweep the world. His opera had an easier line than *Figaro*, one that would be more accessible to Viennese ears. Yet despite the charming music and Da Ponte's attempts to please all, rehearsals were once again beset with divisions and rebellion – this time centred on Martín, whom Francesco Bussani suspected of dalliance with his new wife Dorotea. According to Da Ponte, he dodged the venom himself as his authorship of the libretto was still secret, but the singers never ceased 'to grumble in little groups, criticizing and cursing the Spaniard and his music'. He gives us a glimpse of a tetchy, unhappy company:

The moment the parts were distributed, all hell broke loose. This one had too much recitative, the other not enough; for one the aria was pitched too low, for the other too high; these did not get into any *concertati*, others had too many; this one was sacrificed to the prima donna, another to the first, second, third and fourth buffo. A general conflagration!

The anonymous author, on the other hand, was praised to the heavens. 'Learn, Signor Da Ponte,' a singer advised the theatre poet one day, 'how a comic libretto is written!' Da Ponte kept quiet. He was waiting until after the premiere.

Una cosa rara was greeted on its opening night, its librettist writes, with 'a roar of applause, cries of delight, howls of enthusiasm' – and it seems he was not exaggerating. Even the claque that the cabal had paid to hiss forgot themselves and joined in the general acclamation, and the Emperor broke his own ban on encores by calling to hear the duet '*Pace mio caro sposo*' again. The tunes were delightfully memorable. Melodies from *Una cosa rara* surfaced in house-concerts all over town, and not only the upper ranks were enthralled. Wherever one went, Johann Pezzl noted, shopkeepers and cellar-hands whistled the arias – even tough prisoners joined in the song. A pedestrian passing the Militär-Stockhaus was astonished to hear a lusty rendition of the love duet that had so pleased Joseph ringing out from behind the walls. Dedicated theatre-goer Count Zinzendorf was thoroughly charmed, enthused that '*Pace mio caro sposo*' was '*voluptueux*', and even after the fourth time he saw the opera remained moved by the duet long after the final curtain. Zinzendorf found the Spanish pastoral costumes (some especially made, others donated by Martín's protector, the Ambassadress of Spain) dazzlingly pretty. A craze for *Una cosa rara* dress and hairstyles swept through Vienna. The entire city wanted to see the show, but the Burgtheater's repertory system made it difficult to squeeze in any extra nights, despite the huge demand for tickets. Johann Pezzl, surveying the 1786–87 season, noted that '[*Una cosa rara*] was the piece that virtually took the town by storm; at every performance 300 to 400 people had to be turned away.'

The fashionable ladies in the parterre at the premiere clamoured for the librettist; *he* was the man who ought to be poet to their opera. Yet the booklets printed for distribution in the theatre bore no writer's name. Da Ponte came clean after the final act: he was ceremoniously presented to the clamouring (and now embarrassed) ladies; then, going backstage, he handed to each member of the company copies of the libretto booklet – this time emblazoned with his name in capital letters. These events, recollected years later by Da Ponte in 'luminous triumph' at his enemies' humiliation, are perhaps less useful as an historical record than as a revelation of character. A jest is a jest, but there is a tang of malice in the way he behaves, a smirking glee, as not content with mere victory he must needs shame his opponents in a way that could only alienate them further. If previously he suspected he was disliked by his colleagues, he could now guarantee it.

Increasingly, Da Ponte was beginning to cast himself at the centre of a violently drawn melodrama. The language he uses to describe Count Rosenberg's reaction to the dance incident in *Figaro*, that it 'redoubled the hatred of my powerful persecutor and whipped his thirst for vengeance to a frenzy', reveals more of Lorenzo's perceptions of the world in which he was having to do battle than of the character of the count, who, schemer and intriguer though he may be, was a respected and highly competent statesman. Clearly there is verity in Da Ponte's sense of his troubles – intrigue in the Burgtheater was rank, and he was certainly deeply entangled in it – but the lens through which he viewed the situation distorted his perspective, leading to histrionic reactions that could hardly help his cause. Lorenzo had never truly been part of the group – not in Ceneda, Venice, nor now in Vienna – but this sense of not belonging was beginning to curdle into destructive self-absorption. His touchiness, impulsivity, and the youthful cockiness now dried out into vanity, could only make life more bitter.

Yet after *Figaro* and *Una cosa rara*, Da Ponte was once again on the ascendant. Vienna loved success, and those who lived by their talents had of necessity to court it. Martin and Da Ponte found themselves fêted not only by members of the Italian opera company but by the German faction at the Burgtheater and society at large – especially women.

The ladies in particular, who desired to see nothing but the *Cosa rara* and dress only in the styles of the *Cosa rara*, believed that Martini [*sic*] and I were in truth two 'rare things' ourselves. We might have had more amorous adventures than had all the Knights of the Round Table in twenty years. No one was talked about other than us, no one was praised other than us. That opera worked the miracle of revealing graces, beauties, rarities that had not been detected in us before, and that were not to be found in other men. Invitations for walks, lunches, suppers, jaunts in the country, fishing parties; billets-doux, little gifts accompanied by enigmatic verses – it simply did not stop!

Da Ponte records that Martin 'was much amused at all this and profited from it in every way', but adds primly (and surely quite untruthfully): 'As for myself, I laughed, reflected sagely on the human heart, and turned my mind to writing some other *Cosa rara* . . .' Chaste, moralizing St Lorenzo is an unfamiliar, if not unbelievable, figure – though it is true that women barely feature in his memoirs of the first years in Vienna. It could well be that he was staying faithful to the invisible, unmentioned mother of Felice – though his subsequent behaviour does not bear this out. Soon, he would be dallying with a sixteen-year-old nymph; and not long after that yet another of the destructive, consuming passions of the sort that had marred his life in Venice awaited him.

The year 1786 had been a magnificent one for Da Ponte. Of the twenty-two Italian operas staged at the Burgtheater between January and December ten had been new, and of these he had written the libretti for six – one of which would later be placed with the greatest operas of all time, and another that would be among the most spectacularly popular operas of the last part of the century. After the wild success of *Cosa rara*, even Count Rosenberg proved more tractable, offering the theatre poet a 'Bravo!' and hearty handshake in street. Professionally, prospects could hardly have looked better for Lorenzo, with composers lining up for his libretti. Even Salieri repented of his vow and considered working with Da Ponte again.

For Stephen Storace, Lorenzo adapted Shakespeare's *Comedy of Errors* as *Gli equivoci*, deftly reducing five acts to two, introducing arias, building up ensembles, creating magnificent finales, while retaining the essence of Shakespeare's comedy. Michael Kelly, who had a leading role, was impressed with what Da Ponte had done with 'the main incidents and characters of our immortal bard', noting that he adapted the play 'with great ingenuity', skilfully working it to make it 'operational' as an opera. It premiered on 27 December 1786, to quite some success, largely (an admittedly partial Kelly writes) because 'the music of Storace was beyond description beautiful'. Two months later, the happy quartet of Michael Kelly, the Storace siblings, and their mother (sestet if you count their friend the singer Thomas Attwood, and Nancy's ever-present lapdog) set off in a coach-and-four piled with luggage for London, where Nancy had been offered an engagement as comic prima donna with the Italian opera company at the King's Theatre.

Past favours and present obligations meant that it was not always easy for Da Ponte to exercise choice over which of the importunate composers he accepted. *Gli equivoci* had been taken on at the express request of the Emperor, who had been prevailed upon by Nancy to give her brother a commission (Joseph had probably agreed in a vain attempt to keep her in Vienna). Da Ponte writes that he chose to adapt Shakespeare 'to get the matter out of the way quickly'. Next, Da Ponte was persuaded against his better judgement to write a libretto for Francesco Pittichio, a third-rate composer well connected with ladies at court and a close friend of his doctor, who did the persuading. The commission was for an adaptation of an earlier libretto by Gaetano Brunati to music Pittichio had already written. *Il Bertoldo*, which opened on 22 June 1787, was remarkable only for the fearlessly enlightened shepherd of the title, who believes that all men are born equal and is brave enough to tell his king so. Zinzendorf found it 'very long', though pleasant enough. It was mildly popular, lasting for eight performances before (like the rest of Pittichio's work) sliding from view. 'Da Ponte,' said the Emperor a few days after the premiere, 'write operas for Mozart, Martín, Salieri; but drop these *potacchi, petecchie, pitocchi, peticchi* – whatever his name was. Casti was smarter than you: he wrote a libretto only for a Paisiello or a Salieri.' Da Ponte took his sovereign's advice – quite literally, it would appear. He tells us that in the summer of 1787 he began working on three operas simultaneously, for just the trio of composers that Joseph had recommended:

> The opportunity was offered me by *maestri* Martín, Mozart, and Salieri who came all three at the same time to request libretti of me. I loved and esteemed all three of them, and through all three I hoped for a remedy for past failures and for some increment in my theatrical glory. I wondered whether it might not be possible to satisfy all three and to write three operas at one spurt.

For the court composer he embarked on *Axur, re d'Ormus* – an adaptation of *Tarare*, Salieri's opera with libretto by Beaumarchais that had opened in Paris that June; for Martín y Soler he wrote *L'arbore di Diana*, one of the few libretti he created from scratch, and with Mozart he began *Don Giovanni*.

In his version of events, Da Ponte casts himself as a scholar-poet, rather in the Romantic mould, alone in his room, fuelled by wine, snuff, coffee and his muse – the latter in the form of a compliant sixteen-year-old, a 'perfect mistress in loving tenderness' with a pretty face that was 'just the thing to excite poetic inspiration and witty thoughts'. To an Emperor sceptical of his abilities to succeed with the feat of writing three operas contemporaneously, he had said:

> I shall write in the evening for Mozart, imagining I am reading the *Inferno*; mornings I shall work for Martin and pretend I am studying Petrarch; my afternoons will be for Salieri. He is my Tasso! [. . .]
>
> I sat down at my table and did not leave it for twelve hours at a stretch – a bottle of *tokai* to my right, a box of Seville snuff to my left, in the middle an inkwell. A beautiful girl of sixteen (I should have preferred to have loved her only as a daughter, but . . .) was living in the house with her mother, who took care of the family, and would come to my room at the sound of the bell. To tell the truth, I rang the bell quite often, especially at moments when I felt my inspiration flagging.

His young Calliope brought coffee, cakes and kisses as he worked twelve hours a day for two months on end – though eventually he had to ration her visits as they were too distracting from the task at hand.

Salieri and Beaumarchais's *Tarare* had been highly experimental in form and revolutionary in content. Salieri had earlier worked closely with Gluck, whose protégé he was, and who had blasted fresh air and a greater naturalness into moribund *opera seria*. As musical drama, *Tarare* took Gluck's reforms even further, its recitative only occasionally drawing into passages of arioso, and never breaking out into aria. Beaumarchais's story of Tarare's overthrow of a cruel despot ends with the gods proclaiming: 'Man! Your greatness on this earth derives not from your social standing but solely from your character!' – this at the Paris Opéra just weeks after the Assembly of Notables had been dissolved. (The meeting of the first Assembly of Notables at Versailles in February is considered the beginning of the 'pre-Revolution'; the Assembly was dissolved in May.) Originally, Salieri and Da Ponte had intended a straight translation, but after they began to work on it realized that an adaptation was needed as there was a difference between 'music for French singing actors and music for Italian acting singers'. In converting *Tarare* to *Axur*, they added arias and ensembles to soften the impact of its musical oddity for a Viennese audience, and removed the inflammatory epilogue – though as with *Figaro* the central political focus remained.

L'arbore di Diana also had a political barb hidden in the folds of its lacy fantasy and eroticism. Da Ponte writes that part of his intention was to provide an admiring parallel to 'certain policies of my august protector and sovereign', namely Joseph's dissolution of the convents, reflected in the opera in Endymion's subversion of Diana's temple. The reluctant abbé, it may be remembered, was no friend of the Church. He recalls that on catching the political allusion, Joseph was delighted and sent him an extra 100 sequins, nearly doubling his normal fee.

Stylistically, if *Cosa rara* curtsied towards Goldoni, *L'arbore di Diana* cast a lingering glance at the fairy-tale works of Carlo Gozzi; yet the libretto is entirely Da Ponte's invention. It gave him opportunity to display his classical grounding. Diana, goddess of chastity, has a tree in her garden whose fruit grow large and begin to glow if virtuous nymphs pass under its branches; yet if a nymph has been sinful, the apples grow blacker than coal and pelt down on her, disfiguring her face or breaking her limbs (in proportion to the crime). Amore, unable to endure this affront to his divinity, enters the garden dressed as a woman, teaches the gardener to seduce the nymphs each in turn, and for good measure brings along the beautiful Endymion, with whom Diana herself falls in love. A priest, suspecting something is amiss, demands Diana and her nymphs subject themselves to the judgement of the tree; but the goddess wrong-foots her minion by having the give-away vegetation felled, and Amore, 'appearing in a radiant cloud, ordains that the Garden of Diana be thenceforward the Realm of Love'. Cold, unloving chastity is defeated. Throughout the opera Lorenzo reiterates a phrase he had first used in a sonnet written with his friend Michele Colombo for their rector in Ceneda, an expression of a lesson that was taught him with varying degrees of pleasure and unpleasantness all through his life: '*Quanto è possente amor!* [How powerful is love!]' Da Ponte, in later life, thought this the best of all the operas he had written, both in its conception and its verse, noting that 'it was voluptuous without overstepping into lasciviousness'. A contemporary pamphleteer disagreed, calling it 'a miserable, botched-up piece of double entendre, smut and abomination'. When Count Rosenberg acidly asked him how he had come up with '*quelle belle cose* [all those pretty things]', he retorted that he found them 'on the backsides of my enemies!' (Or so he coyly reports – one might imagine his expressing the sentiment more pithily.)

L'arbore di Diana had its premiere on 1 October, in a gala performance to mark the arrival in Vienna of the Emperor's niece, the Archduchess Maria Theresa, on her wedding journey to Dresden. Count Zinzendorf enjoyed the opera, but thought it hardly decent for such an occasion. Later in the month, Mozart received similar criticism from a 'very high and mighty' lady when *Figaro* was given to celebrate the Archduchess's passage through Prague. The lady had prematurely cried, '*Ho vinto!* [I have conquered]' from her box on hearing the opera had been withdrawn, but an announcement was made a few days later stating that, at Their Highnesses' specific request, *Figaro* would be performed after all.

Both Zinzendorf and the high-and-mighty lady of Prague were being stuffy and old-fashioned. They belonged back in the days of the Empress Maria Theresa, when wedding operas were one-off events performed before invited audiences as part of court ritual. Times had changed. A public gala performance was a different sort of occasion from an exclusive court spectacle, and as Mozart commented in his letter back to Vienna, 'No opera in the world, unless it is written specially for it, can be exactly suitable for such an occasion and . . . therefore it was of absolutely no consequence whether this or that opera were given, provided that it was a good opera and one which [the Archduchess] did not know.' The opera had, after all, to remain in the repertoire, and the public, at least, enjoyed *L'arbore di Diana*. It received fifty-nine performances over the next four years.

On the day that *L'arbore di Diana* opened, Wolfgang and Constanze Mozart left Vienna for a visit to Prague. Mozart carried with him his fulfilment of the commission given him by the impresario Pasquele Bondini after the Prague success of *Figaro* the previous season – a working score (ready for rehearsal, at least) of *Don Giovanni*.

If 1786–87 had been a glory time for Da Ponte, it had been a pretty dismal period for Mozart. Not only had his *Figaro* been eclipsed by *Una cosa rara* in Vienna, but there had been a sudden and catastrophic slump in invitations to perform. The private concerts that contributed so much to his income dwindled almost to nil. (Some put this sudden change in taste among the nobility of Vienna down to the revolutionary politics of *Figaro*, though that did not adversely affect Da Ponte's popularity.) This collapse left Wolfgang heavily reliant on money from teaching – and that, too, dried up in the summer, when rich families left the city. On 7 April some hope arrived in the form of a sixteen-year-old pupil who had travelled to Vienna from Bonn especially for lessons, but Ludwig van Beethoven had to return home two weeks later because his mother was sick. On 24 April 1787, the Mozarts had suffered the humiliation not just of moving from their sumptuous apartment in Schulerstrasse but of emigrating across the green glacis, to a humbler house in the suburbs, where the rent was just fifty gulden. The move made Mozart ill. Then in

May, Leopold Mozart died. 'After God,' a young Wolfgang is supposed
to have said, 'comes Papa.' As time went on their relationship had
become more contentious: Leopold increasingly self-absorbed and
accusing; Wolfgang docile, craving favour, but bursting periodically
into defiance. Wolfgang sincerely mourned Leopold's death; but though
this beloved antagonist had left the field, the feelings of guilt and financial
obligation with which father had tormented son were weapons effective
from beyond the grave. Distress about debt and fears of poverty would
dog him as long as he lived.

If Mozart felt unappreciated by the people of Vienna, Prague presented a different prospect entirely. Prague had adored *Figaro*, had sung
it, danced to it, fêted its composer on his previous visit. The city itself was
not particularly appealing, having declined from its seventeenth-century
days of splendour as home to the imperial court to become – as the
Bohemian nobility removed themselves to Vienna – a grubby, unfashionable backwater. Mozart's pupil J. N. Hummel found Prague 'very
dirty with narrow streets'. John Moore thought it 'retain[ed] some marks
of former splendour, but many more evident symptoms of present
decay'; and Hester Piozzi was even less impressed, writing that the
whole town had 'a ragged and half-ruined melancholy aspect', where
(sin of sins) the shops shut for most of the afternoon, and everything
seemed 'at least five centuries behind-hand' – except, that is, the ladies in
their boxes at the opera, whose dress, she sniffed, 'reminded me of a
fashion our lower tradesmen had in London about fifteen or eighteen
years ago'. Yet for Mozart, Prague shone – even if 'the stage personnel
here are not as smart as those in Vienna' and would fail to get his opera up
on time.

Earlier that summer, Da Ponte – scratching away with his quill, wine
to his right, snuff to his left, eyes wandering towards his hand-bell, the
spirit of his absent friend Casanova stalking his tiny room on the Graben
– had lighted on the old story of Don Juan. The original Spanish tale of a
lascivious aristocrat who meets his doom dated back 150 years to Tirso de
Molina's *El burlador de Sevilla*, and had appeared in a variety of versions,
including at least four operas, countless puppet shows, plays by Molière
and Goldoni, and a ballet by Gluck. Over the years, the tale had become

in most instances little more than an excuse for a bawdy pantomime
romp with a flash of hellfire, a crackle of devils and clever stage
machinery – all with tremendous popular appeal. In 1787, there was
a resurgence of interest in the Don Juan story around Italy. Goethe noted
that an operatic version in Rome:

> . . . was played every night for four weeks, which excited the city so
> much that the lowliest grocers' families were to be found in the stalls
> and boxes with their children and other relations, and no one could
> bear to live without having fried Don Juan in Hell, or seen the
> Commendatore, as a blessed spirit, ascend to heaven.

Cognoscenti regarded this public zest for Don Juan as displaying un-
enlightened irrationality and a base predilection for the obscene. Goldoni
had undertaken the task of adapting 'this bad Spanish play' only
reluctantly, stating: 'I have always regarded it, in Italy, with horror,
and I have never been able to understand how this farce could hold its
own for such a long time, could draw crowds, and could be the delight of
a cultivated nation.' Italian actors, he continues, joked that the original
author must have made a pact with the Devil to gather such support.
Goldoni writes that he tackles the subject himself 'in order to fulfil the
contract with the devil a little more fittingly', and his changes are a model
of eighteenth-century rationalism – he does away with walking, talking
statues of the Commendatore, and ends with Don Juan being struck by
lightning rather than dragged down to hell, as this could equally be
explained as the wrath of God, or a natural phenomenon.

None of this disdain for Don Juan appears to have put Da Ponte off.
Luckily for the time-pressed poet, a new operatic version of the tale had
surfaced at that year's Venice Carnival, with music by Giuseppe Gazzaniga and libretto by Giovanni Bertati. In days innocent of copyright laws,
that made it ripe for the plucking. Both composer and librettist were
familiar to Da Ponte. His own opera for Gazzaniga, *Il finto cieco*, had sunk
without trace the year before, but Bertati was author of *La villanella rapita*,
one of the first operas at the Burgtheater to point the way to the
possibility of giving opera buffa a more serious remit.

Bertati, in his *Don Giovanni Tenorio, o sia Il convitato di pietra* (Don Giovanni, or The Stone Guest), had evidently been cautious about using the coarse tale, setting it as an opera within an opera. In the first part of what is in effect a double bill, the impresario of a collapsing Italian troupe touring in Germany decides to revive company fortunes by staging Don Juan as a last resort (a scenario not unlike the real-life one in Prague, as Pasquale Bondini's ailing company eagerly awaited the new Mozart opera to give it a financial boost). The piece is described as '*una bella e stupenda porcheria* [a marvellous bit of filth]' just right for wooing provincial audiences. Several of the cast in this imaginary company immediately develop sore throats (again, a tactic not unfamiliar to Da Ponte), but are finally cajoled into singing. The second part of the double bill is presented as the company's rehearsal of the opera itself.

If it were not for the ready availability of the Bertati libretto to speed up the writing process, Da Ponte might never have considered the Don Juan myth as suitable subject matter for an opera – almost certainly not for the sophisticated patrons of the Burgtheater. But time was short, and the Prague audience was a different matter. (Mozart, for one, does not appear to have expected the opera to transfer to Vienna.) By comparison with the beau monde that sparkled in the Burgtheater's boxes, a large element of the Prague opera public were ordinary burghers, or from the provinces. While musically appreciative, they were open to more boisterous entertainment than the fettered tastes of aristocrats encouraged in Vienna – and they were also no doubt enjoyably familiar with earlier versions of the Don Juan story. What was more, Pasquale Bondini wanted another *Figaro*, and Don Juan fitted comfortably in a buffo tradition. Mozart's own sense of humour was at times earthy: he wrote some notoriously scatological letters; his brother-in-law Joseph Lange accused him of frivolity, outbursts of vulgar platitudes and 'jests of a nature one did not expect of him'; Caroline Pichler, daughter of a Privy Counsellor at whose house Mozart played, remembered his 'everyday turn of mind' and 'insipid jokes'. In 1783 he had himself appeared in a romping pantomime, written especially for him, at a ball in the Redoutensälen, and there is every likelihood that he delighted in the idea of an opera full of rough-and-tumble and stage trickery. Da Ponte records that when he suggested *Don Giovanni* to Mozart, 'it was a subject that pleased him mightily'.

In Da Ponte's version of the tale, *Il dissoluto punito, o sia Il Don Giovanni* (The Rake Punished, or Don Giovanni), the amorous Don, in making his escape from Donna Anna, a woman he has attempted to seduce, kills her father the Commendatore. When, together with her betrothed Don Ottavio, she discovers the body, Donna Anna swears vengeance. Don Giovanni meanwhile shrugs off the admonitions of Donna Elvira, whom he had once gulled into a pretend marriage, and pursues Zerlina, the peasant bride of Masetto. As ever, he entangles his manservant Leporello in his schemes. The peasant couple are invited into a masked ball at Don Giovanni's estate. The Don continues his pursuit, but is unmasked and exposed, and his victims tell him vengeance is nigh. A series of buffo-style disguises and confusions of identity follow, culminating in a graveyard where there is a statue of the dead Commendatore, whom Don Giovanni mockingly invites to supper. That night when Don Giovanni is at table, the stone guest appears at the door, invites him to repent and, when he refuses, offers a return invitation to dine. Don Giovanni accepts, takes the Commendatore's hand and is removed screaming down to Hell, as an invisible chorus of devils warns of the torments that await him. Leporello describes these events to the others, who turn to the future: Don Ottavio to renew his suit to Donna Anna, Donna Elvira to life in a convent, Masetto and Zerlina to a cosy dinner with friends, and Leporello himself to a tavern to find a better master. They all join together in a resounding damnation of the sinner.

As with *L'arbore di Diana*, it was Gozzi's magic rather than Goldoni's rationalism that held the guiding lamp for Da Ponte. Unlike Goldoni, Da Ponte retained walking, talking statues and the fires of Hell, yet like Goldoni he appears to take a severe moral stance, subtitling the work 'The Rake Punished' rather than a more neutral 'The Stone Guest' (as Bertati had done), and ending with the full ensemble singing the lines:

Questo è il fin di chi fa mal!
E de' perfidi la morte
Alla vita è sempre ugual!

[This is the fate of all who do wrong!
Evildoers always come
to an equally evil end.]

An aspect of this condemnation is the punishment (as in *Figaro*) not merely of a sinner but of a nobleman who abuses his power. Da Ponte appears to have been more consciously engaged in politics than Mozart (who like Jane Austen barely mentions major current events), but the spirit that had informed *Figaro* was once again behind *Don Giovanni*, emerging most pointedly at such moments as Leporello's opening aria, in which he speaks scathingly of the contrast between his lot and his master's easy life, and bursts out repeatedly, '*Voglio far il gentiluomo / E non voglio più servir* [I'd like to live the life of a gentleman / And no longer have to serve]'; and even more so, when Don Giovanni welcomes the peasant couple to his ball with a possibly ironic '*È aperto a tutti quanti / Viva la libertà!* [It is open to all / Long live freedom!]' In Mozart's hands this '*Viva la libertà!*' is snatched from Giovanni's mouth by the crowd, and to the accompaniment of drums and fanfares of trumpets becomes a stirring triumphal march that soars from the context of the opera to settle as shivers down the spine.

Bertati's instinct for a buffo plot that offered possibilities of a more serious – and socially critical – tone was already evident in *La villanella rapita*, and he displayed it again in his *Don Giovanni Tenorio*. It is a quality Da Ponte picked up on. Da Ponte followed Bertati's libretto closely, though he dispensed with its pussyfooting structure, ignoring the fictitious touring troupe and expanding the second part into a full two-act opera. This is one reason for long buffo games of disguise and confusion at the beginning of Act II, stock scenes – perhaps the result of Da Ponte's haste – which some said caused a lull in the opera's momentum. At the same time, because there were fewer singers in the Prague company than had been available to Bertati in Venice, Da Ponte had to reduce the

number of characters. As he did this, he deftly pithed out the roles of the
pairs of lovers (Don Ottavio and Donna Anna, Zerlina and Masetto),
broadening the canvas so that the opera encompassed more of the world
around Don Giovanni. All this was no doubt done with a spirited
exchange between composer and librettist, the same modus operandi
that had been so successful for *Figaro*. Mozart had long expressed a desire
to give female roles a subtler, deeper turn. The Countess in *Figaro* is a
product of how Da Ponte responded to this, of how together – one
providing skeleton, the other flesh – they had created a full character. In
Bertati's *Don Giovanni*, Donna Anna retires to a convent in the first scene,
leaving Don Ottavio to exact vengeance on her behalf. In Mozart and Da
Ponte's opera she stays the course, becoming Don Giovanni's most
tenacious adversary, a richer character than in Bertati, and one who
throws a more revealing light on the Don himself.

Though strictures of time forced Da Ponte into a close rendition of the
Bertati original, he managed to produce some of his most lyrical poetry
for the opera – verses, like the psalms he had written in Dresden, that sing
of themselves. It must have been a delight for Mozart to write a duet for
words so tender, beguiling and precise as:

DON GIOVANNI: *Là ci darem la mano,*
                Là mi dirai di sì;
                Vedi, non è lontano,
                Partiam, ben mio, da qui.

ZERLINA: *Vorrei, e non vorrei,*
                Mi trema un poco il cor;
                Felice, è ver, sarei,
                Ma può burlarmi ancor.

[DON GIOVANNI: There we'll take each other's hand,
                and you will tell me 'Yes'.
                See, it is not far:
                So, let's go, my dear.

ZERLINA: I'd like to, and also not;
              my heart is fluttering a little.
              I know I would be happy;
              but perhaps he's just making fun of me.]

A comparison of the two librettists' versions of Leporello's famous
'Catalogue Song' reveals just how transforming Da Ponte's touch could
be. In Bertati's version:

> Dell'Italia, ed Allemagna
> Ve ne ho scritto cento, e tante.
> Della Francia, e della Spagna
> Ve ne sono non sò quante . . .

> [From Italy and Germany
> I have listed a hundred or more.
> From France and Spain
> I don't know how many.]

And Da Ponte:

> In Italia sei cento e quaranta,
> In Lamagna due cento e trent'una.
> Cento in Francia, in Turchia novant'una,
> Ma in Ispagna son già mille e trè.

> [In Italy six hundred and forty,
> In Germany, two hundred and thirty-one.
> A hundred in France, in Turkey ninety-one,
> But in Spain already a thousand and three.]

Rape, murder and eternal damnation may seem tough meat for an opera
buffa, and indeed later in life Da Ponte would maintain that Mozart
originally wanted to cast the work as an *opera seria*, and had to be
dissuaded. Whatever the truth of this claim, it is clear the Don Juan stage

tradition had long been a comic one, and the two highly competent stagecraftsmen knew full well that their paymaster Bondini wanted a rousing, comic follow-on to *Figaro*. The surprise came in the way that in their hands comedy and tragedy proved such compatible bedfellows, as they often do in Shakespeare (whose works both men knew). The changes of mood, strands of seriousness, and profundity of characterization evident in their 'new kind of spectacle', *Figaro*, became in *Don Giovanni* even more complexly intertwined with humour, some of it quite knockabout (though in Da Ponte's version centred almost entirely on Leporello). Different emotions vie for dominance; contrasting perspectives demand attention. As with life, Mozart and Da Ponte's opera favours variety over uniformity. They had taken a step beyond *Figaro* into new territory, though neither had a word for what they had created. Da Ponte labelled his *Don Giovanni* a *dramma giocoso* (literally a playful or jesting drama), but other poets had used the term before to describe works largely comic. Mozart, in his thematic catalogue, settled simply for opera buffa.

Da Ponte's voluptuous young muse would appear to have fired his imagination. The priapic presence in his libretti swells from *Figaro*, through *L'arbore di Diana*, to reach full tumescence in *Don Giovanni*. In measures of lust and ruthlessness, Cherubino and Count Almaviva seem pale prototypes of the degenerate Don – but Don Giovanni emerges from their opera as an elusive, ambivalent character, one (like Hamlet) open to all manner of turns in meaning, shades of interpretation; one who snaps whatever cords bind him to a single story and transcends the bounds of plot to become a figure in the human psyche. Is he mere philanderer, or demonic force of sensual energy? He may be *il dissoluto punito*, yet there is something heroic in his continued defiance as he is dragged down to Hell, an alluring animal vitality akin to that found in such complex villains as Shakespeare's Richard III. He has all the elements of a Romantic hero, and it is no wonder that in cities where *Sturm und Drang* and Romanticism were already making an impact, the opera was soon being performed without the moralizing final sestet, but ending on Don Giovanni's descent to Hell. Don Giovanni dominates the opera. Even when he is not on stage his presence lingers like a sharp aftertaste, yet he does not (apart from the brief, energetic '*Fin ch'han dal vino*') even really have his own aria. Instead, like Shakespeare's Richard, he can 'add colours to the chameleon / Change shapes with Proteus' – when seducing Donna Anna, his music reflects her own; then he adopts the Commendatore's more dignified line, woos Zerlina to her own peasant rhythms, and counters Leporello's request to leave his service with similar buffo terseness. He is no one and he is everyone.

As soon as *L'arbore di Diana* had opened, Da Ponte followed Mozart to Prague, arriving on 8 October. *Don Giovanni* was scheduled to premiere on 14 October in a gala performance which, like *L'arbore di Diana* in Vienna, was to celebrate the visit of the Archduchess Maria Theresa on her wedding tour. On arrival Lorenzo discovered (as Mozart had done a few days earlier) the Prague company to be in a state of disarray. *Don Giovanni* with its gaping gates of Hell, leaping flames and walking statue challenged the stage personnel beyond their resources. Not only were they 'not as smart as those in Vienna when it comes to mastering an opera of this kind in a very short time', but, Mozart wrote to his friend Baron Jacquin, 'I found on my arrival that so few preparations and arrangements had been made that it would have been absolutely impossible to have produced [the opera] on the 14th.' *Don Giovanni* was postponed until 24 October, and *Figaro* staged in its place for the Archduchess – it was this performance that the 'high and mighty' lady of Prague protested so crowingly against (quite what she would have made of *Don Giovanni* as a wedding opera must be left to the imagination).

Bondini had put the Mozarts up at '*Zu den drei Löwen*' (The Three Lions Inn). Da Ponte lodged in a room at the rear of the adjoining *Platteis* hostelry – composer and librettist could speak to each other through their windows. Comfortable though the *Drei Löwen* was, Mozart spent as much time as he could at Villa Bertramka, the country seat of his musical friends the Duscheks, where he could indulge his delight in billiards, English punch, dancing, and fine ladies (the latter not quite as stylish as Hester Piozzi might have liked, but still the cream of Prague's fashionable intelligentsia). Da Ponte was invited, too, and the aging Casanova on a visit from nearby Dux had a chance to unfold his now rather old-fashioned charm, and buff up his antique flirtatious patter. Professor August Meissner, who held the chair of classical literature at Prague University, was a guest, both at a magnificent ball and an afternoon party at which, although winter was coming on, 'the sky shone clear and blue on the earth below and people lingered happily in the open air with the feeling that days like this were a rare blessing'. The composer and librettist of *Figaro*, in town for a new opera that was sure also to have resounding success, were the centre of attention. Meissner, recounting his reminiscences to his grandson Alfred, remembers Mozart, grown podgy with good living, as short with 'unusually thick hair in a big knot', chatting vivaciously, quite unaware of the stir he caused. 'He anticipated the day of the premiere as though it were a carnival. He paid extravagant court to the ladies, played all kinds of tricks, talked in rhyme, which gave him especial pleasure, and everyone let him do anything he wanted as if he were a child or very young man.' Da Ponte, the professor thought, was 'in his forties'. (Lorenzo was only thirty-eight – hard times, hard living and the nitric-acid mouthwash had no doubt aged him prematurely.) Nearly a decade in German-speaking lands had not improved his ability in the 'language that would frighten St Francis', and he lapsed frequently into Italian. 'People called him Abbé,' Meissner recalled, but was doubtful of the verity of the title. Slender, with 'quicksilver movements and dark, fiery southern eyes', the poet 'seemed to be paying court collectively to the singers who were there' and, unlike Mozart, 'seemed always to be watching what impression he was making'. The abbé's friend Casanova, despite his sixty-odd years, was 'of Herculean build and vigorous stance . . . [He] and Da Ponte had much in common. Both of them had lived in Venice when they were young, both had travelled the world restlessly, in both there was an unmistakable vein of vanity. They both boasted of the honours that had been heaped upon them, and took pleasure in talking about the potentates with whom they had had dealings.' Da Ponte had the edge in that he could brag of present favours, whilst Casanova's royal patrons had all dropped him. What was more, 'The ladies, every one of whom had ambitions to leave Prague for the first theatre of the German empire, lavished their especial favours on Da Ponte, as the "poet of the theatre" in Vienna.' When Casanova heard Da Ponte speak of 'my uncle the Bishop', he could not resist a wicked side-thrust, letting slip the odd word about the poet's Jewish origins, and his true relation to the late Bishop Da Ponte. The bishop's namesake countered with the remark that his good friend was no true bird of court, but 'an adventurer who has spent his days playing cards, brewing elixirs and fortune-telling' and revealing that he had performed his elevation to Chevalier de Seingalt himself.

Life was not simply sweetmeats and soirées. There was a complicated opera to stage. Time was short, even with the postponement of the opening night – and if the stagehands were dim, the singers were unco-operative. They refused to rehearse on opera days, and Bondini, who according to Mozart was 'in a perpetual state of anxiety', was running his company on skeleton lines, and could not afford to upset or lose a single person. When one of the singers fell ill (shades of Bertati's fictional troupe), the opera had again to be postponed, this time to 29 October.

Don Giovanni had been specifically written with the Prague company in mind, and its structure and casting reflected the roles they had played in *Figaro*. The prima donna was Bondini's wife Caterina – darling of the Prague public and as good an actress as she was a singer. She had been a delightful Susanna in *Figaro*. At her benefit performance, poems in her praise thrown from the gallery 'positively rained' down on the stage. The correspondent from the *Prager Oberpostamtszeitung* caught one and published it a few days later:

> Bondini sings
> And pleasure brings
> To th' melancholy heart;
> Sorrows at least depart
> The while Bondini sings,
> The while her roguish art
> Its vocal changes rings.

As with most opera companies of the time, a strict pecking order operated when it came to distribution of roles among female singers.

Caterina was to sing Zerlina – an indication that Da Ponte and Mozart considered this, rather than Donna Anna, the leading female role (and, indeed, that Susanna had the edge over the Countess in *Figaro*). Donna Anna was given to Teresa Saporiti, famed for her vocal artistry and beauty, who would go on to a triumphant career in Italy, and died in Milan at the age of 106. Felice Ponziani, who had played Figaro, was taking the part of Leporello; the tenor Antonio Baglioni, highly praised for the purity and expressiveness of his voice, was to be Don Ottavio (a part, coincidently, he had played in the Gazzaniga/Bertati *Don Giovanni* in Venice).

For their first Don Giovanni, Mozart and Da Ponte had a godsend: the dashing and talented 22-year-old, Luigi Bassi – a 'most beautiful but utterly stupid fellow', alas, but possessed of a voice that (according to the 1792 Bondini Company register) was as mellifluous as his acting was masterly. He was the perfect Don Giovanni, and ideal for the complex mix of tragedy and comedy that Mozart and Da Ponte had produced. A Prague report from the 1790s reveals his prowess:

> [His voice] range is between tenor and bass, and although its sound is somewhat bright, it is always flexible, full and agreeable. Bassi is also a very skilful actor, who handles tragedy without being absurd, and comedy without lapse of taste . . . He never spoils a part and is the only real actor in the present Italian company.

Bassi was not a man to be thrown off balance by a role that demanded subtle acting skills, though he did complain bitterly at the lack of a real aria. Although Mozart did not allow singers to interfere in ensembles, recitatives and arias were often tailored during rehearsal (which was why Da Ponte had come to Prague), but in this case the composer appears to have remained adamant.

The orchestra in Prague was a good one – the trombones in particular were given a moment of glory as instruments of retribution, introducing real terror to the music as the Commendatore comes to condemn Don Giovanni. Music appears as part of the onstage action in Mozart's musical jokes for the supper scene at the end of Act II, when Don Giovanni dines to the sounds first of a tune from *Una cosa rara* (the opera that had so upstaged Mozart's efforts the previous year), then a popular aria from Sarti's *Due litiganti*, and finally, with a nod to his beloved Prague audience, Wolfgang's own '*Non più andrai*' from *Figaro* – as Leporello comments, 'Now that is a tune I know only too well.' But Mozart's ultimate compliment to the musicians' ability came in the ball scene, when three bands play for the dancers, entering one after the other until all three are playing simultaneously, in different time signatures, in an extraordinarily complicated contrapuntal arrangement – first an aristocratic minuet for Anna and Ottavio, then a middle-class contredanse for Zerlina and Don Giovanni, and the third band (after tuning up) letting fly with a heel-kicking peasant dance as Leporello whisks a protesting Masetto from the scene. As Don Giovanni dances with the peasant Zerlina, Donna Anna expresses her disgust, realizing that to the lecher she is no different from a servant. She is told by Don Ottavio to pull herself together and play the part ('*Simulate . . . Fingete, per pieta*'). In a real-life correlate of such an occasion some years before, the advice might well have been given to Joseph II. In December 1781 the Emperor had thrown open the doors of the Schönbrunn Palace for a public ball. Over 3,000 people attended, including '*friseurs* and housemaids' (sniffed the *arriviste* Mozart). Enthusiastic revellers 'pushed themselves so roughly' into a contredanse that they jostled the Emperor, forcing a grand duchess from his arm. Joseph 'began to stamp furiously, cursed like a lazzarone, pushed back the crowd of people and dealt blows right and left', refusing help from his Hussars. 'All I can say is that it serves him right,' Wolfgang wrote to his father. 'For what else can you expect from a mob?' Egalitarianism went just so far. Mozart, like his sovereign, was no revolutionary.

Prague awaited *Don Giovanni* eagerly, and as news of two postponements spread, gossip about goings-on in rehearsals was rife. No sooner had Luigi Bassi been calmed down about his dearth of arias than he began to complain about the duet '*Là ci darem la mano*'; it was said that Mozart had to produce five versions before he was satisfied. La Bondini refused – was 'unable' – to utter the scream required of Zerlina in the first finale. After several vain attempts, Mozart came to stand quietly beside her on stage as the passage was yet again repeated, and at the vital moment grabbed her unexpectedly and with such force that she shrieked in terror. 'That is the way!' he said. The situation became even more fraught when, after only eight days in Prague, Da Ponte received a 'fiery letter' from Salieri saying that the Emperor had ordered him home as work on *Axur* had to be completed at once, in time for the nuptials of Joseph's nephew and designated heir the Archduke Franz. It would appear that Da Ponte's old friend Casanova stepped into the breach, coming to Prague from nearby Dux as if winched in on Cupid's radiant cloud, to help with final adjustments. A version, in Casanova's hand, of Leporello's escape from Donna Elvira in Act II was found among his Dux papers many years after his death. Casanova was working on his memoirs, and must have found an odd resonance between Leporello and his own rascally servant Costa, between the catalogue aria and the conquests he himself was listing. *Don Giovanni* and Casanova's reminiscences mark the turn of the tide, as an age of erotic flamboyance gave way to more prudish times. As a grey-haired Casanova watched the opera (and he surely did), he may well have caught a glimpse of a future in which his name would become synonymous with that of the rakish Don.

Don Giovanni opened on 29 October, just the flicker of a footlight away from yet another postponement, as Mozart worked frantically to the very last moment, finishing his dramatic overture with its audience-quelling opening chords the night before the final rehearsal, so that the orchestra had to play almost sight unseen from uncorrected parts. Nevertheless, the reception was rapturous. The *Prager Oberpostamtszeitung* for 3 November reported that 'Herr Mozard [*sic*] conducted in person; when he entered the orchestra he was received with threefold cheers, which again happened when he left it.' The opera was, the newspaper admitted, 'extremely difficult to perform', but singers and musicians 'strained every nerve to thank Mozart by rewarding him with a good performance'. Herr Mozard, according to the *Provincialnachrichten*, 'was welcomed joyously and jubilantly by the numerous gathering'. The little man himself, who had been so terrified before the performance that the leader of the orchestra Johann Kucharz had to calm him down and speak some courage back into him, wrote in relief to his friend Baron

Jacquin of the 'loudest applause' the opera had been given. Special copies of Da Ponte's libretto bound in gold paper were sold at the theatre for twice the normal price, and audiences swelled far beyond their usual numbers. Mozart wrote to his librettist in Vienna saying that Domenico Guardasoni, Bondini's second in command, had burst in on him after the performance with: '*Evviva* Da Ponte, *evviva* Mozart! Every impresario, every virtuoso must bless them. As long as they live it shall never be known what theatrical destitution means.' The words were to gather bitter irony for both composer and librettist.

Chapter Ten

EMPEROR JOSEPH II believed he was 'the unhappiest mortal alive'. Malaria racked his frame, cysts and suppurating sores tormented him, his diseased lungs so pained him he could hardly breathe, and he was plagued by piles. Worst, he was bitter to the soul. Twice a week he sent desperate missives across the Alps to his brother Leopold in Tuscany. 'I am unfortunate in everything I undertake,' he wrote, 'the appalling ingratitude with which my arrangements are received and I am treated – for there is now no conceivable insolence or curse that people do not allow themselves to utter about me publicly – all this makes me doubt myself, I no longer dare have an opinion and put it into effect . . .' For years as co-ruler with his forceful mother he had restrained his reforming impulses. The incense of her funeral mass had barely wafted away before he let his pent-up radicalism loose upon his domain. But his domain had not at all reacted in the way he had expected. Now, just a few years on, a sense of failure shrouded his early fervour; a dull blade of resentment hacked at his affection for subjects who seemed truculent and resistant where they should have been grateful. The outlook was gloomy on a broader front, too: his two attempts to invade Bavaria had been unsuccessful; the Low Countries threatened revolt against his policies; and his alliance with Russia was drawing Austria inevitably into war with the Turks. The initial flourish of patriotism this conflict excited was soon crushed by drawn-out and dispiriting campaigns, draining recruitment drives, and a war tax. The talk in the coffee-houses (which of course reached the royal ear) was of a pamphlet entitled *Warum wird Kaiser Joseph von seinem Volk nicht geliebt?* (Why is Emperor Joseph not loved by his people?)

One of the reasons that the people had lost affection for their monarch was that in his absolutist zeal for reform he had trodden over peasants and feudal lords alike. Edicts such as the one that restricted rural wedding feasts (real-life versions of the jolly celebration at the heart of *Figaro*) to just one day, when in peasant society they would have gone on until few were left standing, may have been seen by Joseph as a boon for rationalism and productivity, but were viewed by his bewildered subjects as arbitrary, puritanical and severe. 'The best among people would wish that the Emperor may be more patient with the lesser faults of men and with their weaknesses,' the hurtful pamphlet had proclaimed. The upright burghers of Vienna, on the other hand, found that together with the easygoing tolerance of Joseph's regime went uncertainty and moral laxity. Some even began to hanker after Maria Theresa's rigorous, but clear, code. Mozart's song *Die Alte*, written in the early summer of 1787, gives wry expression to this mood as an old woman considers how everything was different and better '*zu meiner Zeit* [in my time]'. Foreigners, too, felt the nostalgia for everything being in its proper place. Looking back on the Empress's reign, Dr Charles Burney opined, 'Her piety has been thought to border on bigotry, but if we may judge of its effect by the tranquillity, happiness and affection of her people with their turbulence, discontent and detestation of her unprincipled, philosophical, and disorganizing successor, we suppose that too much religion is less mischievous in a sovereign than too little.' The old aristocracy had, of course, opposed Joseph from the start and those ministers antipathetic to his reforms were only too quick to take advantage of his flagging personal morale to propel their 'advice' into law.

By 1785, Joseph was beginning to give up the struggle. Gradually, as one hand continued to push forward reforms (particularly with his campaign against the nobility), the other tightened in unexpected repression, or reversed earlier edicts, which the Emperor now considered 'to undermine all religion, morality, and social order'. In 1787 Joseph abolished the death penalty, yet came up with horrific physical punishments in its place. He made prostitution (for which Vienna had become famous) a crime against the state, set up a secret police force, and stage by stage reintroduced censorship.

It was the reforming hand that made Lorenzo Da Ponte a gift of 100 ducats on his return to Vienna, seemingly (as had been the case with *L'arbore di Diana*) in acknowledgement of the support Da Ponte's libretto tendered to his sovereign's ideals. Mozart also received his reward. Early in December 1787, the Emperor instructed Count Rosenberg to engage him as chamber musician – a post previously held by Gluck, who had died in November – at an annual salary of 800 gulden. That was not nearly the amount Gluck had received, but the demands on Wolfgang's time were minimal, and the guaranteed income something he had longed for. The Mozarts moved back from the suburbs to the inner city.

Mozart had already heard talk in Prague that *Don Giovanni* might be given in Vienna. At the Emperor's behest, though to Rosenberg's apparent displeasure, Burgtheater performances of the opera were scheduled to begin in May. Before rehearsals had begun, Austria was drawn into the war against the Turks, and Joseph left Vienna for the field.

As *Don Giovanni* had been composed specifically for Bondini's Prague troupe, Mozart and Da Ponte had changes to make to tailor it for the company at the Burgtheater. Luisa Mombelli (née Laschi) had taken over as prima donna when Nancy Storace left, so she took the role of Zerlina (she had been the Countess in Figaro, but seniority rather than vocal suitability governed the casting). Da Ponte and Mozart wrote a flippant little duet for her and the popular comic buffo Benucci in which Zerlina catches Leporello, drags him by his hair and ties him to a chair, followed by a scene in which Leporello tricks the peasants into releasing him. Salieri's mistress Caterina Cavalieri, as Donna Elvira, demanded – and got – an extra aria ('*Mi tradì quell' alma ingrata*'), which she then refused to tackle in E flat as composed. Mozart had to concede to her singing it in D – but then he was used to her foibles; when he wrote Constanze for her in *Die Entführung* he had had to 'sacrifice an aria a little to her flexible throat'. Her new scene added little, and was if anything harmful to the plot. Michael Kelly having left the company along with Storace, and good tenors being difficult to find, Mozart wrote a new, easier, but extraordinarily beautiful aria for Don Ottavio, '*Dalla sua pace*'. The most radical change was the cutting of the final, affirmative sestet, so that the opera ended tragically, with Don Giovanni's descent into Hell, thus widening uncertainty about its meaning and opening the way to Romantic interpretations of his character.

The Emperor kept up a busy correspondence from the field with Count Rosenberg, following progress in rehearsals closely. Begrudgingly, Rosenberg had to admit that the music was exceptional, to which Joseph replied acidly, 'Your taste is beginning to become reasonable.' When the count reported that the cast were struggling with the demands the music made, he received the terse admission: 'Mozard's [*sic*] music is certainly too difficult for the singers.' It would be unsurprising, the Emperor remarked, if the opera were to fail; he knew the taste of the Viennese public.

Don Giovanni had its Vienna premiere on 7 May 1788. The Emperor's prediction proved correct. 'The opera did not please!' recalled Da Ponte. Count Zinzendorf's companion, Madame de la Lippe, found 'the music learned, little suited to the voice'. That word 'learned' was a kiss of death among the frivolous opera audience. People had gone to laugh, looking forward to a rolicking rendition of the Don Juan legend, and did not expect to be challenged intellectually. The *Wiener Zeitung* remained dryly silent, simply reporting that the opening had occurred. The Archduchess Elizabeth did not attend, but 'was told that it did not have much success'. At a party thrown after the premiere by one 'Prince R', later reported in the *Allgemeine Musikalische Zeitung*:

Most of the musical connoisseurs of Vienna were present, also Joseph Haydn. Mozart was not there. There was much talk about the new work. After the fine ladies and gentlemen had talked themselves out, some of the connoisseurs took up the work. They all admitted that it was the valuable work of a versatile genius and was of an endless imagination; but for one it was too full, for another too chaotic, for a third too unmelodic, for a fourth it was uneven, etc. In general one cannot but admit that there is something true in all these opinions. Everyone had spoken by now only – not Father Haydn. At last they

asked the modest artist for his opinion. He said, with his usual
fastidiousness: 'I cannot settle the argument. But one thing I know'
– he added very energetically – 'and that is that Mozart is the greatest
composer that the world now has.' The ladies and gentlemen were
silent after that.

Wolfgang was silent on the matter, too, though he is said to have
remarked that he had written his opera 'not for Vienna, a little for
Prague, but mostly for myself and my friends'. In June, the Mozarts
moved back to the suburbs.

The Emperor was still in the field for the premiere of *Don Giovanni*,
and although he was back in Vienna shortly before the final performance
on 15 December, he was ill that night and did not attend. He may,
though, have had parts of the opera performed for him privately, even
before he left, for Da Ponte relates that Joseph said to him, 'The opera is
divine; possibly, just possibly even more beautiful than *Figaro*. But such
music is not meat for the teeth of my Viennese!' When Da Ponte
repeated the remark to Mozart, the composer quietly replied, 'Give them
time to chew on it!' The public certainly had opportunity to do so. At
Mozart's suggestion and Da Ponte's instigation, *Don Giovanni* received
fifteen performances in 1788 – quite extraordinary for an opera that had
been given a lukewarm reception. Da Ponte writes that 'at each
performance the applause grew, and little by little even Vienna of the
rotten teeth came to savour its taste and appreciate its beauties' – but the
opera was not staged in Vienna again in Mozart's lifetime, though it was
widely performed in cities in the German-speaking world over the next
few years.

Da Ponte, buoyed by fame and favour, collected the pick of his life's
poetry into two volumes, which he published under the title *Saggi Poetici*.
Vienna's literary world did not take to his poems with quite the fervour
he had hoped. But soon the theatre poet had his attention distracted by
other affairs entirely. At the beginning of August, Johann Thorwart,
vice-director of the Burgtheater, 'mortal foe to the Italians' and lynchpin
of the German cabal, walked in on a rehearsal for Cimarosa's *Il fanatico
burlato* bearing a letter from the Emperor, and ('in great glee', Da Ponte

thought) announced that the Italian opera company would be disbanded at the end of the season.

'Three buffo singers,' Joseph had once wistfully written to Count Rosenberg, 'cost as much as 100 grenadiers, and the grenadiers give better service.' War with the Turks was proving a drain on Austria's coffers, and the Emperor was having to economize. Joseph had already closed the old Kärntnertortheater and suspended the *Singspiel* company, then in February 1788 had given Count Rosenberg control of the Hofkapelle in addition to the Burgtheater, in order to consolidate numbers of musicians in court. The costly Italian opera company was the next in line. An 80,000-gulden deficit, run up during a shaky start to the 1788–89 season, did not help matters, nor did the demands of some of the leading singers for higher fees. The flint that set spark to the Emperor's decision was the behaviour of the soprano Celeste Coltellini. La Coltellini swooped upon the company in April 1788, expensive, belligerent, and late. She cost the theatre a considerable sum by causing a postponement of the season's opening premiere. On an earlier engage-ment with the Burgtheater, in the 1785–86 season, she had been favourite (if not mistress) to Casti, Count Rosenberg and possibly the Emperor himself. Now she presumed upon her privileged status, clashed with Salieri, fought with Rosenberg, and fired off raging letters directly to Joseph in the field. He responded by shortening her term of contract (eliciting more fiery letters); then, in a billet to Rosenberg on 29 July, the Emperor declared that the current season would be the company's last.

Thorwart's announcement, as he callously interrupted rehearsals just a few days before a premiere, shuddered through the theatre. Everyone felt the jolt, from lamp-trimmers and the men trundling painted scenery across the stage to seamstresses and the box-keepers who stood guard on loges and sold libretti; all the way to the musicians, singers and the theatre poet himself. Opera, perhaps more than any other activity of the time, brought people of different ranks together to work towards a common end. Now all their livelihoods were in some measure under threat, though the stage staff might be able to find some employment with the German drama. For Da Ponte, the shock reached even further, as it rocked the very foundation of the new life he had created for himself. '[M]y hope [is] scattered to the wind in that moment that I was to gather its fruits,' he wrote in a verse letter to his father Gaspare soon afterwards. 'I am losing my work, my title . . . and to crown it all my monthly stipend.'

Da Ponte's loss of income had clear implications for his father and 'nostra Famigliuola' (our Little Family), as he had been making remittances home not just to Gaspare and his brood of ten but also to his eldest half-brother Agostino's family. With a piety that is hardly justified by his own past record, Lorenzo chided Agostino in the letter, hoping that he would 'place aside the lies, the loves, the cards, to at least think about feeding the three children he has brought into this world'. Another of his half-brothers, Paolo (for whom he had a special affection), appears to have been in Vienna at the time, enjoying his protection while studying music. All would feel the impact of the closure of the opera company.

Da Ponte had a dream to uphold, status to maintain, and an extended family to support. He also had a mistress to impress. It appears that Lorenzo had leapt headlong into an affair with Adriana Del Bene, called La Ferrarese after her home town. She had recently arrived Vienna for the revival of L'arbore di Diana. By Lorenzo's own admission Adriana was a woman 'of somewhat violent disposition', every scratch, spit and tantrum the equal of Angela Tiepolo, the fiery fury who had first captured his heart back in Venice. The phrase that is reiterated through-out his opera, 'Quanto è possente amor! [How powerful is love!]' was once again showing itself to be true. This spitfire Diana had admittedly 'no great merits of beauty', nor had she the 'most graceful of figures' (the Emperor, who had seen her before, also remarked in a billet to Rosenberg on her 'laide figure', her ugly figure). She was not even a very good actress – but Lorenzo thought she had the most beautiful eyes, the most charming lips, and he was delighted by her voice. She became the third great passion of his life, after Angela and then Anzoletta in Venice, and he was determined to protect her position. Lorenzo Da Ponte was an old hand at battling adversity. He would not be defeated by any diktat borne by a smirking Thorwart. The optimism and blind enthusiasm that had carried him through earlier trials was intact. 'A triumphant faith within my soul [he wrote to his father] always tells me, "Do not fear, you will be happy".' His heart 'rejoice[d]', and he believed that the moment was not far away when he would once again have purses of gold. Even before the Emperor returned from the field, the theatre poet had set to work.

Da Ponte's scheme was imaginative and revolutionary. Only in London had anything like it been tried before. He would take the opera company off the Emperor's hands entirely. It would run without subsidy, funded by expensive subscriptions to the boxes – a uniform 500 gulden per loge, which would raise 100,000 gulden annually, doubling previous income from that source. He also planned subscriptions for different packages of single tickets. A box at the Burgtheater was a social necessity, as Joseph barely maintained a court and the theatre was Vienna's main forum for display of rank and riches. Diplomats in particular saw a box at the opera as an essential setting for representing their countries. Lorenzo would have no problem in selling his subscriptions.

The old Da Ponte charm came back into play. He had a word with the leading singers. Although most of them would be able to find work elsewhere, it would be hard to match the prestige of the Vienna company. A snip here, a modest shrink in salary there, a little cost-cutting elsewhere, and he was able to come up with a proposal that reduced expenditure by one third. The prominent banker Jakob von Gontard agreed to take control of the finances; Da Ponte would take on day-to-day running of the theatre in addition to his role as theatre poet. Making use of the terms of Joseph's *Schauspielfreiheit* of many years before (by which the Emperor had opened the Kärntnertortheater to all comers), all Da Ponte requested was that the Italian company be given the Burgtheater rent-free. All further concerns about the running of the company would be lifted from the Emperor's shoulders. Opera would take one more step away from court into the public domain.

As soon as Joseph returned from the field, Da Ponte requested an audience. He already had a full subscription list. While he was speaking to the Emperor, lamenting the demise of the Italian company and the numbers of families that would affect, he drew from his coat a large sheet

of *carta reale* (the most expensive sort of paper), meticulously folded.
Joseph noted this and asked him what it was. Da Ponte said it was a brief
memorial to the opera. The Emperor was wary:

> 'Brief?'
> 'Very brief.'
> 'On such a huge sheet of *carta reale*?'
> He unfolded the document with a rather long face, but on all that
> spread of white, there were but two lines, by Casti:
>> *Proposizioni ognuno far le può*
>> *Il punto sta nell' accettarle o no.*
> [Anyone can make proposals
> The point is whether they are accepted or not.]
> He could not hold back a laugh, and asked what proposal I had to
> make.

Da Ponte then unfolded his plan, producing two further sheets of paper,
this time showing his expenditure cuts and full subscription list. Joseph
was impressed. 'Well,' he said finally, 'go to Rosenberg and tell him that
I give you the use of the theatre.' Da Ponte was elated – even the director
of spectacles showed 'great jubilation' – but Thorwart came in with a
clatter of petty objections: the stock wardrobe and scenery were
insufficient without further royal patronage; Italian singers and German
actors would fight (as if they did not already); it was all too uncertain and
confusing. Soon Thorwart had Rosenberg chiming in with his, 'It
cannot be done, it cannot be done.' Undaunted, the prospect of poverty
and the scorn of La Ferrarese driving him on, Da Ponte ran back around
the corner to the palace, before the Emperor, too, might change his
mind. Breathless, before his sovereign had even the chance to speak, Da
Ponte burst out:

> 'Sire, Thorwart says, and the Count echoes him, that it cannot be
> done!'
> 'Give me your plan,' said he.
> I handed it to him, and he wrote at the foot of it:

My dear Count,

Tell Thorwart that it can be done. I am keeping on the theatre according to the plan of Da Ponte, whose salary you will please double.

Joseph

Back I went to the Count's office. He received me with greatest joy, and could not refrain from crying:

'Bravo, bravo! Hurrah for our Da Ponte!'

For a while, Lorenzo rose high in the esteem of the city. Grateful members of the opera flocked to his house. Count Zinzendorf records in his diary for 15 January 1789 that on a visit to Count Rosenberg's, he discovered the count and the Abbé Da Ponte discussing this new project of subscriptions, and that all the ambassadors in Vienna wanted a box. Word spread rapidly through the coffee-houses, and the press soon took up the story. On 24 January the *Rapport von Wien* enthused: 'At last the business with the opera buffa is decided! We have pleasure in giving all the friends of the Italian theatre the delightful news that this temple of comedy – will not be profaned!'

Da Ponte was not alone as he discussed subscriptions with Count Rosenberg. 'La Ferrarese was there,' Zinzendorf noted dryly. 'She was wearing a pelisse. You couldn't see her figure, and she didn't look too bad.' La Ferrarese may have been no beauty, but she could sing. She had trained under Antonio Sacchini at the Ospedale dei Mendicanti in Venice, where – in 1770 when she was just sixteen – Charles Burney was impressed by her range:

The performers [at the Mendicanti] are all orphan girls; one of them, *La Ferrarese*, sung very well, and had a very extraordinary compass of voice, as she was able to reach the highest E of our harpsichords, upon which she could dwell a considerable time, in a fair, natural voice.

Thirteen years later, Casanova gossiped in a letter to Count von Smecchia: 'The son of the Roman Consul in Venice has fled with

two young women from the Ospidale dei Mendicanti, Adriana La
Ferrarese and Bianchi Sacchetti. The father has had them followed
. . .' Consul del Bene was not quick enough. His son Luigi married
Adriana, and followed her through London and Milan to Trieste and
Vienna, as her career blossomed. As Diana, La Ferrarese had taken
Vienna by storm. Rosenberg thought her singing 'ravishing', and the
newspapers, like Burney, were astonished at her range. The *Rapport von
Wien* raved: 'In addition to an unbelievable high note, she has a striking
low, and connoisseurs of music claim that such a voice has not been
heard within the walls of Vienna in living memory.' *Wiener Neueste
Nachrichten* was even more enthusiastic, stating that a visit to *L'arbore di
Diana* was to 'see, hear and marvel'.

La Ferrarese relished her fame and nurtured her new paramour. Her
husband Luigi del Bene knew his place. He was apparently aware of Da
Ponte's attentions to his wife, but compliant. Da Ponte, for his part,
began to insist that Adriana be given certain roles – an insistence that
carried quite some weight now that he had saved the opera from closure.
But rivalry at the Burgtheater remained vicious. La Ferrarese may have
been good, but there were other sopranos in the company who (certainly
in their supporters' eyes) could match her. On the one hand was Salieri's
mistress Caterina Cavalieri, who despite her name was German and had a
strong following from that cabal; on the other was Dorotea Bussani (the
original Cherubino), who, Da Ponte snorted, 'though a vulgar woman of
little merit, had purely by means of pulling faces and silly clowning, and
perhaps by methods more theatrical still, built up a great following
among cooks, ostlers, waiters, lackeys and wig-makers . . . and in
consequence was thought a gem'. New factions bristled and, after the
halcyon moment when the entire company had been grateful to Da
Ponte, old enmities began to reassert themselves. The theatre poet's
championing of La Ferrarese further riled those who previously 'with
their teeth, and with canine boldness had joined together to tear into me,
to skin me, to devour me'. Lorenzo's capacity for scheming redoubled, as
the hatreds and suspicions that fuelled it intensified. Apt to self-drama-
tize, Da Ponte tended to magnify his enemies' malice, and then return it
tenfold. In his new position of importance, his conceit burgeoned. La

Ferrarese, by her lover's admission, was of a disposition 'rather calculated to irritate the malevolent than to win and retain friendships'. Together, they must have been the operatic couple from Hades.

For the carnival of 1789 Da Ponte wrote two libretti for La Ferrarese. *Il pastor fido* (The Faithful Shepherd) with music by Salieri sparked off muttering behind the scenes, but it was *L'ape musicale* (The Musical Bee) that really caused backstage uproar. *L'ape* was a musical pastiche beje-welled with popular past arias from a variety of composers. On the well-tried framework depicting vocalists, impresario, poet and composer getting together to stage an opera, now bickering, now going into raptures about each others' work, Da Ponte set songs by some of Vienna's favourite composers, and assigned them to singers in the company – all chosen by himself. It was a recipe for gunpowder. The singers who were left out, Da Ponte writes, were furious, as were the composers who received no money for the works used. That the first few performances were given as personal benefits, with all takings going to La Ferrarese, Da Ponte, Benucci, Luisa Mombelli and her husband Domenico, turned disgruntled mumblings to venomous rage. Salieri had a double grievance, both on his own part and that of La Cavalieri, and his friendship with Lorenzo, which had slowly been rehabilitated in the years since *Burbero*, once again soured.

Da Ponte made sure that most of the scenes in *L'ape musicale* were changed in some way for every performance – a boon to a fashionable audience who usually found themselves seeing the same opera night after night out of social necessity – but *L'ape* became a showcase for La Ferrarese and Luisa Laschi. To exacerbate the situation, the opera was a sensational success. Da Ponte's text was trenchant and very funny, full of witty banter and wicked gossip, poking fun at the singers, the musicians, the public, and the poet himself. The arias splendidly displayed the singers' talents. The whole marvellous motley was a triumph of Da Ponte's understanding of the theatre, his extensive knowledge of the repertoire, and his perception of the singers' strengths. The audience loved it. *L'ape* ran for an unprecedented eight opera-nights in succession.

In August *Figaro* was revived with La Ferrarese, as Susanna, insisting on two new arias. Mozart obliged – though he was less enamoured of her talents than others in Vienna. After lunch at her house, and what would appear to have been a prickly try-out, he wrote to Constanze (who was away taking a cure at Baden):

> The little aria, which I had composed for Madame Ferraresi [sic], ought, I think to be a success, provided she is able to sing it in an artless manner, which, however, I very much doubt. She herself liked it very much.

The public liked it as well. The revival of *Figaro* was so popular that, in the autumn, Mozart and Da Ponte began work together on a third opera, one in which there was a fine role especially written to display La Ferrarese's vocal range and talents – they called the new work *Così fan tutte, ossia La scuola degli amanti* (Women Are Like That, or The School for Lovers).

Chapter Eleven

B EFORE WORK ON *Così fan tutte* began, while rehearsals for the revival of *Figaro* were just getting under way, events were unrolling that would turn carefree, tolerant Vienna into a very different place. On 14 July 1789 a mob in Paris had stormed the Bastille. France was in the grip of a revolution. Joseph II heard of the fall of the Bastille within days. The news blew out the last vestiges of the sick Emperor's impulse for reform, and he appeared to take the revolt as a personal affront to his sister, Marie Antoinette. He lashed out as he had done when, years before, he had been jostled by the crowd at his own public ball. '[The news] excited a transport of passion,' reported the British chargé d'affaires of the Emperor's reaction, 'and drew from him the most violent menaces of vengeance in case any insult had been, or should be offered to the person of his sister'. In the coffee-houses, by contrast, the mood was jubilant. As early as May, the *Wiener Zeitung* had noted:

> In France, a light is beginning to shine which will benefit the whole of humanity. Necker has persuaded the King to leave the throne of despotism, and to set an unprecedented example which is of such a nature that all countries will hence follow it sooner or later.

Such public euphoria was short-lived. Ailing, frightened, his spirit crushed, Emperor Joseph II repealed his earlier reforms in swathes, bending to the will of his advisors. The reactionary Count Pergen became minister of police and introduced vicious censorship. Books were suppressed and sunny articles, such as that in the *Wiener Zeitung* that encouraged other countries to follow the lead of France, became a thing of the past. The changes happened swiftly, surprising the Viennese and devastating those abroad who had seen the city as a centre of tolerance. Johann Pezzl observed that in the new Vienna on social occasions 'one never speaks openly, and never about matters of importance. It is known that walls have ears'. Drawing up a list of the differences between Vienna of 1790 and of the decade before, he included:

Old Vienna	*New Vienna*
Spies — in wartime and against the enemy.	Spies — in peacetime and against the state's own employees and subjects.
The state body politic sick from constipation.	The state body politic becoming sick from too many purges.

Da Ponte, like all foreign residents in Vienna, was now subject to scrutiny by Pergen's secret police, yet he and Mozart seemed unmindful of the distant turning of the larger cogs of history, focussing more on the machinery of their own lives, where the wheels ticked forward slowly, affected fractionally and at far remove by the broader churn of events. As the gloom gathered over Vienna, they concentrated on an opera that seems peculiarly detached from the changes going on around them.

Da Ponte had originally begun work on *Così fan tutte* with Salieri, but this project was suddenly abandoned. During 1788 and 1789, Da Ponte had worked almost exclusively with the court composer. Following *Axur*, he had in September 1788 adapted a Goldoni play as *Il talismano*; for the carnival of 1789, while he was busy with *L'ape*, he had also adapted for Salieri *Il pastor fido*, a Guarini play that he knew well from his days in the seminary in Portogruaro. Neither *Il talismano* nor *Il pastor fido* was particularly well received. In the autumn of 1789, the pair were already working on *La cifra*, another adaptation, written especially for La Ferrarese, but their collaboration lacked spark. It is quite possible that after the successful revival of *Figaro* Joseph II commissioned *Così* from Da Ponte and Mozart instead, and that Salieri did not give up his work by choice. Mozart received an astonishing 200 ducats (900 gulden, double the usual honorarium for an opera), and Niemetschek writes that it was 'not within [Mozart's] power to refuse the commission' and that the text was 'expressly served on him'. Indeed, the title of the opera comes from *Figaro* – in the Terzetto in Act I scene vii, a cynical Don Basilio sings, '*Così fan tutte le belle, non c'é alcuna novità* [That's what all beautiful women do, there's nothing new in that]'. Salieri's relinquishing the work to Mozart would have done little to improve their relationship, especially if it were not done voluntarily.

The story goes that the Emperor also suggested the subject for the opera, based on gossip of the year before. At a masked ball at the Redoutensaal two young officers had pretended to their respective ladies that they were called up to fight the Turk, but had instead disguised themselves as part of a wager, had themselves 'introduced' to their ladies (each to the other's partner) and successfully effected a seduction. The tale has the quality of an urban myth (some versions have it set in Istria on the Adriatic coast), yet is one that would have appealed to Joseph's misogynistic tendency. Da Ponte (rarely for him) penned the libretto himself rather than adapting it from another source, and, if not dramatizing the Emperor's gossip, was clearly inspired by the age-old plot of a wager struck with a man too confident of his wife's fidelity (such as in the ninth book of Boccaccio's *Decameron*), and stories of suspicious husbands disguising themselves to test their wives' virtue – as occurs in Ovid's version of the myth of Cephalus and Procris, and in Ariosto's *Orlando*. Lorenzo was a passionate admirer of Ariosto, and from his early days in the seminary in Ceneda had immersed himself in the classics. There are elements, too, of Gozzi's *Le droghe d'amore* (The Drug of Love) – a work not in his customary fairy-tale style, but a satire of love and jealousy. Da Ponte was also not shy of purloining a theatrical device from his rival Casti's *La grotta di Trofonio*, in the use of two rather than one pair of lovers to give an extra turn to the drama.

Ferrando and Guglielmo, two young officers, boast to the world-wise Don Alfonso of the fidelity of their lovers, the sisters Dorabella and Fiordiligi. Don Alfonso maintains that the sisters would be no more faithful than any other women if put to the test, and the soldiers enter a wager with him, promising to do anything he requires for a day. Don Alfonso pretends to the sisters that their betrothed have to go to war, and after taking their leave the men return in disguise as moustached Albanians, each to woo the other's fiancée. The sisters put up stout resistance against a relentless onslaught – even when the Albanians take poison and pretend to die for love. Their maid, Despina, enters into the game disguised as a doctor and revives the men using a huge magnet, following the techniques of Dr Mesmer (Mesmerism had been the rage in Vienna, but was just going out of fashion so was ripe for parody). Whenever either the women or men flag, they are egged on by Despina and Don Alfonso. The sisters are battered by all manner of tricks and some quite vile emotional blackmail. Guglielmo, with an histrionic performance as a forlorn lover, wins over Dorabella, but Fiordiligi is fraught and sincerely troubled. Though Fiordiligi appears unassailable, Don Alfonso persuades Ferrando to make one last attempt. Ferrando redoubles his efforts when he hears his Dorabella has succumbed to Guglielmo's advances. Fiordiligi tries to escape in military uniform, thinking to join her fiancée in the field, but is intercepted by Ferrando, and finally yields to him. Don Alfonso has won his bet; the men have to admit that all women are the same. At a fake wedding (with the ever-versatile Despina as notary), military music from the returning army causes the Albanians to flee. Ferrando and Guglielmo contrive their reappearance as themselves, and reveal all. They pay Don Alfonso his 100 sequins (a considerable sum equal, incidentally, to the amount a composer would be paid for a new opera at the Burgtheater). Mortified, Fiordiligi and Dorabella beg forgiveness, and are reunited with their original lovers – improbably quickly perhaps, but the buffo form required reconciliation.

Fidelity and forgiveness were much on Mozart's mind. In August, while Constanze was taking her cure in Baden (a spa noted for its effervescent social atmosphere and mixed bathing), he had written

anguished letters after rumours reached him of her behaviour with a
certain 'N.N.':

> [D]earest little wife! – let me talk candidly – you have no reason
> whatever to be sad – you have a husband who loves you, who does
> everything he possibly can for you . . . and you know, I am glad when
> you are having fun – I truly am – I only wish you wouldn't lower
> yourself so much at times – you are a bit too familiar with N.N . . . A
> Woman has to always behave properly – otherwise people will talk –
> Dearest! – forgive me for being so frank, but it is necessary for my
> peace of mind as well as our happiness together – just remember that
> you yourself confessed to me that you *give in too easily* – and you know
> what the consequences are – so do remember the promise you gave
> me – Oh, dear God! – make an effort my love! – be merry and happy
> and loving, *with me* – and don't torture yourself and me with
> unfounded jealousy – trust in my love, for you do have full proof
> of it! – And you'll see how happy we'll be together and, believe me,
> only a woman's proper conduct can tie a man firmly to her – adieu –
> tomorrow I shall be kissing you most tenderly.
>
> Mozart

Da Ponte's story of women separated from their true partners, left alone
to be besieged by men with seduction in mind, and of their inevitable
capitulation, must have wrung at Mozart's heart. Wolfgang had married
for love, and was hurt that Constanze might dip her toe, be it ever so
daintily, into the pool of erotic flirtation in fashionable Baden. His
jealousy reflected a modern attitude towards companionate marriage,
one emerging among the intellectual bourgeoisie, while notions of a loss
of honour had to do with breaking the delicate rules of conventionalized
sexual predation in Baden. This ritualized flirtation and seduction
belonged in the realm of Count Almaviva and Don Giovanni, of
aristocrats whose arranged marriages shifted desire and sexual satisfaction
away from the conjugal sheets. From one angle, *Così fan tutte*, as a light-
hearted opera about seduction, fitted with this atmosphere of *ancien
régime* acceptable impropriety. Mozart could bring to Da Ponte's text a

sense of the ruthless, brittle sexual scheming as existed in such other works of the period as Laclos's *Les Liaisons dangereuses*, yet weave into it strands of warmth and sincerity.

Da Ponte's situation was more ambiguous, though closer to the old regime. His was the world of the *cicisbeo*, one built on artifice. Though a reluctant priest, he was nevertheless forbidden the marriage and stability his operas ultimately had to affirm – strictly, he was even denied physical love. Passion, for him, meant participation in such games of indiscretion as played by the old nobility, where a blind eye was turned to the antics of certain abbés. Love and deceit were inextricably linked. His own great loves had shown an odd duality: on the one hand, besotted debauchery with Angela Tiepolo, and on the other, the tenderness of his life with Anzoletta, which though illicit had all the trappings of marriage. In Vienna, he was violently in love with an adulterous La Ferrarese, yet his illegitimate son Felice (now aged six) and Felice's mother Annetta still hovered somewhere behind him. Part of him revelled in the world of mistresses; part never stopped seeking the security of family.

The Casanova-like dalliances with women in gondolas and German innkeepers were fleeting ardours, minnows that swam around the rocks of Angela and Anzoletta, Annetta and La Ferrarese. Lorenzo could not live without love. He could say with Don Giovanni that women were more necessary to him than the bread he ate, than the air he breathed. He loved wholeheartedly and distractedly, yet even love was not free of his overwhelming sense of others' perfidy. As an old man he would write: 'My heart was not, and perhaps is not, able to exist without love; and regardless of the many deceits and betrayals I have suffered at the hands of women in the course of my life, I truly cannot remember having passed six months in the whole course of it, without loving someone and loving – I would like to boast – with a perfect love.' Coupled with this sense of the perfection of his own love is one of the inevitability of a woman's disappointing him. All too often ardour led (as Fiordiligi discovers) to 'madness, anguish, remorse, repentance, fickleness, deceit and betrayal', and that was invariably the woman's, never Lorenzo's, fault.

Though he could love with a reckless, consuming passion, Da Ponte

had not always been kind to women in his writing. It may be remembered that in the preamble to the *Canzonetta* published in a Trieste
newspaper in 1784, Da Ponte had, the editor wrote, dedicated his poem
'to the Fair Sex as an apology for his way of writing against the same and
proof of the respect which he professes to have towards it'. Lorenzo's
attitude to women was at least as ambivalent as that of his monarch. As
early as 1791, the actor Friederich Schröder noted in his diary, after
reading a German translation of the libretto of *Così*, that it was 'a
miserable thing, which lowers all women, cannot possibly please female
spectators, and will therefore not make its fortune'. If the prudish
nineteenth century was to condemn *Così fan tutte* for obscenity, the
next age would complain that it was trivial and misogynistic. Part of Da
Ponte is indeed in the cynical Don Alfonso laughing in the background
as Dorabella and Fiordiligi succumb with apparent inevitability to their
seducers, in the cold plotting of the women's ruin and the outrageous
parodies of serious love arias; and Da Ponte preferred the more sardonic
alternative title for the opera, 'The School for Lovers'. Yet he is also there
in genuinely beautiful arias, in affirmations of love not treated ironically,
in Fiordiligi's long resistance to Ferrando's advances and her real anguish
as she finally yields.

Mozart's music enriched Da Ponte's libretto with shades and further
ambiguities, softening crueller edges, adding lacquer-layers of meaning
and affection, pointing moments of satire. As before, composer and poet
delicately stitched the comic and the serious together, and made their
mix even more complex by an interplay of real and faked emotions,
histrionic bombast and moments of transporting beauty. At times the
parody is delicious, at others the opera is clearly serious; sometimes it is
hard to tell which. Mozart and Da Ponte created a work that would have
critics arguing for centuries, berating it then rescuing it, damning it for its
cynicism and triviality, lauding it for its complexity. It is, as one
commentator put it 'iridescent, like a glorious soap-bubble' in the
changing colours it presents to the world. *Così* was indeed in part
frivolous and worldly, an unwitting swansong to a life that was disappearing even as Mozart and Da Ponte were writing, a farewell billet-
doux to the old Vienna. Yet it was infused with a warmth that was

lacking in other, more cynical texts of the time. *Così fan tutte* was *Les Liaisons dangereuses* with heart.

After *Don Giovanni* and the revival of *Figaro*, Da Ponte and Mozart knew the abilities of the Burgtheater company well, yet in the early stages of *Così* they worked closely with the singers, apparently exploring possibilities in arias that were later abandoned. Mozart replaced a superb, high-spirited buffo aria for Benucci (as Guglielmo), which interrupted the flow of the first act, with a shorter one that was more dramatically appropriate. Skilful stagecraft was again to the fore. Together they created an intimate opera, with just six characters in a simple setting. *Così* was poised and concentrated, comprising numerous tight ensembles – short scenes (often involving just two or three singers) that intensified the drama. As ever, Da Ponte tailored and cut each scene, moulded each aria to suit the shape of Mozart's music, fitting words to notes or creating forms that gave the composer freedom and matched his style. Well paced and finely structured, *Così fan tutte* was perhaps the best libretto the theatre poet had yet written.

La Ferrarese was given ample opportunity to display her remarkable range, and in the rondo '*Per pietà*' had the most genuinely moving aria in the opera, as Fiordiligi sings in real anguish over an infidelity she has not yet committed, yet is finding hard to resist. The singer's arch-rival Dorotea Bussani (she who Da Ponte dismissed as a 'vulgar little woman' of clown's antics and facial contortions) no doubt relished her role as Despina in her various guises. Mozart could once again make rich use of violas (for *Don Giovanni* in Prague he had been constrained by an orchestra with only two viola players, but the Burgtheater had a strong section). Anton Stadler and his brother, both virtuoso clarinet players, had joined the orchestra, helping to give respectability to what had previously been a wind-band instrument, and allowing Mozart a glorious palette of orchestral colouring. *Così* makes sumptuous use of the clarinet.

They worked quickly. Mozart sorely needed the money – he had written very little in 1789 and was in debt – and he and Da Ponte surely realized that should the ailing Emperor die, their opera would be in jeopardy. They were adept at speedy production, and by the end of December *Così fan tutte* was ready for musical rehearsals. In a letter that hints at the possibility that Salieri was angry at not being allowed to

complete *Così* himself, Mozart wrote to Michael Puchberg, asking him
for a 400-gulden loan until the fee for the opera came through and
offering an invitation to his house:

> I invite you, you alone, to come along on Thursday [31 December] at
> 10 o'clock to hear a short rehearsal of my opera. I am only inviting
> Haydn and yourself. I shall tell you when we meet about Salieri's plots,
> which, however, have completely failed already.

Three weeks later he wrote, again to Michael Puchberg:

> We are having our first instrumental rehearsal at the theatre tomorrow.
> Haydn is coming with me. If your business allows you to do so and if
> you care to hear the rehearsal, all you need to do is to be so kind as to
> turn up at my quarters at ten o'clock tomorrow morning and then we
> shall go there together.

Così fan tutte opened on 26 January 1790, and Count Zinzendorf, at least,
was beguiled. 'The music by Mozart is charming,' he wrote, 'and the
subject rather amusing.' The Viennese public appears to have been
lukewarm, but it did not have much opportunity to enjoy *Così*, for after
only four more performances, on 13 February, the Burgtheater was
closed as Joseph II was dangerously ill.

Over the next week, Da Ponte slipped in and out of the palace, pacing
silently with a handful of others in an antechamber as Joseph grew
weaker. Everyone, even the Emperor's harshest critics, was impressed by
the monarch's dignity and fortitude in his final hours. Self-effacing to the
end, Joseph ordered that the catafalque and other royal trappings that had
just been used for the burial of the young wife of his nephew Franz be
left in place for his own funeral. He used his last energy to compose
letters to his closest friends. To his chamberlain he wrote:

> My dear Count Rosenberg!
> Friendship normally has limits, but yours has been given to me
> entirely. I could not leave this world without first expressing my

gratitude for how much you have done for me, for all you have done to console me, and for the sacrifices you have made to help me bear the weight of this long illness. The wisdom of your excellent suggestions, and the devotion you have shown me under all circumstances, to the very last, fills me with gratitude and friendship. Accept my assurance of these feelings, and believe me when I say that the only thing I regret upon departing this world is the small number of friends that I must now leave behind, and whom I have inconvenienced. So farewell. I embrace you with a loving heart. Remember me as your sincere and loving friend.

Joseph

PS Only the trembling of my hand prevents me from personally writing these lines.

On 20 February 1790, Emperor Joseph II died. Casanova wrote that he had committed suicide, through overwork and disappointment: 'Although he did not do so intentionally, he killed himself nonetheless . . . What he pretended to know, but did not know, rendered what he did know useless, and the intelligence he sought spoiled the one he possessed.' The poet Johann Gottfried Herder was more sympathetic: 'I could have wept when I learnt the details of the end of his life . . . what a fate was that monarch's, who, confronted with his death, was forced not only to renounce the aim he had set himself during his noblest years, but also to disavow, formally, the whole of his life's work, to annul it solemnly, and then to die.'

Da Ponte had lost not just a patron but the man who 'created a new fire' in him: a father, muse and protector. Life for Da Ponte under Joseph's successor, his brother Leopold, would be very different. With careful pragmatism, the poet composed a *canzone* on the death of Joseph and the accession of Leopold – a grandiose, conservative piece that was less an expression of grief than an overture to the new ruler, curiously out of step with both events in France and his own earlier egalitarian expressions. It is not clear whether Leopold even read the poem. Whatever Da Ponte's suspicions might have been over how the new monarch might treat him, they could hardly have been worse than what transpired.

Emperor Leopold II did not appreciate music as Joseph had done, and tended to leave decisions in this area to his wife. The Empress Maria Luisa's tastes were old-fashioned: she thought opera buffa vulgar, preferring stately, formulaic *opera seria*. A ripple of unease ran through the Burgtheater. At first, Leopold was far too busy with affairs of state to concern himself with the frivolities of opera. On 12 April, after a suitable period of mourning had elapsed, the theatre reopened with its former personnel in place and Da Ponte's new scheme for running the company still operative. Everyone from the director of spectacles Count Rosenberg to the prompter Sgrilli realized their positions were in danger, but the season proceeded as normal. *Così* was revived, but the cogs in Vienna had turned and it seemed out of place, lasting for only five performances before dropping from the repertoire. Reruns of *Figaro* and *L'arbore di Diana* met with more success. Da Ponte worked on three new operas over the next few months – with music by Paisiello, Guglielmi and Salieri's protégé Joseph Weigl – but none made much of a mark. Weigl's piece, *La caffettiera bizzarra*, was given in the Prater on 15 September in celebration of the visit of the King and Queen of the Two Sicilies, who were in Vienna on an extended visit to celebrate the betrothal of two of their daughters to two of Leopold's sons. For Weigl and Da Ponte, the evening was a dismal failure. The royals arrived an hour and a half late, and the by then fidgety public was more interested in getting a good look at the visitors than in any contrived entertainment. Weigl admitted that neither music nor libretto deserved a better fate, marvelling that such an 'Unding' (worthless absurdity) with music by a relative beginner be chosen to mark so important an event. Nevertheless, as theatre poet, Da Ponte still carried some status. Early in 1791, two diverting commissions – also connected with the royal visit – allowed him to shine a little more brightly.

On 9 January, the Neapolitan Ambassador the Marquis Marzio del Gallo drew up outside Da Ponte's house in the power and glory of a coach-and-six, and delivered himself of 'a ministerial oration'. To a twitching of curtains and an edging-open of shutters the haughty marquis – 'young, handsome, well built and with an exceptionally lively wit' – approached the theatre poet. His Excellency was about to throw a party for the birthday of the visiting King of the Two Sicilies. Piticchio had composed a cantata, but the librettist had failed them. There were three days before the feast. Would Da Ponte help? Would he fit words to a pre-existing score? The Marquis lowered himself so far as to 'implore'. Three days was short, even for Da Ponte, but the poet was quite aware in these delicate times of the dangers of appearing unwilling. *I voti della nazione Napolitana*, presented on 12 January, was a notable success, but the dashing marquis was not nearly so generous as he was sensational. Two days later he sent Da Ponte a grandiloquent letter of praise – and a paltry fifty gulden. Da Ponte gave the money as a tip to the messenger. Furious, the marquis demanded an explanation and when Lorenzo sidestepped with the excuse that a 'Bravo, Da Ponte!' was reward enough, Del Gallo saved face by insisting he accept the gift of a watch – worth not much more, Da Ponte reckoned, than the original fifty gulden. His contrariness now prickling, Da Ponte gave the watch away to a 'verse-inspiring muse' (perhaps the Calliope who had murmured sweet silliness to him as he wrote *Don Giovanni*, for La Ferrarese would surely not be impressed by such trinkets). It was a rash move. Word got back to the Ambassador's residence. Da Ponte made a relentless enemy of the Marquis del Gallo, a man who had the ear of Emperor Leopold. Lorenzo had already heard that the new Emperor disliked him. Antagonizing Del Gallo would certainly not help his cause – especially as Leopold buffeted himself with bureaucratic barriers and was not nearly as accessible as his predecessor had been. Good favour and connections in court were now important.

Just a week after the marquis's party, the Prince von Auersperg also hosted a soirée for the visiting royals. Not to be outdone he, too, asked the theatre poet for a cantata. The prince was renowned as the most prestigious patron of private entertainments in Vienna, encouraging lavish productions. Da Ponte was given free rein with staging and the choice of singers and composer. Walking to view the private theatre the prince had in his garden, Da Ponte spotted a rotunda with nothing in it but a sculpture of Flora on a pedestal. Immediately, he had the idea for his cantata: a festival of flowers in the middle of winter (the prince no doubt also had a well-stocked hothouse), staged not in the theatre, but in the rotunda. Perhaps to make up for his sorry literary effort for *La caffettiera bizzarra*, he chose Weigl as composer. That afternoon Da Ponte came up with the verses:

Di gemme e di stelle	If I had jewels and stars
S'avessi abbondanza,	In abundance,
Corona di quelle	A crown of them
A te vorrei far.	Would I make for thee.
Ma il fato non diemmi	But Fate gave me
Che impero de' fiori;	No more than an empire of flowers;
Son questi i tesori,	So these treasures
Che a te posso dar.	I offer thee.

When the young Joseph Weigl heard these words it was, Da Ponte says, 'as if a celestial fire swept through him'. Composer and librettist worked together through the night, and finished *Il tempio di Flora e Minerva* (The Temple of Flora and Minerva) by morning.

The rotunda, with its lone statue, had given Da Ponte inspiration for staging the cantata. Even with 300 people in it, there was still enough room for an orchestra and a small acting space. Da Ponte had Flora removed, and had his singer stand on the pedestal 'motionless so that the spectators took her to be the same marble goddess' (one doubts, at this point, that the role was taken by the not particularly well-sculpted La Ferrarese). The rotunda was in total darkness, but for a single lantern that lit the aisle as the royal party took their seats. Behind a curtain, the orchestra played quietly. At a signal from Da Ponte, the rotunda was suddenly flooded with light from little lanterns fixed to the cornice, and the royals realized they were sitting on thrones of flowers. After Flora's first aria, little Cupids distributed roses and myrtles to the betrothed princes and princesses, while Minerva protested that her olives and Apollo's laurels were a more appropriate gift. As contention reached its height, Flora descended from her pedestal to present a garland to the visiting Queen. (The Queen returned it, as a gift to the singer rather than to Flora, with a kiss to the forehead.) The audience, the visitors, and their host were delighted. Next day, Prince von Auersberg made handsome gifts to the singers and presented Da Ponte with a gold box, a sculpted stag with gold-leaf horns, and a purse containing 225 gulden.

At the Burgtheater, tensions grew. Joseph had involved himself minutely with the running of the theatre, and through Rosenberg the link to the imperial mind and ear was immediate. Now nobody quite knew what the Emperor – or more likely the Empress – planned to do with them. The mood was taut. Old factional loyalties were simultaneously intensified and made fragile, as at base everyone was fighting for his or her own position, no matter to whose detriment. Eyes narrowed, muscles tensed, hackles rose. Some couples stood back-to-back against the others – the Mombellis, the Bussanis, Salieri and Caterina Cavalieri, Da Ponte and La Ferrarese. Da Ponte identified his most deadly enemies as Salieri, whom he said wanted to take over running of the theatre, and whose antagonism was sharpened on behalf of Cavalieri; Thorwart, a long-standing foe, who Da Ponte was now also accusing (to his face) of embezzlement; the Bussanis, in a feud that dated back to Francesco Bussani's attempts to scupper the ballet in *Figaro* and was sustained by the couple's belief that Da Ponte excluded them from parts that were their due (a confidence in their own talent that does not seem entirely warranted); and even the prompter Sgrilli, who Da Ponte said conspired with Piticchio to spread slanders about him. Outside Burgtheater circles was Giuseppe Lattanzi, a shady character once convicted for forgery, who wrote for the newspaper *Vox Populi*. He had come to Vienna with Leopold as a private secretary, and was a member of the Emperor's secret cabinet. Through him Da Ponte attempted access to his monarch. To make matters worse, his old rival Casti was back in town, restored to favour under Leopold and set at long last to achieve his aim of becoming imperial poet.

No doubt to the delight of the other sopranos, La Ferrarese's contract was due to expire in February, but that glee was soon tempered by the news that two outside singers had been appointed: Irene Tomeoni, a successful buffa singer from Naples, and (more ominously) Cecilia

Giuliani, a *seria* soprano renowned for her interpretation of tragic roles. Some fogginess surrounded the origin of these appointments, but it seemed to the company that the Empress was imposing her staid tastes for *opera seria*. They did not know it, but they were right – both Tomeoni and Giuliani had been summoned at Maria Luisa's express command, and Giuliani and the Empress were personally acquainted. Both sopranos immediately began to receive anonymous letters, graphically depicting the intrigues and stifling atmosphere of the Burgtheater, poisoning them against Vienna and urging them not to come. The letters reached Maria Luisa's desk. All Vienna got to hear about them, and rumour was that the hand of the theatre poet had held the quill – for Da Ponte had, with apparent blindness to his own fate, passionately taken up the cause of La Ferrarese. In the face of company fury he was doing all he could to have her contract renewed.

In December 1790, Da Ponte had written a long petition to Count Rosenberg, imploring him to keep La Ferrarese on. He wrote, he assured the count, objectively, entirely from love for the theatre, without 'private interest, personal malice, partiality or ulterior motives', to persuade him of the tremendous financial and artistic loss La Ferrarese's departure would mean. He argued at length of the programming and administrative difficulties the new arrivals would entail, mentioning – by the way – letters from certain impresarios that had chanced to fall into his hands which had it that the talents of Tomeoni and especially Giuliani were not all they had been made out to be. He warned of 'empty theatres, enormous losses, a bad start [to the season], and as a result deadly consequences for the whole year' should the company lose La Ferrarese, but beseeched the count not to tell a soul – not even the singer herself – of the petition.

The mood at the Burgtheater gave no space to secrets. Soon the contents of the petition were scorching from salon to coffee-house, from street-corner to dressing-room. Intrigue grew to a tumult. Da Ponte noticed that 'the number of my enemies was increasing in proportion to my zeal for La Ferrarese, who, to foment passions further, was wooing audiences daily on stage'. Fiery letters about the theatre poet's unfair support for his favourite reached the imperial couple. Da Ponte was told that Leopold had exploded with a 'To the devil with this disturber of the peace!'

Da Ponte and La Ferrarese began quietly to consider alternatives to an uncertain future at the Burgtheater. La Ferrarese's father-in-law — the Roman Consul in Venice, who had once pursued his son and the runaway orphan girl but been unable to prevent their marrying — had died, and Luigi was attempting to secure his father's old position (such posts were often considered hereditary). While Da Ponte was busy with his cantatas for the Marquis del Gallo and Prince von Auersperg, petitions were being made to the Pope on Luigi's behalf that would enable him and La Ferrarese to put the trials of life in the opera behind them:

> [By granting this request] Your Holiness with an act of His well-known munificence will come to free him [Luigi] and his wife from a painful, uncertain, and always risky life, one that out of sheer necessity he had to embrace in the past, a life abhorred no less on his part than on that of his companion.

Such a move need not break up the cosy *ménage à trois*. Da Ponte contacted his family to ask them to begin petitioning to have his banishment from Venice revoked. But he could not rely on this happening, and the ground was beginning to move beneath his feet. While he was waiting for news from Venice, a way to deliverance opened itself in a letter from his old friend Martín y Soler. Martín was now director of Italian opera to the court in St Petersburg, where (he wrote) *Cosa rara* and *L'arbore di Diana* had greatly pleased, both at court and in town. He suggested that Da Ponte come to Russia, where he could not fail to be appointed theatre poet – but he would have to act quickly. Da Ponte went immediately to hand in his resignation. Count Rosenberg was away, so Da Ponte had to ask his enemy Thorwart to approach the Emperor to have his contract terminated early. One might have thought Thorwart would have been only too pleased to rid himself of the troublesome theatre poet, but either his malice ran so deep that he could not bear Da Ponte moving on to further success and wanted to see him destroyed, or he was not able to convince the monarch that the inconveniences of suddenly losing the theatre's manager and poet were surmountable. Word came back that permission was refused.

Frustrated, Da Ponte wrote to Martín saying that he could not come. The vitriol, public insults and 'nefarious conspiracies' which he claimed had dogged him all his years with the Burgtheater were growing rampant; the enemies who 'joined together to tear into me, to skin me, to devour me' were becoming unstoppable. He hated, bred hatred, and seethed with righteous fury, once again the outcast. Desperate to put his own case directly to Leopold, he tried to persuade Giuseppe Lattanzi, that murky intimate of the Emperor's, to arrange a private audience. According to police surveillance records, Da Ponte visited Lattanzi on 24 January. Lattanzi told him an audience was not possible, but offered to ensure that Leopold would see anything that Da Ponte cared to write. Anxious, indignant, defensive of his self-worth, Lorenzo penned a verse letter that – unlike his memorial ode to Joseph – was in the same spirit as his revolutionary *accademia* in Treviso, or his sonnet in support of Pisani in Venice. Once again his poetry landed him in trouble. At a time when revolution in France was on the brink of toppling Louis XVI and denying his right to rule, it was not a good idea to write to an emperor (especially one whose goodwill one was trying to win, and whose sister was married to the French King) that, 'My destiny does not depend on you, because all your power and that of all possible kings has no rights over my soul. If I feel no guilt, if my conscience is clear, I can adore you, I can love your name and your virtues, but I cannot fear you.' Da Ponte frankly told the monarch that he was surrounded by flatterers and false counsellors, and that good intentions were 'not enough for a man, and you are a man, subject like other men to fraud'. He did not beseech mercy, like a subject, but implored justice, like a fellow man. To underline his point, Da Ponte used the familiar '*tu*' instead of more formal registers of the pronoun 'you'. This was *lèse-majesté* that would have astonished the radical Joseph; it would fire outrage in his more conservative brother.

Whatever Lattanzi's hidden grudge against Da Ponte was, it must have been a hard one. Instead of discouraging the poet from such folly, he had the poem circulated publicly. His covering note, when he submitted the letter to Leopold, read: 'The entire city is reading with absolute amazement the letter, which, so it is said, Da Ponte has circulated. It is written in such vehement terms that one can't imagine how anybody could be so foolhardy as to address the Sovereign this way unless he were involved in some very dangerous intrigue.' Some days later a sixty-eight-page pamphlet in German entitled *Anti-Da Ponte* appeared in the coffee-houses. In it the letter was reproduced in full, followed by a report of an imaginary court case in which such accusers as Beaumarchais claimed that Da Ponte did not understand his play, 'else he could not have made such a changeling of it', and 'Salieri and Mozart complained loudly about the tasteless, jolting and disjointed opera texts'. Vienna was laughing at its theatre poet. On 9 March, Da Ponte was dismissed.

Da Ponte's letter spurred Leopold to action on the Burgtheater, much in the way that Celeste Coltellini's missives to Joseph had sparked the decision to disband the Italian opera three years earlier. Within weeks Leopold had replaced Count Rosenberg with Count Johann Ugarte as director of spectacles, relieved Salieri of active duty as kapellmeister, created a ballet troupe, and hired not two but three new *opera seria* singers.

Da Ponte still had obligations to fulfil in the current program. Two days after his dismissal, he staged an oratorio entitled *Il Davide*, with the first three performances as benefits for La Ferrarese; then from 23 March *L'ape musicale rinnuovata* (a reworking of the original pastiche) again filled seats, with most shows given as benefits for poet and singers. After that Da Ponte's work at the Burgtheater came to an end. He received some compensation for the months of his contract still to run, and for printed libretti yet to be sold, but remained in Vienna as if stunned, unable to fathom exactly what had happened to him. His *non grata* status began to hit home when one evening he was refused entry to the opera. He had bought a ticket (not something he had had to do in the past), but the embarrassed ticket-taker said that Thorwart had given orders not to let him in. Quietly, Prince von Auersperg, who had overheard the exchange, took him by the hand and led him to his own box.

In April, Da Ponte heard that the Council of Ten had refused permission for him to return to Venice – perhaps it had not been wise to choose his errant half-brother Agostino to present the petition, despite the additional support of Bernardo Memmo and Count Zaguri. Besides being a womanizer, gambler and neglecting his three children, Agostino had already spent a month in prison in Venice for threatening the life of a man who had restored one of his conquests to her husband. Da Ponte did not hold out much hope that a position in St Petersburg might still be vacant, as he had long since turned down Martín's offer. With these avenues closed, Da Ponte spoke to Mozart, suggesting the two go to London together. This took up an idea originally mooted to the composer by Nancy Storace and Michael Kelly when they had left Vienna. For a while Mozart appeared to have been seriously considering the move, and Da Ponte no doubt hoped to reawaken his interest in the idea, but by now the security of Mozart's position as chamber musician bound him to Vienna. He asked Da Ponte to give him time to consider the proposal, but would soon be working on *La clemenza di Tito* and *Die Zauberflöte*.

Vienna was 'full of a thousand conflicting rumours' about its former theatre poet. The handwritten newspaper *Heimlicher Botschafer* reported: 'The Italian court poet [*sic*] Abbé Da Ponte has had his dismissal and in a few days will leave for Italy in the company of Madame Ferrarese.' On 7 April the *Gazetta urbana Veneta* announced, prematurely, that Giovanni Bertati (the librettist of *Don Giovanni Tenorio*) had replaced Da Ponte as poet to the opera. In Ceneda, Gaspare Da Ponte heard the rumour that his son had committed a grave crime and been given twenty-four hours to leave Vienna. Lorenzo was desperate and tormented by his conviction that he was conspired against. Familiar sights around town that might have reminded him of better times instead filled him with 'disgust and loathing'. Enemies at the Burgtheater continued to conspire against him, not wanting him to meddle and create cabals in the new season. '[M]y presence [in Vienna] seemed dangerous,' he wrote. 'The new Director, at the instigation of several of my enemies, sent me a written order to leave the city.' Shortly before Easter (either as a result of this pressure from Count Ugarte, or as a consequence of his letter to the Emperor) Da Ponte received two peremptory police injunctions, the second of which commanded that he leave the city within days. In mid-April he informed the cashier at the Burgtheater he would be gone by the twentieth of the month – before the new season began. He delayed his departure by a few days, to reassure his old father that gossip of his grave crime and banishment were untrue, but before the end of the month, Lorenzo Da Ponte – once again homeless, without work and on the road – set off for Brühl-bei-Mödling, a village in the woods outside of Vienna.

Count Zaguri, gossiping in a letter to Casanova some months later, wrote that he had seen Da Ponte's 'insane' verses to the Emperor, and went on to put his finger on a cause of this strange and difficult man's misadventures: 'He carries within him, and will always carry, a wood-worm in his soul, gnawing away at every root of his good fortune. I had hardly read the verses when I cried: This is too bad! This is too much! He deserves only one thing – contempt. Some things are so extreme that they do not wound at all.'

Mozart had dreamed of meeting an able poet, 'that true phoenix' with whose words his music would meld. The qualities of the mythological bird he was evoking were those of rarity and beauty, but the phoenix had another trait: it invariably set fire to its own nest. Lorenzo Da Ponte was indeed a true phoenix. Yet he also possessed that best-known attribute of the bird. Time and time again, he could rise from the ashes.

PART THREE
LONDON
Pigmies on Parnassus

Chapter Twelve

D A PONTE REMEMBERED his first day in Brühl as 'one of the most terrible of my whole life'. He was just an hour's journey from the heart of Vienna, yet cast as far from his former existence as it seemed possible to be:

> Sacrificed to hatred, envy, the interests of evildoers; driven from a city where I had lived on the honourable earnings of my talent for eleven years! Abandoned by friends . . . slandered, cursed, disgraced by idlers, hypocrites, triumphant foes; chased, to crown it all, from a theatre which would not have been in existence save for my efforts! I was many times on the brink of taking my life by my own hand. My true conviction of innocence, instead of consoling me, intensified my despair . . . I spent three days and three nights in tears and desolation.

A friend who met Da Ponte in the woods where once he used to take strolls for pleasure wrote that the theatre poet was barely recognizable, that one could not look on him without feeling the strongest emotions, that 'every feature of his face seemed crazed', and that over and over again he would express torment at his rejection, his worry that he was dragging his father and siblings into his downfall. That friend was Major Thaddäus Stieber, a former soldier and aide to Joseph II, who was intervening with the Emperor Leopold on Da Ponte's behalf – for after those first three days and three nights of tears and despondency, Lorenzo's coursing energies began to cut a new channel to survival.

Only a handful of people knew where Da Ponte was. Casanova's brother Francesco (whom Lorenzo met in Dresden) lived in the village, and Da Ponte mentions just two friends visiting him from Vienna. To Major Stieber he had already written two letters of appeal. With a third (on 8 May 1791) he had included a memorandum to the Emperor pleading his case. He admitted to Stieber that he had 'written a letter which perhaps [he] should not have written', but implored the major to help him to restore his reputation. Stieber had agreed. With military thoroughness he began his investigation, uncovering malice, intrigue and cabals at the Burgtheater, very much as Da Ponte had outlined. He contacted people who knew the former theatre poet, finding two eminent citizens and two leading churchmen who quite spontaneously spoke of Da Ponte's good character and generosity to his family. All this Stieber included in his own report to the Emperor, stating that 'Da Ponte's enemies therefore hastened his banishment from Vienna and barred all doors which might give him opportunity to throw himself at Your Majesty's feet and reveal to your great insight and future judgement a large number of malpractices in public affairs'. Da Ponte's 'earthly fate' and the well-being of his family lay in the Emperor's hands, and Stieber appealed for clemency on his behalf.

Leopold was in Italy at the time, and friends advised Da Ponte to wait until the monarch returned to Vienna before petitioning him – but Stieber's efforts had not halted the machinations of Da Ponte's enemies. At the end of May, two police commissioners appeared suddenly in Brühl and hauled Da Ponte back to Vienna, where – after being kept waiting in suspense that he might be thrown into jail – he was given twenty-four hours to be gone 'from the capital and all adjacent and surrounding towns'. When Lorenzo asked from whom the order came, he was told dryly: 'From the one who gives orders here.' Persistence gained him an interview with Count Pergen's deputy, Count Saurau, whom Lorenzo thought 'one of the wisest, most just and estimable citizens of his country'. Saurau informed him that he was 'only the executor of orders from others' and that Da Ponte 'had powerful enemies

at the Opera who had painted [him] in black colours at Court, especially
to the Empress'. With all the fervour he could muster, and any residue of
charm he had, Da Ponte pleaded with Saurau for a week in which to
clear his name. On 3 June, Leopold's son Franz, who was regent in the
Emperor's absence, granted Da Ponte a stay of eight days in order to
prepare a defence. Da Ponte appears to have edged out his period of
grace, as more than a fortnight later he was still in Vienna, writing to
Casanova to inform his old friend that his sights were now set on Venice.
La Ferrarese was there, and he hoped she would 'act for [him] with more
judgement and interest' than his brother Agostino had done in attempting to have his banishment revoked. He was mistaken to expect loyalty
even from La Ferrarese. She appears to have re-hitched her barque to her
husband's now-promising career, done nothing to further Da Ponte's
cause, and remarked to Count Zaguri when she met him in Venice that
Lorenzo was 'a madman'. Franz had more sympathy. He told Lorenzo he
was only carrying out his father's wishes regarding his expulsion, but
suggested that Da Ponte go to Trieste, where the Emperor was due
shortly on his way back from Italy, and present his petition there, so as to
forestall his enemies in Vienna.

At the end of June, Da Ponte left Vienna for Trieste. He was joined by
two of his half-brothers (Paolo and, presumably, Agostino), and faithfully
accompanied in his misfortune by 'a sweetheart of ten years' – most likely
the mother of Felice, the shadowy Annetta who here receives her only,
albeit glancing, mention in his memoirs. Felice and Annetta later
returned to Vienna, though the boy would eventually be taken to live
with his wicked uncle Agostino in Venice.

Count Zaguri wrote that Trieste was 'the usual refuge of those in
disgrace'. Although in the Austrian Empire, Trieste was close to Venice
and on a main route to the Balkans, combining the cosmopolitan to and
fro of a busy port with the more nefarious activities of a frontier town.
Sailors from faraway lands caroused in its taverns; transients, spies and
adventurers took up temporary residence along the narrow, cobbled
streets that climbed up to the Castello di San Giusto, which overlooked
the harbour. The Emperor was most displeased when, on a visit to the
opera at the Teatro San Pietro soon after his arrival, he caught sight of the

scurrilous Abbé Da Ponte in the audience. Leopold told Baron Pietro Pittoni, his chief of police in the city, that he was pained and astonished to have spotted the poet (who was no doubt trying his utmost to be noticed), and that 'it could not be tolerated, that he was a scoundrel and had been banished from Vienna on his orders'. The Governor of Trieste, Count Brigido, was present (Pittoni related to the insatiably curious Casanova) and put in a good word for Da Ponte, informing Leopold that the poet had come expressly to Trieste for an audience, and to answer the accusations made against him. The Emperor 'absolutely refused to see him, and repeated and confirmed his initial orders'.

Da Ponte had already cornered Count Brigido. During days of 'continuous mortal paroxysms' between his own arrival in Trieste on 5 July and that of the Emperor a few days later, he had toyed with the idea of dragging along his 72-year-old father and a horde of dependent siblings to confront Leopold *en tableau* in public and demand justice. (Logistics rather than logic halted that course of action, as it was too difficult to bring them all from Ceneda.) Eventually, he had settled for a cooler approach and had appealed to the Governor for help. In Brigido he had found unexpected warmth and support – and apparently an effective ally.

On the morning after the opera, Da Ponte was roused by a banging on his room door. Count Brigido (and yet another missive from Vienna complaining of continuing intrigue at the Burgtheater) had softened the Emperor's resolve. Da Ponte was summoned to an audience at eleven o'clock. He ran all the way to the royal hostelry, and was ushered through an antechamber crowded with supplicants into the sovereign's presence. The door was left open. Leopold was looking out of a window, with his back to Da Ponte. He turned with an icy: 'Might one know the reason why Signor Da Ponte never chose to call on the Emperor Leopold at Vienna?' Taken aback, Da Ponte answered that Thorwart had told him that the Emperor refused to see him. Yet Thorwart, it seemed, had informed the Emperor that Da Ponte had refused the offer of an audience. Da Ponte had done this, Thorwart told his sovereign, to portray Leopold as a tyrant. The ice thawed a little. Da Ponte revealed Thorwart's misdemeanours with Burgtheater finances, and was shocked to hear his enemies had accused him of writing a book against Leopold, 'something on the style of Madame Lamotte's against the Queen of France'. They spoke of Rosenberg and Salieri, of the Bussanis, Ugarte and Lattanzi, and finally Da Ponte heard the words: 'I understand that you are not the man they wanted me to believe you were.' He asked permission to return to Vienna, but Leopold told him it was too early for that, the bad impressions were too fresh; besides, the post of theatre poet had been given to Bertati. Da Ponte would have to wait in Trieste until Leopold had returned to Vienna and set matters right. On his knees, the author of egalitarian verse implored his monarch for something, anything – 'some other post, send me to serve the lowliest of Your Majesty's servants' – but this without delay, for the well-being of his family. Four times the Emperor commanded him to rise before the desperate man gave up his pleas. After an audience lasting an hour and a half – every word of which could be heard by those waiting in the antechamber – Da Ponte left with nothing but the hope that his name would soon be cleared, and a vague assurance from the Emperor that 'I believe you have been persecuted, and I promise you compensation.'

For Da Ponte, that was enough. He remained in Trieste as the Emperor had suggested, and waited. Two of his brothers and his 'sweetheart of ten years' (and no doubt also Felice) formed a small household that drained his resources as the weeks passed, and the little money he had saved during his extravagant life in Vienna began to run out. Soon his purse was empty, and as he had done a decade earlier in Venice, he began to pawn his more spectacular clothing and write begging letters to friends. Few responded, save Giuseppe Lucchesi, a Trieste lawyer with whom he shared much-welcomed meals, all the time guilty that his little entourage could not do the same.

On 20 July, Da Ponte wrote to Stieber (who was still acting as a go-between) to reiterate plans he had outlined to Leopold for the better running of the Burgtheater. Da Ponte also put forward (as the Emperor had requested) a suggestion for Thorwart's successor: his generous lawyer friend Giuseppe Lucchesi. On 27 July, a week after returning to Vienna, Leopold dismissed Thorwart. Later in the summer, Lattanzi, too, was given walking orders and Ugarte offered a year's salary and urged to leave

Vienna. But these were slow developments to a poet desperate for money. Weeks of waiting became months. With his old rival Casti as imperial poet and Bertati as theatre poet, Da Ponte began to realize there was little prospect for him in Vienna. Though not yet completely giving up hope, he began to consider alternatives. Once again, his mind turned to Venice.

La Ferrarese had not even attempted to help Da Ponte in his petition to the Council of Ten. Instead, he writes, she began another liaison entirely, in pursuit of riches that 'filled her naturally romantic head with a thousand illusions of vanity and grandeur'. Indeed, she 'forgot not only every sentiment of affection and gratitude, but used every dishonourable means she could to have withheld from me the sweet pleasure of returning to my country'. He was vehement at 'this act of feminine iniquity'. In the heat of the summer, Da Ponte hit on a plan that might gain him credit in the eyes of the Council, and simultaneously destroy La Ferrarese's hopes in Venice.

Under cover of darkness on 14 August, in a secret spot near the Venetian border, a little over an hour's journey south of Trieste, Da Ponte met Zan Francesco Manolesso, *podestà* (mayor) of Capodistria, a seaside town just within Venetian territory. It was a Sunday, so the mayor would not be missed; the moon was full, so he could read what Da Ponte had brought him. Some days earlier, Da Ponte had told Carlo Maffei, an agent of the Serenissima in Trieste (whom he probably knew through contacts in the theatre), simply that he had 'a matter of some importance' to communicate. Maffei had passed this information on to Manolesso, who had contacted the Inquisitors. Ever vigilant and suspicious, the Inquisitors had speedily sanctioned the rendezvous, but advised caution. Da Ponte unfolded four letters – given to him by La Ferrarese, or stolen from her. The only really damaging revelation in any of them was in a letter from Luigi Del Bene to the Pope, as part of his supplication for his father's post of consul, offering to furnish the Vatican with information and secrets of Venetian government, which he planned to obtain (as his father had done before him) through contacts, bribes, and splendid dinner parties. Da Ponte would not give the letters to Manolesso, but agreed to send copies. On 20 August he appears to have had an attack of conscience, and wrote to Manolesso withdrawing the offer, on the advice (he said) of his protectors in Venice. On 8 September, still having had no word from Vienna, Da Ponte changed his mind again and submitted a grovelling memorandum to the Inquisitors, denouncing Luigi, and a priggish one to Manolesso, enclosing the letters and saying that he had struggled with compassion and a sense of honour, but that duty had won. Rather inappropriately, he quoted Pilate's words from the Gospel of Matthew, as he washes his hands of the innocent Christ's blood.

Desperation or a desire for vengeance had driven Da Ponte to an act that was an enormous personal betrayal, but one that was just wheat-husk to the world of espionage. Luigi Del Bene was not given the Roman consulship – though what role diplomatic pressure from Venice had in that decision is unknown. Nor, when the Council of Ten discussed his case in the autumn, did Da Ponte have his banishment lifted. Perhaps his offering had been too paltry; perhaps the councillors had a distaste for disloyalty. Count Zaguri was astonished when news leaked out. On 12 October he wrote to Casanova:

If it is true that Da Ponte has been banished, as he is capable of having been an informer, God knows which country he will go and disturb next. He was madly in love with La Ferrarese; he said he had lost everything for her; she dropped him, and never wrote to him again.

Back in Trieste, Da Ponte cast around for means of earning money. In October, he published a sonnet on the ingratitude of man, and the following month revived a tragedy he had once worked on with his brother Girolamo, but never finished. He gave *Il Mezenzio* a happy ending – a *coup de théâtre* in which the hero is rescued at the last minute from the jaws of circus lions – dedicating his play with a loving poem to Giuseppe Lucchesi and his wife. *Il Mezenzio* opened at the Teatro Regio on 5 December – the night that, in Vienna, Wolfgang Mozart died, suddenly, at the age of thirty-five. Audiences enjoyed *Il Mezenzio*, and the play received a good review from none other than Giuseppe Coletti – the man Lorenzo suspected of penning the forged letter that had taken

him in haste to Dresden so many years before. There was yet no word
from the Emperor. Still in Trieste in the new year, Da Ponte staged a
version of *L'Ape musicale* for the 1792 carnival.

Lorenzo does not record his reaction to Mozart's death, but whatever
he may have felt at the loss it was clear that yet another door in Vienna
had slammed shut. To make matters worse, by early 1792, Stieber had
also fallen from grace with Leopold (some said on grounds of excessive
support for democracy). In February, Da Ponte wrote a letter directly to
the Emperor, beginning, 'My cries of despair should by now have
reached the august Throne', complaining of 'desolating poverty', and
imploring some response, some decision. None came. Finally, Da Ponte
decided to go to Vienna himself to seek another audience. Count
Brigido gave him twenty-five sequins to pay for the journey. Da Ponte
arrived at the city gates on 1 March to find the city in mourning. Leopold
II had died earlier that day.

For three weeks Da Ponte stayed on in Vienna, but Leopold's
successor, his son Franz, was not giving audiences. La Ferrarese was
also in town, but (as Count Collalto gossiped in a letter to Casanova)
Luigi Del Bene wouldn't allow Da Ponte in the house. Lorenzo's stay
was enlivened slightly when he paid a surprise visit to Bertati, and found
the new theatre poet at work with 'a tome of French comedies, a
dictionary, a rhymer, and Corticelli's grammar' to hand. Da Ponte only
too gleefully reported these signs of what he considered poetic ineptitude
(for him, snuff and Tokay being the only prerequisites for good verse) to
the Abbé Casti. Da Ponte and the new imperial poet – now that all
danger of competition had been removed – appeared to be getting on
most cordially. Casti even helped Lorenzo, through the auspices of the
kind Count Saurau, to petition the monarch for some sort of compensation so that he could begin a new life. A reply came from His Majesty
that the Abbé Da Ponte, 'as he will be remaining at a distance [from
Vienna]', be paid 200 ducats (900 gulden) towards settling his debts in
Vienna and travel expenses – a generous but firm hint for Da Ponte to
move on. At the end of March, Da Ponte returned to Trieste.

About this time, Lorenzo was introduced to a young woman who had
just arrived in Trieste and was being referred to in society as '*la bella*

inglesina'. Ann Celestine Grahl had been born in London in 1769, though her mother Antoinette was French, and her father John Grahl was a Jewish convert from Dresden, who had anglicized his name from Johannes Krahl on moving to England. John Grahl and his son Peter were merchants and chemists, selling drugs, spices and medicines, but also turning their hand to distilling. In addition they were moneylenders, speculating in bad debts and dealing in mortgages and real estate. As a result, family fortunes, though often buoyant, sometimes hit turbulent waters. When Da Ponte met Nancy (as Ann was generally called), the Grahls were rich. He was introduced to her by Nancy's sister-in-law Elizabeth, Peter Grahl's wife, an Englishwoman with whom Lorenzo was already friendly. The meeting was a mishap. Encouraged by the free-and-easy gaiety that ruled in the younger Grahl household, Da Ponte said to Nancy that the veil she was wearing was not in fashion. When she enquired, 'How should it be worn to be in style?' he replied, 'This way, signora,' lifting the edges and draping it back over her head, to get a glimpse of whether the *inglesina* was indeed as *bella* as all had been saying. Nancy was affronted and did not speak to him for some days, though Elizabeth assured him that 'the pout would soon pass'. It did, and in no time at all Nancy and Lorenzo were swapping French and Italian conversation lessons, and he had lined up a friend of his – a young Italian merchant from Vienna called Galliano – as a prospective husband for her. Letters were exchanged, and then portraits, and matters had reached the point where the young man was coming to Trieste to talk about marriage, when he sent Lorenzo a note asking if he knew how large Nancy's dowry would be. According to Da Ponte, John Grahl seized the letter in a fury, tore it up and threw it on the fire, exclaiming angrily, 'So, Signor Galliano is after my money and not my daughter!' Still enraged, he offered his daughter's hand to Da Ponte. Lorenzo laughed nervously. He looked at Nancy, who lowered her eyes and blushed. In past weeks they had been lingering over their language lessons, 'inclining them to last somewhat longer than they usually do between friends and language students'. Not a word of love had been spoken, but there had been 'affectionate glances, significant sighs, halting words, and above all the need we felt of always being together'. After her initial bashfulness at her father's suggestion, Nancy raised her eyes, smiled and looked directly at Lorenzo. 'Nancy is yours!' exclaimed John Grahl; then, to his daughter, 'Da Ponte is yours!' The rest of the family, who were sitting around the fire, broke out in spontaneous applause, but Da Ponte writes that he and Nancy were so overwhelmed that they were not able to say another word to each other for the whole evening.

Lorenzo Da Ponte had fallen in love for the very last time. At the age of forty-three, penniless, toothless, and with no prospects, he had won the heart of a beauty twenty years his junior, and the acquiescence of her wealthy family to the match. Clearly something of the Da Ponte charm was still intact. He still trailed enough of his former glory, his important friends and famed achievements to impress. As for his bride, the allure and independence of Englishwomen was renowned – and Nancy indeed had spirit. She must have seen beyond Da Ponte's anguished battles, beneath what La Ferrarese – and later Zaguri, too – called his madness, to recognize a similar soul of indefatigable energy, tapping through to Lorenzo's core of optimism, which seemed uncrushable no matter how over-layered it became with anger, desperation or despair. Theirs would be a thoroughly modern marriage, one reflecting a vision that had emerged from the Enlightenment of a couple bound by sentiment rather than convention. Like that of Wolfgang and Constanze Mozart, and of Rousseau's Sophie and Emile, their union was based on affection, the 'right of nature' prevailing – though being a man's companion did not mean being his equal. Like Sophie, Nancy would learn 'early to endure even injustice and to bear a husband's wrongs without complaining'. Da Ponte's days of dalliance were over, but his life was by no means an easy one. Nancy would remain with him, through it all, for the next forty years.

Nearly two decades earlier, Lorenzo had turned down the hand of the daughter of a beggar king because he was a priest. Now, his clerical bonds seemed magically to have evaporated. In his memoirs Da Ponte writes that 'after social ceremonies and formalities, [Nancy] was entrusted to me by her parents on the twelfth day of August 1792, about two o'clock in the afternoon'. A clue to what might have occurred comes in a letter from Count Zaguri to Casanova:

Apropos Da Ponte, do you know that this Nancy is an English Jewess, whom he married in Trieste to the utter amazement of a man I know, one Savordello, who could not imagine what it was all about when he saw her married to an ordained abbé, in a synagogue according to Jewish rites. I'll wager you did not know about that, as Da Ponte would have kept it quiet. It is possible that Savordello may have been hoaxing me, but that is hard to believe, since he said it quite casually, speaking of Da Ponte and his affair with La Ferrarese.

Some weeks later, he dismissed his doubts and wrote, 'How the devil did Da Ponte manage to pass himself off as a Jew in Trieste, where he has been living for a long time?' Trieste had a thriving and expanding Jewish community, who had just built themselves a sparkling new synagogue. Nancy and Lorenzo could easily have been reaching into the well of their earliest childhood religious experiences to find a meaningful ceremony to mark a marriage that was impossible in the Roman Catholic Church, and could even have presented difficulties for Nancy's Anglicanism. Whatever way they found, it was a rite solemn enough to satisfy all parties concerned, including her parents, and significant enough to be assigned an exact time and date.

Overnight, the Abbé Da Ponte had become plain Signor Da Ponte – a detail on which he had pointedly (and repeatedly) to remind Casanova when it came to the addressing of letters. It was a dangerous step. An abbé as *cicisbeo* might be acceptable; however, a priest with a wife was not only excommunicable but socially intolerable – and so unemployable. At first Da Ponte pledged Casanova to absolute secrecy about the marriage, and in correspondence referred to Nancy as his 'sister-in-law' (Nancy was soon adding affectionate postscripts to Lorenzo's letters to his friend). Casanova advised Da Ponte to 'flee Rome and all Italy forever'. Lorenzo had already decided to go to Paris. He had a letter from the late Joseph II mentioning that his sister the French Queen 'likes your *Cosa rara* very much', and thought this 'should be sufficient to help me find some position congenial to my studies'. Travelling to Paris in late 1792 with a letter bearing a recommendation from Marie Antoinette was not the wisest of moves. Even Casanova, tucked away in the castle at Dux, knew that – but there would be time to dissuade the newlyweds from their course, as they were coming to visit him on their journey.

Soon after the ceremony, Nancy and Lorenzo set off in their own calash, drawn by a single horse and driven by a boy of about fifteen. Da Ponte had around 700 gulden to his name. With the fate of his friend Galliano in mind, he had told his new father-in-law that 'satisfied with winning his daughter, [he made] no pretensions to a penny of his money'. He had been given none, though as they left, Nancy's mother pressed a purse of gold coins into her hand. They spent their wedding night at an inn in Leibach (now Ljubljana), then headed on towards Prague. One evening, descending an Alpine pass in drizzle, as they were walking under an umbrella beside the carriage (to ease the load on the horse), Nancy spotted two armed men coming towards them. She slipped her purse of gold (worth around 100 gulden) down the front of Lorenzo's shirt. The bandits turned out to be farmers, their guns merely Alpine staves. The couple were still laughing about their mistake when they reached the inn at the foot of the mountain, only to discover that the purse had slipped between Da Ponte's shirt and waistcoat, and fallen out on to the road. A frantic search by torchlight revealed nothing, nor had they any success the following morning – though the local abbot promised to inform his congregation of the loss, and to forward the purse to them if it was found. They pushed on to Prague, waited a few days, but when they had no word journeyed out to Dux, where as well as introducing his new wife to Casanova, Da Ponte hoped to claim an old debt of several hundred gulden from his friend.

Now nearing seventy, Casanova was lonely and frustrated at Dux, flotsam from the Age of Debauchery and Adventure, laughed at and taunted by the Count Waldstein's servants when the count was away, querulously demanding of a bowl of macaroni a day, bored witless by the village priest, barely acknowledged by his patron, and destitute. Yet young Nancy was swept away by his stories, 'dazed by the vivacity, the eloquence . . . and all the many ways of that extraordinary old man'. For the rest of the journey, Da Ponte entertained her with further tales of Casanova's life. Far from being able to repay his debt, Casanova wheedled money out of Da Ponte as commission on the sale of his coach (an act he had pretty much forced Da Ponte into in the first place). In return Casanova gave his friend three pieces of advice: to go to London instead of Paris; when there never to set foot inside the *Caffè degli italiani* (the Prince of Orange coffee-house, 'famous for its clientele, all the worst Italian troublemakers in London'); and never to sign his name to anything.

Now in the discomfort of a diligence, Nancy and Lorenzo travelled on to Dresden, where they were warmly greeted by Mazzolà and Father Huber, but where Mazzolà made it clear that he did not want competition from another Italian poet. In Dresden, Da Ponte paid off his young coachman (who had clung to him tenaciously, despite their lack of conveyance) with a pair of fine leather breeches. Da Ponte still seemed set on Paris, but the inns they stopped at after Dresden were awash with news of a massacre at the Tuileries and the overthrow of Louis XVI and Marie Antoinette. Da Ponte finally decided to heed Casanova's advice and go to London instead – much to Nancy's delight, as her sister Louisa lived there. It was becoming necessary to economize. Travelling by diligence ate into their reserves, and as well as having had no news of Nancy's lost purse they had also had their luggage robbed just outside Dux. Along the way, Da Ponte had been given a magnificent gold watch by a love-struck count – for whom he had written a sonnet that helped the man win the hand of his beloved – but it was with a much-depleted stock of gulden that the Da Pontes arrived at the coast early in October 1792, to wait for a packet to take them to England.

Nancy had crossed the Channel before, but it was Lorenzo's first sea voyage. He leaves no record of the crossing – though another first-time traveller, Joseph Haydn, on his way from Vienna to London the previous year, had not enjoyed the experience. Becalmed for a full four hours, he had not at first been nervous, but then (he wrote in a letter to Maria von Genzinger), as 'the wind grew stronger and stronger, and I saw the monstrous high waves rushing at us, I became a little frightened, and a little indisposed, too. But I overcame it all and arrived safely, without vomiting, on shore. Most of the passengers were ill, and looked like ghosts, but since I went on to London, I didn't feel the effects of the journey right away; but then I needed two days to recover.'

'The moment one sets foot in England one is struck by the speed, willingness, and propriety with which all one's desires are fulfilled, and by the number of handsome girls,' wrote Georg Lichtenberg, a professor from Göttingen University, arriving for the first time in the 1770s. More than one newcomer remarked on the 'fine rosy girls', and many were impressed by the speed and efficiency of the stagecoaches, in comparison with lumbering Continental transport (though a crabby J. H. Campe, a German schoolmaster, complained bitterly of the torture of a fifteen-hour journey from Yarmouth to London, with only one half-hour break along the way). Christian Goede, arriving ten years after the Da Pontes, noted that as one neared the metropolis:

> . . . the high road becomes more and more lively. Travellers in carriages and on horseback follow after each other in rapid succession. They press onward with the utmost expedition, and seem universally actuated by the same restless principle of industry . . . On every side, post-coaches of various forms meet together, and vie with each other in the velocity of their movements; crowded not only with inside-passengers, but also completely occupied by travellers without.

Themselves pressing onward with the utmost expedition, Nancy and Lorenzo headed directly for London, through the shabby outer sprawl to the house where Nancy's sister Louisa lived with her husband, Charles Niccolini, on Silver Street (now Beak Street) off Golden Square – once a nouveau-riche quarter of the fashionable West End, but by the 1790s just a little on the turn.

Like Haydn, Da Ponte had no doubt been warned of the 'English disease' (melancholic gloom), of 'English rheumatism' (especially painful – Haydn countered it by the local custom of wrapping himself in flannel from head to foot), of the London fog ('so thick you could have spread it on bread', the composer complained), and of the nation's reputation for excessive drinking (that Da Ponte would have experienced first-hand, as at one point in the 1780s young Englishmen in Vienna found it great sport to get drunk, then break all the lanterns on the Graben, where he lived). Lorenzo was in a strange land. For the first time in his wanderings he was truly in the position of being foreign – Gorizia and Trieste, though in Austria, were strongly Italian in tone; in Vienna, and even to some extent in Dresden, Italian was an important language of court and culture. Here, few people spoke his tongue, and he knew hardly any English. In England, he was on the margins. When Casanova suggested he teach Italian to earn some money, Da Ponte snorted that was 'a profession currently practised by waiters, cobblers, exiles . . . who by way of payment are insulted with a few pennies, or a shilling, or sometimes a measure of beer'. Yet he found himself in a city larger and in many ways more advanced than any he had lived in before, a vigorous metropolis clamouring in pursuit of progress. 'Improvement' was the word of the moment, whether it meant rebuilding one's house in the current fashion or expanding one's mind. Writing later of his London life, Da Ponte said, 'So strange, so varied, so new are the things which happened to me in that city, that to give an idea in a brief compendium would be like trying to enclose an ocean in a walnut.'

So much of London was startlingly novel. John Soane's Euclidian Bank of England was rising in the city, stark and majestic. People were fascinated by the magnificent houses John and Robert Adam had built in the West End in the 1770s and 1780s, the style delicately distilled from ancient Rome, interiors painted in astonishing reds, greens and yellows, resplendent with motifs lifted from Pompeii. Rebellious John Nash, the inspired advocate of the asymmetrical 'picturesque' style, was hot on the Adams brothers' heels. New streets and squares were appearing; wide, raised, flagstone pavements now protected pedestrians' shoes from mud, their clothes from the splatter of passing carriages – at least in the smarter parts of town. Yet in the midst of this novelty was a strong note of conservatism, the beginnings of a strain of staidness that would characterize the next century. After 1791, 'she-dog' rather than 'bitch' was used in polite society; euphemisms for underwear and pregnancy abounded. Ideas germinated by Enlightenment *philosophes*, which bore fruit in American independence, had been brought closer to home by the revolution in France – and many who had supported the cause of the faraway colonists now became fearful of massacre and found the existence of the newly proclaimed French Republic unacceptable. Edmund

Burke's reactionary *Reflections on the Revolution in France*, published in
1790, prescient of the horrors of the Reign of Terror, found many
readers and a popular following. The kingdom was on the brink of war
with the republic.

Yet London glittered. Visitors to the metropolis marvelled at the
variety of goods on sale, the glass-fronted shops and the brilliant
illumination. One traveller declared that Oxford Street alone contained
a greater number of lamps than the whole of Paris. Goede was impressed
by 'the spacious streets, the magnificent causeways, the transparent
windows which reflect the beams of day-light with two-fold lustre,
the shops elegant beyond all description, the vast concourse of well-
dressed people ebbing to and fro, and above all a great number of green
lawns and public gardens, which enliven the finest parts of town by the
pleasing image of rural scenery . . .' As nightfall arrived, he was even
more taken by the 'thousand twinkling lights [that diffused] a bright
stream of glory over the main streets' and by the ingenuity of shopkeepers who replaced in their display-windows objects that might look
dull by candlelight with those that 'borrow[ed] an additional beauty from
the glare of the light that surround[ed] them'. Professor Lichtenberg was
quite swept away by life in the city, in comparison with his native
Göttingen, as he wrote to his friend Ernst Baldinger:

Imagine a street about as wide as the Weender in Göttingen, but,
taking it altogether, about six times as long. On both sides tall houses
with plate-glass windows. The lower floors consist of shops and seem
to be made entirely of glass; many thousand candles light up silverware,
engravings, books, clocks, glass, pewter, paintings, women's finery,
modish and otherwise, gold, precious stones, steel-work, and endless
coffee-rooms and lottery offices. The street looks as if it were
illuminated for some festivity: the apothecaries and druggists display
glasses filled with gay-coloured spirits . . . [that] suffuse many a wide
space with purple, yellow, verdigris-green, or azure light. The con-
fectioners dazzle your eyes with their candelabra and tickle your nose
with their wares, for no more trouble and expense than that of taking
both into their establishments. In these hang festoons of Spanish

grapes, alternating with pineapples, and pyramids of apples and oranges, among which hover attendant white-armed nymphs with silk caps and little silk trains . . . All this appears like an enchantment to the unaccustomed eye; there is therefore all the more need for circumspection in viewing all discreetly; for scarcely do you stop when, crash! a porter runs you down, crying 'By your leave', when you are lying on the ground. In the middle of the street roll chaises, carriages, and drays in an unending stream. Above this din and the hum and clatter of thousands of tongues and feet one hears the chimes from church towers, the bells of the postmen, the organs, fiddles, hurdy-gurdies, and tambourines of English mountebanks, and the cries of those who sell hot and cold viands in the open at street corners. Then you will see a bonfire of shavings flare up as high as the upper floors of the houses in a circle of merrily shouting beggar-boys, sailors and rogues. Suddenly a man whose handkerchief has been stolen will cry: 'Stop thief', and every one will begin running and pushing and shoving – many of them not with any desire of catching the thief, but of prigging for themselves, perhaps, a watch or a purse . . . That is Cheapside and Fleet Street on a December evening.

Arriving in London for the first time in the autumn of 1792, Lorenzo's 'unaccustomed eye' was surely just as enchanted by all he saw. In the now familiar position of being in a new city, without employment, looking for a home, and with little money, he quickly set to work. He and Nancy moved out of the Niccolini's house on Silver Street to a small room just around the corner, at 16 Sherrard Street (now Sherwood Street). Though not on a square – always more fashionable – they were nevertheless a step up from a court, row or close. As in Vienna, rooms on the middle floors were most in demand; poorer families crowded into the cellar and garret. Indoors, a strict hierarchy operated. The housekeeper (the chief lessee of the building) ruled; below him came various roomkeepers, who sublet parts of their multi-chambered domains; and below that still were lodgers like the Da Pontes, cramped into a single furnished room, often with a skilfully crafted bed that folded away and masqueraded during the day as a bureau, cupboard or bookcase. The rent for such a room would have been at least five shillings a week. Da Ponte had (he wrote to Casanova, who, more than ever, was becoming his confidant and father-figure) arrived in London with the equivalent of just a few guineas; Nancy's '*putana borsa*' with its 100 gulden had never been found. Lorenzo needed work urgently.

Fortunately, London was famed for its cosmopolitan music scene, and had a thriving Italian opera company. From Handel and Gluck through to Cherubini and Haydn (who had an enthusiastic reception the year before the Da Pontes arrived), foreign musicians were lauded in London – and handsomely paid. As early as 1713, Johann Mattheson had noted in his *Neu-eröffnetes Orchester*: 'He who in the present time wants to make a profit out of music betakes himself to England. The Italians exalt music; the French enliven it; the Germans strive after it; the English pay for it well.' Foreign musicians echoed this sentiment (and local ones, too, begrudgingly) throughout the century, especially in the final decades. Such assured fame and fortune were prime reasons why Nancy Storace had left Vienna for London in 1787. Prospects looked rosy for Da Ponte. *Una cosa rara* had been performed in London in 1789 to some acclaim, so his name was not unknown, and the post of librettist to the Italian opera had recently fallen vacant. La Storace had influence, and her brother Stephen (with whom Da Ponte had enjoyed quite some success in 1786 with *Gli equivoci*) together with Michael Kelly held positions of management at the King's Theatre on the Haymarket, home of the Italian opera company (*see* Appendix). This promised well for employment. Lorenzo approached his old friends immediately. Disregarding Casanova's advice, he also began to visit the Prince of Orange coffee-house, just across the way from the opera house and not only the haunt of 'Italian trouble-makers', but also of literati and denizens of the theatre world.

Da Ponte's rival for the post of theatre poet was the 72-year-old Carlo Francesco Badini, whom Da Ponte muttered knew less about writing libretti 'than did the shoes of Bertati' (his disdained replacement in Vienna). Badini, '[a master] of satire and malicious gossip', had been intriguing around the Italian opera in London since the 1750s, and had influential friends. By the time Lorenzo arrived on the scene, Badini's appointment was as good as made, and the younger poet chose to support his rival's claim, provided that he himself was offered two libretti a year at the usual London rates. Da Ponte proposed this, he told Casanova, to avoid unpleasantness – though as that was not a usual course of action for him, it may be assumed that he saw the battle already lost and deduced that such gallantry would stand him in good stead. With such an aged occupant, the post of theatre poet might soon fall vacant again. For a month or two Da Ponte was hopeful his proposal might be accepted, but both Kelly and Storace snubbed him. 'I believe the air in London,' Da Ponte wrote bitterly to Casanova, 'has something of the nature of the waters of Lethe.'

Uncowed, Lorenzo unleashed his energies. Within weeks he had applied, albeit with scant success, for patronage from Prince Lichtenstein, the Marquis of Salisbury, and the Duke of Bedford (who was closely involved with the Italian opera). Bedford and Salisbury he hoped to persuade to back his bid not only to become the next theatre poet, but also manager of the company. Casanova's patron Count Waldstein was in London, horrifying society with his tales of escape from the mob in Paris. Da Ponte managed to squeeze four guineas from him over five months, but the count was himself in difficulties, and after he returned to Dux no further help was forthcoming, despite Casanova's intervention. Da Ponte found better fortune with various foreign diplomats, Count Lamberg, the imperial ambassador, and the minister for the King of Naples. In addition, he had plans to open a room in which to give Italian readings, which he thought could net him fifteen guineas a month, and to start a review, *La bilancia teatrale*, which would appear the morning after each opera performance (no doubt wreaking public revenge on Badini, Kelly, the Storaces and their ilk). Neither plan came to anything. He conceived the idea of writing his memoirs – which he thought would be most lucrative – though that idea would not reach fruition for some years. He wrote an ode on the death of Louis XVI – an event that shocked him and swayed him towards more conservative views (as it did many) – and he entered into a sabre-fight of obscene satires with Badini (sending some of his more outrageous thrusts on to Casanova). By the beginning of May, he had spent his way through ninety guineas, 'though whether they sprang from the earth or fell from the sky only an angel could tell you'. Just then, he and Nancy heard the good news that her lost purse had been recovered intact, and that the money was in the hands of a dyer named Mardegani in Prague, though they had to work out the safest way of transferring it to London. In the meantime, ever careful to keep his top spinning, Da Ponte managed to maintain such a hum (as he had done decades before in Padua, and in his early days in Vienna) that 'everyone thinks I'm pretty well off'. The little room in Sherrard Street was a retreat and a refuge. Over and again in his letters to Casanova, Lorenzo writes of how he could not manage this life without Nancy, of the depth of their affection for each other, of how she understands him and gives him support.

Of Lorenzo's Orange coffee-house friends, only one really came forward with support, money and practical assistance. Carlo Pozzi, a second-rung composer who paid his way mainly from writing insertions for revived operas, introduced Da Ponte to Gertrud Mara. Madame Mara was one of the great singers of the century. Born in the same year as Da Ponte, she was now in her mid-forties and her voice was beginning to lose its grandeur, but she still commanded enormous fees, adoring audiences, and general respect. Madame Mara commissioned an opera from him, and he adapted his Trieste play *Mezenzio*, for which she paid him a handsome thirty guineas. Sensing that 'no favourable wind was blowing for me on the banks of the Thames', Da Ponte decided to use the money to travel to the Low Countries. He had heard that the French troupe there had disbanded, and he dreamed of starting an Italian opera company in its place. He left his dear Nancy in London with part of Madame Mara's money, and set off back across the Channel.

With barely enough money to support himself, let alone any capital; with no backing and few contacts in a land entirely foreign to him; with only the fire of his eternal optimism and inventive energy, Da Ponte arrived in Brussels in early July 1793. '*Audaces fortuna juvat* [Fortune helps those who dare]', he wrote to Casanova, and within eight days had 140 of the 300 subscribers he needed. But convincing subscribers (and especially good singers, who demanded part of their fees up front) of the credibility of the venture demanded a display of financial stability, and Da Ponte was beginning to falter. His plans were further disrupted

A letter written by Lorenzo Da Ponte when he was still Emanuele Conegliano to Don Pietro Bortoluzzi (14 July 1763). It is the only existing letter signed with his former name.

Lorenzo Da Ponte in his youth. Lithograph made from a watercolour in the second half of the eighteenth century.

Giacomo Casanova, the self-styled 'Chevalier de Seingalt'. By the time Da Ponte met him the rakish adventurer's sheen was beginning to fade.

Wolfgang Mozart, as he appeared when Da Ponte arrived in Vienna. From a portrait of the Mozart family by Johann Nepomunk, 1780/81.

The singer Nancy Storace, the first Susanna in *Le nozze di Figaro*. Famed for her voice, she was a close friend of Michael Kelly, who travelled to London with her.

Emperor Joseph II at the clavier with his two sisters Maria Anna and Maria Elisabeth, by Joseph Hauzinger. The family were all competent musicians.

The tenor Michael Kelly, known for his bouffant blond hair as well as his fine voice. The portrait is by John Neagle, after Sir Thomas Lawrence.

The Michaelerplatz, from a watercolour by Carl Schütz (1783). The Burgtheater, where Da Ponte worked as poet to the opera, is the modest building on the right of the picture, alongside the imposing Spanish Riding School.

Interior of the Burgtheater, *circa* 1830.

Portrait of Antonio Salieri by Heinrich Eduard von Wintter. Salieri was a year younger than Da Ponte – just six years older than Mozart – and a highly successful composer in his time.

A portrait of Mozart painted in 1790, the year before Da Ponte left Vienna, in which the effects of high living are clear. The painting – discovered in late 2004 – is by Johann Georg Edlinger.

Costumes for 'Urson', 'Atar' and 'Semira', from Salieri's opera *Axur, re d'Ormus*, designed by Friederich Anton Lohrman.

A 1791 cartoon satirizing the opera battles that preceded Da Ponte's arrival in London. Rival impresarios Robert Bray O'Reilly (left, backed by King George III and Queen Charlotte) and William Taylor (right, backed by Sheridan, the Prince of Wales and Mrs Fitzherbert) square up to each other.

A ticket for the premiere of Mozart's and Da Ponte's *Le nozze di Figaro*, 1 May 1786.

Anna Celestina Ernestina 'Nancy' Grahl. Nancy was known as Da Ponte's wife for the latter part of his life, though details of the ceremony by which they were married (Da Ponte was a Catholic priest at the time) are unclear.

The notoriously raucous area known as Five Points, north-east of City Hall in New York, in the late 1820s. Grocery shops were sources of alcohol – in his own shop Da Ponte recalls measuring out cobblers' and carters' morning drams.

New York's Italian Opera House, the first purpose-built opera house in the city, opened in 1833. Da Ponte was a driving force behind establishing the theatre, but had been sidelined from any part in management by the time it opened.

The interior of the Park Theatre, from an 1822 painting by John Searle. The Park was the city's most fashionable theatre.

Lorenzo Da Ponte in his professorial robes at Columbia College (later Columbia University). He was the first professor of Italian at Columbia.

A portrait of Da Ponte in old age, from a miniature by Nathaniel Rogers (1788–1844).

A view of New York from Brooklyn Heights. Print by William James Bennett after a watercolour by John William Hill, done in 1837, the year before Da Ponte's death.

by the resounding defeat of Anglo-Hanoverian and Austrian forces by
the French Army at Hondschoote, near Dunkirk, a decisive battle in wars
with revolutionary France begun the previous year. Da Ponte moved
north to Rotterdam, then later Amsterdam and The Hague, where
Nancy joined him. Da Ponte managed to convince the Dutch Stad-
holder to support his project, but could not persuade leading singers to
take him seriously. Nancy Storace first accepted an offer, then withdrew,
and La Ferrarese did not even answer his letter. A bitterly cold autumn set
in, as Nancy's 100 gulden ran out. In the streets and coffee-houses people
talked of the execution of Marie Antoinette, and the excesses of the
revolutionaries in Paris. By mid-October the venture had all but
collapsed, leaving Da Ponte and Nancy (who was pregnant) stranded
in The Hague. In Rotterdam Da Ponte sold the gold watch given him by
the grateful count on his journey to London, then he began to sell his
clothes, fraught with concern for Nancy's well-being. Towards the end
of the month, a kindly landlord took them in on credit:

> [W]e lived [there] for more than a week, she and I: our breakfast was
> bread, and bread our dinner. And sometimes not even bread, but tears
> made our supper! But it was not my companion shedding those tears!
> She endured everything with angelic patience, did her utmost to laugh
> and jest, obliged me to play chess with her, and for huge stakes, with
> whoever lost to pay the winner in caresses and kisses. These artifices of
> her tenderness, which in other circumstances would have been the
> delight of my life, served only to intesify my grief and desperation.

Da Ponte scorned Casanova's cynical suggestion that Nancy exploit her
charms for money, replying, 'As far as I'm concerned: *Yes to anything, but
not horns*. I believe that God has given me a heart and a brain: that is
enough for me to suffer all of fortune's reverses; to open one or another
road to me that will enable me to live with integrity, without having to
reproach myself for anything base or dishonourable. *Aude aliquid* [one
needs to dare], but not at the expense of virtue.' Nancy managed a
remarkably restrained postscript, saying that Casanova was not married,
so perhaps that was why he had offered such advice, and suggesting his

attempts at help be better directed to getting money for them out of Count Waldstein.

The situation appeared hopeless when, on 30 October, a letter arrived from Nancy's sister Louisa informing them that Badini had been sacked, and that the new manager of the King's Theatre, William Taylor (known as 'Opera' Taylor), had offered Lorenzo the post of theatre poet at a salary of 200 guineas. By mid-November, Lorenzo and Nancy were back aboard a Channel packet bound for England.

Chapter Thirteen

'THE CHARACTER OF Mr Taylor,' wrote John Ebers, manager of the King's Theatre in the early nineteenth century, '[was] one of the most singular of mankind.' Opera Taylor was a practical joker, an incorrigible meddler, impressively adept at talking money out of people, a man whose whole life was a continued bluff. 'It seemed his delight to involve himself as much as it was possible to perplex others. He quarrelled with everybody, ridiculed everybody and hoaxed everybody.' Haydn called him 'that miserable cur'. Da Ponte thought that '[l]eft to himself he was humane, noble, generous', and that his faults were the result of the influence of others.

Born into a poor family, Taylor had started professional life as a bank clerk, working his way into the management of the King's Theatre, eventually to buy it outright. When the old theatre burned down in 1789 (*see* Appendix), his conniving and Machiavellian scheming to reopen it under his control had been astonishing. With obscure thrusts and ingenious tactics he wreaked total confusion among his opponents (some of them the highest legal minds in the land), a state he then subtly used as leverage to get his way. Taylor's *coup de grâce*, given that he held only a leasehold on the old site, set to expire in 1803, was to buy up adjacent land freehold, then build a large new theatre in which the auditorium occupied the former site, but the stage was on land owned by himself. Anyone who planned to buy him out after 1803 would then be left with a theatre without a stage, or would have to allow him to name his price. Here was a man after Da Ponte's heart.

Taylor had frequent bouts of bankruptcy, managing to bend the King's Bench Rules (which confined debtors to gaol, or to prescribed limits outside prison walls) to jaunt off on fishing trips, and even on one occasion to travel to Hull to stand as an MP. When Ebers asked him how he managed to continue running the theatre while under King's Bench Rules, he replied:

> My dear fellow, how could I possibly conduct it if I were at liberty? I should be eaten up, Sir, devoured. Here comes a dancer – 'Mr Taylor, I want such a dress,' another, 'I want such and such an ornament.' One singer demands to sing in a part not allotted to him; another to have an addition to his appointments. No, – let *me* be shut up, and they go to Masterson [Taylor's secretary]; he, they are aware, cannot go beyond his line, but if they get at *me* – pshaw! no man at large can manage that theatre; and in faith no man that undertakes it ought to go at large.

Taylor had quite a task on his hands. In London, opera was entirely detached from court. Privately owned, the King's Theatre survived by whatever patronage it could attract, and on a scheme of subscriptions very similar to that Da Ponte had implemented in Vienna. The theatre Taylor had built was, after La Scala in Milan, the largest opera house in the world, very different for Lorenzo from the cosy proportions of the Burgtheater. When it reopened the press erupted in superlatives, marvelled at 'the stupendous fabric' that would 'rank among the finest pieces of architecture in Europe', and were agog at the total absence of pilasters in an auditorium wider than Westminster Hall. Especially impressive were the five tiers of individually curtained boxes, arranged as a lyre and staggered upwards, 'by which means every person in the boxes will be visible from any part of the house'. This was a distinct advantage rather than criticism, as 'there are many who think a clear sight of the boxes an essential part of the entertainment'. Goings-on in the auditorium were quite as much a focus of attention as those on stage. The Italian opera was 'the rendezvous of all that is gay and pleasurable in the Metropolis'.

Fashionable dandies, the 'puppies' and 'loungers' paraded themselves in Fops' Alley (a broad space running down the centre of the pit, almost to the orchestra) and sported about on stage – a practice long since stopped at the theatres in Covent Garden and Drury Lane. The frequent presence of the Prince of Wales, the pivot of London's *haute monde,* made attendance at the opera absolutely de rigueur in society. Names appeared in screeds in the next morning's press, as eager social climbers scoured the papers to see whether they had made mention, or to sift out grist for gossip. 'The Prince of Wales was present the whole evening with Mrs Fitzherbert,' noted *The Times* in its report of the opening night of the first season of Italian opera in the new theatre. Reviews went into as much detail on the audience as of the performance, such as the critique of Cimarosa's *La locandiera,* which veered off to note:

> The Duchess of Gordon's box at the Opera was honoured by the alternate visits of the Prince of Wales and the Dukes of York and Gloucester. They sat with her for half an hour each. The Prince of Wales, the Duke of Gloucester, and Prince William of Gloucester were dressed exactly alike in blue, with gold *Brandenburghs.* The Duke of York was in *scarlet,* and his Grace of Cumberland in the *old green and narrow embroidery.* The Princess Sophia of Gloucester was in a *gauze bonnet,* composed of *light-blue* and white gauze, decorated with coloured ribbons and feathers.

Da Ponte was used to similar social display at the Burgtheater, and audiences were not nearly as raucous as those he remembered from Venice, but Londoners, it seemed to him, lacked the Viennese and Italian love for the opera itself. Haydn also opined, 'The English are not too fond of Italian opera, because they don't understand the language.' In Fanny Burney's *Evelina,* the ill-bred Mr Branghton puts it more bluntly:

> 'What a jabbering they make!' cried Mr. Branghton; 'there's no knowing a word they say. Pray what's the reason they can't as well sing in English? – but I suppose the fine folks would not like it if they could understand it.'

The critic Thomas Wilkes brought a similar dose of stolid English common sense to bear: 'The absurdity of managing the commonest matters of life by way of sing-song is glaring,' he wrote in his *General View of the Stage*. 'Who is there, in his right wits, that ever sung out his commands to his servants? or imparted, in that manner, a secret to his friend?'

There had long been opposition in England to 'this *exotic monster* the Italian Opera' – when the old King's Theatre had burned down there had been those who agreed with Horace Walpole that there was no occasion to rebuild it, as, 'The nation has long been tired of operas, and now has a good opportunity of dropping them.' Some of this opposition was sheer chauvinism – something only too familiar to Da Ponte from clashes with the German faction at the Burgtheater – but many people preferred the more down-to-earth ballad operas (such as John Gay's *The Beggar's Opera*) that were common fare at Drury Lane, with spoken text instead of recitative and interpolated songs in English. It was a divide similar to that between *Singspiel* and Italian opera in Vienna, but in London riven even more deeply along class lines. The general populace crowded into the pit at Drury Lane for ballad operas; the elite preened itself at the King's Theatre, where (though standards were slipping by the 1790s) evening dress was required in all but the uppermost gallery and the cheapest tickets were equivalent to a clerk's daily wage. Here they gossiped in their curtained boxes, secretly preferring the ballet interludes and for the most part not understanding a word of what was sung on stage. 'The Italian opera would instantly be abandoned,' wrote Goede, 'notwithstanding the talents of the singers and the beauty of the music, if dancing were not the powerful magnet which attracts the Londoners. All Italian operas are, therefore, abridged, divertissements introduced between the acts, and the ballet considerably lengthened, in order to gratify the public taste.' Da Ponte's primary task was to hack, paste and alter rather than create new works. His status as theatre poet was nowhere near as high as it had been in Vienna. He was modestly paid, rarely mentioned in reviews and seldom featured in the playbills. But it was work.

Nancy and Lorenzo moved back to the house in Sherrard Street. Their daughter Louisa was born early in 1794. Da Ponte spent most of his first season at the King's Theatre tinkering with other men's libretti, including a version of the old Gazzinga–Bertati *Don Giovanni Tenorio*, done, despite his pleading 'in bestial preference to the *Don Giovanni* of Mozart'. He managed to insert his and Mozart's infinitely superior 'Catalogue Song' in place of Bertati's, but on the whole thought the opera a dismal affair. Audiences appear to have agreed, as *Don Giovanni Tenorio* lasted only two performances – though the *Morning Chronicle* (run by a friend of Taylor's, and ever happy to puff the King's Theatre) did admire the 'practicable hell', which used red-tinted transparencies and fiery torches that 'threw flashes of light into the boxes, which had a most superb effect, in the way of spectacle'. Don Giovanni's funeral procession, with a ballet executed by dancers in Spanish dress, was on the first night joined by so many unofficial mourners that the artists could not move, and a ban on audience members swelling the parade had to be enforced for subsequent performances.

After the first flush of euphoria at his new employment, Lorenzo was having to temper his expectations. London opera was old-fashioned in comparison to that at the Burgtheater. *Opera seria* still held a position in the repertoire, and just three years previously audiences had seen intense rivalry between Marchesi and Pacchieroti – two of the greatest castrati of the day. Castrati had long since given way to tenors at the Burgtheater, as Vienna set the new taste for buffa, and even in England opponents of Italian opera reserved special venom for the practice (though, it must be said, far more often on grounds of their improbability in heroic roles than for humanitarian reasons). Acting standards at the King's Theatre were not of the best. Nancy Storace and Michael Kelly had brought with them from the Burgtheater a more subtle, naturalistic performing style, but it had been slow to catch on. A critic at the first night of *Don Giovanni Tenorio* was moved to comment: 'The Italian gentry must *pantomime* it more – they really stand as dull as some of our own actors, with one eye on the Prompter, and the other on the Leader of the Band, beating time with both hand and foot like children in the science.' Most dispiriting of all to Da Ponte was the London taste for *pasticcio* – the patching into an extant opera of singers' display pieces, popular arias to please the public, bits and pieces garnered, invented and stolen, until the final product bore little resemblance to the original and often did not even make much dramatic sense. The practice was widespread, but though falling from favour on the Continent survived at the King's Theatre, where few of the audience could understand Italian. Still worse, Da Ponte had to take a hatchet to otherwise good libretti, sometimes pruning a hundred lines of recitative to a mere twenty, in order to reduce full-length operas to a size the local audience would be equal to, and to make room for the ever-popular ballets. London opera cried out for a good composer to bring it some original music, a poet that was his match, and a strong guiding hand from management (something neither Kelly nor Taylor, for all his financial scheming, seemed able to give).

Da Ponte's work at the King's Theatre was considerably enlivened by the arrival that spring of Brigida Banti and Anna Morichelli. La Banti, 'an asp, a fury, a demon of Hell, capable of throwing an entire empire into confusion, let alone a mere theatre', sang chiefly *opera seria* and was celebrated for her voice. La Morichelli, 'an old fox' whose principle divinities were Pride, Envy and Profit, was a prima donna buffa renowned for her acting skills. She had been Da Ponte's first Diana in *L'arbore di Diana* in Vienna.

Banti, who had grown up as a street-singer and (according to Da Ponte) retained 'all the habits, manners and customs of a brazen Corsican', read music badly (if at all) and had exhausted any number of teachers with her obstinacy and laziness. On stage, she had the distracting habit of 'conversing *mezza voce* with performers in the orchestra, instead of attending to the business of the scene'. She also had a fondness for the bottle. Yet she had a voice that the *London Chronicle* described as 'ecstasy to listen to', commenting that 'more perfect, more impassioned, more divine singing, perhaps, was never heard'. The informed and discerning opera-goer Lord Mount Edgcumbe recalled: 'Her natural powers were of the finest description: her voice, sweet and beautiful throughout, had not a fault in any part of its unusually extensive compass. Its lower notes, which reached below ordinary sopranos, were rich and mellow; the middle, full and powerful; and the very high totally devoid of shrillness . . .' It was a voice, Da Ponte said sourly, that was 'the single gift she had received from Nature'.

Banti had, according to the painter Vigée-Le Brun, a bosom shaped like a pair of bellows, and was 'tiny and very ugly, with such a lot of hair that her chignon looks like a horse's mane'. Yet her opening salvo was to establish her position within the company by embarking on an affair with Opera Taylor. An anonymous pamphlet entitled *Veritas* sneered at the theatre proprietor's 'blind attachment' to this 'antiquated siren' (Banti was in her thirties), calling Taylor 'a doting Cicesbeo with an Harreden, who had children in every town in Italy'. Da Ponte noted that La Banti had 'her secret young Adonises and changed them oftener than other women change their hat', yet she had the proprietor under her thumb, demanding – and getting – most Saturday-night performances, while driving Morichelli back to the less popular Tuesdays.

Morichelli, too, had a taste for 'voluptuous pleasures', but was wary and cunning. Although around the same age as her rival, she managed 'to play the part of a modest and retiring virgin of fifteen'. Like Banti, she had a sharp temper, but, wrote Da Ponte, she was a stealthy fighter: 'the more bitter the gall she harboured in her soul, the smoother and more honeyed shone the smile on her face.' The composer Gaetano Andreozzi had a different experience when he made overtures towards her one day: 'I found her [he told Michael Kelly] in a *motivo penseroso*. I approached her in *adante Siciliano*, followed by a movement *allegretto vivace*, when she ran up a division of abuse *con spirito*, and came out with two false fifths and a change of key so discordant that I was obliged to quit the house in a *motto prestissimo*, to *volti subito* and run down stairs, leaving her screaming *in tempo furioso!*'

Both singers were, Da Ponte wrote, 'idols of the public but the terrors of composers, poets, singers, and impresarios'. And they had descended on London simultaneously. Not only were their contracts at the King's Theatre running concurrently, but they had come over from Spain on the same packet boat, and travelled from Southampton in the same coach. By the time they reached the metropolis, the artillery was bristling – and Da Ponte was in the direct line of fire.

Each demanded an opera that ensured her debut outshone that of her rival. 'God help you,' Banti threatened Da Ponte one day, 'if Morichelli gets a better reception in [her debut] than I do in mine!' Morichelli conducted her campaign through leers, pouts and curt phrases. Da Ponte (and no doubt the rest of the King's Theatre) set to work 'all of a tremble'. La Banti mobilized first, appearing on 26 April as the murderous Assyrian queen in Francesco Bianchi's *La Semiramide*, a role she had triumphed in some years earlier in Naples. Da Ponte made his usual additions and adaptations to a text by Ferdinando Moretti, based on Voltaire's tragedy. To the outside world, Banti 'gave exquisite delight' and 'convinced every hearer of her being the finest singer in the world'. Her appearance marked a groundshift in London opera. Previously, the star of an *opera seria* had been the castrato. Now, for the first time, a soprano enjoyed the top billing, the adulation, the cosseting, and the outrageous fees. Mount Edgcumbe points out that Banti 'was but poorly supported' by male singers in the opera. The best castrato the company could come up with was the second-rate Agrippino Roselli, and no available tenor could rank with Michael Kelly, who was too busy with management and with performing in English opera at Drury Lane to appear. *La Semiramide* took London by storm. 'No opera ever had greater success or a longer run than this,' wrote Mount Edgcumbe, 'indeed, it was one of those of which it is impossible to tire.'

Later in the season Banti won over her audiences even further, when after a gala performance of *La vittoria* – a cantata especially written by Da Ponte to music by Paisiello, celebrating Lord Howe's victory over the French fleet off Brest – she rounded off the show with a rousing version of 'Rule Britannia'. This was a wise gesture in a city edgy at the ongoing war against republican France. Rumours of invasion and of Jacobins secretly stirring up insurrection against the King had led to anti-French hysteria in which, if they were not careful, all foreigners could end up being tarred with the French brush. Banti may not have been (as Da Ponte once put it) exactly the person who invented gunpowder, but she was astute enough to see what was needed to win a following. On other occasions she impressed audiences with her rendition of the newly established national anthem 'God Save the King', singing 'with as perfect articulation, as if she were a native of England, and never were the few notes of the anthem so exquisitely uttered'. The first conquests were to Banti.

On 17 May, Morichelli counter-attacked. She made her debut in

Martín y Soler's *Il burbero di buon cuore*, the opera that had been Da Ponte's breakthrough at the Burgtheater, and in which she had previously enjoyed high favour. Morichelli introduced two songs by Vittorio Trento and G. G. Ferrari, while the buffo Morelli had an additional aria by Da Ponte's ally and benefactor Carlo Pozzi. Together they sang a duet by Haydn, taken from his opera *Orlando Paladino*, but with new words by Da Ponte. The Haydn duet, especially, drew critical acclaim, but Morichelli's reviews could not match those of her rival. Banti held her position as favourite. Morichelli took some solace in the news that Martín y Soler was himself soon to arrive in London from St Petersburg, at Da Ponte's instigation and Kelly's invitation. She knew what a public success his work could be. She had shone in Martín's operas before – and now he would be creating roles especially for her. Having been defeated in the skirmish for Opera Taylor, La Morichelli realigned her sights. Soon after arriving in London, Martín y Soler became her lover.

Lorenzo welcomed the advent of an old friend. Martín reached London towards the end of 1794, and went to stay with the Da Pontes. By now, Nancy and Lorenzo, though remaining in Sherrard Street, were apparently acting as roomkeepers in larger lodgings. Martin had made it a precondition of his appointment that Da Ponte – poet for his three most successful works – be his librettist. The two men set to work immediately. By the end of the year Morichelli had a new opera. *La scuola di maritati* (The School for Spouses) opened on 27 January 1795, with Martín leading from the harpsichord. The opera 'did wonders' according to *The Times*, as it was 'particularly adapted to the taste of an English audience'. The *Morning Chronicle* noted, approvingly, that the music pleased both the popular and the learned ear, and that 'many pieces . . . will assuredly come to the barrel organ'. All the opera needed, wrote the critics, was 'the pruning knife', as it was too long.

Da Ponte had surmounted 'composers' jealousy, rivals' badmouthing, women's cabals, the directors' ignorance, national prejudices' to bring Martín to London, and a first-night Italian cabal paid to hiss this usurping Spaniard in their midst was drowned out by rapturous English applause. The 'Italian troublemakers' at the Orange coffee-house seethed. Da

Ponte must have regretted ignoring Casanova's advice not to have anything to do with them when an obscene and dangerously revealing satire began circulating from the pen of Badini, entitled: 'Brief news of the opera buffa entitled *The School for Spouses, or rather of the Cuckold* : written by the famous Lorenzo Da Ponte, who after having been Jewish, Christian, Priest and Poet in Italy and Germany, finds himself being Secular, Married and a Jackass in London.' Da Ponte retorted with an equally filthy batch of verse.

Such ordure-flinging apart, the Da Ponte that Martín found in London was more subdued than the friend who had joined in his carousels with the ladies of Vienna. Nancy was pregnant again (though she appears to have lost the baby), and the doting husband and new father drew back from his friend's bachelor dalliances. A tension crackled between them that exploded halfway through their work on a second opera for Morichelli. The second act of *L'isola de piacere* (Island of Pleasure), Da Ponte said 'was written on an Isle of Ice'. Part of the reason for this is that Morichelli had insisted on a mad scene (following on her success with one in Paris), which 'fitted about as appropriately there as Pilate in the Lord's Prayer', but the prime cause of the frost was Martín's lechery. A servant girl ('neither pretty nor interesting' according to Lorenzo) was carrying the composer's child. When she reported this to Morichelli, Martín said the child was Da Ponte's – and the word had spread. Da Ponte was furious that Martín had 'painted me with the colours of his own black soul in the face of my friends'. Martín treated it all as a joke, paid the girl off and went to live with Morichelli. Work on *L'isola de piacere* limped on, but in the end it was poorly received, staggering through only four performances. Haydn harrumphed that the music was simply the overture from *L'abore di Diana* and then 'a lot of old stuff from *Cosa rara*'.

L'isola de piacere was the last mainpiece of the season. Morichelli made a strategic retreat to Italy, taking her new operas with her (and later giving *La scuola di maritati*, especially, with some success). Martín y Soler left London without saying goodbye. 'Oh! Monster without character or heart!' wrote Da Ponte to Casanova on 25 August 1795, in what was to be his last letter to his old friend and counsellor (who, increasingly frail, died in 1798). Da Ponte had heeded one and ignored another of the three nuggets of advice that Casanova had given him: to go to London, not to associate with the Italians at the Prince of Orange coffee-house, and never to sign his name to anything. He was soon to disregard the third, with devastating consequences.

The following three seasons would prove uninspiring for Da Ponte, comprising the usual cut-and-patch work, revivals of his old libretti (such as *La cifra*, which he had written for Salieri in 1789), two translations, and just four new operas. A revival of *L'abore di Diana* in April 1797 drew by far the best notices of the period, and Da Ponte received rare personal mention in a review for his work on Sacchini's *Evelina*, originally written in French and 'very ably translated into Italian by the Poet of the Theatre'. Reception of his new operas was lukewarm, and indeed *Merope* (composed by Bianchi, based on the Voltaire tragedy), which premiered in June 1797, was thought 'stale, flat and unprofitable', despite a build-up that had led the *Monthly Mirror* to expect 'a very grand, scientific [i.e. accomplished] and impressive performance'.

Banti still reigned, more unpopular than ever backstage once she had decided that the musicians' candle-stubs, formerly theirs to take home at the end of an evening, were now the prima donna's prerogative; and La Storace returned to the Italian stage (she had been appearing mainly at Drury Lane), sweeping up the applause with her performance in *Diana*, even though time had taken its toll, and one critic thought that 'as this lady's figure is not of the most exquisite form, we submit to her better judgement, the propriety of not again coming forward in *Breeches*'. Storace's new lover, the young tenor John Braham, so impressed the *Morning Chronicle* with his debut in Grétry's *Zemira e Azore* (in a new Italian translation by Da Ponte) that the critic hoped 'he will give us an example, that shall induce us to chace from an English stage the degrading and disgusting form of a *Castrato*'. As for the theatre poet, Da Ponte was beginning to find life in London a strain on his meagre income, and started to look around for additional ways of earning money.

London was expensive. Haydn had complained of that as early as 1791, and ongoing conflict with France had hiked prices even higher.

Crop failures and the exigencies of war caused a 90 per cent soar in the cost of wheat between 1793 and 1794, and rising taxes took another bite from the family budget. In October 1795, a 200,000-strong, hungry mob had attacked King George III as he drove through St James's Park in his state coach, drawn by 'eight fine Cream-Coloured Horses in Red Morocco Harnesses', breaking its windows and yelling, 'No King, No War' and, 'Give us Peace and Bread.' Even the well-fed were tense, as rumours of an imminent French invasion shot periodically through the city. Fears were not in any way allayed by news that a brilliant young commander called Napoleon Bonaparte, already made a general in his twenties, was – as 1796 raced on – notching up victory after victory across northern Italy.

Da Ponte decided that one path to extra income would be to buy a printing press and publish the King's Theatre libretti himself. He had already discovered the exorbitant cost of having anything printed in London, when making plans to bring out the review *La bilancia teatrale.* Cutting out the middleman by having his own press would edge up the 50 per cent cut of profits from all libretti sold at the theatre that he already enjoyed. During 1796 he raised the backing, and set up shop just around the corner from the theatre, at 134 Pall Mall. Da Ponte's debut as a publisher was with the libretto for *Evelina*, in January 1797. Soon after that, he claims, Vincenzo Federici – director of music at the opera and Banti's secret lover – persuaded the singer to convince Taylor that he should be assigned Da Ponte's 50 per cent share of libretto sales, a privilege Federici enjoyed for two years.

No demure stay-at-home, Nancy also began to bring in money. Da Ponte secured from Taylor a lease on the coffee-room at the King's Theatre, and Nancy and her sister Louisa took over its management. The coffee-room, billed as 'one of the most beautiful Rooms in the Kingdom', with a lofty ceiling, 'and the whole . . . simply magnificent', had for some years been inoperative owing to a dispute over the cost of extra lighting, but the theatre underwent extensive renovations at the end of 1796, and Nancy's coffee-room opened to general approbation in January 1797. 'The paintings and decorations are very elegant,' noted one first-nighter, 'Lipparati, who was many years a painter to the late

Empress of Russia, executed the figures.' The *Morning Chronicle* welcomed the coffee-room as a magnet to the fashionable, drawing the 'Puppies in pantaloons' away from parading through the pit and on the stage: 'This Coffee Room will be an admirable resort for a lounge, and may be the means of reducing Fop's-alley, as well as the Stage, from half their nocturnal tenants. It is certain that, in this more remote haunt, the elegant Beau may indulge in his promenade with less interruption to the Audience, and fashionable *badinage* may be reconciled with decorum.' 'Madame Daponte's' coffee-room brimmed with the cream of society, not only on opera nights but on the mornings of open rehearsals, not only in the hour before the show began (when ticket-holders who did not have reserved places in boxes crammed the corridors, waiting for the inside doors to open) but all the way through the performance, as those – like Fanny Burney's Mrs Harrel, whose 'love of Opera was merely a love of company, fashion, and shew' – heedless of the artistes on stage, 'to the coffee-room readily led the way'. The end of the evening was busiest of all, as people delayed their departures to avoid the heave-ho of carriages and sedan chairs outside the theatre. The coffee-room became one of the most glittering assemblies in town. Soon Nancy was also catering for the enormously popular masked balls held periodically in the theatre (where on at least one occasion in the coffee-room, 'several parties kept up the Highland Fling until morning'). At the outset, Lorenzo had estimated an annual income from his wife's venture of £100. Nancy was clearly earning more than that.

Da Ponte's initial relations with Taylor had been cool – the proprietor had all but ignored him when first introduced – but now they heaped friendship upon one another. They went for long walks together, called at each other's houses. Taylor asked Da Ponte's advice 'on various matters, theatrical or financial, and seemed to be most pleased, as much by my observations, as by my calculations'. Flattered, Da Ponte drew closer. Taylor became a shadow of Joseph II, Da Ponte the eager acolyte, anxious for approval, braced by their association. In the background was Banti, generally drunk and slyly taunting. One day Taylor, half-jestingly, asked Da Ponte if he could raise some money for him, producing a bill of exchange for £300 endorsed by Federici which he wanted transformed

into cash. 'If you can do that,' said Banti, 'your fortune is made!' Taylor
was yet again in financial trouble, and, as the *Monthly Mirror* raged, even
'the dear little infants behind the scenes . . . [the] flying and dancing
Cupids, whose astonishing exactness entitles them to our support, have
not received a shilling salary during the season'.

Da Ponte took the bill to 'a very smooth young man' who operated
from a shop with the sign 'Money' over the door (where, on first arriving
in London, he had pawned a ring for six guineas). The young man sold
him a watch for twenty-two guineas (worth fifteen) and drew up an
order on the Bank of London for the remainder of the money. Da Ponte
reached out to take it, and was presented instead with a pen. He had to
endorse Federici's bill of exchange. Casanova's advice thrust out of his
mind, he put his name to the paper. In England, that made him liable for
half the sum.

Da Ponte's action earned him a '*Bravo, poeta!*' from Banti, who
pocketed the watch, which Taylor had been about to present him.
In his earlier life, Da Ponte might well have become besotted with such
'an asp, a fury, a demon of Hell' as Banti; now he had Nancy. Instead it
was Banti who began to rain favours on him, praising his unselfishness,
his hard work and his talent, eulogizing his beautiful eyes. With arch
looks and suggestive glances, Banti invited him to spend some time with
them at Holywell, Taylor's country house. Taylor gamely agreed.
Embarrassed, Da Ponte accepted, but arrived at Holywell with Nancy
– younger and more attractive than her hostess – earning himself the
threatening aside: 'With your wife! Well . . . so much the worse for
you!' Banti and her secret lover Federici, for whom Da Ponte harboured
an intense dislike, were dangerous opponents, but Lorenzo was becoming the agent of his own undoing.

The bill he had encashed at the 'Money' shop was to be the first of
many. In one year, Da Ponte claims, he raised in this way a sum
approaching 6,500 guineas, ingratiating himself ever more fervently
to his proprietor. He became aware of Taylor's shadier dealings – such
as buying goods on credit and then pawning them, selling free passes, and
overselling season tickets – but, with the dogged loyalty he was capable
of towards those he loved, remained convinced that, 'left to himself and

provided with plenty of money, [Taylor] would have been one of the best men in the world'. Lorenzo professed innocence of the financial danger he himself was running: 'I a poet by trade . . . scarcely knowing what an acceptance, an endorsement, or a note is.' If that was so, one can but imagine Nancy's frustration – her father and brother were, after all, moneylenders who had operated in England – as, time and time again, she tried to dissuade her husband from such folly.

Taylor, for his part, dispensed friendship and favour. At the end of the 1797–98 season he suggested Da Ponte make a journey to Italy, offering 100 guineas towards travel expenses. Nancy Storace and John Braham had left London for the Continent, and no fitting replacement had ever been found for Morichelli. Taylor commissioned Da Ponte to recruit a buffo tenor and soprano. Lorenzo was elated. It was nearly twenty years since he had been in Italy. His banning order had expired, so he could once again go to Venice and, more importantly, he could visit his family in Ceneda. As fast as they could, he and Nancy scraped together £1,000 in money and jewels (much of it, surely, earnings from the coffee-room), and bought a small carriage. Baby Louisa was sent to stay with her eponymous aunt. By October, Nancy and Lorenzo were aboard a boat bound for Hamburg.

Chapter Fourteen

NOT EVEN THE notoriously dreadful German roads could hold Lorenzo back in his enthusiasm to see his family. He and Nancy set off directly from Hamburg, and by 2 November were rattling into Castelfranco, about fifty kilometres from Venice. Lorenzo told Nancy to rejoin him in Treviso in two days (best not to present her immediately to his father, who most likely still thought Lorenzo to be an abbé), and started immediately for Ceneda in a hired wagon. He arrived there as evening fell, and for a while simply stood, breathing in old aromas, looking up at a familiar sky. Leaving the wagon some distance from his father's house, so its creaking wheels would not alert anyone, he covered his head with a scarf and made his way across the cobbles. Then he knocked at the door.

I heard someone cry from a window:
'Who is there?'
I tried to alter my voice, and answered just:
'Open up!'
But that was enough for one of my sisters to recognise my voice, and cry with a scream to the others:
'It's Lorenzo!'
They were down the stairs like lightning, flinging themselves around my neck and almost suffocating me with their kisses and caresses. Then they bore me in to my father who, on hearing my name

and even more at the sight of me, remained completely immobile for a
good few minutes.

It was All Souls' Day and the entire extended family had gathered to
celebrate the feast. Just a short while earlier, Da Ponte's 76-year-old
father (once again widowed) had proposed a toast: 'Let us drink to the
health of our Lorenzo, and pray God that He may give us the grace to see
him before I die.'

That night Lorenzo shared his father's bed, waking in the morning to
find Gaspare had slipped softly out at dawn to the market, and that the
family were nudging and shuffling outside the bedroom door, waiting
for his first stirrings. 'I know not whether I had occasion to spit, or cough,
or make the bed creak: all I know is that the next moment I could see a
phalanx of men, women and children, marching into my room, flinging
the windows wide open, and then leaping on to my bed . . . A little
while later my father came in. The good old man was laden with fruit
and flowers, the latter being strewn by the family all over my bed till I
was covered with them head to feet; surrounded by a general hubbub of
squeals of merriment and happiness at all that jubilant festivity.' A servant
girl brought in coffee, and then everyone sat around the bed for
breakfast. 'In very truth I remember having seen neither before nor
since that morning a happier spectacle. It was though I were the centre of
a circle of angels rather than of mortal folk.' Lorenzo was living the idyll
of 'nostra Famigliuola', of which he had dreamed so often.

Word spread quickly through the village. Old friends and former loves
came to call. Two days later, Da Ponte left for Treviso with his youngest
half-sister Faustina and his favourite Paolo, to introduce Faustina to
Nancy, who – he had told his family – was a friend, a pretty young
dancer from the opera company. Paolo, who knew Nancy from Trieste,
may well have known about the marriage, but Lorenzo is coy in his
memoirs about whether or not he revealed Nancy's true status to the rest
of his family. Whatever Gaspare's initial motives had been for converting
to Christianity three decades earlier, he was, as an old man, extremely
devout and would have been deeply upset at the news.

In Treviso Da Ponte met up with former pupils, with his old friend

Giulio Trento, who had helped stitch and unstitch some of his earliest poems, and with Bernard Memmo, who was temporarily in town, and still utterly ruled by Teresa Zerbin. The mistress who had been behind Memmo's split with Da Ponte was now grown old, ugly and fat. Enjoyable though these reunions were, Treviso offered little opportunity to hear new singers. Da Ponte may also have got wind of the fact that the local assistant police commissioner was uneasy about his presence, and on 13 November had received instructions from the imperial authorities to eject him. (Treviso was in Austrian hands, and Da Ponte must still in some way have been *non grata* in Vienna.) By the time the commissioner replied to his seniors four days later, Da Ponte had left. He sent Nancy to Ceneda with Paolo and Faustina, and travelled south to Venice, where he had been told two good prima donnas were singing.

Venice shocked him. The year before, the city had been occupied by the French, the first foreign army in its thousand-year history to cross the lagoon. Within months, Napoleon had bartered off the glorious Serenissima like unwanted chattels to the Hapsburg Empire, and French soldiers had hacked and hammered at anything feasibly movable and taken it away. Even the four bronze horses above the great west portal of St Mark's had gone. The French had ransacked altars, stripped the Doge's splendid state barge of its trimmings, and for no reason at all smashed all the fine plasterwork and the great marble staircase in the Arsenal. Most patricians had retreated to their country estates on terra firma, and the Venetians who remained were stunned, dismayed, scarcely able to comprehend what had happened to their city. As Lorenzo walked across the Piazza San Marco, once a font of gaiety where he had jostled with mountebanks and ballad singers, where Matilda's boatman had twitched his sleeve with news of his mistress, he could hardly believe what he found: 'As I turned my eyes in every direction, I could see only melancholy, silence, solitude, desolation. I could see no more than seven people as I entered the Piazza . . . and my surprise increased at seeing that even the coffee shops were empty. In eleven of them, I counted exactly twenty-two people and no more.' In low voices, fearful of arrest, the Venetians discussed new taxes, high prices and police thuggery.

Always a small town, Venice had shrunk further, and it was not long before Lorenzo began to encounter people he knew. In the fish market, an old man, 'very pale, haggard, unkempt, stained by smoke, who had every appearance of being a beggar', turned out to be Girolamo Tiepolo, the imperious twin brother of his first great love Angela, now offering to carry purchases home for strangers. Angela was dead, said Girolamo. Without the public offices of the old order, which had been the mainstay of so many patrician families, *barnabotti* like him had subsided into indigence. Da Ponte also recognized the jutting nose of Gabriele Doria, brother-in-law to his second Venetian love Anzoletta, and the man he believed to have been behind the denunciation that lead to his banishment. Da Ponte spoke warily to Doria, and learned that Anzoletta was still alive, and with the husband she had returned to after their affair. He visited them, and was received 'as joyfully as a loving sister might welcome a brother'. La Ferrarese was also in town, and more than happy to meet Da Ponte again once she discovered he was recruiting singers for London. She said to him, 'You know, Da Ponte, you are handsomer than ever?' To which he ungallantly replied, 'I'm afraid I'm not able to say the same of you!' He then apologized and told her about Nancy. Together they attended *Il re Teodoro*, by Da Ponte's old adversary Casti, for Lorenzo to hear some singers. The prima donna that evening was good, but already contracted for the Carnival. Da Ponte did not offer to sign La Ferrarese. He was not progressing very far with his mission for Opera Taylor.

Two nights after Da Ponte arrived in Venice, Anzoletta and her husband came to his inn for supper, and Anzoletta slipped him a note warning him to beware of Gabriele Doria, now her *cavaliere servente*, and still insanely jealous of him. Later that night, Da Ponte relates, Doria arrived at the inn with a police officer and warrant instructing that, 'By order of His Imperial and Royal Majesty, Signor Lorenzo Da Ponte will be pleased to leave Venice tomorrow before evening.' This may have been a trumped-up charge, instigated by Doria, or else the earlier eviction letter pursuing him from Treviso. He left Venice before dawn, sending word to Nancy that he would not be coming to Ceneda and that she should join him in Padua. Lorenzo would never see his Ceneda family again.

As soon as Nancy arrived, they set off for Bologna, then Italy's foremost market-place for singers, dancers and musicians. They had hardly begun their journey when the carriage was halted by two imperial soldiers who, because Nancy addressed one in French and the other in Italian, accused her of being a spy.

> 'The young lady,' remarked one of [the soldiers] ironically, 'is adept in many tongues!'
>
> 'Oh sir!' she answered, 'I speak other languages, and among them my own.'
>
> 'Of what nation are you, signora?'
>
> 'I am English, sir! I speak French because I lived for a time in France; German because my father was born in Dresden; Dutch, because I lived in Holland for a while, Italian because it is the language of my consort.'

The situation was saved by the appearance of an officer who had known Da Ponte in Vienna. He endorsed their passports, and they continued their journey. En route to Bologna they stopped at Ferrara, where Da Ponte met another old friend, Giorgio Pisani, now freed after many years in prison. Da Ponte, who had once supported Pisani's political stance with a fervent sonnet, was growing crustily conservative, and thought Pisani no longer 'the wise, sapient citizen of the Republic, but a rabid, and desperate revolutionary'. In Bologna he met a young poet on the rise, Ugo Foscolo, whose work he would come to admire much. Da Ponte was thoroughly enjoying himself feasting with the literati of Ferrara and Bologna, but still had no singers – and winter was falling. A letter from London announcing that Banti and Federici had made up after an earlier split (an alliance that did not bode well for Da Ponte) further focussed his mind.

Leaving Nancy (who was again pregnant) in Bologna, Da Ponte travelled on to Florence, where he most likely met the renowned dramatist Vittorio Alfieri (who on reading his *Il Mezenzio* commented that Da Ponte had read too much Metastasio, and ought instead to consider the Greeks). Still he found no singers. In freezing cold, he headed back north, the 'rickety carriage and two miserable horses' (the only one willing to carry him in such weather) capsizing along the way, tipping him into the snow. He completed the journey on a sturdy little horse. Back in Bologna, he signed up the only two artistes he could find: Maddalena Allegranti, a former friend of Casanova's, and Vitale Damiani – neither by any means 'singers of the first class', as he claimed.

Travelling with him by this time was an eleven-year-old son of Banti's, whom he was escorting back to England, and also young Felice, his own illegitimate son from Vienna. Felice had been living with Lorenzo's dissolute half-brother Agostino. Two years earlier, when he was twelve or thirteen, Felice had stolen a necklace and run away to join the French Army, then after being caught and spending time in a correction centre ran away again, to become a drummer boy. In Bologna he and Banti's son stole some of Nancy's jewellery and again absconded, to be found by soldiers a few days later in the house of a peasant near by. In his memoirs, Da Ponte mentions Felice only as 'a lad of the same age [as Banti's boy] who was with me', though in a letter to Paolo of 29 November 1798 he complains of the sixty-five zecchini he has had to spend to buy Felice out of the army and clothe him. In a later letter to Paolo he laments Felice's wickedness and implies that the boy has been sent away to school in England. We never hear of him again.

After the slight delay caused by Felice's flit, the party set off for Hamburg. A particularly harsh winter was tightening its grip over northern Europe. Rumours of new hostilities between the Austrians and the French were growing more persistent every day. Villages along the way had been razed by passing soldiers. Inns were hard to come by. One night near Brunswick, the women and children had to sleep in the carriages, while the men shivered in their cloaks in a stinking stable to the accompaniment of 'splutters and snores from people sleeping on a number of tables hung about on cords in all parts of the room . . . suspended directly over our heads, at a continual and imminent risk of falling on top of us and crushing our bones'. At Harburg they found the River Elbe completely frozen over, and following local advice continued their journey over the ice in carriages, passing along the way a spot where the ice had cracked, swallowing up a coach and all its passengers, drowning six horses. To their horror, parts of the coach still poked out through the ice. They found Hamburg bound in by the freeze, and accommodation at a premium as people crowded the city waiting for ships to leave. Having at last found an inn, and after a contretemps over who should have the best room (which nearly ended in a duel between Da Ponte and Allegranti's husband), they settled in – and there they stayed. For over a month they waited for the ice to break, as Da Ponte's money dwindled to the last few guineas.

It was March 1799 before Lorenzo arrived back in London, with a pregnant wife, an empty purse, and two very mediocre singers. Taylor had expected him back after three months. He had stayed away nearly six, and had little to show for it.

London was hurtling towards the new century. Scientific discoveries of the Age of Enlightenment were reaching the street. Goede, surprised while out walking by 'a number of bucks of the first class issuing from an apothecary's shop with bursts of laughter', discovered that the young men had 'intoxicated themselves with the fumes of oxygen, which is prepared and sold as a powerful aphrodisiac at half a guinea per dose'. Another newly isolated gas, carbon dioxide, had recently been put to good use by a Swiss gentleman living in London, one Jacob Schweppe. The French Revolution, like many social upheavals, had its effect on fashion as well as on thought. Courtly splendour was passé, though cutting a dash most certainly was not. Younger men discarded wigs and powder for wildly combed mops of hair. They wore impossibly high collars, voluminous neckscarves, round hats (rather than tricorns), and variations on the simple 'John Bull' country style of clothing, for some years much imitated on the Continent. Women appeared to have changed shape. They had cast off hoops and panniers for the astonishingly flimsy *robe en chemise* – high-waisted, near-transparent and sometimes with the fabric dampened so as to cling to the body in imitation of the folds in the robe of a classical sculpture. Both genders swept aside the elaborate embroidery and brocades of the *ancien régime* with the cry, 'Return to Nature' (an aim not fully realizable in polite society). Literary coffee-houses hummed with outrage at a similar call for simplicity by two young poets, Samuel Taylor Coleridge and William Wordsworth,

in their new *Lyrical Ballads*. Wordsworth, particularly, caused controversy with his attack on the 'gaudy and inane phraseology of many
modern writers', by the 'low', everyday subjects of his poems, and their
supposedly banal language. That, and Coleridge's focus on the super-
natural and 'romantic' heralded a new literary era in England. This was a
far step from the nymphs and goddesses, the complex allusions and
highly wrought style of the poetry Da Ponte was steeped in. But the
niceties of poetic diction were not Da Ponte's most pressing problem in
1799. He had been sacked.

Exactly when and how Da Ponte was dismissed is uncertain. It is clear
that none of his works was performed at the King's Theatre in 1799, and
that 1800 saw only a revival of his *La Semiramide*. His successor as official
librettist, Serafino Buonaiuti, had already made an appearance while Da
Ponte was in Italy. The abysmal failure of the singers Lorenzo brought
back with him would not have aided his cause. Allegranti was way past
her prime. According to Mount Edgcumbe 'she had scarcely a thread of
voice remaining, nor the power to sing a note in tune'. After just four
performances, she disappeared from view. Damiani did not even make it
to the stage, having entered into immediate conflict with Taylor over a
clause Da Ponte had (without authorization) inserted in his contract
allowing him the right to choose the opera for his debut, and then
embarking on further claims for free tickets, new clothes for every opera,
and the right to sing at other theatres in town. He squabbled on for a few
weeks, then flounced back to Italy.

Da Ponte blamed intrigue, mainly that of Banti and Federici, for his
downfall; he said that Buonaiuti undercut him by agreeing to work for
half his salary, and maintained that a creditor of Taylor's had somehow
garnished the salary of the theatre poet, so that only old operas could be
performed (a claim borne out by the fact that no fewer than eight of his
earlier works were performed in 1801). Taylor ignored his letters, and
shrugged off his pleas and tears. Federici was still skimming off profits
from the sale of libretti.

The loss of his theatre income was not the worst of Da Ponte's
troubles. On the morning of his fiftieth birthday, while he was still in
bed, a stranger burst into the room, demanded that Da Ponte dress and

leave with him immediately. Lorenzo grabbed the loaded pistol he kept by his bedside, and the rest of the conversation was conducted through a closed door, with the stranger in the corridor. It transpired that Da Ponte was under arrest for a note he had endorsed for Taylor which had not been paid. He spent the night behind bars, and when he at last found somebody to stand bail for him the next day, was immediately rearrested for a second note, and later that evening for a third. All in all, Da Ponte writes, he was arrested no fewer than thirty times over the next three months for bills endorsed on behalf of the impresario, spending further funds on 'usurers, lawyers, and constables of all the courts of London'. Taylor was even more financially pressed than usual by battles surrounding a grandiose development scheme for the streets around the King's Theatre, and in January 1800 by the Lord Chamberlain's temporary refusal to grant the opera house a licence for the new season, as salaries from the previous year had not been paid. Having at last secured election to Parliament (as member for Leominster in 1797), Taylor was immune from the claims of creditors. Others who had signed notes for him, such as Federici and Gallini, were being thrust into bankruptcy.

Nancy, who had given birth to their second daughter, Frances (Fanny), in 1799, still had money from the coffee-room, but even this was for the moment, according to Da Ponte, 'not in her hands and the person who had possession of it would not give it up'. With no income from the theatre, Da Ponte turned to printing, moving his press from 134 Pall Mall to number five, and setting up shop with his brother-in-law Charles Niccolini (Louisa's husband) and one Daniel Bastie. He also had dealings with the instrument makers and music publishers Corri and Dussek, which further compounded his problems when they went bankrupt, Dussek fleeing the country and Corri going to prison in Newgate. On 18 February 1800, Lorenzo wrote to Paolo in Ceneda, asking him to send harp and violin strings, which he could sell in London, and saying how much he wished Paolo were with him. He writes that he had been hoping to arrange work for Paolo in a piano shop he had an interest in (possibly Dussek's), but that this, too, had run into difficulties: 'If it had not been for recent mishaps I would maybe have made some good money.' On 22 February, Da Ponte declared himself bankrupt – a common ploy to keep creditors at bay and oneself out of jail for a few months. Most of his furniture was removed, his printing press was impounded, and his last pennies were sucked up by legal costs. On 27 May, he was granted a Certificate of Conformity, which stated that at least four creditors were satisfied, effectively discharging him from his debts, but he found himself having to pay a guinea a month to reclaim his press, and 'without property, without employment, without credit, and without friends other than Providence and my own courage'. And, he might have added, with a family of five to support, for in 1800 Nancy gave birth to their first son, Joseph. Despite her pregnancies, the gallant Nancy appears for a while to have been the family's sole breadwinner. It is not clear for how long she continued to run the coffee-room, but it seems likely she was still doing so in the early 1800s, given the savings she was able to build up.

Yet again Lorenzo was having to rise from ashes of his own making, and as ever it was his starry optimism that gave him the energy to do so. One day in the early autumn of 1800, Da Ponte was walking down the Strand when he had suddenly to dodge into a bookshop to avoid a charging bull – or so he says, and though the tale is not unlikely as animals did escape from Smithfield meat market, the sight of a creditor seems a more plausible cause of flight. Inside the shop, Da Ponte discovered a stash of hundreds of Italian books, taking up an entire upstairs room. It was the childhood moment in his father's attic in Ceneda writ large. The bookseller was contemptuous of Italian books, said he needed the space, and that Da Ponte could have the complete stock for thirty guineas. The dusty pages, the smell of leather bindings, some beautiful engravings, reawakened a passion for Lorenzo. He could see himself as proprietor of London's premier Italian bookshop, and agreed to the bookseller's terms on the spot – with just the slightest twinge of concern that he had not examined the works, and that the seller seemed overly keen to be rid of them. Da Ponte raised the money by endorsing another of Taylor's notes (for the singer Benelli, who was desperate to cash it in order to get his hands on his own salary), and pocketing sixty pounds commission. It does not need much imagination to picture Nancy's reaction when he arrived home.

For once, though, Da Ponte had made a commercially viable decision. As he examined his purchase more closely, he turned over tome after valuable tome – a sixteenth-century copy of *Orlando furioso*, and works by some of his most loved authors: Dante, Metastasio, Goldoni and Petrarch. His find was worth many hundreds of pounds. He spent the rest of his sixty pounds acquiring similar bargains around town. In November he compiled a detailed catalogue of his finds. By March 1801, 5 Pall Mall was a well-stocked bookshop.

Pall Mall and Piccadilly bookshops were 'fashionable lounging places' according to *The Picture of London for 1802*. Whigs lounged at Debrett's on Piccadilly, Tories lounged at his rival Stockdale's two doors further down. A short walk away on Pall Mall, Da Ponte's illustrious clients included 'Lord Douglas and Lady Devonshire' (the latter most likely the doyenne of London society, Georgiana, Duchess of Devonshire), as well as 'Lord Spencer' (presumably the bibliophile George Spencer, who later became Duke of Marlborough). These noble customers, according to Da Ponte, 'in less than a week despoiled my shop of four hundred volumes at least, and enriched my purse with as many guineas'. Little by little, 'the booksellers of London began to scent the pudding, and the price of Italian books, especially of old editions, began to rise out of all proportion'. By this time Da Ponte had amassed a stock of some 8,000 books, had paid off the bond on his printing press, and begun publishing once more – both libretti for the King's Theatre and work closer to his heart. Later in 1801 he brought out a new edition of *Saggi Poetici*, his collection of poems, and began work on an abridged and annotated edition of *Gli animali parlanti*, by his old rival the Abbé Casti (whose work, despite their mutual enmity, he had always admired). One day in the bookshop, a stranger picked up and admired *Saggi Poetici*, and was delighted to discover he was speaking to its author. Thomas James Mathias – a royal official and renowned Italian scholar – became a revered and useful friend. In a letter to the scholar Samuel Henley, enclosing a copy of *Saggi Poetici*, Mathias wrote that he thought Da Ponte a genius, and admired his learning and taste. He was one of the few men not to receive a lashing in Da Ponte's memoirs.

Two others in this select band came to London at the time: Paolo at last arrived to work with Lorenzo; and into the shop one day walked Michele Colombo, Lorenzo's beloved boyhood companion from his days at the seminary in Ceneda. Colombo and his charges (he was tutor to two young Italian aristocrats) visited the shop day after day during their stay. One of the young Italians took news back to the Abbé Casti in Paris of the expurgations Da Ponte was making in *Gli animali parlanti* (cutting or even changing lines he considered 'too filthy or at least too free'), and that he was providing annotations explaining some of the allusions. This intelligence brought a furious letter from Casti, berating Da Ponte not only for his audacity in changing lines, but for unravelling allusions to contemporary figures (among them Napoleon, by now First Consul, and other powerful people in France, where the ancient Casti needed friends and support). In December 1802, Da Ponte replied, justifying his actions by saying teachers of Italian could not have used the original in staid England; but Casti probably did not receive the letter, as he died toward the end of the year of indigestion after a particularly extravagant meal at the Spanish Ambassador's residence. Da Ponte published *Gli animali parlanti* in April 1803.

Lorenzo's success could not be tainted, even when Michael Kelly began to publish opera music and opened a shop on Pall Mall with a door that lead directly on to the King's Theatre stage, offering special access to fee-payers who wanted a private route to their carriages and sedan chairs. Da Ponte moved around the corner, renting from Corri a larger shop with an excellent location, at 28 Haymarket. Nor had he entirely lost connection with the opera house. He had a hand in one or two adaptations in 1801 (including Salieri's *Angelina*, for which he is again billed as 'Poet to the Opera-House' on the libretto); and in the early summer of 1802 wrote a new *opera seria*, *Armida*, his last for Bianchi and for Banti. *Armida* was panned by *The Times*, with: 'If a modern Italian Opera could be considered as a legitimate object of criticism, we should be disposed to speak of this in terms of more than usual severity for it is certainly one of the worst which has of late been exhibited.' It was Banti's last opera in London. She left England soon afterwards, dying in Bologna in 1806 at the age of forty-seven.

Banti was replaced by one of the few singers who could match her:

Elizabeth Billington (known as Mrs Billington), then at the height of her fame. Mount Edgcumbe thought her voice sweet, flexible and agile, though not as full as Banti's; her interpretations were skilful and intelligent, but somehow wanting in feeling. 'Her face was handsome and her countenance full of good humour,' he wrote, 'but it was incapable of change, and she was no actress.' Mrs Billington was joined by the equally renowned Giuseppa Grassini, a soprano who had some-how lost her upper ranges and become a contralto (Kelly called her a counter-tenor; Mount Edgcumbe admired her 'deep tones'). Grassini was a 'very handsome woman' and 'an excellent actress', wrote Mount Edgcumbe, continuing that, were they to appear on stage together, 'no doubt the deaf would have been charmed by Grassini, while the blind must have been delighted by Mrs Billington'. The two divas were quite as fierce rivals as Banti and Morichelli had been before them, but this time Da Ponte, at a safe distance on the Haymarket, was less affected by the fur-flinging. He wrote his last three operas for Mrs Billington and the Bavarian composer Peter von Winter. The first of these, *La grotta di Calipso* premiered on 31 May 1803, with great success. *The Times* particularly admired Mrs Billington's recitative, where 'she soars above all competition . . . and ennobles the sentiment expressed by the Author, with a richness of tone, a spirit and animation, that elevate her to the summit of the art'. The second, *Il trionfo dell'amor fraterno*, which opened on 22 March 1804, was also well received. The third, *Il ratto di Proserpina*, the only opera in which Grassini and Mrs Billington sang together, had its premiere on 31 May (two weeks after Napoleon Bonaparte had been declared Emperor of the French). Michael Kelly called it a 'grand triumph', and duets and trios that featured both Grassini's sonorous tones and Mrs Billington's agile brilliance were lustily encored.

William Taylor, meanwhile, was beginning to lose his battles on all fronts. The trustees of the opera house were at last having some success in their long-held aim of ousting him from power. In 1803, the lease on the auditorium half of the King's Theatre expired, but Taylor was not able, as he had hoped, to use his freehold ownership of the stage as a lever in negotiations. The chief reason for this was that he was desperate for money, and that everyone knew it. He had failed to be re-elected to parliament, was now liable for his debts, and was forced to sell one-third of his interest in the King's Theatre to an old schoolfellow of Michael Kelly's, Francis Gould. By the end of 1804, Taylor was in such dire financial straits that he mortgaged his remaining interest in the theatre to Gould, and handed over to him entire responsibility for the running of the theatre. He fled to France. Taylor's swirling cloud of notes and promises burst, raining down upon Da Ponte (and many others in town) a flurry of double-endorsed bills of exchange. There followed a maelstrom as various creditors and debtors claimed and counter-claimed, borrowed, promised and lent. James Mathias very generously met a large debt for Da Ponte, on at least one occasion. Da Ponte, 'in spite of the cries of my wife, of all the family', to the very end desperate to please, went so far as to bail Taylor (now back in England) out of a constable's lock-up, only to be snubbed and hoaxed by the ex-impresario yet again.

In April 1804, in an auction that lasted ten days, Da Ponte took the drastic step of selling some 2,000 of his finest books, a 'Superb & extremely valuable Collection', read the catalogue, 'Consisting of almost every Author in the Italian Language many of which are of the greatest rarity, and some Editions may be said to be UNIQUE in this Country'. The reason given for the sale was that Mr L. Daponte was 'Retiring from the Bookselling Business'. A second sale was fixed for May. In August, Nancy left for America.

Nancy's father John Grahl was in America (her mother had gone there, but appears to have died before 1804), and so were her brother Peter and his wife Elizabeth (who had introduced Da Ponte to the family). Whether Nancy had simply had enough of her impetuous, quixotic and hopelessly gullible husband, was genuinely going to visit her family for a year (Da Ponte's version of events), or was making a hasty escape with money from the book sales and her savings from the coffee-room, is not clear. She sailed on the trade ship *Pigou*, taking with her Louisa (then aged ten), Fanny (five), little Joseph (four) – and baby Lorenzo, who was barely a few months old. The journey took fifty days, and could not have been an easy one.

Da Ponte accompanied his family to Gravesend, and as he left the *Pigou* after their last embraces, felt 'a hand of ice on my heart that tore it from my breast'. Beset by sorrow and remorse, he made a lonely journey back to London. Without Nancy and his children, 'the house where I was living, the city in which I dwelt, in truth everything about me became so odious and unbearable that I was at countless times on the point of leaving and flying away to America'. Over the next few months he wrote again and again to Nancy, imploring her to return. Not even Paolo could console him. His love for his half-brother, and for James Mathias, kept him in London, but 'held me nailed down . . . in a kind of inferno'. Da Ponte's financial situation deteriorated. Further endorsed bills fell due, and he complains of business partners cheating him on book deals. On 1 April 1805, he held a meeting of his creditors that ended in mumblings of 'we shall see' and 'we'll talk it over'. Just before midnight, a friendly constable banged on Lorenzo's door and tipped him off that he would be arrested the next day. Da Ponte hurried to Francis Gould, told the impresario that he was disappearing to America until Taylor's affairs were put in order, and managed to talk 100 guineas 'advance salary' out of him for work he would do on return. At dawn he left home for the City, found a passage to Philadelphia, and somehow managed to persuade the director of the Alien's Office to give him a passport. Then he took a post chaise to Gravesend. Paolo went with him, but when he heard Lorenzo was leaving for America 'his sorrow was so great that I thought he [Paolo] would die'. Da Ponte gave Paolo a solemn promise that he would either return to London after six months or find some way of bringing Paolo to America. He did neither. Paolo continued to run the press but died a few years later, driven to his end, Da Ponte believed, by moneylenders.

On 7 April 1805, on Captain Abishai Hayden's *Columbia*, Lorenzo Da Ponte sailed off towards the New World.

PART FOUR
NEW YORK

Mozart's Grocer

Chapter Fifteen

S AILORS CALLED THE westbound Atlantic crossing the 'uphill' passage, as ships sailing to the Americas fought constantly against headwinds. Da Ponte remembered his 'long, disastrous' voyage, full of 'annoyances and anxiety' as lasting sixty days, then eighty-six, and later (as the horrors of journey burgeoned in his memory) over three months. In reality, the *Columbia* made the crossing in fifty-seven days – but the experience was none the less gruelling for that.

In his haste to leave, Lorenzo had taken with him a curious collection of portable items that might have resale value: violin strings (his old standby), a good violin (later valued by American customs at $189.50), a carpet ($50), a tea urn ($18.90) and a trunk of books. He had not taken any bedding, and had neglected to ask Captain Hayden just what his forty-four-guinea fare bought him, beyond passage and provisions on the way. The honest answer would have been: 'Nothing, and very little of the latter at that.' Lorenzo (dubbed 'Signor Italiano' by Hayden) had to make 'a kind of litter of the shirts and clothes' he had with him, in the narrow, worm-eaten wooden niche that was his sleeping quarters. His first meal was of broth that looked like the water from boiled chestnuts, in which floated the carcass of a chicken scrawny enough to have been a crow, served on a pewter plate and eaten with a rusty spoon. There was a little cheese and some strictly rationed wine.

It would appear that Da Ponte hid on board for two days, before the *Columbia* set sail from 'the last town of the River Thams', Gravesend – 'a

right name as every body of Sailors knows,' noted Captain 'Ramblin'
Jack' Cremer in his journal some decades earlier, it being where 'many
Never returne again'. Transatlantic travel had been made a little safer
since Ramblin' Jack plied the main, partially through the publication in
1802 of the *New American Practical Navigator* by the astronomer Nathaniel
Bowditch. This (trusting that Captain Hayden was up to date in his
reading) allowed for far greater precision in plotting and keeping a
course. But other dangers were rife. Admiral Nelson's defeat of the
French Navy at the Battle of Trafalgar was still six months away. Like
John Aspinwall crossing the Atlantic in the *Hope* in 1794, those aboard
the *Columbia* would have viewed unflagged ships near the French coast
with distinct unease. Aspinwell noted a small flotilla of which 'the
foremost ship was on our lee Bow, which would intercept us, and
accordingly we all prepared for France not doubting but we should be
taken, knowing we could not get away. Capt. Hayley prepared all papers
on board which might endanger any property or persons for a preasent to
Davy Jones.' Fortunately, the ship raised a friendly flag and allowed them
passage.

The *Columbia*, like the *Hope*, passed by France unmolested, but
beyond the Casquets – the three oil-burning beacons that marked
the southern limit of the English Channel – further hazards awaited
in the form of rough seas and the notorious Atlantic storms. Day after day
Aspinwell notes in his diary such entries as 'Felt seasick this morning',
'Sick all this day', then a long succession of 'sick', 'Sick' and '*Sick*', before
a brave 'I felt a little better' is again overwhelmed by nausea. Gales
smashed the *Hope*'s earthen bottles of water and wine, and 'broke the hen
Coop to Shatters'. Other voyagers record unfortunate hogs (like the hens
carried live for food) 'reeling and spewing about the decks'. Janet Schaw,
a Scot sailing to North Carolina, encountered such an appalling storm
that one of her journal entries ends simply, 'Thy will be done'; on other
days (the storm lasted over a week) she records a little boy crying because
he fears God will not be able to pluck him from the ocean if he drowns,
and 'the last of our poultry, a poor duck, squeezed as flat as a pancake' by
a sliding harpsichord that had broken its moorings. Icebergs were also a
hazard at this time of year. Sailing just a few weeks ahead of the *Columbia*,

Captain Law's *Jupiter* had been struck by floating ice near Nova Scotia and had sunk within hours.

Captain Hayden of the *Columbia* was a Nantucket man, an old whaling hand used to rough weather, now in command of a packet that regularly ferried cargo and passengers between European and American ports. He treated his passengers, Da Ponte complained, 'like the vilest sailors', and his unfortunate crew like 'monsters of the sea'. Da Ponte recalls only one other fellow traveller (though the *Columbia* at times carried up to fifty): the Philadelphian merchant Richard Edwards, whom he first encountered as a 'sleepy Bacchus', dressed in white linen like a miller and apparently in mid-hangover. 'Signor Italiano' and 'Signor Oduardo' (as Edwards became to the captain) were soon inseparable, and as Hayden relaxed his vigilance over the wine bottles they drank and gambled to ease the trials of the journey. By the time the boat creaked up the Delaware River to reach Philadelphia, on the morning of 4 June 1805, Da Ponte did not have enough money left to pay the duty on his motley possessions. Edwards came to his aid, but kept the goods as guarantee. This was hardly an auspicious new beginning.

Da Ponte stepped off the sea-tossed *Columbia* on to terra firma of the world's newest nation. America was a land apart, one where the most exalted ideas of recent times had found form, as many in Europe watched with a fascination tinged with awe. Joseph Priestley, the discoverer of oxygen and an English radical, enthused to his friend Theophilus Lindsey, soon after emigrating to America: 'I feel as if I were in another world. I never before could conceive how satisfactory it is to have the feelings I now have from a sense of perfect security and liberty, all men having equal rights and privileges, and speaking and acting as if they were sensible of it.'

Not only did America have no king, no established church, and no censorship, but it had suffered no Reign of Terror, nor bred a Napoleon Bonaparte. The daring experiment in democracy was proving successful. By the time Da Ponte arrived, the nation had without serious mishap elected Thomas Jefferson, leader of an opposition party, as its third president, and had given him a second term. The United States had learned the first crucial lesson of a new democracy: how to accommodate dissent. America was not merely surviving without a monarch; it was prospering, plunging into the new century, its growing population already pushing south and westward to distant territories over the mountains and across the plains.

Many years earlier, Lorenzo Da Ponte had presented a brave and dissenting *accademia* on freedom and the nature of happiness to the seminarists at Treviso, beginning with the elegy 'The American in Europe'. The poor boy from Ceneda had since rubbed fur with princes, and lapped at the cream of sophisticated society in Venice, Vienna and London. Now he was the European in America. Still excited by ideals, though grown more conservative since his youth, he came trailing remnants of the Old World with him. 'I well knew that my dramatic talents would avail me but little in this country, in which the knowledge of Italian was so limited,' he wrote soon after his arrival, 'but I felt a sympathetic affection for the Americans. I had, besides, suffered so much in aristocratical republics, and monarchical governments, that I pleased myself with the hope of finding happiness in a country which I thought free.' It was a country custom-made for those who wished to slough off the past and reinvent themselves, an art at which Da Ponte was a master. He stepped ashore penniless, but he was among the very first to feel the tug of the American Dream.

Philadelphia, beyond the tar tang, the barrel-banging, the shouts, whinnies, striding and scuttling of its harbourside, presented a composed and sober prospect to the new arrival, a tone set by its Quaker founders. Neat brick buildings – touched with white on shutters, pilasters and window-frames – were laid out on a regular grid, quite a contrast to the higgledy-piggledy streets of London. Mansions and monumental stone buildings proclaimed the city's status. From 1790 until 1800, Philadelphia had been capital of the fledgling United States, and the country's biggest and richest city. Some compared it with London or Paris, even with classical Athens. 'At Philadelphia, "the city of Brotherly Love",' noted travelling Londoner Charles Joseph Latrobe, 'you are struck with the regularity of the streets, – their numberless handsome mansions, – the lavish use of white and grey marble, – pleasant avenues and squares . . .' Charles Francis Adams (grandson of John Adams, the country's second

president) felt there was something solid and comfortable about Philadelphia, 'something which shows *permanency*. Every thing looks neat, the
steps are white, the entries are clean, the carriages nice, the houses bright
. . . the eyes of strangers cannot be denied to be cheerful and inviting.'
Another visitor thought there was 'a general air of sombreness' about the
city, 'increased perhaps by the quantities of Quakeresses and weeping
willows you meet at every turn'.

Da Ponte hurried from the harbour to the house of Captain Collet in
Walnut Street. Collet was master of the *Pigou*, which had brought Nancy
and the children to America, and his was the address Lorenzo had been
using for correspondence. To Da Ponte's consternation, Collet told him
that Nancy had moved to New York. Lorenzo was now not only unable
to pay Richard Edwards and reclaim his possessions, but most likely had
to touch Edwards for a loan to cover his journey north. At one o'clock
that afternoon, he took the stagecoach (fare $4) from Mr Anderson's at
the sign of the Sorrel Horse, squeezing in with eight other passengers on
three transverse seats (or, if he was lucky, perched up beside the driver).
'Bones of me, what a road!' exclaimed the actress Fanny Kemble on her
way to New York, as late as the 1830s. Abigail Adams, the wife of
President John Adams, travelling in the same season as Da Ponte, found
the stretch between Philadelphia and New York the worst road she had
ever experienced: 'The soil is all clay. The heavy rains and the constant
run of six stages daily, had so cut them up, that the whole was like a
ploughed field, in furrows of two feet in depth, and was very dangerous.'
Hapless stagecoach passengers were called upon by the driver to lean
their bodies halfway out of the carriage, first on one side then the other,
with a 'Now gentlemen, to the right!' or a 'Now, gentlemen, to the left!'
to balance the vehicle as it rocked through the ruts. Twenty-one
juddering hours after setting off, Da Ponte arrived in New York. This
city presented a very different prospect from the one he had left the day
before.

At around this time a talented young New Yorker named Washington
Irving, who had a taste for the new century and an inventive touch with
words, playfully compared his city's streets (yet to be straightened into an
orderly grid) and its people with those of Philadelphia:

. . . the people of New York – God help them – tossed about over hills and dales, through lanes and alleys, crooked streets – continually mounting and descending, turning and twisting – whisking off at tangents, and left-angle-triangles, just like their own queer, odd, topsy-turvy rantipole city, are the most irregular, crazy-headed, quicksilver, eccentric, whim-whamsical set of mortals ever jumbled together in this uneven, villainous revolving globe, and are the very antipodeans to the Philadelphians.

Somehow, Lorenzo found his way through the rantipole tangle to the house where Nancy and the children lived. 'There is no need to tell how I was received,' writes Da Ponte, and indeed, Nancy's response to the unexpected appearance of her impecunious, travel-bruised and bedraggled husband on the doorstep that early June morning is un-recorded. Later, she gallantly paid off his debt to Richard Edwards and handed Lorenzo nearly $7,000 (apparently her savings from the coffee-room in London) so that he might set their family up in a new American life.

Thomas Jefferson's private secretary earned just $500 that year; Jefferson's annual salary as secretary of state, before he became president, was $3,500; in 1800 you could have had a ship built to order for $11,000 and bought a smart carriage for $1,500; a skilled worker in New York was lucky to earn $1.25 a day. Nancy's $7,000 was a considerable sum of money. On her father's advice, Lorenzo invested it in a grocery shop, diving headlong into the turbulent waters of New York commerce.

By 1804, New York had overtaken Philadelphia as the country's largest city, its population having more than doubled in less than a decade, climbing to 80,000. New York generated overwhelming first impressions of activity and speed. 'Everything in the city is in motion,' exclaimed one visitor. 'Everything was in motion; all was life, bustle and activity,' wrote another. 'Whoever visits New York feels as he does in a watchmaker's shop,' commented a third, noting that it had the effect on a man 'as if he had been wound up or regulated anew . . . He hears a clicking, as it were, on all sides of him, and finds everything he looks at in movement, and not a nook or corner but what is brim-ful of business.'

Even garbage was disposed of actively as hogs snuffled and gobbled about the streets (despite frequent attempts to have them banished to the countryside). Merchants were as much in their counting houses as at the wharves, aprons around their waists, rolling hogsheads of rum and molasses, 'flying about as dirty and a diligent as porters'. At the Tontine coffee-house on Wall Street, underwriters and brokers, traders and politicians, sold, purchased, trafficked, insured, and swapped news. Unlike Quaker Philadelphia, New York had been founded upon trade, and on commerce it thrived. People were beginning to make money from the ground itself as men took a cue from John Jacob Astor, who bought up every piece of undeveloped land north of the city limits he could get his hands on, later to sell at phenomenal gain and make himself the richest man in the nation. All was haste, show, energy, splendour and profit. New York was well on its way to becoming what Washington Irving would call 'one of the most rucketing cities in the world'.

Da Ponte seemed somewhat bemused by his new role as a merchant grocer. 'Let him who has a grain of sense imagine how I must have laughed at myself,' he wrote, 'every time my poet's hand was called to weigh out two ounces of tea, or measure half a yard of "pigtail" [plug tobacco], now to a cobbler, now to a carter, or pour out, in exchange for three cents, a morning dram.' The leatherworker's son from Ceneda had refined for himself a fine strand of snobbery. A similar distaste for the company he would be associated with had been his prime objection to teaching Italian in London. Together with other genteel European travellers, he must have been shocked during stops on his ride to New York that the stagecoach driver sat at the same table to dine as the passengers. Yet the society Da Ponte now lived in was not quite as egalitarian as it might initially have seemed. In New York, especially, a powerful moneyed elite was making its mark. Here, more than in any other city in the country, life bore out the opinion of the French Consul-General, Louis-Felix de Beaujour, that the guiding principle of the new republic was 'a frantic love of money . . . a result of the political equality which reigns there, and which, leaving people no other distinction besides wealth, invites them to acquire it by every possible means'. Those who rose by their riches formed a distinct upper crust (a term first used in

America, as the century hurtled on); they were founders of clubs and learned societies, builders of fine country houses and places of entertainment. This was a class of people to whom the erstwhile abbé, denizen of 'aristocratical republics', bird of royal courts, poet with a nose for patronage, was instinctively drawn.

In the beginning, despite his protestations that being a grocer was below his station, Da Ponte made a success of the enterprise. This novel and heady situation did not last. Just a few months after opening shop in New York, Lorenzo sold up and moved his family to Elizabethtown in New Jersey, ostensibly to avoid yellow fever (an epidemic raged in New York during the summer of 1805), though lured also by what he saw as a lucrative partnership offer from one H. Micheli. Louisa and Charles Niccolini arrived from London in 1806, and also settled in Elizabethtown. Da Ponte bought a small house with a garden, and carried on trading as a grocer with Micheli. An all-too-familiar tale of perfidy, betrayal, promissory notes and financial disaster followed, with Micheli fleeing to Jamaica, and other business associates cheating mercilessly. 'Sometimes deceived by feigned distress, sometimes by false promises, I sold my goods to those who were never prepared when their payments became due,' moaned Da Ponte. 'I was sometimes obliged, rather than lose all, to take for notes, due long before, lame horses, broken carts, disjointed chairs, old shoes, rancid butter, watery cider, rotten eggs, apples, brooms, turnips, potatoes.' Within a year he had lost $6,000. Da Ponte implies in his memoirs that Charles Niccolini had something to do with this downfall, and began to take against Nancy's family with a bile that grew ever more venomous as the years went by. He now began to consider other ways of making money, and visited New York to investigate the possibility of earning a living by teaching Italian or Latin. It did not take him long to discover that, as far as Latin went, New Yorkers saw no point in having a foreign teacher, and 'as far as the Italian language and literature were concerned, they were about as well known in this city as Turkish or Chinese.'

The great wave of Italian migration to New York was a few decades away; even in the years from 1820 to 1830 only 438 Italians, most of them political exiles, came to live in the city. Advertisements in the

Evening Post mention a D. Mazzinghi, who sold imported pianofortes at 11 Murray Street in 1804; and Parri, Rinaldi and Company, who dealt in art objects, prints and paintings from 1810; but when Da Ponte arrived in New York only a handful of his countrymen lived there. Few in the city showed much interest in the language which he believed 'from its united sweetness, delicacy, force, and richness, compares with every ancient language, and surpasses every modern tongue; which equals in sublimity the Greek, the Latin in magnificence, in grandeur and conciseness the Hebrew, the German in boldness, in majesty the Spanish, and the English in energy.' If English-speaking New Yorkers were to be bothered learning another tongue, French and Spanish were commercially more useful to them.

Complaining about this lack of local interest in Italian and the unavailability of Italian books, one day in December 1806, in Riley's booksellers on Broadway, Da Ponte was interrupted by a genteel New Yorker. 'Ah, sir,' said the gentleman, 'modern Italy is most unfortunately not the Italy of ancient times.' The stranger went on to opine that there had been at most five or six Italian writers of note over the past six centuries: 'Dante, Petrarch, Boccaccio, Ariosto, Tasso . . . and to tell the truth, a sixth does not occur to me just now.' Da Ponte recalled:

He had been counting the names off on his fingers, thus he paused, with his little finger held tightly between the forefinger and thumb of his right hand, in the manner of a person thinking. I laid hold of all of those fingers and said boldly:

'You would not let go of that finger for a whole month, were you to allow me to clasp your hand like this until I have finished naming one by one the outstanding men of the last six centuries in Italy!'

'We do not know them,' he said.

'So I perceive!' I replied. 'But do you suppose a teacher of Italian would find any favour and encouragement . . .?'

The gentleman thus charmed was Clement Clarke Moore, then twenty-seven, a member of an old and highly respected New York family, the son of Bishop Benjamin Moore (who was Episcopal Bishop of the

Diocese of New York for thirty-five years) and proprietor of Chelsea, the largest country estate in the area. Some years later, he would write a poem for his children entitled 'A Visit from St Nicholas', beginning ' 'Twas the night before Christmas, when all through the house / Not a creature was stirring, not even a mouse' – arguably the best-known verse ever written by an American. Clement Moore was to become a close and loyal friend. Within days, Lorenzo Da Ponte was giving his first Italian lesson, at the home of Bishop Moore, to a group of young gentleman that included Clement, his cousin Nathaniel F. Moore (an accomplished classicist, one day to be Professor of Greek at Columbia) and John M. MacVickar (who became Professor of Philosophy at Columbia). Back in Elizabethtown, nine days later on 24 December 1806, Nancy gave birth to a son. He was christened Charles Grahl Da Ponte, though his father always called him Carlo.

Carlo's birth and Clement Moore's support spurred Da Ponte to action. Well-to-do New York families were beginning to place a high priority on the education of their daughters, equipping them to meet their new social and organizational responsibilities; youthful merchants and professionals were finding the time and cultivating the inclination to become men of letters as well as men of commerce, and forming cultural societies to further their aspirations. Respectable women at reputable addresses were opening boarding schools for young ladies offering instruction in music, French, drawing, and sometimes more daringly in 'Elements of Chemistry and Astronomy'. Surely it would be possible to add Italian to such a curriculum, and with Clement Clarke Moore's connections perhaps also to establish lessons for young gentlemen. Suddenly, teaching patrician offspring in New York seemed an infinitely more viable prospect than propping up a failing grocery business in the provinces. Early in 1807, Da Ponte sold up his house, shop and garden in Elizabethtown to pay off his debts, and moved back to New York.

The year 1807 was a bad one for the city. Talk of American involvement in the Anglo-French conflict led to a 'fortification fever', as the people of Manhattan built defences against invasion from the sea, and an embargo on vessels leaving American ports throttled trade. The galloping economy stumbled, and would not fully recover until well into 1809. By 1808 the Tontine coffee-house, the wharfs and quays, would be gloomy and forlorn. Da Ponte wrote a *canzone* entitled *Agli Stati Uniti d'America*, urging intervention against the French and describing Napoleon in terms reminiscent of Dante's *Inferno*. He had given up his career as a grocer just in time.

Despite the financial tribulations, New York's cultural life was taking sturdy steps forward. Prospects for Da Ponte's Italian classes remained good. Samuel Latham Mitchill's 1807 travel guide, *The Picture of New-York*, went out of its way to point out theatres, booksellers, literary societies, scientific organizations and other evidence of the city's cultural maturity. Throughout 1807, Washington Irving together with his brother William and James Kirk Paulding brought out a series of paperbound volumes entitled *Salmagundi; or The Whim-Whams and Opinions of Launcelot Langstaff, Esq. & Others* – whimsical, verbally acrobatic, irreverent commentaries on New York life with (in Irving's words) an 'eye to the *picturesque*'. A new spirit of American literature was being born, one closer to that of Coleridge and Wordsworth (with, perhaps, a spark more bonhomie) than to Da Ponte's revered Italians. *Salmagundi* – and much else besides – grew out of riotously convivial clubs formed by young men attracted to New York by the energy and freedoms the city offered, centred on such haunts as Thomas Hodgkinson's Shakespeare Tavern, on the corner of Nassau and Fulton Streets (very near where Da Ponte lived). Rather like the *Accademia Granellesca* that had so enthralled Da Ponte in his youth, the clubs mingled revelry with literary pursuits. In their more serious moments, budding poets pondered the relationship between reality and romance, and whether the American landscape possessed sufficient romantic association to render it a fit subject for poetry. In the midst of these young men, Da Ponte must have felt, and appeared, very old-fashioned. Yet many of them – such as the poet Fitz-Greene Halleck (a member of the Ugly Club, established to 'advocate ugliness in all its hideous forms') – became not only his pupils but friends. The quaint old man from a distant world had vitality enough to engage them together with the respectability of a venerable culture, for those uncertain moments when young adventurers have to look back over their shoulders for reassurance.

On 10 March 1807, to celebrate his fifty-eighth birthday, Lorenzo Da
Ponte held a *conversazione* at his home on Partition Street, a delightfully
Old World occasion at which Clement Clarke Moore read his own
translation of Da Ponte's *Introduzione* in praise of Italian letters; a four-
year-old Joseph Da Ponte appeared suitably clad as Cupid during a short
dramatic conversation between Psyche and Hebe, translated by Nathaniel Moore; John MacVickar recited Petrarch; and Nancy (still beautiful in
her late thirties) gave an epilogue, dressed as Venus. Da Ponte published
the evening's poems in parallel text, appending a suitably abridged
Compendium of the Life of Lorenzo Da Ponte, the first evidence of his
memoirs. The volume was published in New York, and became a set
work for his Italian classes.

Da Ponte writes that within a month of his beginning teaching, the
number of his pupils had risen to twenty-four, and continued to increase.
The Moores' endorsement and Da Ponte's European background gave
his school a certain tone – and respectability was crucial, as the Da
Ponte's took in boarders. Advertisements for their Manhattan Academy
for Young Gentlemen and the Manhattan Academy for Young Ladies
began to appear in New York papers, alongside those assuring anxious
parents that 'N.B. The Rev. Mr. Magee has promised to visit and
examine the School frequently'. 'Madame Duponte' offered to instruct
young ladies in French, Italian and the making of artificial flowers, while
ensuring the attentions of the finest music and dancing masters. Mr Da
Ponte treated his young gentlemen to Italian, Latin and French, while
undertaking that 'a very able person' would provide them with writing,
ciphering, geography and the other rudiments. He promised that 'every
attention will be paid to the morals of those entrusted to his care'.
Respectability was certainly enforced when it came to his own offspring
– in 1809 his daughter Louisa, then fifteen, married one of the lodgers,
Martin Franklin Clossey, the son of a shopkeeper and on his way to
becoming a lawyer. Bishop Moore conducted the ceremony.

The last time Da Ponte had been a teacher, at the seminary in Treviso,
his pupils had loved him for his passion, his learning, his quick tongue
and lively imagination, and had been 'fired with the joy' of studying
literature. In New York, wrote a contemporary, he 'takes the glory of

those who are breaking new ground in the poetic career he once chose for himself, and cherishes it as his own'. It is clear that Lorenzo had lost none of his skill as a teacher – nor any of his charm. His friend Clement Moore noted that his pupils would declare that 'the hours passed in pleasing conversation with their elegant and cultivated tutor, as among the sweetest moments of their existence'; at least one of Lorenzo's young ladies (whom he referred to as his 'flowers') recalled his distinguished manner, and 'how the schoolgirls all admired him, and how some of them sighed for him in secret'. Da Ponte's lessons, and his 'day and evening assemblies', where only Italian was spoken and where some of 'the most dignified and respected young ladies in the city' recited passages of poetry and performed in short comedies and operas, became not only popular, but fashionable. Arthur Livingston notes:

> There is no doubt at all that this was an important moment for the American mind. Da Ponte made Europe, poetry, painting, music, the artistic spirit, classical lore, a creative classical education, live for many important Americans as no one, I venture, had done before. And his classical scholarship, his competence as a creative Latinist, dazzled quite as much as his fame as an Italian poet . . . It was not so much Da Ponte, as Da Ponte and his setting – the cultural atmosphere of his home that survived in his children and thereafter . . . It has happened to me thrice, a near century after Da Ponte's death, to hear some New Yorker boast, not knowing quite the significance of the words, that his grandmother, or his mother 'studied with Da Ponte'.

The Da Pontes were the find of the 1807 social season, and (according to Livingston) Nancy's Italian cooking the talk of the town. The Livingstons, the Hamiltons, the Duers, Ogilbies, Verplancks and Onderdocks – some of New York's greatest families – were over the following four years exposed to the Da Ponte charm, their sons and daughters to his learning. But fashions fade, and customs change.

On two evenings in succession, Da Ponte writes, at the height of the popularity of his Italian entertainments some time in 1810, his charges performed Vittorio Alfieri's tragedy *Mirra* on a stage he had set up in his house, to audiences of over one hundred past pupils, parents and friends. But a prudish twinge was already on its way to becoming the puritan cramp that would afflict the new century. People began to talk. Such behaviour did not perhaps befit young ladies aspiring to gentility. Da Ponte's assertion that Venetian nunneries and even the rigidly ascetic Empress Maria Theresa indulged in theatricals was unconvincing – the attitude of a decadent era and (to overwhelmingly Protestant New York) a corrupt religion. Lorenzo brought a little too much of the Old World with him, and was losing his footing in the new one. *Conversazioni* at the Da Ponte household began to tail off, numbers of students to decrease. To make matters worse, Da Ponte had sunk much of his new-found wealth into a distillery business (one can almost hear Nancy's cries of protest), which by 1811 had crashed on the usual rocks of 'betrayal', 'avarice', and 'the baseness of the wretch' who had been his partner. A letter from Nancy's sister Louisa, extolling the virtues of the village she and Charles Niccolini had recently moved to, in rural Pennsylvania some 160 miles west of Philadelphia, set Da Ponte – until now unassailably urban – dreaming of a pastoral idyll. Impulsively, he sold up in New York and in June 1811 bundled his family – including daughter Louisa and her new husband – off to Sunbury, on the banks of the Susquehanna River.

Louisa Niccolini had clearly not expected her paean to Sunbury to have quite the effect it did. She was surely pleased to see Nancy and the children, but the welcome she accorded her brother-in-law was 'neither as tender nor as enthusiastic' as he would have liked. The Grahls were a nomadic yet close-knit family, scattering across the world but regrouping in London, Trieste and then America. After wandering through Baltimore, Gettysburg and Carlisle, Nancy's father John Grahl had moved to Sunbury, and would live there until his death in 1814. Her brother Peter had set himself up there as a doctor, with his wife Elizabeth, before Louisa arrived. Both the Niccolinis and the Grahls had made a healthy fortune in property speculation along the Susquehanna at the turn of the century. Sunbury had become a Grahl clan stronghold. Da Ponte was perhaps hoping for a little family generosity to be directed his way, but if he found Peter Grahl hard-hearted, 'not at all, at Sunbury, the man I had known in Trieste', the family in turn were decidedly less embracing than once they had been of Nancy's scapegrace husband, who seemed at a single touch to turn gold to dust.

Though the Grahls' reception of their errant relative was cool, Sunbury itself was every bit as beautiful as Lorenzo might have hoped. He was entranced:

> One arrives at the foot of a mountain . . . which though steep and alpine has been made of safe and easy ascent by the art of man. The waysides are garlanded with fronds, bushes and trees of every sort, resplendent among them is an incredible quantity of wild laurel, which in the springtime and during part of the summer offers (its flowers perhaps the most delicate and graceful of all) the spectacle of one continuous garden. The flanks of the mountain present on both sides a theatre of rustic magnificence. Brooks, cascades of water, hillocks, crags, masses of marble rock and multiform copses of trees stretch away in two broad, deep valleys, which come to an end at other mountains of not dissimilar aspect.

The clear cool waters of the Susquehanna yielded trout more tasty than those of lakes Como or Garda; the forests teemed with deer, partridges, pheasant and other game. Wolves, bears and rattlesnakes only added to the allure, giving 'a certain delightful terror' to the Eden, 'a certain aura of solemnity to that majestic solitude'. The women in this paradise, thought the old roué, were 'almost all amiable, virtuous, and, for the most part, pretty enough'. Da Ponte's brief sketch of Sunbury is the only sustained description he ever gives of a town in which he lives, in the entire length of his memoirs. Now into his sixties, he had found a reposeful setting in which to while away the remainder of his years. Or so he thought.

Da Ponte had realized some $3,000 to $4,000 dollars on selling up in New York. On Peter Grahl's advice, he again invested the money in tradeable goods, especially medicines. When the family arrived in Sunbury, Da Ponte rented a small house beside the river, from where

he began to sell the general merchandise, while Doctor Grahl took care
of the pastes and potions. As he had done in New York, Da Ponte
gravitated towards the most solid families the town had to offer – the
Grants, the Enoch Smiths, the Buyers, and most especially Charles Hall
and his wife Elizabeth. Charles Hall was rich, a celebrated lawyer and
something of a squire of the county. Elizabeth Coleman Hall, just a little
younger than Nancy, was a gentlewoman of the old school, descended
from one of Maryland's most eminent families. Da Ponte began to
prepare their son Robert for Princeton, and later tutored his brothers,
too.

The Da Pontes' first year in Sunbury passed 'in perfect harmony',
marred only by the death of Charles Niccolini in February 1812. Da
Ponte proposed setting up a college for young gentlemen, employing
two other teachers and taking in borders at $200 a year. Although this
scheme does not appear to have been realized, he did give lessons to 'a
number of young ladies of the village' and from the neighbouring town
of Northumberland. In the evenings the Da Pontes and their new friends
passed their time in 'nightly *conversazione*, country dances, convivial
dinners' and other 'amusements of genteel company'. The war that
broke out between America and Britain in 1812 appears not to have
disrupted this rural idyll. If anything, Da Ponte – who was still trading
from his home – managed to benefit from the rising prices that ensued.

Cash was in short supply among the farming community, and Da
Ponte was often paid in kind. Logwood and almonds, sausages and
prunes appeared in his storeroom. With a surplus of grain, he again set his
hand to distilling, gaining a reputation for producing a spirit akin to a
good French brandy. He began transporting skins, butter, wax, fruit and
grain to the pristine markets of Philadelphia, and returning with nails,
medicines, oil, shoes, and yards of dimity for sale. Peter Grahl persuaded
Da Ponte to deal with cash-strapped farmers on credit, and his turnover
burgeoned. Da Ponte moved his business to larger premises on the east
corner of Market (Sunbury's central square), rented from one Thomas
Robins, who was known around town as 'Big Tom Hundred Legs' – a
dissolute character, 'a drinker, gambler, schemer, sunk deep in filth,
inured to vice', who spent much of his time in a dubious house across the

square. Nearly every Saturday night, all through 1812 to 1815, Big Tom created some sort of rumpus about town. Whatever happened, Robins was always guilty and paid everybody's fines. There was still something of the frontier town about Sunbury.

In 1814, Da Ponte built his family a home that was 'the finest edifice in all the town'. He was by now the second largest taxpayer in Sunbury after Charles Hall and the house on the west corner of Market was appropriately grand – built in brick, and for years the only three-storey structure in the county. At this time, 'L. de Ponty's Wagon' was a common sight along the pike-road to Philadelphia, at its helm the wispy, white-haired sexagenarian himself, tunes of Mozart trippling through his mind as his span of horses slipped on steep descents, or strained on their load up agonizing hills. Da Ponte recalls that he crossed 'the Ridge' seventy-two times in those years, travelling through country as beautiful as it was rugged and remote. Twice, he was involved in terrible accidents. On the first occasion the shafts of his wagon broke, the horses took fright and dragged the vehicle over a stump in the road, catapulting Da Ponte to the ground. He broke a rib and collarbone and his skin was lacerated. It was three months before he fully recovered, treated in the final stages in Philadelphia by the famous Dr Philip Physick, the 'Father of American Surgery'. Just a few months later, travelling at night with a drunken driver on a stagecoach that overturned in a ditch, Da Ponte again broke a collarbone and so injured his back that he could not move for three weeks. This time he was treated by Benjamin Barton (Da Ponte had not approved of Physick's dietary regime of only two potatoes and four oysters a day). Lorenzo relished Barton's learned company, as he did that of his Sunbury physician Doctor Sam Jackson, who described him at this time as having 'a good figure, very handsome, and with a noble manner. An extremely honest man, delightful company, witty, and often deceived by rogues into embarrassing situations.'

Rogues there were aplenty, whether real or imagined. From the start of his time in Sunbury, despite his initial success as a trader, Da Ponte bewailed his customary woes. There was the Italian merchant in Philadelphia who sold him a lame horse and a damaged chaise, and who cheated him out of profits on a sale of spices; the friend bailed from jail who turned against him; the reappearance (stolen, he says, from among his papers) of an old Opera Taylor promissory note; a night spent in a Sunbury jail for debt. Staff, he complains, stole from him, merchants cheated, and people whom he had trusted with credit could not pay. Taxes sucked unfairly at his profits from distilling (this is certainly true, as the law discriminated against small-scale seasonal distillers). Finding himself – in 1814, after some shaky dealing – the unwilling possessor of a quantity of lace and fancy fabrics, he opened a millinery store at 29 North 2nd Street in Philadelphia, no doubt relying on Nancy's skill at making artificial flowers. The store was probably tended by his second daughter Fanny (now fifteen), who preferred life in the city to rural Sunbury and appears to have boarded in Chestnut Street with Frances Papegay, a friend of Louisa Niccolini's. (Fanny married in Philadelphia in 1815, though divorced her husband three or four years later and returned to live with her parents.)

Prices of goods slumped dramatically (in some instances by up to 50 per cent) after peace was declared with Britain in 1814, and sea-trade routes reopened. This created panic among grocers and middlemen, but news of the peace – and the commercial crisis – spread slowly, not reaching some parts of the country until a good few months into 1815. Thinking he was cutting an excellent deal on a large consignment of goods, Da Ponte discovered that the sellers (who had information about plunging prices that Da Ponte had not yet heard) had unloaded their wares on him at a cost he could not hope to realize. At the same time the value of the three-storey house he had built for $5,000 dropped to $3,000. The birth in 1815 of Lorenzo's first grandchild, a girl named Matilda (whom he adored) to Louisa and Miles Clossey, added some cheer to life, but there was no escaping the losing battles. From 1815, Da Ponte spiralled through 'a continued series of calamities', as it became clear that the odd loan from Charles Hall or sale of his gold watch and pianoforte were no bolsters against collapse. The old man was no match for Sunbury rough justice. A violent Big Tom Hundred Legs raided his home while he was away (though the unfortunate Nancy was still there), making off with stoves, furniture, horses and a cart in lieu, he said, of monies owed him. The court case that followed, as Da Ponte tried to reclaim his goods, was delayed when the sheriff retired and no one had the courage to take his place. Forcibly ejected from the three-storey house by one creditor (a man known for arranging settlement of debts with his fists and gun), Da Ponte moved his family to a small wooden house next door – and even that was later stripped of all its furniture by Big Tom's henchmen (the dispute was ongoing). After pleading in tears, all Da Ponte got back were the beds.

In addition to his court battle with Big Tom, Da Ponte was embroiled in litigation involving his in-laws. Louisa Niccolini died a rich woman in January 1815, leaving $5,000 to Nancy in a trust to be administered by Charles Hall, guaranteeing her an income from the 6 per cent annual interest, whatever her husband's adventures. On Nancy's death, the principal was to be divided among the children, who would all also receive a $600 bequest upon attaining their majority. Until that time, interest on these legacies would go to Nancy, for her personal use. If any of the children died, their share would either go to their own offspring or be divided among the other siblings. Louisa left Peter Grahl $1,000 and her late husband's property, and $1,000 to her friend Frances Papegay. She bequeathed her wardrobe to Nancy, and her not insubstantial collection of furniture to young Louisa. Any residue from the estate would be added to Nancy's capital. Louisa Niccolini had stitched her will carefully and tightly, making absolutely sure that Da Ponte would not get his hands on a cent. Lorenzo was livid. Friend though Charles Hall was, he – and later his son Robert – relentlessly implemented Louisa's wishes, despite Da Ponte's anguished and persistent attempts to release the money. Even when Nancy herself intervened, asking Hall to buy on her children's behalf, using their share of the inheritance, the three-storey house which was being sold by creditors at below its market value, Hall did not budge. Louisa's will was not all Lorenzo disputed. When Peter Grahl died in 1816, Da Ponte hoped he would be relieved of a $500 debt he owed his brother-in-law, but found himself dunned for it by the executors. In fury, he brought a suit against Peter's widow Elizabeth – the woman who had so delighted him in Trieste, and who had introduced him to the Grahl family – claiming a share of the jewellery left her years earlier by Nancy's mother. In addition to all this, Da Ponte was involved in a dispute with one Giuseppe Mussi over property left by John Grahl – a case that would drag on for years.

Bitter, disillusioned with Sunbury, and seething against his myriad injustices, Da Ponte left for Philadelphia in August 1818 with his fifteen-year-old son Joseph, hoping to find sufficient teaching work there to support his family. Nancy – with the more astute business mind – remained behind for a few weeks to finalize sales of property and try to collect some of the money owing them. Unlike her husband, Nancy appears to have found her métier in this new land, and had investment interests of her own – though having lost her father, brother and sister in the space of a few years, and suffering the public humiliation of Da Ponte's decline, she was perhaps pleased to leave Sunbury. Young Joseph, on the other hand, who had been witnessing deeds and mortgages since he was twelve, and who helped his mother with her business correspondence, had lived half his life in Sunbury and wrote a curious, sorrowful poem entitled 'Farewell to the Susquehanna', which was published some time later in the *Northumberland Times*.

Philadelphia failed to deliver the redemption Da Ponte had hoped for. In September he wrote urgently to Nathaniel Moore in New York, saying that he had found only two pupils in the course of a month, and (hiding momentarily behind the mask of a quatrain of comic verse) that the old woman he and Joseph were lodging with was pestering them for unpaid rent. He implored Moore to find friends, former pupils or a publisher who would advance him some money on a book he was writing. In a letter to his old friend Michele Colombo (of whom, to his delight, Lorenzo had heard news from an Italian traveller) Lorenzo revealed that the book was the story of his life. Moore, who had left law to become a teacher of Greek at Columbia College, sent 'not twice but twelve times' the amount Da Ponte had hoped for. In a letter thanking 'Signor Nataniello' for his 'boundless generosity and angelic ways', Da Ponte went on to congratulate him on his new appointment, adding: 'Would to God I should in my old age find a similar post in Italian! This dream has passed so often through my mind, but I fear in America it will always be a dream.'

Da Ponte's windfall was consumed in an icy winter. By January 1819,

Da Ponte was writing desperate letters to Charles Hall, pleading for release of capital from Louisa Niccolini's estate, and begging for help in calling in money still owed him in Sunbury. In March he wrote again to Nathaniel Moore, stating that he had given up all hope of teaching Italian in Philadelphia – and that he was in a little trouble involving a promissory note. An Italian traveller through Philadelphia had brought with him the most splendid books, a series of classics called *Classici Italiani di Milano*, beautifully produced and with a wealth of annotations. Da Ponte was enraptured. As the traveller was about to leave town, Lorenzo had bought the entire collection with a note dated to expire in three months, hoping to sell some volumes to the local library. Although Zaccheus Collins, a trustee of the Library Company of Philadelphia (the 'Mother of all American Subscription Libraries') had expressed interest in the collection, he had clearly been thinking in terms of a bequest. Shortly before Da Ponte's promissory note was about to expire, a curt letter arrived from Collins stating that 'the Library does not buy books'. Da Ponte then sent Joseph to New York with a few of the volumes – and Joseph returned within days, having made a handsome profit. The young man also brought a letter from Clement Moore, urging Da Ponte to return to New York and devote himself 'to the cultivation and diffusion of [Italian] language and literature'.

Da Ponte did not hesitate. Leaving Nancy and rest of the family behind to wait until funds permitted them to travel as well, Lorenzo departed town with Joseph (whom he feared had been falling into dissipated company while studying law in Philadelphia) in April 1819. He had with him just a few clothes and some books, including 140 volumes of the *Classici*. It was with 'a heart overflowing with hope and joy' at the prospect of a fresh start that Da Ponte saluted 'from the opposite bank of its beautiful stream, the noble, populous, and to me beloved, city of New York'. He had just turned seventy.

Chapter Sixteen

Lıke washington ırvıng's Rip Van Winkle – who fell asleep one night and woke after twenty years to discover a much-altered, more complicated world – Da Ponte found the city once so familiar to him utterly changed. Steamboats now ferried passengers across the river. New York astonished even its residents by the rapidity with which buildings were put up, pulled to pieces, razed, repaired and transformed. Just a few weeks before Da Ponte left town in 1811, the street commissioners had unveiled an eight-foot-long map depicting a daring, extraordinarily far-sighted city plan. Manhattan's hills, dales and twisting alleys were to be subsumed under a rectilinear grid. The rantipole city confined below Canal Street and containing 100,000 souls would acquire a framework of straight roads and regular blocks with room for a million people – a layout to equip New York for expansion well into the future; a scheme of admirably democratic design with no 'circles, ovals and stars' to cuddle nooks of elitism; and with throughways given numbers rather than being named after families of rank or fortune. By the time Da Ponte returned in 1819, the ironing-out of Manhattan was well under way. A year earlier, Clement Moore had been indignant to find Ninth Avenue thrusting itself into his Chelsea estate – though even he, too, would soon be carving out lots for genteel purchasers.

With the Moores' energetic support, Da Ponte acquired twelve students within a week of arriving, and had doubled that number in less than a month. His students purchased 80 of the 140 volumes of classics Da Ponte had brought with him, and together funded the donation of the remainder to the New York City Library. Da Ponte rounded off the gift by adding fourteen editions of modern Italian literature – the first stone, he said, of a literary edifice he had dreamed of erecting ever since arriving in America. He also went to great lengths to persuade booksellers in Italy to grant him credit, so that he could open an Italian bookshop in New York, but to no avail.

Da Ponte's mission to bring Italian culture to the New World was taking on heroic proportions; it was 'a miraculous enterprise' aimed at 'introducing the Italian language and literature into the most vast and remote portion of the globe, and of making known, diffusing and establishing there our divine literature'. In pursuit of this dream, Da Ponte had, he wrote, to expose himself to vexations and fatigues, endure hardships and make sacrifices. He does not mention the effect his mission had on the long-suffering Nancy and their children. Lorenzo loved his family deeply – as poems he wrote for them reveal – but in his travails with fortune, in his battles with life in following his visions, his self-absorption was complete. Traits that may not be bothersome when we are young become exasperating as we age, either because they amplify, or because they become salient as other more attractive characteristics fade, rather as physical features – ears, a nose – become more prominent as a face droops and withers. Thus childhood insouciance may grow to youthful cockiness, and later arrogance in a man, to become an all-consuming egoism as he ages. Da Ponte's self-obsession not only flooded his life but spilled into his memoirs.

Lorenzo's new-found fortune did, though, enable him to rent a small house on Chapel Street, and bring the rest of his family up from Philadelphia. He hired a room near by for his lessons, and they settled back into city life. Da Ponte found tutors for Charles (Carlo) and young Lorenzo, and sent Joseph to a college to improve his Latin and Greek, subjects neglected while he had been studying law in Philadelphia. In October 1819, he enrolled Joseph at Columbia College, though the new prosperity did not stretch quite that far – in November he had to write to the president of the college, William Harris, admitting that he could not

pay fees in advance, and might have 'to deprive [Joseph] of the benefit of
tuition in the College'. Quite possibly Clement Moore, or John R.
Livingston – a member of one of New York's leading families (and
landlord of five of the city's best-known brothels) – came to the rescue,
as Joseph took up his college place in the autumn. Da Ponte was
enormously proud when, at the end of the academic year, Joseph came
third in his class – but the young man pleaded to return to Philadelphia to
study law with the firm he had originally been attached to, and finally
Lorenzo relented and let him go.

Since the previous occasion that Da Ponte had lived in New York, the
city's Italian population had grown. As Napoleonic Italy dissolved back
into its constituent states after Bonaparte's defeat in 1815, restored rulers
crushed sedition and prized out dissenters from what were on the whole
reactionary new regimes. Many fled to the democratic New World, and
though numbers were by no means large, there was enough of an Italian
presence in New York by the mid-1820s for a *Società di Unione e
Benevolenza Italiana* to form, to help the poor and 'keep alive a true
feeling of nationality'. Despite his mission to establish Italian culture in
America, Da Ponte dismissed his countrymen as 'a swarm of exiles', and
resented the competition from those 'who had exchanged their bayonets
and muskets for dictionaries and grammars and turned to teaching
languages' – an unfair accusation, as many of the new arrivals were
cultured men. Lorenzo had lost none of his ability for making 'relentless
enemies'. One newcomer, a defrocked priest named Marco Antonio
Casati, circulated a letter among the parents of Da Ponte's pupils
criticizing the old man's pronunciation and education, his habit of
plagiarizing, his birth and even his teeth (or lack of them). He accused
Da Ponte of debauchery, murder, swindling and intrigue, maligned his
servants, pronounced his son Joseph 'familiar to every vice', and further
revealed that Da Ponte had in his youth been made to quit Venice for his
misdemeanours. The claims seemed too far-fetched for polite New York
to believe, though Da Ponte did ask some prominent men – such as past
pupil Samuel Jarvis, then a professor at Yale – for testimonials to refute
Casati's slanders. (About expulsion from Venice, Da Ponte was tactfully
silent.) He also continued to work on his own version of events, which

would become five volumes of memoirs suitably cleaned up for a more puritanical age, and infused with more than a tang of the bitterness he had come to feel against the world. Believing himself constantly obstructed, Lorenzo did not temper his high hopes but instead turned sourly against those who thwarted them. If his dreams could not be realized, it was invariably someone else's fault, or the perversity of Fortune. Yet his optimism and enthusiasm remained undiminished, a constant burning core that formed a crust of rancour where it met the world. Some of those who knew him – such as Joseph II or Clement Moore – could tap through to the core. Da Ponte was, noted one such contemporary, 'truly a good man . . . who preserves in old age the warmth of youth'.

While ploughing on with his memoirs, Da Ponte, having read an article in the *Edinburgh Magazine* on *Don Giovanni* (which premiered in London only in 1817) and noting that the piece made no mention of him at all, published in a blaze of self-justification, *An extract from the life of Lorenzo Da Ponte with the History of several dramas by him, and among others, il Figaro, il Don Giovanni and La scuola degli amanti* [Così fan tutte]; *set to music by Mozart.* It was in English (most likely translated by Joseph or Fanny) and ran to forty-six pages. In all his years in Sunbury, Da Ponte had brought out only one poem – a *canzone* to his London friend Thomas Mathias, which was probably privately printed in Philadelphia. After the appearance of *An extract*, his literary activity intensified.

A similar sense of outrage to that which fuelled the appearance of *An extract* lay behind Da Ponte's *Discorso Apologetico* on Italy, which followed an attack on the Italian nation in an open letter to the King of England, by the lawyer and member of the New York City Council Charles Phillips in 1821. The letter began by maligning the royal consort Queen Caroline for taking an Italian lover during an extended visit to Europe, then broadened to encompass an assault on the Italian nation as a whole. Da Ponte prepared a public reply to this 'barbaric diatribe', which he delivered, in English, at the Lecture Room on Barclay Street on 13 February. The college newspaper the *Columbian* reported that the oration was delivered before 'one of the most numerous assemblages of wit and fashion which ever graced an apartment in this city', and that

the audience listened 'with delighted attention'. One of the company,
Dr John Francis, admired 'the earnestness and animation of a great
speaker', as well as Da Ponte's clear passion for the language and its
literature, and the 'copious stores' of his reading. *Discorso Apologetico* was
published in both English and Italian in 1821. The public oration had an
immediate benefit for Da Ponte, in that it encouraged Henry James
Anderson, a young man of very good family and of 'marvellous keenness
of wit', to apply to him for lessons. Young Anderson had a glittering
career ahead of him, as Professor of Mathematics at Columbia and a
distinguished astronomer, and his advent brought change to the Da
Pontes' lives. Anderson's two brothers and three other young gentlemen
followed his example in seeking lessons from Da Ponte, and as they all
lived some distance from town asked if they could not be taken in as
boarders. This was all the encouragement Lorenzo needed to move to
Greenwich Street (a most fashionable address) and open 'Ann Da Ponte's
Boarding House' for the accommodation and tuition of young ladies and
gentlemen.

Barely had the boarding school opened when Joseph, who had
returned unexpectedly from Philadelphia looking pallid and emaciated,
died 'of a strange and painful illness, which the most experienced
physicians either could not identify, or found greater than their skill'
– the disease appears to have been consumption, the malaise that would
become the plague of the nineteenth century. Da Ponte was pierced by
'the most heart-rending grief', finding Joseph's death at the age of twenty
so 'bitter, strange and overpowering' that it plummeted him 'into the
depths of most desperate misery'. To compound Da Ponte's distress,
Joseph had died leaving debts in Philadelphia, just four months short of
his twenty-first birthday, when he would have inherited $600 from his
aunt Louisa's estate. Lorenzo paid the debts, and considerable doctors'
bills, but was unable to lever any money out of Robert Hall, leaving him
not only mourning but yet again seething against that 'vindictive
woman' his late sister-in-law, and her perfidy.

One of the kindly young men Da Ponte taught, seeking some means
to distract him from his sorrow, gave Lorenzo a copy of Byron's poem
The Prophecy of Dante, an impassioned vision of an Italian *risorgimento* by a

poet very much of the new generation. Da Ponte thought the poem
sublime, was struck by its 'sweet melancholy' and read it voraciously in
one sitting. Immediately, he determined to translate it. The Livingstons
suggested that he spend some time in their country estate at Staatsburg on
the banks of the Hudson River, where he had passed 'two blissful
months' the year before. Da Ponte retreated there with his family, and
some of his students. Each day he would breakfast with his children and
pupils (among whom were two of John R. Livingston's daughters), then
he would 'find some spot, now under a peach, now under an apple tree,
and still weeping translate a portion of that poem which would ever add
a touch of sweetness to my tears'. By the end of the summer he had
finished his translation, and found that the companionship and kindness
of his student hosts had helped ease his anguish. He dedicated *La profezia
di Dante* to one of them, Julia Livingston, and to her sister Eliza he wrote
a pretty, if slightly old-fashioned poem that his pupil and young friend
Fitz-Greene Halleck (he of the Ugly Club) translated, beginning:

> Eyes with the same blue witchery as those
> Of Psyche, which caught Love in his own wiles;
> Lips of the breath and hue of the red rose,
> That move but with kind words and sweetest smiles . . .

Da Ponte published his *La profezia di Dante* in 1821. The subscription list
boasted some of the most influential names in New York, including seven
members of the Livingston family, Clement and Nathaniel Moore, the
Verplancks, Lennoxes, and President of Columbia College, William
Harris. A second edition in 1822 contained an appendix of touching
poems to his family and observations of everyday life, translated by one of
his daughters (probably Fanny) in the literary workshop that the Da Ponte
household was becoming. Lorenzo sent *La profezia di Dante* to Lord
Byron with a letter begging forgiveness for his audacity, but confessing he
had not been able to withstand the temptation to translate it. No reply
from Byron exists, but Giacomo Ombrosi, the American Vice-Consul in
Florence, wrote to Da Ponte praising the translation and saying that he
had delivered a copy to the poet on encountering him in Livorno.

Da Ponte immediately made use of Ombrosi's goodwill to ask him to persuade a Florentine bookseller to send a large stock of books to New York at a good price – though Da Ponte still had to pay in advance. In order to raise the requisite sum of $100, he notes (with characteristic self-focus): 'I did not hesitate to deprive myself of many objects necessary to the decorum of my family.' At the same time, a French firm at last allowed him credit, and Messrs Fusi and Stella, publishers of the *Classici Italiani di Milano*, 'made certain very fair offers and proposals' which he was most happy to accept. In June 1823, Da Ponte drew up a *Catalogo ragionato di libri*. He had over a thousand volumes to hand. Together with his youngest son Charles, now seventeen, Lorenzo was back in business as a publisher and bookseller, initially selling from home and from a gig that he used to drive around the city, later from a shop at 336 Broadway. Almost immediately, Da Ponte began to bring out the first volumes of his memoirs, a process he was to continue through to 1826. The second volume lists over one hundred subscribers, including a certain 'Count Survilliers' – in reality Joseph Bonaparte, Napoleon's brother and former King of Spain, now living in America, who ordered fourteen copies. But the triumphs of 1823 were marred when Lorenzo's eldest daughter Louisa, the family's 'most graceful ornament', died of consumption in July at the age of twenty-eight. Louisa's second baby, a boy named Franklin, had died the year before after a life lasting only five months, so she was survived by her husband Miles and the eight-year-old Matilda.

After the anguish of the loss of Louisa, in Da Ponte's words: 'Fortune seemed to have struck a truce with me.' The family found stability and reasonable prosperity, and Lorenzo some equanimity as he sold books, taught, and composed verses. 'I am old, as you well know,' he wrote to Girolamo Perucchini, a friend from his days in the Ceneda seminary, 'yet though seventy-three years have passed, they don't weigh heavily on me, neither on my soul nor on my shoulders. I still eat well, drink even better, and sleep peacefully, and – which amazes people – spend six, eight, ten and sometimes twelve hours a day working and writing poetry. I won't say the verses are especially beautiful, and I don't dare to believe it when some of my friends say so, because after forty years absence from

Italy I find it impossible to believe that I have not lost that modest skill I perhaps once had.'

Da Ponte taught Italian not only at his own house (assisted by Fanny and Matilda, young though she was) but at other schools for young ladies around the city – at Mrs Green's, Miss McClenahan's and Mrs Okill's. His methods were extraordinarily effective. An enormous chart of irregular verbs together with 'a rule which [Da Ponte] had himself discovered' enabled one student to master over five hundred of the fiends 'in a flash'; and a technique of teaching grammar through translation accomplished the dual task of imparting the language and its literature simultaneously. In April 1825, Da Ponte took a step towards realizing a long-held dream and wrote through Clement Moore to the trustees of Columbia College, asking permission to teach Italian to students of the college on the premises. He was willing to do so for free. By this time a number of his former pupils were attached to Columbia – Clement Moore was a trustee and Professor of Biblical Learning, Nathaniel Moore was Professor of Greek, and Henry James Anderson was librarian and Professor of Mathematics. Anderson had also just founded the *New York Review and Athenaeum Magazine*, to which Da Ponte had contributed an academic 'Critique on certain passages in Dante'. After some discussion, the trustees reached a decision. In September 1825, Lorenzo Da Ponte was appointed Columbia's first Professor of Italian Language, simultaneously becoming by default probably also the first Jewish-born member of teaching staff and the first Roman Catholic priest to take up an academic appointment.

The new professor was not to be considered a member of the college board, attendance at classes was voluntary, and though Da Ponte received no remuneration from the college, he was required to charge students for tuition (conditions not markedly different from those granted to other professors of modern languages). In the first months, twenty-three young men came to his lessons, but Da Ponte did not have as much success with them as he did with his feminine 'flowers'. Young men wishing to get ahead in the world were better served by French and Spanish (especially now that neighbouring Mexico had gained its independence), and had no time for an Italian teacher bent on literature.

Numbers dwindled to nil, and at the end of the academic year Da Ponte resigned. The trustees would not accept his resignation, and though ruefully acknowledging in a witty Latin verse that he was 'a shepherd without sheep . . . a priest without a temple / a professor without precedent', Da Ponte maintained his association with Columbia for the rest of his life, inaugurating a series of Dante lectures, selling books to the college library, and continuing to press for Italian language and literature to become an established part of the college curriculum rather than an addendum. One of the schemes Da Ponte came up with proposed that Columbia require 100 students to register at a fee of $15 each, while he would indirectly reimburse the college with a donation to the library of Italian books to a value equal to the total amount (no doubt still pocketing the profit his bookshop would make). His importunate letters in this instance became so pressing that Clement Moore replied in exasperation:

> It seems to me that you are a little overanxious as regards the memory that you long to leave behind you. For what you have already done for Italy and the cause of letters, so long as there remains a spark of taste among us for the belles-lettres, the name of Da Ponte, *clarum et venerabile nomen*, will be held in veneration; and his scholars of our, as well as of the gentler sex, will remember in the decline of life, the hours passed by them in pleasing conversation with their elegant and cultivated tutor, as among the sweetest moments of their existence; and it is, therefore, my dear sir, that I pray you to let this suffice, and not aspire, like Bonaparte, to acquire for yourself alone the whole glory of the universe.

Soon after he was appointed professor at Columbia, Lorenzo sent a copy of his memoirs to his sisters in Ceneda (his father had died in 1806) with a trippingly rhymed verse letter, asking them how they were, if they were married, whether their husbands were honest or not, rich or poor, ugly or handsome. He described his life teaching, selling books and writing poems, and enclosed a lock of Fanny's hair for his favourite, the youngest, Faustina, as they were both so beautiful they could be twins.

Life was pleasant, he writes, though '*Non sempre è carnovale / Non sempre si può ridere*' – it is not always a carnival, and we cannot always be laughing.

Towards the end of 1825, life – and the mission to establish Italian culture in New York – took a dramatic upward turn, when Lorenzo learned that an Italian opera company was coming to town, under the leadership of the celebrated Spanish singer and composer Manuel Vicente Garcia.

The Garcias were the first family of Italian opera. Manuel Garcia was a tenor, just edging past a magnificent prime. In Paris his voice had captured the attention of Gioachino Rossini, who created the role of Count Almaviva for him in his *Il barbiere di Siviglia*. He excelled at ornate vocal decoration, one contemporary complaining that the progress of a melody could sometimes scarcely be perceived 'through the dust of Signor Garcia's gambols'. Of his acting, a French singer had enthused: 'I love the Andalusian frenzy of the man. He puts life into everything.' Off-stage he had a ferocious temper. Garcia's wife Joaquina was a gallant soprano famed less for her voice than for her progeny. Their twenty-year-old son, also called Manuel, had an exhilaratingly clear baritone that deepened into a bass, but had not yet made his debut. He would live to be 101, invent the laryngoscope, and become a legendary singing teacher, counting Jenny Lind and Mathilde Marchesi (and thus by descent Nelly Melba) among his pupils. Even more impressive was the Garcias' precocious daughter Maria Felicia, whose voice soared from contralto to soprano, and who although just seventeen was already gathering bouquets of adulation. At the King's Theatre in London just a few months earlier, she had stepped out of the chorus to replace an unwell Giuditta Pasta as Rosina in *Il barbiere di Siviglia*, and had so seduced audiences that she was engaged for the remainder of the season for an astonishing £500. While perhaps not yet 'the finest singer in Europe' (as an eager supporter dubbed her in the New York press), she would very soon, under her married name of Madame Malibran, indisputably merit such acclaim. To New Yorkers, she became 'the Signorina'. Little Pauline – just four when the packet-ship *New York* docked at Manhattan on 6 November 1825 – was the only non-performing member of the family, but as Pauline Viardot she too would become a fabled diva (and Turgenev's heart-throb). Along with the Garcias came Madame Barbiere from Paris (an untried singer, referred to both as a soprano and a tenor), the much-admired basso Felice Angrisani (who had emerged from retirement for the occasion), and a colourful band of (mostly fledgling) singers and stagehands. The more experienced members of the company were past their best, and the younger ones had yet to prove themselves, but there was no doubt that New York's first taste of Italian opera would be a rich one.

Garcia's company had been lured to New York by the combined efforts of the manager of the Park Theatre Stephen Price, and the wine merchant Dominick Lynch – 'the greatest swell and *beau* that New York had ever known', whose fine manners, refined behaviour and royal dinners set the tone and established the fashion in Manhattan society. 'A man was nobody in those days if he had not subscribed for a box [of Lynch's Château Margaux],' wrote the journalist Joseph A. Scoville in the 1860s. 'The subscription lists for three hundred cases contained all the principal people in New York.' Lynch was, recollected Julia Ward Howe (author of 'The Battle Hymn of the Republic'), himself without rival as a ballad singer: 'His voice, though not powerful, was clear and musical, and his touch on the pianoforte was perfect. I remember [as a child] creeping under the instrument to hide my tears when I heard him sing the ballad of "Lord Ullin's Daughter".' It is quite possible that Da Ponte first met Lynch at the Howes' home, as (though she was aged only five or six) Julia recalls the old man, and was later taught Italian by young Lorenzo.

The Italian opera company arrived without the drums and trumpets of pre-publicity, but New York was soon buzzing with news of their presence – fired by an article in the *American* heralding one of the 'highest and most costly entertainments' of the Old World. The exotics themselves were the subject of great curiosity. Dr John Francis (who had so enjoyed Da Ponte's discourse on Italian, and who became the company physician) was surprised to discover the artistes neither lazy nor dissolute, but that '[t]hey had not crossed the Atlantic twenty-four hours ere they were at their notes and their instruments', and until the day's work was over they partook only of '[a] taste of claret, a glass of lemonade, eau

sucrée . . . and scarcely a particle of animal food'. To Lorenzo, the troupe
carried a fragrance of his old life in another world. The story spread that
when Da Ponte introduced himself as the author of *Don Giovanni*, Garcia
clipped the old man to his arm and danced around the room in childlike
glee, singing the 'Champagne Aria'. Da Ponte wasted no time in
suggesting that Garcia stage his opera, but the company lacked a suitable
singer for the part of Don Ottavio. Lorenzo promised to do what he
could to rectify that. He also made sure that, at their lodgings in Canal
Street, the Italians in the company would have a taste of home. They
boarded at the house of one Mrs Meigs, together with a friend and pupil
of Da Ponte's, William Cullen Bryant, poet and then assistant editor of
the *New York Evening Post*. Nancy – famed for her Neapolitan macaroni
with Parmesan, and her beef with garlic, its 'aroma fragrant enough to
awaken appetite in the dead' – taught Mrs Meigs's cook 'Aunt Sally' to
prepare Italian food. Another pupil of Da Ponte's recalls that Aunt Sally's
cooking (later at her own establishment on Broome Street) was renowned among Italian visitors to New York well into the 1860s. Most of
all, Da Ponte conducted a one-man publicity campaign among his
influential friends and pupils to ensure the success of the Garcia
company's visit.

The excitement spread. A correspondent signing himself 'Musœus'
took it upon his shoulders to enlighten the public through the pages of
the *American* and the *Evening Post* with 'some general information
touching *Italian Music*, a style seldom heard in this country, and less
understood than any other'. On 10 November he whipped through an
explication of regional styles, and a history from Italian sacred music
through madrigals to theatre music, assuring readers of his experience and
credentials when it came to opera. The following week, because there
were 'but few, very few, amongst us who have any idea of the Italian
Opera', he gave a quick run-down of opera terms, helpfully explained
the difference between aria and recitative, and hastened to assure New
Yorkers – who were beginning to shuffle uneasily at the thought of
hours of incomprehensible singing – that the glorious Italian language
'glides through melody [and] melts at once into a dream of pity or of
love'.

As Musœus bombarded future opera-goers with advice on how best to appreciate the music, he was joined by 'Cinderella' on the social front. Cinderella opined that 'a few remarks upon the propriety of the appearance of the ladies and gentlemen who attend [the opera] will not be irrelevant'. She eschewed the European custom of appearing in full dress for opera (as the boxes of the Park Theatre were too crowded to admit such display), but asserted that ladies should pay special attention 'to the dressing of their hair and bust, in order that the theatre might have a gayer appearance'. Bonnets with feathers and muslin caps were most definitely out, as were coloured cravats and hats for men. Young, beautiful women might ornament their hair as showily as they pleased, while those more advanced in years were advised to resort to a turban. Advertisements began to appear in the press offering 'operatic head ornaments' as well as 'London Opera Cloaks & Shawls' and a wealth of other accoutrements especially imported for the occasion. The Park Theatre upped the price of a box from $1.00 or $1.50 to $2.00, and announced a stylishly late curtain time of eight o'clock rather than the usual seven or seven-thirty. The stage was set for grand opera to make its debut as a leading player in the New York social scene.

The Park Theatre, rebuilt after a fire in 1820, was a fashionable vortex for theatre-loving Knickerbockers – old-stock Anglo-Dutch and Huguenot families who had taken their tongue-in-cheek monicker from the imaginary author of Washington Irving's *A History of New York*, and who jostled for place in the lower tier of boxes. (The upper tiers and gallery were occupied by the artisan and shop-keeping class, the pit largely by European immigrants.) As such, the Park was an appropriate venue for this new event in the social calendar – though Cinderella could not resist a sideswipe at the theatre's not being as clean or as handsomely maintained as it might (it was not unknown for rats to put in an appearance during performances), as this discouraged ladies from wearing their better robes. She also took the opportunity to dismiss the concern that language might be a problem as 'trifling', because 'no one who can read Italian will regret the loss of [the words], as they must necessarily be, in a great measure, nonsense, from the constant repetition to which they

307

are subject'. It can only be hoped that Da Ponte did not read that issue of the *American*.

On 17 November advertisements appeared in the press announcing that *Il barbiere di Siviglia* was in rehearsal, and that from 29 of November opera would be given at the Park Theatre every Tuesday and Saturday. A twenty-four-piece orchestra was put together locally (though it seems no oboist could be found in the entire country), rehearsing five or more hours a day to master Rossini's music, then considered daring and difficult. Members of the troupe built and painted sets, sewed costumes, and rehearsed their roles. Chorus master Crivelli marshalled a group recruited from immigrant English factory workers who had sung in church choirs and so could read music. On the morning of the premiere the *American* announced that the troupe were in high spirits, that rehearsals had been most satisfactory, and that (despite a severe snowstorm a few days previously) the evening's performance would be fully attended.

Under the blue-and-gold domed ceiling of the Park Theatre that night gathered 'one of the most full and fashionable houses ever witnessed in New-York'. Leading Knickerbocker families were splendidly represented; Joseph Bonaparte was there, and next to him sat Da Ponte's young friend Fitz-Greene Halleck and James Fenimore Cooper, whose novel *The Last of the Mohicans* would be published a few days later. Da Ponte was surely there, as were any number of his students. The *Spectator* observed that the audience contained 'an unusual number of ladies, arrayed with great taste and elegance, whose bright eyes sparkled with delight during the whole evening'; the *American* was pleased to perceive that 'no unsightly bonnets marred the view of those occupying the back seats, or detracted from the array of beauteous and smiling faces, decked in native curls, or embellished with wreaths of flowers, or tasteful turbans'. Cinderella's heart was gladdened.

The overture produced immediately a 'gratifying silence' among the audience, and according to the *American*, 'no sign of restlessness, or fatigue' appeared for the remainder of the performance – though 'A Spectator' was moved to write to the paper that the constant conversation of a pair of Frenchmen in the pit, 'that after the dulcet tones of

Signora Garcia, sounded like the croaking of frogs', had driven him to the second tier, from whence the know-it-all comments of two local lads had further impelled him to seek the seclusion of a box. The Signorina, much talked-about around town, was 'greeted with great and long continued applause' before she even opened her mouth, and Garcia, Angrisani, and even the chorus and orchestra were warmly received.

In the newspapers, critics were cautious, and a little nonplussed. They were on new ground. 'In what language shall we speak of an entertainment so novel in this country?' inquired the *Evening Post*, continuing, 'All have obtained a general idea of opera from report. But report can give but a faint idea of it.' The *Albion* admitted frankly that it would have to withhold comment until it had received a 'scientific critique' promised by a professor; the *American* more confidently proclaimed that '[t]he whole opera was performed in a style and with a spirit that cannot, we are persuaded, be surpassed at this moment on either the Paris or the London boards'; and Henry James Anderson predicted in his journal a glorious future for Maria Garcia, marvelled at her acting as well as her vocal skills, and saw the evening as a significant milepost in the progress of American culture. To the man brave and foolish enough to call the music 'monstrous', Da Ponte issued a public rebuke in a lengthy open letter praising Rossini. At home the day after the premiere, Dominick Lynch dashed off a quick note to Giuditta Pasta in Paris, extolling the triumph of the evening and the 'truly astonishing' singing and performing skills of 'the little Signorina'.

Italian opera had made its mark. People came from Boston and Philadelphia to hear the Garcias. One Signora Bartoline of 403 Broadway lost no time at all in offering singing and guitar lessons, with all the 'airs as sung in "Barbiere de Seviglia"', and the Park's rival, the Chatham Theatre, attempted a spoiling campaign by reviving its dreadful, mangled English-language version of *Don Giovanni*. Garcia followed *Il barbiere* with one of his own compositions, *L'amante astuto*. It failed, and the company quickly returned to Rossini. Then in May notices appeared announcing the American premiere of *Don Giovanni*, in its original Italian. Da Ponte had persuaded a group of his friends and pupils to pay for a tenor to sing Don Ottavio, but the company – and especially the orchestra – were not up to the challenge. Garcia, perhaps under pressure as a tenor coping with the baritone title role, flew into a fury on the opening night as the band disintegrated under the strain of the finale at the end of Act I, rushed to the footlights sword in hand, and commanded that they begin again.

The *Albion* had no great regard for Garcia's own performance, considering him 'not much at home in the simple melodies of Mozart', and only the Signorina worthy of praise. Otherwise, the New York press appears to have remained silent on the topic of *Don Giovanni* (which ran for a further three performances), though the Garcias' housemate and *Evening Post* editor William Cullen Bryant wrote to his wife that the opera was better than he had expected (not much of a vote of confidence for his friend Da Ponte), that the Signorina had a liquid voice and acted well, despite her skinny arms, but that Monsieur Milon (Da Ponte's find for Don Ottavio) was 'intolerable'. Da Ponte, on the other hand, was delighted and proudly exclaimed, 'Everything pleased, everything was admired and praised – words, music, actors, performance; and the beautiful, spirited, and amiable daughter was as distinguished, and shone as brilliantly, in the part of Zerlinetta as her father seemed incomparable in the part of Don Giovanni.' At last the part of his life that meant most to him could be something tangible to his friends and 'flowers'.

Da Ponte published a copy of the libretto, with a translation by the younger Lorenzo, which was sold at the theatre, and later brought out *Una tragedia et tre drammi*, a compilation of his play *Il Mezenzio* with three operas – *Le nozze di Figaro*, *Il Don Giovanni* and *Axur, re d'Ormus* – which he described as 'the three most precious gems of the lyric/comic theatre of Italy'. In the introduction of *Don Giovanni* he proclaimed, with customary absence of modesty, how marvellous it was that

> . . . the three operas of Mozzart [*sic*] are almost the only ones which no modern Composer has succeeded in supplanting; the only ones which with every day that passes are more highly esteemed and valued, in every theatre in Europe; the only ones which can cry out in triumph, WE ARE ETERNAL.

The words of these operas were written by me. To that immortal genius I gladly yield all the glory which is due to him for writing such miraculous works; for myself, may I hope that some small ray of this glory may fall on me, for having provided the vehicle for these everlasting treasures, through my fortunate poetry.

Garcia's troupe stayed in New York for nine months, giving nine different operas over seventy-nine performances, and ending as they had begun with *Il barbiere di Siviglia*. The fizz of the first night had not lasted the season – only adulation for the Signorina, 'the magnet who attracted all eyes and won all hearts', continued to bubble. A bitter winter followed by a scorching summer took their toll on audience numbers, and the eerily synchronous deaths of both Thomas Jefferson and John Adams on 4 July 1826 (the fiftieth anniversary of the signing of the Declaration of Independence) temporarily closed the Park Theatre. Takings ranged from $1,962 on the best night to $25 on the worst, and overall receipts were a perfectly respectable $56,685, not the pot of gold Garcia might have dreamed of but quite enough to take the company on tour to Mexico – all except the Signorina, who had made a disastrous marriage to a man older than her father, a French merchant named Eugène Malibran, who turned out to be bankrupt and a wastrel (some say Maria only married him to escape her father's tyranny, and that Da Ponte introduced them to each other). The Signorina (as New York persisted in calling her) stayed on to sing ballad operas in English to adoring audiences at the New York (Bowery) Theatre, before leaving her husband the following year to return to Europe and embark on a magnificent career as Madame Malibran. Dominick Lynch, despite the middling success of Garcia's season, hatched a scheme to build an opera house and employ the company permanently, but enthusiasm had waned and the committee set up to form a 'New-York Opera Company' gave up on the idea by the autumn.

Glittering though the opening night of *Il barbiere di Siviglia* had been, New York was sceptical about Italian opera. Some of the opposition came from quarters familiar to Da Ponte after his experiences of cultural nationalism at the Burgtheater and in London. Hostility from local theatre companies expressed itself in direct competition, as (in a conflict reminiscent of clashes with *Singspiel* and German drama in Vienna, and with ballad-opera companies in London) not only the Chatham Theatre but the Park itself offered English-language versions of such operas as *Don Giovanni* and *The Barber of Seville*. Ballad opera and pastiche had a long and successful history in New York, dating back to the 1750s. Before the Revolution, English operas that had been popular with London audiences made it across the Atlantic just as fast as a packet-ship could carry the score. French operas on tour from New Orleans were also happily consumed in New York and Philadelphia – though French was more widely understood and performances were often given in an English translation. New York's reluctance wholeheartedly to embrace Italian opera lay deeper than mere cultural chauvinism; it was the result of the audience's reluctance to endure an entertainment in a language it did not understand.

Da Ponte had seen glimmerings of such rebellion in London, where Italian was not nearly so much a shared language of the governing class as in continental Europe. In egalitarian America this opposition was even stronger. Much though a Knickerbocker upper crust might preen itself at this 'highest and most costly entertainment' of the Old World, the bulk of the populace was more forthright in its dismissal of an evening conducted in a foreign tongue, and at the irrationality of a drama entirely sung. The assurances of 'Musœus' and 'Cinderella' notwith-standing, many New Yorkers agreed with Fanny Burney's Mr Brangh-ton that Italian opera was simply a lot of jabbering, and with the anonymous English critic of the 1780s that unintelligible recitative was 'too dull to keep us awake, yet too noisy to let us fall asleep'. Da Ponte tells the story of one of his friends making a very similar complaint, though admitting after a performance of *Don Giovanni* that 'not only [was] there no sleeping during the performance, but there [was] no sleeping afterwards, the whole night long'.

At the premiere of *Il barbiere di Siviglia*, Chancellor Kent had stormed out of the theatre shouting, 'It's an insult to human nature!' Philip Hone, Mayor of New York in 1825, agreed that 'recitative is an affront to common sense' and encapsulated local opinion in an entry in his diary:

I went to the opera . . .! The house is as pretty as ever, and the same faces were seen in the boxes as formerly; but it is not a popular entertainment, and will not be in our day, I fear. The opera did not please me. There was too much reiteration, and I shall never discipline my taste to like common colloquial expressions of life: 'How do you do madame?' or 'Pretty well, I thank you, sir,' the better for being given with orchestral accompaniment . . . The Italian language is among us very little understood, and the genius of it certainly never entered into with spirit. To entertain an audience without reducing it to the necessity of thinking is doubtless a first-rate merit, and it is easier to produce music without sense than with it; but the real charm of the opera is this – it is an exclusive and extravagant recreation, and above all it is the fashion.

> Italian music's sweet because 'tis dear,
> Their vanity is tickled, not their ear;
> Their taste would lessen if the prices fell,
> And Shakespeare's wretched stuff do quite as well.

Only fashion and its purse could save the opera. If that purse were not large enough, in the absence of royal or aristocratic patronage opera would fail, because, in the words of Da Ponte's friend Samuel Ward, 'no harmonious influence had educated the taste of the multitude on whom theatrical and operatic success depend. The boxes [are] filled with applauding *virtuosi*, the pit with a thin, bewildered people, whose surprise [is] divided between the actors before and the performers behind them.'

The more serious admirers of the genre fought back with arguments of the combined power of music and drama, no matter whether the language was understood or not, and lauded the ability of opera to transcend to a new plane of aesthetic experience; but others simply saw the Italian opera for the social kudos it delivered, and were thus fickle supporters. A few subscribed to the shattering intellectual snobbery of the American composer Thomas Hastings in his 1822 *Dissertation on Musical Taste*:

It has sometimes been objected against the opera that it is offered to us in a foreign language; but what if it is? This only proves that those who know nothing of Italian, are not the proper persons to listen to it. It has been composed for a different class of individuals; and if others, through the mere affectation of taste, are willing to go, and to laugh and cry at the wrong places, or to regulate their emotions by the example of those around them, whose fault is it? They obtain the object they are seeking, and the rest are doing no more.

In a sense, opera in America became a battleground for a clash between eighteenth- and nineteenth-century values, between the Old and New Worlds, the scene of a struggle for cultural as well as political independence. In Vienna, when Joseph II lamented that 'three buffo singers cost as much as 100 grenadiers', Da Ponte had found subscribers and helped opera take a step away from court – but it had still been essential for ambassadors and aristocrats to be seen at the Burgtheater. In London, the King's Theatre was technically quite distinct from the Palace, yet was still the possession of an aristocratic class bound to opera through a set of social expectations and obligations. They were patrons, not investors, and expected nothing more in return for the money they poured into it than an affirmation of their social position. It remained to be seen whether such an expensive amusement for an elite could survive in a New World atmosphere, and by just what means. The question in a republic was who should pay for opera, and would the price be worth it? There was a creeping opinion that it would not.

Undeterred by Dominick Lynch's failure to establish the Garcia troupe in New York on a permanent basis, Da Ponte continued to dream of a resident Italian opera company in the city. His mind turned to his niece Giulia, the daughter of his wayward half-brother Agostino. Travellers to New York had brought word that she was an excellent singer and was studying with an old friend of Lorenzo's – Antonio Baglioni, the first Don Ottavio in the Prague *Don Giovanni*. Lorenzo had 'a hankering to see some of my own people after thirty years of separation', and saw an opportunity not only to do that but simultaneously to take another step in his quest to bring Italian culture to America. He began to put the word about that he was bringing Giulia to New York to sing. As ever, just as his life was beginning to find an even keel, Da Ponte did something to capsize it.

Chapter Seventeen

B Y THE LATE 1820s, though the number of his pupils was again
dwindling, Da Ponte was making a respectable living from the
sale of books. Henry James Anderson had bought two healthy
consignments for the Columbia College library, and through Gulian
Crommelin Verplanck, a former pupil who was now a congressman, Da
Ponte sold some costly editions to the Library of Congress. A plan to
establish a permanent Italian library in New York had not come to
anything, but business was good enough by 1830 for Da Ponte to cease
selling from his gig and storeroom and to open a proper bookshop on
Broadway (a fashionable address, where the family also came to live).
Here he would take his chair 'at cock's crow, never leaving, save for a
few moments, staying on into the late hours of the night' and entertain
such customers as the poet and Harvard professor Henry Wadsworth
Longfellow, then in his twenties, for whom Da Ponte autographed two
volumes of his own poems, which he had recently published.

Lorenzo continued to write, publish others' work, translate, and bring
out volumes of his memoirs (completing the final one in 1830). A
favourable review of his reminiscences in the prestigious Florentine
journal *Antologia* in 1828 at last brought his name back into prominence
in his native land – but led to the *Memorie* immediately being banned in
Venice, Trieste, Naples and throughout the Austrian Empire. As a result
of the review, Da Ponte entered into correspondence with new admirers
such as Anthony Panizzi (later principal librarian at the British Museum,

and responsible for its magnificent reading room), and Domenico
Rossetti, a Trieste lawyer who remembered seeing Da Ponte as a
boy. Rossetti became a lucrative source of books for Da Ponte, roused
the literati of Trieste to donate their works to his cause, and in the course
of a barrage of letters was a helpful and seemingly indefatigable recipient
of all manner of Lorenzo's demands. It was he who gathered a bundle of
letters for Lorenzo from long-lost friends. The gesture overwhelmed the
old man, who did not know where to begin in reading them, and replied
to Rossetti that he felt as 'a Turk must do when he is surrounded by the
beauties in his harem and bestows his kisses and caresses first on one and
then on another'. Lorenzo bestowed his kisses once more on his former
schoolmates Michele Colombo and Girolamo Perruchini. He was nearing eighty, but apart from the odd twinge of rheumatism and a fall on an
icy step – which left him badly bruised and laid up for a month – he was in
the pink of health. In 1826, his son Lorenzo (known in America as
Lorenzo L. Da Ponte) had married Cornelia Durant, a niece of the wife of
President Monroe, bringing the family the wealth and social cachet of
which Da Ponte had long dreamed. Fortune was at last being gentle with
him, when he took it into his head to act as impresario for Giulia.

Agostino had tried as early as 1823 for a passport to America, but his
long record of disruption in Venice, not to mention the many creditors
clamouring in protest around his door, had stayed the hand of the
relevant Austrian official. It was not until Lorenzo, fired with enthusiasm
after the Garcia troupe's visit to New York, intervened with a *canzone* to
the Emperor Francis in person (copied in a fine hand in Venice, and sent
on to Vienna) that cogs began to turn, and even then they moved slowly.
Agostino would only be allowed out of Austrian territory if he could
prove he had left adequate funds to support his wife Caterina and elder
daughter Pasquetta while he was away. Negotiations lurched on for
years, with Da Ponte along the way advising Agostino to bring silkworms, vine cuttings and books on viniculture with him – as he foresaw
silk and wine as becoming leading American products – and the noble
Rossetti arbitrating through a great deal of brotherly ill will when
Lorenzo claimed that Agostino had frittered away money that he had
sent to Venice to pay for the journey.

In the meantime, in 1828 (the year that Noah Webster's dictionary proclaimed independence for American English), Da Ponte had acquired US citizenship. He does not mention why he did this – he had been eligible for naturalization for nearly a decade. The banning of his *Memorie* in Europe may well have sharpened his focus on the benefits of being a citizen of a country with a free press, or he may have reasoned that the move strengthened his standing in his attempt to bring Giulia to New York. In any event, it was as an American national that he launched out on his new career as an impresario.

As time dragged on and still Giulia did not appear, Da Ponte's pupils began to tease him, pretending to believe she did not exist, giggling in class when one young lady read from the *Purgatorio* the lines:

> *Una donna soletta, che si già*
> *e cantando, e scegliendo fior da fiore*

> [A lady all alone who wandered
> Singing and plucking flower from flower]

'Signor Da Ponte,' they asked, 'this singer who is picking the flowers – couldn't she be your niece?' Certain that Giulia would be in New York by June 1829, Da Ponte urged his son Lorenzo to negotiate hiring the Bowery Theatre for her, but June passed with no sign of the young singer and Da Ponte was forced to pay a substantial sum as forfeit – so much that it consumed his remaining capital, and Nancy had to travel to Sunbury, presumably to plead face to face with Robert Hall to free up some money from Louisa's estate. Da Ponte's letters to Rossetti became ever more frantic, declaring that unless Giulia come to New York soon, he would be ruined.

When Giulia and Agostino finally did arrive on 18 February 1830, Da Ponte was faced with further financial difficulty. He had authorized Rossetti 'not to look too closely at expenses' in arranging passage, and had promised to settle all accounts on sight when their ship came to New York. The pair must have travelled royally, because Lorenzo found himself faced with a bill for $420, an amount which made him 'tremble from head to foot, not seeing the fount from which such a sum must gush'. Da Ponte raised what he needed from a moneylender, at over 30 per cent interest, and Giulia was given a rapturous welcome by his friends and pupils. Even the 'frank and offhand' Agostino was politely received. Giulia gave one or two private concerts, and sang during her uncle's eighty-first birthday celebrations. Against his family's advice, and unbeknown to those who maintained that Giulia's introduction to the public should be gradual, Da Ponte signed a contract for her to appear at the Park Theatre at the end of March, and raided Rossini and other composers to create a new *L'ape musicale* pastiche for her.

Giulia had previously sung only in private concerts. She was a shy young woman and, though her voice does appear to have been a good one, she was, Da Ponte admitted, 'not made for the stage, nor the stage for her' (which, in fairness to Agostino, he had warned Lorenzo would be the case). *L'ape musicale* was a failure, and Giulia spent most of the ensuing weeks weeping. She and Agostino stayed on in the Da Ponte household for some months, running up considerable expense and occupying rooms that would otherwise have been let out. Lorenzo and Agostino argued bitterly – as they always had done – and the pair moved out of the house on Broadway when Giulia met and married a Trieste merchant named Giuseppe Staffler, who was passing through New York. All three later left for Europe without even saying goodbye.

Da Ponte's spirits were raised by some measure when in August 1831 Fanny at last married Henry James Anderson, who would appear to have been courting her for nearly a decade, since the days when he was a boarder in the Da Ponte household – another very favourable match for the family. But four months later came the most shattering blow of all. Nancy, who was just sixty-two and in good health, died suddenly of pneumonia, after an illness of just six days. Lorenzo was crushed. The loss of the 'angelic woman' who had reformed his rakish ways, who had channelled his need to belong into paternal pride, who had put up with his folly and (quite literally) paid for his mistakes, whose resolve, good sense and hard work had been his support for nearly forty years (yet which he had so often taken for granted), left him wrung dry with grief. 'You could not imagine my sorrow at her death,' he wrote to Michele

Colombo, 'nor can I describe it.' He did try, in a collection of sonnets 'dictated by my anguish', bound in a tiny volume, like a private prayer book, and bearing portraits of himself and his beloved Nancy. She was, he wrote, 'kind, candid, sincere, a mortal enemy to lies, pious toward God, compassionate of those in need / Free from envy, virtuous, constant, a humble daughter, wise mother and a faithful friend'. In the forty years they were together, she had been 'wife, friend, companion and consort, through happy times and desperate ones / A loving mother to her children – and anyone in distress was her child, and would cry: "Weep with me for she is dead!" '

Mourn though he might, Lorenzo's mind was never far from the financial consequences of his bereavement. It could not afford to be. He was a very old man, yet at a time when he might expect some repose he was having to scrabble for every cent, drain whatever wells of resourcefulness and courage he could find, and force the final reserves of energy from his frail frame. There was simply no let-up. To Gulian Verplanck he wrote that Nancy's death had 'not only robbed me of my peace of heart, but also of my means of supporting myself in my unhappy old age'. In the introduction to the sonnets that he wrote in her memory, he included a scathing attack on his in-laws, especially Louisa, for the way in which he had been cut off from Grahl family money. He then annotated the poems with explanatory notes, so that the book might double as a teaching aid. More disturbingly, when his adored grandchild Matilda died in October 1832, at the age of seventeen (just the day before she was to be married to a man who hoped to take her to the warmth of the Italian climate to restore her failing health), Lorenzo wrote within forty-eight hours to Robert Coleman Hall to make a retrospective claim on Matilda's trust fund for rent. He considered the money was owed to him for the months since 1830 that she had lived in his house, when her father Miles Clossey had been unable to support her. Da Ponte's callous concern with money is perhaps understandable given his circumstances, but not entirely justified as his surviving children moved to help him. After Nancy's death he went to live with Cornelia and Lorenzo L. Da Ponte and his grandson Lorenzo III in Dey Street. Henry Anderson granted him an annual allowance of $200, and Cornelia Da Ponte continued to run the Greenwich Street boarding house, which no doubt also provided the old man with some income. Lorenzo now saw little of his youngest son Charles, who left New York for New Orleans in 1831, and perhaps later went out West.

One issue was certain to distract Da Ponte from his troubles. As his friend Samuel Ward put it: 'Whenever the words music and Italian were coupled together, the old bard became rejuvenesced, enthusiasm lit up his eye, and love of the literature and song of his native land thus remained a worship and ruling passion.' The battered old phoenix could not lie prone in the ashes for long. At the age of eighty-three Lorenzo was about to embark on his most quixotic adventure yet. Shrugging off the disaster of Giulia's visit, he laid out an even more ambitious plan. He would bring an entire Italian opera company to New York, one to rival Garcia's. He might even open his own opera house. Da Ponte was incorrigible. Far from enjoying his hard-won repose, he seemed unable to sit still. The dream of Italian opera in New York generated extraordinary new energies in him, and fired up by his new mission he made an impressive sight: 'a head of Roman beauty and intelligence, a countenance lit up with vivacity, which readily brightened to enthusiasm or became intense with inspiration, and enframed in a classic profusion of flowing hair, dignity of mien, and the self-possession of conscious talent – these met and arrested the passing gaze'.

Da Ponte had, before Nancy's death, already written in high spirits to the French tenor Giacomo Montresor about the possibility of bringing an Italian company to New York. In the months that followed, flurries of letters brimming with optimism crossed the Atlantic as he assured Montresor that 'a good and well-regulated company of Italian singers will make a fortune in America', though it would have to be 'superb, stupendous, excellent' to top the one Garcia had brought over. Da Ponte had, he assured the singer, over 1,800 influential friends and students on whose support he could draw for subscriptions. They might even be persuaded to build a new theatre for the company (they had once been thinking of such a move, he knew). It could be called the Montresor–Da Ponte Theatre. Even French companies from New Orleans were a success in New York, wrote Da Ponte (in his excitement tactlessly forgetting Montresor's nationality): 'Every year a company of *gatti* [cats], I mean *galli* [Gauls] (sorry, my pen slipped), comes from New Orleans . . . and after a tour of two or three months goes back with their pockets full of silver and with the applause of all those who love French howling, and with cats meowing in time.' Da Ponte had experience of local conditions, and could offer sound advice. Montresor should bring 'a good first violin, a good oboist, a maestro at the harpsichord and a prompter', also scene painters, 'as those that are here charge sixty times what they ought', as well as sufficient scores, as copyists in America were six times as expensive as in Italy. Da Ponte recommended bringing works by Mozart, Salieri and Rossini (including a number of his own libretti). He should come with a bag of arias, duets, trios and quartets – old though Lorenzo was, he was still caressed by the Muses and would take singers' favourite battle horses and make them gallop. The success of the venture depended entirely on the quality of the lead singers. Of choristers New York had plenty, even though they flayed a native-speaking Italian's ears, but a troupe of dancers would be a fine novelty, and surely three or four thousand dollars would be enough to persuade Giuditta Pasta to come. America had its drawbacks, but was an 'Earthly Paradise' compared with Europe. Da Ponte sounded one note of warning: 'The Americans are almost all merchants: they make a business of everything, even entertainment. Come, do your best to please, awaken in some the enthusiasm born of pleasure, in others the hope of profit, and then dare all, hope all.' 'Dare all, hope all' was a familiar Da Ponte motto, and one that befitted a fledgling impresario.

Time went on, and Da Ponte – who was energetically raising funds by subscription – became edgy at the delays. At last, at the height of the summer of 1832, Montresor made an appearance with an enormous company of more than fifty people (Da Ponte had been expecting just twenty), yet with no prima donna. Da Ponte had been wrong about Giuditta Pasta, who had declined to come. Worse, New York was in the throes of a cholera epidemic and anyone who could afford to had left town. The new opera company, wrote Philip Hone in his diary, 'must waste their sweetness on the desert air until the destroying angel has sheathed his sword and our citizens have returned to their homes'. It was autumn before the citizens were back in place, and neither the Park nor the Bowery Theatre was available. Instead the company occupied the Richmond Hill Theatre, recently converted from the old residence of Aaron Burr. For a while, the theatre grandly termed itself the Italian Opera House. The season opened on 6 October 1832 with Rossini's *La Cenerentola*.

A lead soprano, Edelaide Pedrotti, a handsome woman with a warm voice, had hurriedly been imported from Havana. Pedrotti pleased the public – though largely because, the Signorina having left town, they required a new singer to worship. The basso, Luciano Fornasari, was also admired, as was Montresor himself, as a restrained singer who did not tumble through quite as many vocal somersaults as Garcia had done. New York thought the scenery and costumes superior to 'the worn and dirty finery at the Park', and the orchestra was the most proficient the city had heard. But the novelty and something of the glamour of Italian opera had worn off, and houses were poor. A move to the Bowery Theatre in the spring did not improve matters, and a tour to Philadelphia met with even less success. The season collapsed after thirty-five performances. Montresor had not included a single Da Ponte libretto in the company repertoire.

Da Ponte was devastated at the collapse, sinking into despair as once again his dreams disintegrated. He was confronted with terrifying bills as he had lodged Montresor and his son, guaranteed their credit, and met many of the company's expenses. He was also left with thousands of copies of libretti on his hands, which he could not sell. He fell out with Montresor, and when he hurt his leg in Philadelphia and was in bed for three weeks only the leader of the orchestra came to see him. His son Lorenzo came to his aid, and brought him back to New York, but Da Ponte faced ruin. In desperation he was forced to sell the objects he prized above anything on earth: the books in his own precious library. Pouring out his sorrow in a wrenching poem entitled (in an English translation) 'A Sad Farewell to my Books', he wrote:

> The nightingale, mourning his lost mate, does not
> fill the countryside with more desperate grief,

Nor does a father suffer more when from the shore
    he sees his sons take to the sea,

Than I, my heart rent, feel in giving you away; for
    in one moment I lose with you all I cherish.

It was only through you that in the changing course
    of life I was able to give respite to my sorrows
    and to turn them into joys;

And only you could have given birth to my fame,
    and your light remained whole and united.

Having you, I did not expect greater gifts from
    heaven; having you, I did not envy kings their
    riches and their thrones . . .

The poem is a moan of pain from an old man bereft of solace; within its lines hides the lonely child of Ceneda, who escaped through books and found in words a sense of belonging and the means to build himself a fragile fame.

There is a German novel, *Der Amerika-Müde* (The Man Who Grew Tired of America), written by Ferdinand Kürnberger in 1855, which gives a fictionalized account of the journey of the Austrian lyric poet Nikolaus Lenau through the United States in 1833. At night on a street in New York, Moorfeld (as Lenau is called in the book) meets an old man, hungry and cold, wrapped in a frayed coat. Moorfeld asks if summer nights in America are also cold. '*Anchi i giorni,*' comes the reply. All that warms him, the old man says, are his memories. When Moorfeld treats him to a glass of wine, the old man empties it with a solemn '*Evviva Vienna*', and curious as to why he should toast the Austrian capital, Moorfeld engages him in conversation. Slowly it dawns on the young poet who the old man is: 'Da Ponte, rival to Casti and Metastasio, languishing on the shores of Manhattan!' Overwhelmed, Moorfeld takes his hand, saying, '*Signor Abbé*, I beg you to accept the tribute of my fervent esteem. Wherever culture is to be found on this earth, there each man is in your debt . . . For *Don Giovanni* is the finest flower of musical art, the sweetest and greatest message of the human heart in modern times. And, by God, it is no mere chance that this wreath of honour in our times flowered principally from your verses.'

Da Ponte would have relished such praise, and this glimpse of an old man out of place in bourgeois New York – his head filled with memories of Mozart, powdered wigs, embroidered silks – has an air of truth about it, but not the picture of a man trapped by his past. Lorenzo was not sentimental. He became convinced that the only reason the Montresor season had failed was the lack of a proper opera house. The lure he had offered Montresor of a 'Montresor–Da Ponte Theatre' had not been a fantasy. As he drummed up the backing for Montresor's company, he had simultaneously been persuading his influential friends of the need for an opera house. Barely had *La Cenerentola* opened on Richmond Hill than an Italian Opera Association, under the experienced guidance of Dominick Lynch, was drawing up an agreement for ninety-six share-holders to invest $1,000 each to provide for the purchase of land on the north-west corner of Church and Leonard Streets, and 'to erect upon the land a building suitable for an Italian Opera House, with proper saloons and other accommodations, the first cost of which is not to exceed 56,000 dollars'. The shareholders' money was seen as an investment, rather than a donation. The board would not employ a manager, but would rent out the building, 'for the Italian Opera, or French Theatre, or both, and for such other purposes as they may deem proper and profitable'. With a rapidity astonishing even for New York, the city's first purpose-built opera house was designed, built, and made ready for use by November 1833. It should have been the crowning moment of Lorenzo's life in America, but it was the bitterest.

Originally, Montresor was to have been resident impresario, but by early 1833 he was firing off letters of protest to the Italian Opera Association at the usurpation of his position by the Cavaliere di Rivafinoli (a friend of Da Ponte's who had once sold books for him in Mexico). Minutes of the association's board of trustees record that Montresor had given his consent to Rivafinoli's renting the theatre, but Montresor denied this. The true reason for the trust favouring Rivafinoli appears to have been doubt over Montresor's ability to run the new

theatre profitably. In the ensuing acrimony, Da Ponte had taken
Montresor's side, but realizing he was fighting a lost cause Montresor
stormed off to Havana. Da Ponte had already gently been edged out of
any direct managerial or administrative role in the opera house, and now
Rivafinoli took revenge for the old man's support of Montresor by
forbidding him to sell libretti at the theatre – leaving Da Ponte with
4,500 books already translated and printed, which he could not dispose
of. Rivafinoli also denied Lorenzo free entry to performances. Da Ponte
sent a plaintive open letter to the press, appealing to 'the generous
American public, and particularly to my respected pupils . . . to know if
it be just that an *octogenarian* poet, who will soon be a *nonagenarian*, ought
to be deprived of this little benefit and left to this hard fate, after so many
years of faithful devotion to your service'. The *American* was not alone in
urging its readers not to forget 'this venerable individual, whose enthusiasm [o]n behalf of language, literature, and music of Italy' had been
instrumental in bringing the opera to New York, and hoping that 'his
friends and the public will seek [the libretti] at his residence'.

The Italian Opera House opened (appropriately, Da Ponte might have
thought) with a performance of Rossini's *La gazza ladra* (The Thieving
Magpie) on 18 November 1833. Austere from without, with its entrance
reached up a short flight of steps past six tall square columns, the building
offered ticket-holders and subscribers a sumptuous interior, 'one of the
most beautiful houses in the Union', raved the *Star*. The dome was
decorated with paintings of the Muses and Apollo; the first curtain
('splendid beyond example' and applauded by the audience) depicted the
climax of a Roman chariot race. Crimson-and-gold panels divided the
boxes, and elsewhere blue, white and gold glinted in the gaslight (itself an
innovation). Most spectacular of all was the tier of shareholders' boxes.
The purchase of six shares entitled one to exclusive use of a box, and to
decorate it in whatever manner one chose. Competition was intense. In
the weeks prior to the opening, decorators had been busy with gilt
mouldings and satin damask, Naples silk and Wilton carpets, installing
armchairs and soft sofas. The result, noted Philip Hone, was 'a style of
magnificence which even the extravagance of Europe has not yet
equalled', and (commented the *American*) the 'consequent straining of

necks from, rather than towards the stage, had the effect . . . of rendering the audience somewhat cold to the music'. Hone wilted rather at a four-hour performance in a language he did not understand, and wondered, 'Will this splendid and refined amusement be supported in New York? I am doubtful.'

Hone was justified in his concern. After the splendour of the first night, attendance lagged, and when the season ended in considerable deficit, Rivafinoli skipped town. He was replaced by Messrs Porto and Sacchi, who proposed making money by using the opera house as a venue for fashionable balls. Da Ponte composed *Frottola per far ridere* (A Squib to Make You Laugh), a poem pouring scorn on the management and ending with a prose address 'To those Americans who love the fine arts'. He lamented the failure of 'an enterprize for which I have so long and ardently laboured, so calculated to shed lustre on the nation, and so honorable in its commencement, ruined by those who have nor means, nor knowledge, nor experience', warning New Yorkers: 'Do not destroy the most splendid ornament of your city.' For himself, he wished for nothing, but concluded, 'It pains me to see spoiled by ignorance, and imposture and vanity, that which cost me so much or to speak more correctly, which cost me every thing, and you so much, and it will cost you more in fame, as well as in money.'

The Italian Opera House limped on until 1836, when it was sold to new owners and became an ordinary theatre. It burned down three years later. Part of its problem, Hone thought, were the private boxes. Not only did they deprive the theatre of income (subscribers did not have to buy tickets, and often sold on their places for their own profit), but they formed 'a sort of aristocratical distinction'. The ordinary New Yorker's attitude was that the subscribers were welcome to their private boxes, but that better entertainment, in English, was more cheaply obtained at the Bowery or the Park. 'I like this spirit of independence which refuses its countenance to anything exclusive,' wrote Hone. Egalitarian America dismissed opera in a language it could not understand, and scorned the social pretensions surrounding it. The small class of people who might have supported Italian opera did not show the unstinting largesse of a European aristocracy to whom the form had so long been an integral part of society. They wanted their investment to be 'proper and profitable'. Mere fashion could not support such a whim. It was to be half a century before New York, after a few further false starts, gained a permanent opera house in the Metropolitan.

Da Ponte slipped slowly from the public gaze. He moved with his son's family to a house in Spring Street, sold what remained of the books in his shop, continued to teach (but had only one pupil), wrote bitter letters to friends, and worked on a final volume of memoirs, of which no trace remains. He also became an 'ardent promoter' of the Catholic faith. In 1835, he published a poem dedicated to Colombo, part of which he translated into English himself. In the preface, he announced his intention to return to Italy to die, but said he had been dissuaded by a gift of fifty dollars by an American benefactor – a paltry sum, it may seem, but the wily old man no doubt had hopes that admission of such need might encourage further contributions from those who might be surprised to find that he was still alive. Of himself and his attempts to bring Italian opera to America he wrote:

> I believe that my heart is made of a different stuff from that of other men. A noble act, generous, benevolent, blinds me. I am like a soldier who, spurred by the longing for glory, rushes against the mouth of the cannon; like an ardent lover who flings himself into the arms of a woman who torments him. The hope of giving, *post funera*, immortality to my name, and of leaving to a nation which I revere a memory of me which will not be ignoble; and the sweet allurement of arousing feelings of gratitude and goodwill in those who follow an art that was not disgraced by my pen; the desire to awaken love for the beautiful language which I brought to America, and love too for our ravishing music; the longing to see once again on the American stage some of the children of my youthful inspiration, which are remembered in the theatres of the Thames, the Danube and the Elbe; and, finally, a sweet presentiment of joy, encouragement and honour, based on the integrity of my actions, the reliability of my promises and the happy success of a well-organized spectacle, were the powerful spurs which goaded me to this delightful undertaking, and from which nothing, so

far, has succeeded in deterring me. I dreamt of roses and laurels, but from the roses I had only thorns, and from the laurels bitterness! So goes the world!

Lorenzo Da Ponte died on 17 August 1838. In his last days he could barely speak, though he wrote a short poem in gratitude to Dr John W. Francis, who was attending him. His friend Samuel Ward paints a picture of his passing worthy of a nineteenth-century novel:

> It was one of those afternoons of waning summer, when the mellow sunset foretells approaching autumn. The old poet's magnificent head lay upon a sea of pillows, and the conscious eye still shed its beams of regard upon all around him. Besides several of his countrymen, were assembled some remnants of the old Italian troupe, who knelt for a farewell blessing around the pallet of their expiring bard . . . All wept as the patriarch bade them an affectionate and dignified adieu, and implored a blessing on their common country. The doctor, watching the flickerings of the life-torch, stood at the head of the couch, and a group of fearful women at the foot, completed a scene not unlike the portraiture we have all seen of the last hours of Napoleon Bonaparte.

The funeral took place three days later at the Roman Catholic cathedral. The choir sang not Mozart's *Requiem* but Allegri's *Miserere*, over Da Ponte's remains. Clement C. Moore and Gulian Crommelin Verplanck were two of the pallbearers. Fitz-Greene Halleck was among the cortège of men in sombre frock-coats and tall stovepipe hats that followed the coffin to the Catholic cemetery on Eleventh Street. Like his friends Mozart and Casanova, Lorenzo Da Ponte was buried in an unmarked grave.

New York thundered on. Obituaries spoke of the venerable Da Ponte's 'vivacity of temperament', his 'zeal and enthusiasm', and counted him 'as one of the literati of the last century'. In the *Albion*, news of Da Ponte's death had to vie for readers' attention with first-hand accounts of the coronation of the young Queen Victoria, just a few weeks earlier. Steamships were now crossing the Atlantic, and the New York &

Harlem Railroad became the world's first steam-driven urban transit line. Madison Square was laid out. And in an act of self-assertion, the *New York Herald* set up six European correspondents to give an American take on affairs in the Old World.

As surrounding property reached a premium, the bones in the old Catholic cemetery were tumbled up and moved to Queens. It was still not clear just which of the remains belonged to Da Ponte, and no monument was erected to him until 1987.

Appendix

Italian Opera Battles in London

The story of London theatres at the end of the eighteenth century is a tangled one. Unravelling it is made difficult by the similarity of theatres' names, by shifting companies, and by unclear definition of managerial roles. Prior to 1789, straight drama was produced at the licensed theatres in Covent Garden and Drury Lane; and Italian Opera almost invariably at the King's Theatre Haymarket. English-language opera was usually put on at Drury Lane.

In June 1789, the King's Theatre Haymarket burned down – the opera company transferred to Covent Garden for the summer. Technically, the King's Theatre had been operating for years without an opera licence, but people assumed a new building would simply be granted a licence on a claim of precedent. They were wrong. A complex spat involving blackmail, intrigue, and most probably arson developed between the Lord Chamberlain, the palace, patrons of various parties, and rival impresarios wishing to establish a new opera house. There was also conflict between those favouring English and those in support of Italian opera (in some ways divided along class lines, with the *bon ton* backing the Italians). In 1790 work began on a new King's Theatre on the site of the old one, but continued fighting about licences meant opera was not staged there. John Gallini, former manager of the King's Theatre (accused of burning it down to avoid debts) opened an Italian opera at the Little Theatre (also known as the Theatre Royal) on the Haymarket. The company staged opera buffa. Michael Kelly, who was contracted to sing with the English opera at Drury Lane, refused to sing there, though later Nancy Storace did perform. Generally, the quality of performances was poor (Haydn described 'a fellow that yelled an aria so horribly and with such exaggerated grimaces that I began to sweat all over'), and in the 1790–91 season the opera had a strong competitor in concerts given at the Pantheon, a former indoor pleasure garden in Oxford Street, under the management of Robert Bray O'Reilly. In 1791, the Pantheon became temporary home to the opera, was granted royal favour, and so officially became known as the King's Theatre Pantheon (though in common parlance, still the Pantheon). The company staged both *opera seria* and opera buffa, and it was the Pantheon (with the encouragement of Nancy Storace) who in 1790 had tried to persuade Mozart to come to London as resident composer. Meanwhile Gallini, together with William 'Opera' Taylor, another former manager of the King's Theatre Haymarket, had reopened the now re-built theatre, staging singing and ballet, but still fighting for a licence to put on opera.

In 1791, Drury Lane closed for refurbishment (it would reopen only in 1794), and the company moved to share space at the King's Theatre Haymarket. Although the actor John Kemble was by now running the drama company, Richard Brinsley Sheridan was the presiding power at Drury Lane, and appears to have carried some influence over to the running of the King's Theatre Haymarket. On 14 January 1792, the Pantheon suddenly (some say suspiciously) burned down. For the 1792–93 season, the new King's Theatre on the Haymarket appears at last to have been given an opera licence (though again some fudge surrounds whether or not in the first year this was yet legally the case). From 1793 onwards, the King's Theatre Haymarket became London's home of Italian opera, staging both *opera seria* and opera buffa, inaugurated with a revival of Paisiello's *Il barbiere di Siviglia* on 26 January.

The season headnote for the King's Theatre in the *London Stage* lists Taylor as 'proprietor', though it would appear that (owing to conflict among the directorship) he did not really take over the helm until 1794. Sheridan (who was technically renting the theatre from Taylor and

Gallini for the Drury Lane company) would appear to have had direct involvement in its running. He appointed Michael Kelly, who had become his confidant and sidekick, and Stephen Storace as 'acting managers' (according to the *London Stage* – in his memoirs Kelly recalls that he and Storace were 'joint directors . . . with a carte blanche'). This was the situation that reigned when Da Ponte came to London.

Notes to the Text

Chapter One

3   **Gaspare** Not Gasparo as sometimes given. He was named after his proxy godfather at the baptism, the Venetian nobleman Gaspare Lippomano. This was pointed out by Aldo Toffoli at a conference on Da Ponte held at Columbia University, New York in 1988, in a paper which overturns many long-held assumptions about Da Ponte's early life. See Aldo Toffoli, 'Lorenzo Da Ponte e Ceneda', in *Atti del Convegno Lorenzo Da Ponte* (Ministero per i Beni Culturale e Ambientali, 1998), p. 261.
small but not obscure city *Memorie* (Istituto Editoriale Milano, 1916), p. 55. Da Ponte is not quite precise, as Ceneda remained a semi-independent and rather rebellious bishopric until the death of Bishop Lorenzo Da Ponte in 1768, after which the Venetian authorities stepped in to claim the control they had been disputing for centuries (see Toffoli, 'Da Ponte', p. 258). Ceneda and the neighbouring town of Serravalle now form the city of Vittorio Veneto.

4   **ghetto, in the west of town** Toffoli, 'Da Ponte', p. 259, locates it on the mountain slope. It was most likely in the area today enclosed by Via Da Ponte, Via Manin and Via Labbi.
Jewish leatherworker Toffoli argues that he can't have been a tanner, as some biographers maintain, as tanneries existed along the riverside, some distance from the ghetto, and that rather he made domestic and agricultural articles from leather. The *Memorie* do mention 'the dyed leather or calfskin that your father makes' (p. 62), but this could refer to the worked or decorative leather of a cordwainer rather than a tanner. A commercial survey of 1770 (post-baptism) shows him to have a small shop, where among other items he sold salt and flour. See Toffoli, 'Da Ponte', pp. 259–63.
Ahi che la morte From the poem '*Di sospir in sospir . . .*', written for Thomas Mathias in Sunbury in 1816; quoted in Toffoli, 'Da Ponte', p. 264.

5   **like Steropes or Brontes** *Memorie*, p. 56.
    lo Spiritoso ignorante Memorie, p. 56.
    as much honour as Corneille Metastasio's *General View of the Stage* (1759);
    quoted in Frederick C. Petty, *Italian Opera in London, 1760–1800* (UMI
    Research Press, 1980), p. 74.

6   **aroused in [his] soul** *Memorie*, p. 56.
    had to wear red headgear Originally the colour was yellow, but legislation
    of 1739 and subsequent charters of 1750 and 1760 stipulated wearing of a red
    cappello (except for Levantine Jews, who retained the yellow *baretta*), subject
    to a penalty of twenty-five ducats. The ruling applied to Jews in Venice and
    throughout the state. See Benjamin Ravid, *Studies of the Jews of Venice 1382–
    1797*, III (Ashgate Variorum, 2003), p. 198.
    The original Ghetto The derivation of the word from the Venetian
    dialect *geto* is the most commonly accepted etymology, although there are
    other candidates for a source, including the German *gehegt*, meaning
    'enclosed', and Genoese *getto* (jetty); but the Ghetto in Venice is indis-
    putably the first of its kind, and gave its name to all others. See Umberto
    Fortis, *The Ghetto on the Lagoon* (Storti Edizioni, 2001), p. 18. For the
    situation of the Jews in Italy, see Fortis, pp. 110ff; Jonathan Israel, *European
    Jewry in the Age of Mercantilism 1550–1750*, (Clarendon Press, 1985), pp.
    238–53; John Julius Norwich, *A History of Venice* (Penguin Books, 2003),
    pp. 601–2; Cecil Roth, *The History of the Jews of Italy* (Jewish Publication
    Society of America, 1946), pp. 419–20; Marion Steinbach, *Juden in Venedig
    1516–1797* (P. Lang, 1992), pp. 430–1.
    The shopkeepers among those of this nation Quoted in Roth, *History of
    the Jews*, p. 420.

7   **ripples through the entire Republic** In 1768 a law was passed in Ceneda
    further restricting Jewish activity by banning Jews from trading in fodder and
    wine.
    an 'aunt' to Emanuele She is almost certainly the '*Signora Zia Monaca*'
    ('Madam Aunt Nun') he refers to in a letter to Michele Colombo in June
    1772. See Toffoli, 'Da Ponte', p. 260, who lists the other conversions.
    a teacher who in all likelihood In a letter written just before his baptism,
    he refers to a 'Maestro' in the ghetto, who appears to have been converted
    some short time earlier. See Giampaolo Zagonel (ed.), *Lorenzo Da Ponte,
    Lettere, epistole in versi, decicatorie e lettere dei fratelli* (Dario de Bastiani Editore,
    1995), p. 21.

8   **In his report the following year** The relevant Latin text is reproduced in
    Toffoli, 'Da Ponte', p. 261.
    any Jewish man or woman See Fortis, *Ghetto on the Lagoon*, p. 114.
    Orsola Pasqua Paietta Most previous biographers surmise that Geremia
    Conegliano converted to Christianity *in order* to marry Orsola Pasqua, but
    Aldo Toffoli convincingly argues that as a Jew Geremia would not have had
    social contact enough with her to arrange such a marriage, and he presents
    new evidence of the Paietta family's poverty and Andrea's illness, as well as
    pointing to the earlier Conegliano family conversions to support the idea that
    the marriage, was arranged after the decision to convert. In the light of the

situation of Venetian Jewry in the 1760s this seems the most likely order of events – though as Toffoli points out, true religious conviction as a cause cannot be simply dismissed. See Toffoli, 'Da Ponte', pp. 258ff.

9 **stepmother just four years his senior** Orsola Pasqua was born on 5 January 1745 (see Toffoli, 'Da Ponte', p. 261) and was thus eighteen, not 'a young girl not yet seventeen', as Da Ponte remembers in his *Memorie*. The error is perhaps telling.

matrimonio sì disuguale Memorie p. 57.

obtain from the charity of others *Ibid.*, p. 57.

a man of renowned piety *Ibid.*, p. 57.

agreed to pay for their tuition In the event, the bishop appears to have arranged for funding to have come from La Pia Casa dei Catecumeni, a Venetian charitable foundation for converts. Evidence of the payments was recently discovered by Aleramo Lanapoppi, *Lorenzo Da Ponte, Realtà e leggenda nella vita del librettista di Mozart* (Marsilio, 1992), pp. 220–1.

Every day, the more I discover Letter to Don Pietro Bortoluzzi, 14 July 1763; see *Lettere*, p. 21.

10 **a document in the Ceneda seminary** *Distinta Narrazione del solenne battesimo conferito nella Chiesa Cattedrale dei Ceneda ad un padre, e tre figli del ghetto della città*. See Sheila Hodges, *Lorenzo Da Ponte: The Life and Times of Mozart's Librettist* (University of Wisconsin Press, 2002), p. 3.

ten children Agostino Maria (1764), Angela Maria (1765), Silvia Rosa (1767), Maria Celestina (1768), Paolo Pasquale (1770), Augusta Maria (1772), Maria Marina (1775), Maria Constanza (1777), Maria Faustina (1779) and Enrico Lorenzo (1783). See Toffoli, 'Da Ponte', p. 263.

he declared an income A journey from Padua to Venice overland cost about one ducat; wages of a stonemason in Padua were sixty ducats.

11 **capable of composing** *Memorie*, p. 57.

full of fire and poetic valour *Ibid.*, p. 58.

12 **knew Dante's *Inferno*** We have only Da Ponte's word for this, as well as for his prodigious output in the ensuing weeks. See *ibid.*, p. 59.

a bookseller who *Ibid.*, p. 62.

13 **Never was a friend dearer** Letter of 1827 to Daniel Francesconi; quoted in Joseph Louis Russo, *Lorenzo Da Ponte, Poet and Adventurer* (Columbia University Press, 1922), p. 5.

in love with the same girl One Pierina (or Perina) Raccanelli, identified in a letter from Da Ponte to Colombo, 4 August 1828.

a terrible illness *Memorie*, p. 63.

14 **La Pia Casa dei Catecumeni** See Lanapoppi, *Realtà e leggenda*, pp. 220–1.

promise not to duel or dance See Giacomo Casanova, *The Story of My Life* (Penguin Books, 2), p. 500 n2. Even the arch-philanderer and adventurer Casanova had once taken minor orders.

wholly contrary to my temperament *Memorie*, p. 63. One wonders which of Da Ponte's 'principles' were so violated by taking the cloth; if he retained more of a conviction in his old faith than he ever lets on.

floundering through pitfalls Carlo Gozzi describes the conditions of a journey in the area at that time of year in *Useless Memoirs* (Oxford University Press, 1962), p. 148.

15   **Strict rules and a rigorous routine** Dominique Julia describes seminary life in 'The Priest', in Michel Vovelle (ed.) *Enlightenment Portraits* (University of Chicago Press, 1997), pp. 362ff.

the 'wild followers' of Aristarco See letter to Michele Colombo, 20 March 1770; *Lettere*, pp. 27–8. Aristarco Scannabue was the pseudonym of Giuseppe Baretti (1719–89), who propounded his ideas in the journal *Frusta letteraria* (the 'Literary Whip'), which was published in Venice between 1763 and 1765. Da Ponte was momentarily seduced by the idea of overthrowing the old literary order, but soon reverted to more established ideas.

16   **Not because I have spent** Letter to Michele Colombo, 20 November 1770; *Lettere*, p. 34. The possibility of a homosexual relationship between the two men is less relevant to an understanding of Da Ponte than is this breathless indication of his capacity for adoration.

Lorenzo found some consolation In a letter to Michele Colombo of 8 August 1770 (a Wednesday; *Lettere*, p. 32), he says he is leaving for Venice 'next Sunday'; he is still there on 3 September, when he writes again (*Lettere*, p. 33), and would appear to be set to stay a while as he asks Colombo to write to him in Venice. The 'terrible fever' and 'fierce convulsions' that the Da Ponte brothers were sent to Venice to recover from are usually put down to malaria, though as all three fell ill simultaneously, in winter, the ailment is more likely to have been something contagious. Some biographers mistake this visit as also being in 1770, as Da Ponte dates two letters from Venice to Colombo '*19 di Gennaio 1770 m.v.*' and '*3 di Febbraio 1770 m.v.*' (*Lettere*, p. 36 and p. 38). The '*m.v.*' is an abbreviation for '*more veneto*' ('in the manner of the Venetian Republic'), and refers to the Venetian practice of beginning the new year at the Feast of the Annunciation in March – so '*1770 m.v.*' is 1771 by normal reckoning. Da Ponte mentions the brothers' illness in the letter of 19 January.

Wolfgang Amadeus Mozart See Peter Dimond, *A Mozart Diary: A Chronological Reconstruction of the Composer's Life, 1761–1791* (Greenwood Press, 1997), pp. 62–3.

in love with Angela Tiepolo Da Ponte refers to her simply as 'Angela'. She and her twin brother were identified by Hermann von Löhner in 1882, after exhaustive examination of Venetian registers of nobility.

petite, delicate, genteel *Memorie*, p. 75.

17   **What do you think of that?** Letter to Michele Colombo, 23 April 1772; *Lettere*, p. 43.

18   **a wind-bag** '*un parolaio, un verseggiatore senza scienza*'; see *Memorie*, p. 65.

praises and caresses *Ibid.*, p. 65.

very violent passion *Memorie*, p. 66.

began slipping away See Russo, *Lorenzo Da Ponte*, pp. 12–14. There is no direct evidence that Da Ponte met Angela Tiepolo on one of his earlier trips to Venice, but in his memoirs he writes that she kept him 'tied to her' for 'three years', before the relationship ended on 1 January 1775, which would mean that they met while he was still at Portogruaro, and implies close contact between them before he went to Venice. Russo posits that his frequent absences were part of the reason for his seminary colleagues' antagonism towards him.

Greet Baliana for me Letter to Michele Colombo, *Lettere*, p. 56.

refused to recognise the boy See Lanapoppi, *Realtà e leggenda*, pp. 40–50. Nor did he recognise Angela's first child, born two years earlier – though he was forced to accept both as his by a judicial decree in 1775.

Chapter Two

19 **Caterina Querini was dancing** The story is told in Philippe Monnier, *Venice in the Eighteenth Century* (Chatto & Windus, 1910), p. 9.

As for Venice From 'A Toccata of Galuppi's', by Robert Browning (1812–89).

Browning's contemporary Philippe Monnier (1864–1911).

coffin under a heap of flowers Monnier, *Venice*, p. 28.

mistress of the Mediterranean Norwich, *A History*, pp. 583–604.

20 **Fat-pursed foreigners** William Beckford of Fonthill is one of the many travellers to comment on the extraordinary cosmopolitan mix in Venice: 'I observed a great number of Orientals amongst the crowd, and heard Turkish and Arabic muttering in every corner . . . Here the Sclavonian dialect predominated; there some Greek jargon . . . This instant I found myself in a circle of grave Armenian priests and jewellers; the next among Greeks and Dalmatians . . . [then] I was entering into a grand harum-scarum discourse with some Russian Counts or Princes . . .' William Beckford, *The Travel Diaries of William Beckford of Fonthill*, I, (Houghton Mifflin, 1928), pp. 91–2.

Friends gathered in *casini*. Casini [sing. *casino*] were small upper-storey apartments of two or three rooms, mainly in the area around St Mark's Square, where well-to-do Venetians met for informal gatherings, but which were also used for secret romantic assignations. William Beckford wrote: 'To these [*casini*] they skulk in the dusk, and revel undisturbed with the companions of their pleasures[.] Jealousy itself cannot discover the alleys, the winding passages, the unsuspected doors, by which these retreats are accessible.' *Ibid.*, pp. 90–1.

adorned with every excellence From Hester Lynch Piozzi, *Observations and Reflections Made in the Course of a Journey Through France, Germany and Italy* (Ann Arbor, 1967), p. 85. The lines of Milton's are from *Paradise Lost*, Book IV, 639–640.

two fiddles, a violoncello Charles Burney, *The Present State of Music in France and Italy* (Oxford University Press, 1959), p. 110.

all harmony like a nightingale Gozzi and Goldoni quoted in Monnier, *Venice*, pp. 109–10.

21 **the gondoliers singing barcarolles** Michael Kelly, *Reminiscences* (Folio Society, 1972), p. 81. Hester Piozzi was similarly entranced by singing gondoliers – though by 1786 the German man-of-letters Johann Wolfgang Goethe thought it all a bit staged, as by then singing boatmen had to be ordered in advance.

a great many ladies Beckford, *Travel Diaries*, I, p. 92.

illuminated by an eerie iridescence Giacomo Casanova, *Story of My Life*, p. 73.

22 **his fellow clergy** The phenomenon of the *cicisbeo* is discussed by Norwich, *A History*, p. 595; Monnier, *Venice*, pp. 69–73; and Giuseppe Baretti, *An Account of the Manners and Customs of Italy* (T. Davies, 1768), pp. 101–7, from whom the quotation is taken, and who strongly refutes that relationships between a *cicisbeo* and his *cicisbea* were ever anything but Platonic. For the other clerical antics see Casanova, *Story of My Life*, pp. 203ff.; April FitzLyon, *Lorenzo Da Ponte: A Biography of Mozart's Librettist* (John Calder, 1982), p. 44; Goethe, *Italian Journey*, p. 76, Monnier, *Venice*, p. 65; Emmett Murphy, *Great Bordellos of the World* (Quartet Books, 1983), pp. 106–8; Norwich, *A History*, p. 595; Joseph Spence, *Letters from the Grand Tour* (Queen's University Press, 1975), p. 87.

The people [of Venice] are attached Quoted in Maurice Vaussard, *Daily Life in Eighteenth Century Italy* (Allen & Unwin, 1962), p. 76.

grave, yet trifling Anonymous, *A new moral system of Geography containing An Account of the Different Nations Ancient and Modern* (G. Riley, 1792), p. 50.

23 **They baptize themselves** A. von Knigge in 1788, quoted in Andrew Steptoe, *The Mozart–Da Ponte Operas* (Clarendon Press, 2001), p. 17.

lodged with La Pia Casa dei Catecumeni Or at least that was where he had asked Colombo to address his letters.

ease and frequency with which marriages were annulled Norwich, *A History of Cities* (Penguin Books, 2003), p. 595.

some 160, people John Julius Norwich, *Paradise of Cities*, p. 4. The permanent residents of Venice today still complain of the gossip, and that everyone knows everyone else's business.

a good bed-room Kelly, *Reminiscences*, p. 71.

24 **The stone floors were worn** Gozzi, *Useless Memoirs*, p. 59, used by permission of Oxford Univerity Press.

superfluous as they both are Piozzi, *Observations and Reflections*, p. 314.

seat of enchantment! *Ibid.*, p. 113.

an azure expanse of sea Beckford describing his arrival in 1782, in *Travel Diaries*, I, pp. 78–9.

25 **These dear Venetians have no notion** Piozzi, *Observations and Reflections*, p. 103.

the earliest Casino Piozzi, *Observations and Reflections*, p. 99.

a thoughtless giddy transport Beckford, *Travel Diaries*, I, p. 90.

downing quantities of coffee Hester Piozzi reels after seven cups before sundown (*Observations and Reflections*, p. 99). William Beckford complains that 'immoderate use of coffee' renders the Venetians 'weak and listless to like any active amusement'. The magic beverage 'diffused a temporary animation . . . but the flash was soon dissipated, and nothing remained save cards and stupidity'. This, together with all the wafting about in gondolas, and nerves left 'unstrung by disease and the consequence of early debaucheries' belies the Venetians' reputation, so that 'instead of slumbering less than other people, they pass their lives in one perpetual doze' (*Travel Diaries*, I, pp. 92–4).

one of the leading theatres See E. Volpi, *Storie Intime di Venezia Repubblica* (Filippi Editore, 1984), pp. 227–9 and Virgilio Boccardi, *L'Ambiente Teatrale Della Venezia Musicale Del '700* (Filippi Editore, 1998), pp. 20–3.

the first public opera house See John Dizikes, *Opera in America* (Yale University Press, 1993), pp. 35–7.

26   **Get off, you goat!** For first-hand experience of Italian audiences see Kelly, *Reminiscences*, pp. 50–1.

The insolent noise one hears Casanova, *Story of My Life*, p. 177.

Montesquieu and Rousseau, were appalled See Boccardi, *L'Ambiente Teatrale*, p. 64, for the various descriptions of Venetian audiences.

to the inns and coffee-houses *Ibid.*, pp. 70–1.

Venice alone had never burned a heretic See Norwich, *A History*, pp. 593–5.

27   **at youth's boiling point** *Memorie*, p. 66.

She had no great *Ibid.*, p. 75.

feasting, carousal and debauchery *Ibid.*, p. 66.

anyone connected with literature Goethe, *Italian Journey* (Penguin Books, 1970), p. 70.

the *Accademia Granellesca*. See Gozzi, *Useless Memoirs*, pp. 155–60.

false, emphatic, metaphorical *Ibid.*, p. 157.

28   **When we had amused ourselves** *Ibid.*, pp. 159–60.

the *barnabotti* The *barnabotti* were required to wear silk, like other nobles, and entitled to their seats on the Great Council, but were debarred from working as craftsmen or shopkeepers. In a city where more exalted political positions relied entirely on having money or influence (which usually went together) they were effectively excluded from high office. Some were given poor relief but only if they stayed single and brought no more young *barnabotti* into the world. Most lived in the parish of S. Barnabà, hence the name. See Norwich, *A History*, pp. 595–9. For attitudes to the nobility and patricians in Venice, see Stuart Woolf, 'Italy 1600–1796' in George Holmes (ed.), *The Oxford Illustrated History of Italy* (Oxford University Press, 1997), pp. 131–8; on manners and decorum see C. Dallet Hemphill, *Bowing to Necessities: A History of Manners in America, 1620–1860* (Oxford University Press, 1999), pp. 65–8, and Woodman, *Politeness and Poetry in the Age of Pope* (Fairleigh Dickinson University Press, 1989), pp. 12–17.

the Venetian aristocracy was diminishing The number of nobles fell from 6,439 in 1586 to 4,457 by 1642 and 3,557 by 1766; see Woolf, 'Italy 1600–1796', p. 133.

29   **rich and consolatory** Piozzi, *Observations and Reflections*, p. 102. 'Venice treacle' was a combination of drugs and spices (some sources say up to seventy), including viper venom, emulsified in honey or molasses. It was generally used as remedy against poisons, and recommended in Britain, mixed with gin, as a cure for 'stomach gout' (whatever painful malady that might have been). See Elizabeth Burton, *The Georgians at Home* (Arrow Books, 1973), p. 242.

One late autumn evening Da Ponte gives the account in *Memorie*, pp. 66–77. The existence of this mysterious woman has never been proved, and some say the story is a figment of Da Ponte's imagination. It does indeed have something about it of an anecdote from Casanova's memoirs (part of which are made up or embellished), or the clandestine 'third affair' Carlo Gozzi describes in *Useless Memoirs*, and may be Da Ponte's attempt to give his memoirs a literary flourish – though it could also indicate a true incident in Da Ponte's life that, like many in Casanova's, captured the atmosphere of the city and the period. There are also remarkable parallels between the woman's early life and Da Ponte's experience of a young stepmother and parental neglect. If one is to see the story as a fabrication, this raises the question of why Da Ponte would want to make it up (and do so at such length). He was not especially good at plot – hardly any of his operas has an original storyline, they are mostly adaptations of others' works – nor does the tale show him in a particularly good light, except to show that he could play the gentleman. His life story was curious and eventful enough without his having to include such colour. The reason he might have made up such an event then becomes very similar to the reason he might have remembered it and chosen to include it in his memoirs if it were true: it is a telling illustration of his feelings of isolation, of being trapped in the situation he was in, his desire for escape, and his failure to do so.

30   **The strange circumstances** Direct speech is as Da Ponte relates it in his memoirs. *Memorie*, p. 67.

32   **a sinister offshoot** See Norwich, *A History*, p. 597.
      he urinated involuntarily Casanova, *Story of My Life*, p. 236.

33   **contributed to [Matilda's] misfortune** *Memorie*, p. 76.
      The mystery in which *Ibid.*, p. 76.
      discovering what had become of her Da Ponte notes in his memoirs that he heard, twelve years later from Sebastiano Foscarini, the Venetian Ambassador at Vienna, that Matilda had been shut up in the Convent of the *Convertite* at the instigation of her stepmother. Foscarini, Da Ponte writes, said that he succeeded in securing her release after six years – her stepmother having died in the interim – and that she was reunited with her father. *Ibid.*, pp. 76–7.
      nowhere were the stakes higher Norwich, *A History*, p. 585.
      The Ridotto In November 1774, a year after Da Ponte arrived in Venice, the authorities closed the Ridotto – though that simply meant that the faro banks moved to private homes and *casini* around the Piazza San Marco.
      cursing cards *Memorie*, p. 77.
      just before Christmas In his memoirs, Da Ponte recounts the event as occurring at the end of the Carnival, but he must have meant the break in Carnival festivities for the *novena* – the nine days of prayer leading up to Christmas – as a letter in January to Michele Colombo indicates that the events he relates have already occurred. *Ibid.*, p. 77.
      the boatman guessed Gondoliers were renowned for their wit and their cheek. Michael Kelly notes that 'they are a privileged caste, and say what they like to their masters and others, no person taking offence at the jest or repartee of a gondolier'. *Reminiscences*, p. 90.

34   **Go, play your cards** *Memorie*, p. 78.

Lorenzo's account *Memorie*, pp. 78–9.

35   **a beggar king** Again, there is no objective proof of this account, and some believe it to be a fabrication. As with the story of Matilda, the question is then raised as to why Da Ponte would make it up, and the answer is similar. It is a telling illustration of how helplessly he felt bound to Angela, and how powerless he appeared to be to break the spell – although in this case the story does also serve to show Da Ponte in a favourable light as a generous, kind-hearted being. He goes so far as to add a footnote in his memoir, pointing out that like the old man he has been unappreciated and persecuted. See *Memorie*, pp. 79–86.

36   **Sir, the weight of the treasure** *Ibid.*, p. 86.
      Vedi se Amor Ibid., p. 87.

37   **Rousseau's** *Pygmalion* See Boccardi, *L'Ambiente Teatrale*, p. 41.
      Make it, then! *Memorie*, p. 88.
      If you do not have the money Letter to Michele Colombo, 19 January 1774; *Lettere*, p. 57.

38   **I was tied [to him] by bonds** *Memorie*, pp. 88–9.
      in intermittent contact These letters, found among Colombo's papers in the Bibloteca Palatina in Parma, were ignored for many years, because Girolamo signs himself 'Momolo', the Venetian diminutive of his name. The first one from Venice is dated 17 November 1773 – which indicates that he must have joined Lorenzo almost immediately.
      You ask me Girolamo Da Ponte to Michele Colombo, 26 January 1774; *Lettere*, p. 520.

39   **No more gambling** *Memorie*, p. 89.

40   **You are my only ray of hope** Letter to Michele Colombo, 8 October 1774; *Lettere*, p. 59.
      a yearly salary Marchesan, quoted in Russo, *Lorenzo Da Ponte*, p. 19n. He noted the salaries from seminary records.

Chapter Three

41   **William Beckford stopped in Treviso** See Beckford, *Travel Diaries*, I, p. 78. The jarred sensualist was overjoyed, at Mestre, to step on to a gondola 'whose even motion was very agreeable after the jolts of a chaise' and on which he could stretch beneath the awning and enjoy his ease.
      delighted by the appearance Kelly, *Reminiscences*, pp. 103–4.

42   **Thus my liberated soul** *Memorie*, pp. 93–4.
      full of life Quoted in Hodges, *Lorenzo Da Ponte*, p. 22.
      omitting . . . neither artifice nor phrases *Memorie*, p. 92.

43   *che gela fin ai pensieri* A local saying recorded by Piozzi, *Observations and Reflections*, p. 97. Da Ponte recalls that the lagoon was frozen and that a path had to be cut through the lagoon from Mestre by four stocky gondoliers (*Memorie*, p. 92), but Hodges points out that while the lagoons were frozen in 1709, 1755, 1788 and 1789, they were not in 1775 (*Lorenzo Da Ponte*, p. 20n).
      at that moment I rushed Da Ponte's account of the incident is related in

Memorie, pp. 92–3 – whether or not he was exaggerating events, he appears to have broken off all contact with Anglea Tiepolo after January of 1775. Angela had the last word. She gave birth to a boy in March 1776, and called him Pietro Lorenzo.

44 **though not completely lacking** *Memorie*, p. 94.

helping to establish Italian literature In his memoirs claims to have been the first to have established the study of Italian literature at the seminary, but Marchesan refutes this.

At an *accademia* of literati Marchesan posits either the *Accademia dei Solleciti* or the *Colonia Arcadia*. See Russo, *Lorenzo da Ponte*, p. 22.

Il Cechino Published in an appendix to the 1830 edition of the memoirs, as well as in *Saggi Poetici* (Vols I and II, printed by Sordi and Muti; Vol. I only, printed by L. Da Ponte, 1801) in Vienna in 1788.

There was such applause Letter of 13 March 1776; *Lettere*, p. 59.

fired the shot From Ralph Waldo Emerson's 'Concord Hymn' (1837):
> By the rude bridge that arched the flood,
>   Their flag to April's breeze unfurled,
> Here once the embattled farmers stood,
>   And fired the shot heard round the world.

a declaration of independence See Hugh Brogan, *The Penguin History of the USA* (Penguin Books, 2001), pp. 165–80; T. C. W. Blanning (ed.), *The Eighteenth Century* (Oxford University Press, 2), p. 46, p. 132; Olivier Bernier, *The World in 1800* (John Wiley & Sons, 2), p. 16.

45 **quotation from a work by Rousseau** Thomas Jefferson would in turn help his friend the Marquis de Lafayette in drafting the Declaration of the Rights of Man.

Whether Mankind had attained happiness An abbreviated title given in the memoirs. The full text of the theme was: *Se gli uomi per le leggi e per le distribuzioni della civil società abbiano il sentiero della felicità umana appianato o restretto, o se per queste leggi medesime sieno in rapporto alla loro felicità nel primiero stato rimasti.* See Russo, *Lorenzo Da Ponte*, pp. 22–30 for a discussion of the poems presented in the *accademia*.

47 **who had more need** *Memorie*, p. 95.

48 **drew up a petition.** See Hodges, *Lorenzo Da Ponte*, p. 24.

unable to take the situation seriously A modern psychologist might say Da Ponte was in denial.

did not judge it prudent *Memorie*, p. 96.

49 **a hearing before the Inquisition** Kelly, *Reminiscences*, pp. 80–1.

But I laughed at them *Memorie*, p. 98.

50 **sent the Senate a letter** Da Ponte appears not to have known of this betrayal, and there is no evidence that the accusation was true. See Hodges, *Lorenzo Da Ponte*, p. 25.

One of the great curiosities Tobias Smollett, *Travels through France and Italy* (Oxford University Press, 1979), p. 290.

51 **At this juncture** *Memorie*, p. 109.

52 **very disagreeable** Burney, *Present State of Music in France and Italy*, p. 97.

ghost of a great city Spence, *Letters from the Grand Tour*, p. 93.

hordes of beggars Kelly, *Reminiscences*, p. 90.

paid for a stagecoach Dr Burney paid eighteen Venetian lire for the trip from Padua to Fusina (a mainland pick-up point for gondolas) in 1765 – so the trip would have been quite expensive for Da Ponte if he had only fifty lire left when he arrived. See Burney, *Present State of Music*, p. 107.

more in need of receiving *Memorie*, p. 103.

I was therefore able *Memorie*, p. 105.

53 **Caterino Mazzolà** See Lanapoppi, *Realtà e leggenda*, pp. 41–2 and p. 84.

54 **A strange man** Zaguri's negative comments about Da Ponte are from letters written some years later to Casanova (see Pompeo Molmenti (ed.), *Carteggi Casanoviani* (Remo Sandron, 1917), II, pp. 209–10). Casanova and Zaguri were often nasty about Da Ponte behind his back, yet kept friendly contact with him – Zaguri even attempted to help Da Ponte return to Venice in 1790 after years of exile.

she had used family contacts See Andrea Di Robilant, *A Venetian Affair* (Fourth Estate, 2004), pp. 20–1.

He has gained admittance *Ibid.*, p. 169. Her comments seem churlish in the light of her own questionable status as an illegitimate child who had wheedled her way upwards in society, and especially so in that she used Casanova (at risk to his life) to attempt to secure her an abortion, and when that failed to arrange for her to give birth in secret.

55 **dubbed him 'Hercules'** See Iain McCalman, *The Seven Ordeals of Count Cagliostro* (Arrow Books, 2003), p. 28.

prematurely old See Casanova, *Story of My Life*, p. 495.

the happiest moment *Ibid.*, p. 289.

Giorgio Pisani See Norwich, *A History*, pp. 597–603.

the weight of responsibility A point made by Lanapoppi, *Realtà e leggenda*, pp. 67–8.

56 **The family with whom Da Ponte lodged** In recounting events following Da Ponte's return to Venice, his relationship with Zaguri, Pisani and the Bellaudis, and the role of Venetian gossip in the affair, I owe much to Alermo Lanapoppi's dramatic revision of views held by most Da Ponte biographers (especially the euphemistic earlier versions), based on material in the Venetian archives relating to the final depositions made against him. See *Ibid.*, pp. 66–85.

57 **when the Priest took a fancy** From the deposition against Da Ponte: '*quando s'invaghì detto Prete [Da Ponte] di mia nuora, trovò già pronta corrispondenza*'; quoted in Lanapoppi, *Realtà e leggenda*, p. 73.

58 **Too many incidents** '*Troppi casi, Ab. troppi casi!*' From a letter some years later to Casanova, 24 October 1792; see Molmenti (ed.), *Carteggi Casanoviani*, II, pp. 209–10. Zaguri goes on to write that he said: 'I hope this latest [incident], of having to assist a woman pregnant by you in the street, and whose child was born on the pavement, will be the last [one] I hear from you while you are in my house!' – both of which accusations were untrue.

the Pietà orphanage This course of action was by no means uncommon. Rousseau and his mistress Teresa Levasseur had five children that were dispatched to a foundlings' home.

60   **passed on his good wishes to an 'Angioletta'** Luigi Da Ponte to Michele
      Colombo, 12 September 1778; *Lettere*, pp. 536–7.
      squeals of the most advanced sexual nature From the testimony against
      Da Ponte: *'delli strepiti connotanti le più avanzate compiacenze'*; quoted in
      Lanapoppi, *Realtà e leggenda*, p. 80. Lanapoppi points out (see p. 73) that
      the term *'compiacersi'* (to be delighted/pleasured) was a euphemism used by
      court clerks to transcribe dialect references to sex.
      Paolo Renier had a reputation See Norwich, *A History*, p. 601.
61   **full of cobwebs** Burney, *Present State of Music*, p. 111 and n.
      I didn't have the means From the testimony against Da Ponte: *'Non avevo
      modi, di poterla mantenere in convento'*, and, *'Ho un sommo timore di esso Padre
      Lorenzo, e per l'animo suo risoluto, e per le valide protezioni che gode, essendo
      precettore delli figli del Nobil Uomo Giorgio Pisani, dove abita presentemente, ed era
      anche di Casa Zaguri'*; quoted in Lanapoppi, *Realtà e leggenda*, pp. 80–1.
62   **make the young woman leave** *'di là fatta partire la giovine'* and *'che più non
      sarebbe andato da detta giovine'*; quoted in *ibid.*, pp. 80–1.
63   **the woman returned** *'la femmina ritornò da Padova e si riunì al marito'*; quoted
      in *ibid.*, p. 85.

Chapter Four

67   **Towards the end of August 1779** In his memoirs, Da Ponte gives his date
      for arrival in Gorizia as 1 September 1777, but this is either a mis-recollection,
      or an attempt to fudge the affair with Anzoletta Bellaudi (he doesn't mention
      her at all at this point in his memoirs, bringing up the events only at a later
      stage in his narration). The dates of the testimonies and trial, together with his
      own slip in writing that he arrived in Gorizia around the time of the Treaty of
      Teschen (which was signed on 13 May 1779), make a more accurate dating
      possible.
68   *occhiantina espressiva* Da Ponte relates his encounter with the innkeeper in
      Memorie, pp. 115–19.
69   **commissioners of chastity** See Casanova, *Story of My Life*, pp. 192–4; and
      Hilary Evans, *The Oldest Profession* (David and Charles, 1979), pp. 94–5.
      Casanova relates that women who *were* on the streets with perhaps not the
      purest intentions resorted to carrying a rosary so that they could pretend they
      were going to church.
70   **death snatched her** According to Gustav Gugitz, an early twentieth-
      century biographer, there was no record of the death of a young female
      innkeeper in Gorizia for the years 1779–80, raising the possibility that Da
      Ponte's version of events is exaggerated. It seems unlikely, anyway, that an
      inn was in sole charge of a 22-year-old woman, so it could be only that aspect
      of his narrative that is not true, or that she did not die in Gorizia. As with
      Matilda and some other recollections of Venice in the memoirs, it is what the
      incident reveals of Da Ponte's situation that is significant, what his possible
      exaggerations (or even inventions) are telling us about his state at the time –
      in this case of someone meeting his need for care, love and comfort with

kindness and dispelling his loneliness, and of love being snatched from him. In his memoirs he charges this incident with such powerful affection that it is clearly not entirely invented.

popular as a refuge See Lanapoppi, *Realtà e leggenda*, p. 86.

Pietro Zaguri was well-known *Ibid.*, p. 87.

a girl of Gorizianese stock Teresa Tommasini came from Rome, but was most likely of the prominent Tommasini publishing family in Gorizia. Mazzolà married her a few months after Da Ponte arrived there. *Ibid.*, p. 87.

wise, erudite . . . and generous See FitzLyon, *Lorenzo Da Ponte*, p. 70.

71 **Nobody actually read [Coronini's] works** *Nessuno leggeva le sue opera, e si preferiva accordargli gratis il titolo di sapiente piuttosto che prendersi il fastidio di vedere se lo meritasse*; from Casanova's memoirs; quoted in Lanapoppi, *Realtà e leggenda*, p. 89.

72 **no temperament, but** Quoted in FitzLyon, *Lorenzo Da Ponte*, p. 71.

in good health *Sono ripatriato da pochi dì dopo essere stato a Gorizia per mio fratello il quale è colà in buona salute e in situazione non affatto cattiva*; from a letter of 29 March 1780, *Lettere*, p. 534.

the family portraits Much of the story of the conflict between Coronini and the Attemses is revealed in a deposition made later to the Empress Maria Theresa. See Lanapoppi, *Realtà e leggenda*, pp. 93–6.

armed with stick and sword According to Valeri's testimony: *provveduto di spada e bastone per cercare l'abate Da Ponte*. Quoted in Lanapoppi, *Realtà e leggenda*, p. 95.

73 **cruelty, disloyalty, treason** Raoul Vèze (ed.), *Mémoires de J. Casanova de Seingalt*, X (La Sirène, 1924–35), p. 202. The two were rivals over a woman. Torriani challenged Casanova to a duel, but later pulled out of it, and he was to die insane shortly after Da Ponte met him. For Casanova's account of his visit see *ibid.*, pp. 202ff.

A one-time mistress *Ibid.*, p. 215.

The Countess Torriani In his journal of 4 June 1781. Quoted in *Ibid.*, p. 279 n8.

74 **Giorgio Pisani had been arrested** Pisani was arrested on 31 May 1780. He would remain in prison for ten years, followed by periods of house arrest and further imprisonment that ended only when he was freed by French troops in 1797.

tremendous catastrophe *Memorie*, p. 124.

Educated by the Jesuits See *Memorie*, p. 81n; and FitzLyon, *Lorenzo Da Ponte*, pp. 72–3.

75 **Coletti had managed to turn around the business** See FitzLyon, *Lorenzo Da Ponte*, p. 72.

77 **eminently fine** Piozzi, *Observations and Reflection*, p. 366.

suffered greatly from the cold Kelly, *Reminiscences*, p. 87.

While undergoing its [the postilion's] operations Kelly, *Reminiscences*, p. 87.

Per la morte di Sua Maestà A copy is still to be seen in the Vienna Stadt- und Landesbibliothek.

graciously received *Memorie*, p. 127.

a 100-florin note A handsome sum. In 1789 one Franz Heintl was teaching nine hours a day in Vienna for twenty-four florins a month – though he was considered poor (H. C. Robbins Landon, *Mozart: The Golden Years 1781–91* (Thames & Hudson, 1989), p. 111); around the same time, forty-seven florins could buy a 'complete suit of men's clothing, the cloth at 8 fl., lined with double-milled material, and with the buttons covered in the same material' (from Johann Pezzl's *Sketch of Vienna*; quoted in H. C. Robbins Landon, *Mozart and Vienna* (Thames & Hudson, 1991), p. 154).

shook to a jelly Thomas Steavens, travelling in 1748; quoted in Jeremy Black, *The British Abroad: The Grand Tour in the Eighteenth Century* (Sutton Publishing, 2003), p. 114.

78   **The breath of life** Quoted in Richard S. Lambert, *The Fortunate Traveller*, p. 75.

in communal rooms Mozart's pupil J. N. Hummel had such experience travelling in December 1788. The stinking straw is mentioned by William Bentinck on his travels; quoted in Black, *The British Abroad*, p. 58.

When he saw me entering his room *Memorie*, p. 127.

79   **catapulted from Gorizia** Some commentators, such as Armando Torno (editing the Italian edition of Da Ponte's memoirs), believe the entire episode is invented by Da Ponte in order to explain why he left Gorizia without being summoned by Mazzolà.

Outside his tavern window See Piozzi, *Observations and Reflections*, pp. 387ff.

80   **those numberless rules** *Memorie*, p. 130.

the Italians only keep going Donald Burrows and Rosemary Dunhill, *Music and Theatre in Handel's World* (Oxford University Press, 2002), p. 743.

around fifteen Italian operas See Lanapoppi, *Realtà e leggenda*, p. 102.

neither blind, nor unjust *Memorie*, p. 131.

81   ***Signor, di fragil terra*** First stanza of Salmo I, which is given in full with four other psalms in *Memorie*, pp. 94–100.

whose names he disguises The girls' real names were Viktoria Vincentia (who was seventeen) and Josefa Maria (fifteen), and Da Ponte refers to Camerata simply as 'an Italian painter'. The identification was made by Gugitz in the early part of last century. See Lanapoppi, *Realtà e leggenda*, p. 100.

82   **not more than thirty years of age** *Memorie*, pp. 138–9.

Da Ponte has gone to Dresden *Ibid.*, p. 140.

83   **an introduction from Casanova** See Lanapoppi, *Realtà e leggenda*, pp. 105–6. Lanapoppi postulates that the possibility of work with the Abbé Eusebio Della Lena, who was staying with a rich patron in Vienna, and the protection of the rich merchant Johann von Puthon were the reasons for Da Ponte's departure for Vienna – though these could equally have been contributory factors in the decision rather than its prime cause. Lanapoppi's version of events also does not explain Da Ponte's seemingly direct access to Salieri. Besides, Casanova and Da Ponte had long since lost contact with each other, after a squabble in Venice.

a cold October day Most commentators set Da Ponte's departure date as

October 1781, based on the date of Luigi's death, the gift of a warm travel clothing, and Da Ponte's clear presence in Vienna before the end of the year (he published a poem there in 1781).

Chapter Five

84   **The Viennese are very quiet** Johann Pezzl in his *Skizze von Wien* (Sketch of Vienna), reprinted in Robbins Landon, *Mozart and Vienna*, p. 187.

Haydn sorely missed Vienna's stillness See letter to Maria Anna von Genzinger of 8 January 1791, in H. C. Robbins Landon, *The Collected Correspondence and London Notebooks of Joseph Haydn* (Barrie and Rockliff, 1959), p. 112: '. . . I wished I could fly for a time to Vienna, to have more quiet in which to work, for [in London] the noise that the common people make as they sell their wares in the street is intolerable.'

singing and scaramouching The phrase is Beckford's, *Travel Diaries*, I, p. 91.

and then diarrhoea See Pezzl, in Robbins Landon, *Mozart and Vienna*, p. 56.

a common cause of 'wounded lungs' See Piozzi, *Observations and Reflections*, p. 379.

85   **boats built upstream to carry goods to Vienna** The boats were not built to last, but with this single journey in mind. Sometimes they would go on into Hungary, to Buda and Pest before being destroyed. See Pezzl, in *ibid.*, p. 143.

The streets of Vienna Piozzi, *Observations and Reflections*, p. 379.

every street, almost every house William Howitt, quoted in Steptoe, *Mozart–Da Ponte Operas*, p. 14.

a feast for the eyes The various national costumes and variety of goods to be had for a little gold are noted by Pezzl; see Robbins Landon, *Mozart and Vienna*, p. 62 and p. 65.

86   **the Vienna people** Robert Townson, *Travels in Hungary in the Year 1793* (G. G. and J. Robinson, 1797), p. 11. As regards birds, Townson noted everything from robins and blackbirds to woodpeckers and magpies on sale in the markets, as well as such other exotica as frogs and snails. Deciding to be adventurous himself, he purchased some turtles for soup – in the market they were 'lying in all directions like so many stones', but in the warmth of his kitchen, the animals woke up, and his dinner scuttled away.

monstrous contrivance See Pezzl, in Robbins Landon, *Mozart and Vienna*, p. 70. The skirts were out of fashion by the end of the 1780s.

Vienna combined the serious and the frivolous See Steptoe, *Mozart–Da Ponte Operas*, p. 27.

87   **I have never passed my time** From *A View of Society and Manners in France, Switzerland and Germany*, quoted in Steptoe, *Mozart–Da Ponte Operas*, p. 27.

booked into an inn See Kelly, *Reminiscences*, p. 112, and Pezzl, in Robbins Landon, *Mozart and Vienna*, p. 75 and p. 117. The presumption of an abundance of lodging advertisements is based on the generally accepted belief that Da Ponte arrived in Vienna in early October. According to Pezzl, the fortnights after St George's Day (23 April) and Michaelmas (29 September) were 'the two dates on which it is customary for half the city to change quarters'.

His store of social entrées Michael Kelly, by comparison, had at the very least half a dozen letters of introduction. See Kelly, *Reminiscences*, p. 111.

some trifling point *Memorie*, p. 233.

Both these men were intimates of Casanova See Giampaolo Zagonel (ed.), *Lorenzo Da Ponte, Bibliografia* (Dario De Bastiane Editore, 1999), p. 8, and Lanapoppi, *Realtà e leggenda*, pp. 105–6.

It was Della Lena Da Ponte refers to him simply as 'a worshipper of Metastasio' whom he had met in Italian circles in Vienna, but identifies him as the man who had suggested he write *Filemone e Bauci*, and dedicate it to 'an important German nobleman'. Da Ponte locates the meeting as having taken place a few days before Metastasio died – which was on 12 April 1782. See *Memorie*, p. 144.

88   **set every one of his arias to music** Metastasio mentioned setting all his arias to music to Casanova, during the latter's visit to Vienna in 1753. See *Story of My Life*, p. 190.

The mild old man Dr Burney's descriptions of Metastasio's character are given in FitzLyon, *Lorenzo Da Ponte*, pp. 89–90. Burney wrote a three-volume biography of the poet.

so modest that it did not seem natural See Casanova, *Story of My Life*, p. 190. Casanova goes on to write: 'I very quickly perceived, however, that his modesty was genuine, when it disappeared the moment he recited something of his own composition, whose beauties he pointed out himself'.

made a poem Quoted in FitzLyon, *Lorenzo Da Ponte*, p. 90. This does not mean Metastasio knocked off his poems effortlessly. Casanova reports the poet showing him four or five pages covered with corrections, written to achieve fourteen lines of verse; *ibid.*, p. 190.

ranged with such methodical exactness Piozzi, *Observations and Reflections*, p. 378.

I have been a bird of court Quoted in FitzLyon, *Lorenzo Da Ponte*, p. 89.

89   **one God; one Farinelli** See Michael Raeburn, *The Chronicle of Opera* (Thames & Hudson, 1998), p. 45.

adopted twin See Letter X in Charles Burney, *Memoirs of the Life and Writings of the Abate Metastasio*, III (Da Capo Press, 1973), p. 236 and p. 284.

a single biscuit Or so one of the Misses Martinez told Hester Piozzi; see Piozzi, *Observations and Reflections*, p. 378.

Oh! [Metastasio] he looked like a man *Ibid.*, p. 378. Piozzi doesn't name the abbé, but it is intriguing to think it may well have been Da Ponte. There were, after all, not *that* many Italian abbés in town when Piozzi visited, who had been to a Metastasio salon, and had a barb to their wit.

90   **the gentle bird of court** Da Ponte's version of the poet's death, written when he himself was an old man, feeling very unwanted, was that the poet had died of grief after hearing that his pension had been withdrawn. The Empress Maria Theresa was famously extravagant in granting pensions (on

one occasion, according to Da Ponte, even giving an annual allowance to two horses in Gorizia), and had created a gushing hole in the national purse that her successor was determined to stop. Joseph II cancelled a swathe of allowances granted by his mother and introduced severe restrictions on others, and though he wrote personally to Metastasio, Da Ponte says, assuring the poet that his services were still appreciated and that his income would not be affected by the decree, the letter arrived too late. Metastasio died within days of hearing of the new ruling, of a broken heart. See *Memorie*, pp. 145–6.

I'm a poet From Da Ponte's verse letter to Count Zaguri, early 1785; *Lettere*, p. 84. Italian poets of the time often used 'singing' figuratively to refer to recitation of their poems, though Lorenzo could once again have been showing off his skills as an improviser (which was done to music).

91   **Music is the only thing** Steptoe, *Mozart–Da Ponte Operas*, p. 27.

painter, a sculptor See Pezzl, in Robbins Landon, *Mozart and Vienna*, pp. 186–7.

a visit by the Pope Pius VI visited Vienna from 22 March to 22 April 1782, in an attempt to dissuade Joseph II from some of his more radical religious reforms.

Voglio mo' dir che parlano il tedesco From a verse letter from Vienna to Pietro Zaguri, thought to have been written in 1785; *Lettere*, p. 83.

92   **gap between the old town** For details on city and suburban life, see Andrew Steptoe 'Mozart and Poverty: a re-examination of the evidence', in the *Musical Times* (April 1984), pp. 196–201, and Pezzl, in Robbins Landon, *Mozart and Vienna*, pp. 54–60, and pp. 115–18.

cast out beyond the walls Quite literally – after the repulse of the Turks in 1683, burghers had been removed to the new suburbs to make way for the palaces, which are still an impressive feature of city architecture. See Eda Sagarra, *A Social History of Germany 1648–1914* (Methuen, 1977), p. 63.

the annual expenditure for a single man Pezzl; quoted in Robbins London, *Mozart and Vienna*, p. 74.

The court actor Joseph Lange See Steptoe, 'Mozart and Poverty', p. 199. Primary school teachers were awarded a pitiful 100 gulden annually; students from 800 gulden to 1, gulden – though they were often from upper ranks and comported themselves as cavaliers, their dignity demanding that they had servants. See Sagarra, *Social History of Germany*, p. 84.

containing a bed Pezzl; quoted in Robbins Landon, *Mozart and Vienna*, p. 117.

93   **an erudite and cultured youth** See *Memorie*, p. 146. The youth remains unidentified.

he preferred the French See Peter Gay, *Mozart* (Phoenix, 2003), p. 2.

a remarkably small man See Kelly, *Reminiscences*, p. 123. The other aspects of Mozart's appearance come from contemporary descriptions by his friend Franz Niemetschek, and a pupil Johann Nepomuk Hummel. See Volkmar Braunbehrens, *Mozart in Vienna 1781–1791* (Grove Weidenfeld, 1990), p. 122; Gay, *Mozart*, p. 3; Robbins Landon, *Golden Years*, p. 180.

94   **careering towards marriage** See Alfred Einstein, *Mozart, His Character, His Work* (Grafton Books, 1969), pp. 74–80; Gay, *Mozart*, pp. 60–3; Robbins

Landon, *Mozart, The Golden Years*, pp. 76–82.

never seen her really *besoffen* In a letter of 10 April 1782. See Gay, *Mozart*, p. 61n.

Madame Weber was kind enough Letter of May 9 1782; Robert Spaethling, *Mozart's Letters, Mozart's Life* (Faber and Faber, 2), p. 246.

a reasonably pretty daughter Wolfgang wrote of her: 'Her whole beauty consists of two little black eyes and a beautiful figure' – though he may have been trying to play down her attractions in an odd attempt to make his wish to marry her less abhorrent to Leopold. See Gay, *Mozart*, p. 62.

perhaps more attracted by his talents Quoted in Robbins Landon, *Golden Years*, p. 77.

95 **should be put in chains** Mozart quotes from his father's (now lost) letter in one of his own, to Leopold, on 16 January 1782; see Emily Anderson (ed.), *The Letters of Mozart and his Family* (Macmillan, 1989), p. 793. See also Gay, *Mozart*, p. 61.

96 **There is nothing more disagreeable** Mozart to his father, 23 January 1782; see Anderson (ed.), *Letters*, pp. 794–5.

97 **as literacy rates rose** By 1800 adult literacy rates exceeded 50 per cent in many places in Europe, and in 1790 in Vienna the reactionary Count Auersberg advised Joseph II to confine education to the nobility because of the dangerous effect literacy was having on the masses. By 1789 there were no fewer than 200 newspapers in circulation within the Holy Roman Empire, with an estimated readership of three million. See Blanning, *The Eighteenth Century*, p. 4, and pp. 41–2, and Dorinda Outram, *The Enlightenment* (Cambridge University Press, 1995), pp. 17–23.

an expansion in the scale See Blanning, *The Eighteenth Century*, p. 4 and p. 149.

The model for literary activity Among the first to earn any substantial royalties were writers of widely read non-fiction, such as Gibbon and Hume. See Roger Chartier, 'The Man of Letters', in Vovelle (ed.), *Enlightenment Portraits*, pp. 171–5.

98 **composer Karl Ditters** See Steptoe, *Mozart–Da Ponte Operas*, p. 34.

We lunch about twelve o'clock Letter 394, to Leopold Mozart, 17 March 1781 (his italics); in Anderson (ed.), *Letters*, pp. 713–14.

in some becoming way Letter 395 to his father, 24 March 1781 (his italics); *ibid.*, p. 718.

the solitary, unconventional artist Although this is very much a Romantic and nineteenth-century image, it did exist earlier. James Ralph, in a 1758 pamphlet entitled *The Case of Authors by Profession or Trade Stated*, wrote (referring to Grub Street journalists, who worked for extremely exploitative booksellers):

> Thus there is no Difference between the Writer in his Garret and the Slave in the Mines . . . Both must drudge and starve; neither can hope for Deliverance.

See Chartier, 'The Man of Letters', in Vovelle (ed.), *Enlightenment Portraits*, p. 174.

99 **Da Ponte and Mozart had already taken a step** German writers of the next generation, such as A. W. Schlegel and E. T. A Hoffmann, would see

Mozart as one of the first artists in the Romantic sense. See Steptoe, *Mozart–Da Ponte Operas*, p. 41.

insolence and rudeness In a letter to his father of 9 June 1781; repeatedly after that he expressed the desire to return the compliment. Mozart knew this almost at first hand – on 8 August 1781, he wrote telling his father how a friend of his had been sentenced to fifty lashes after striking a nobleman in Innsbruck. After the fifth lash his breeches had split, and he was eventually carried away unconscious and confined to bed for three weeks. See Anderson (ed.), *Letters*, p. 740 and p. 756.

Chapter Six

100 **how the Emperor had dismissed** The story was related in a letter from Count Rosenberg to Count Durazzo, then Viennese Ambassador in Venice, which was read to Michael Kelly; see Kelly, *Reminiscences*, pp. 110–11.
He was an enemy *Ibid.*, p. 116.

101 **He . . . has the truest** Stormont in a letter to Suffolk of 19 October 1771; quoted in Derek Beales, *Joseph II*, I (Cambridge University Press, 1987), p. 308.
It would be hard Noted by Dr John Moore, tutor to the Duke of Hamilton; quoted in Beales, *Joseph II*, I, p. 306. Some criticized the Emperor, saying that this affability was false, an effort to appear democratic. Writing personally to his brother Leopold in 1777, Joseph II was a little more frank: 'I am a charlatan of reason and modesty. I overdo it a bit in these respects so that I seem simple, natural, thoughtful even to excess; and this is what has won me approval.' *Ibid.*, p. 312.
behaviour of other monarchs See Steptoe, *Mozart–Da Ponte Operas*, p. 21.

102 **establish an Italian opera** The background to Joseph's decision, and the history of the Burgtheater, are from Dorothea Link, *The National Court Theatre in Mozart's Vienna* (Clarendon Press, 1998), pp. 1–21; Daniel Heartz, 'Nicolas Jadot and the building of the Burgtheater', in the *Musical Quarterly*, LXVIII, 1 (January 1982), pp. 1–5; Robbins Landon, *Golden Years*, pp. 35ff, pp. 63ff; and W. E. Yates, *Theatre in Vienna: A Critical History 1776–1995* (Cambridge University Press, 1996), pp. 1–15.
staging pompous spectacles Opera was used as a vehicle for display of wealth and power not only in the imperial court, but in other princely houses. See Sagarra, *Social History of Germany*, pp. 28–9. Lady Mary Wortley Montagu left a description in a letter to Alexander Pope (quoted in Sagarra, and more fully in Yates, *Theatre in Vienna*, p. 3) of a performance of Johan Joseph Fux's *Vincitrice di Alcina*, which she witnessed in 1716 in the gardens of Charles VI's summer palace:

> Nothing of that kind was ever more magnificent; and I can easily believe what I am told, that the decorations and habits cost the emperor thirty thousand pounds sterling. The stage was built over a very large canal, and, at the beginning of the second act, divided into two parts, discovering the water, on which there immediately came, from different parts, two fleets of little gilded vessels, that gave the

representation of a naval fight. It is not easy to imagine the beauty of this scene, which I took particular notice of . . . The theatre is so large, that it is hard to carry the eye to the end of it; and the habits in the utmost magnificence, to the number of one hundred and eight.

103 **a school of manners** From a memorandum drawn up in 1795 by Franz Karl Hägelin, censor from 1770 to 1804. The memorandum was based on one by Hägelin's predecessor Joseph von Sonnenfels, who had defined the function of theatre as being a 'school of manners, courtesy and language'. See Yates, *Theatre in Vienna*, pp. 9–10.

Die Entführung aus dem Auge Gottes This is according to an early biographer, Georg Nikolaus Nissen (who married Mozart's widow in 1809). See Robbins Landon, *Golden Years*, p. 72.

104 **a claque paid to hiss** Mozart mentions the cabal in a letter to his father of 20 July 1782 – but the shouts of 'bravo' won out, and the hissing claque could not detract from the fact that the opera was an immediate success.

[*Entführung*] created a stir Quoted in Robbins Landon, *Golden Years*, p. 140. Franz Xaver Niemetschek wrote a biography of Mozart in 1798, based on information given by Constanze Mozart and other authentic sources. 'Too many notes, Mozart, too many notes', Joseph's comment, has entered popular mythology as evidence of his philistinism, but the Emperor was an adept musician. He sang a little and played both the violoncello and the harpsichord, though he did prefer the contrapuntal music of late Baroque or Rococo to the classical style of Haydn and Mozart (see Beales, *Joseph II*, I, pp. 316–17).

Singspiel **slipped off** In 1785 Joseph II allowed *Singspiel* back to the Burgtheater, resulting in a huge increase in ticket sales for the parts of the theatre assigned to non-nobility. See Link, *National Court Theatre*, pp. 490–6.

105 **to find artists** See Kelly, *Reminiscences*, p. 110.

opera buffa . . . was relegated See Steptoe, *Mozart–Da Ponte Operas*, p. 43.

two of the best buffo singers Kelly, *Reminiscences*, p. 111, labels them 'the two best comic singers in Europe', and Mozart called Benucci 'particularly good' (in a letter to his father of 7 May 1783).

instructed Count Rosenberg See Steptoe, *Mozart–Da Ponte Operas*, p. 152. Later Joseph was concerned that Benucci be paid too much. The Emperor kept close control of management of the Burgtheater. His extensive correspondence on the subject with Count Rosenberg (who, apart from a twenty-month gap under Leopold II, remained in charge of theatrical activities until the court divested itself of the Burgtheater in 1794) is reproduced in Rudolf Payer von Thurn (ed.), *Joseph II als Theaterdirektor*, (Leopold Heidrich, 1920).

Luigi Marchesi's vocal trickery See Kelly, *Reminiscences*, p. 65, and Steptoe, *Mozart–Da Ponte Operas*, p. 147–8. Nancy appears to have guyed other male singers, too, and to have carried on doing so in Vienna – both the Emperor and Count Zinzendorf mention their delight at her imitations.

a Neapolitan father and English mother Born in London in 1765, Nancy, whose real name was Anna Selina, was the daughter of Stefano Storace, a violin and double-bass player, and Elizabeth Trusler, daughter of the proprietor of the Marylebone Gardens. She played up both her English and Italian antecedents, according to convenience and opportunity.

a princely 1,640 gulden His exact remuneration for the first year, according to the Burgtheater account books, was 1,641 gulden 30 kreuzers (see Link, *National Court Theatre*, p. 408).

four large . . . wax candles See Kelly, *Reminiscences*, p. 111. Wax candles (as opposed to stinking tallow ones) were expensive, and often formed part of a contractual deal. Theatre staff (and singers and musicians, too) sometimes had an arrangement that entitled them to candle-stubs left over from the theatre after a performance.

106　**You are mistaken, Miss** *Ibid.*, p. 64.

a small, dumpy creature See Pezzl, 'Skizze von Wien'; translated and reproduced in Robbins Landon, *Mozart and Vienna*, p. 137.

the young Garrick The Shakespearean actor David Garrick had died a few years previously, in 1779, at the age of sixty-two. In an age when women singers began their careers very young (Anna Gottlieb was just twelve when she made her debut as Barbarina in *Figaro*), the Soprano's Mother was a recognized type – her fearsome pushiness evinced by Mozart's mother-in-law Madame Weber, and delightfully lampooned by Florian Gassman in his *L'opera seria*.

A Jew . . . or so the gossip went Da Ponte's Jewish origins appear to have been known in Vienna. Kelly writes: 'It was said that originally he [Da Ponte] was a Jew, turned Christian – dubbed himself an abbé and became a great dramatic writer.' (See Kelly, *Reminiscences*, p. 130.)

For 12 gulden p.a. See Pezzl, in Robbins Landon, *Mozart and Vienna*, p. 62.

107　**the finest promenade in Europe** See Kelly, *Reminiscences*, p. 113 and Pezzl, in Robbins Landon, *Mozart and Vienna*, pp. 158–9.

a remarkably awkward gait See Kelly, *Reminiscences*, p. 130 (spelling modernized).

108　**a most cultured and intelligent** *Memorie*, p. 149.

Mazzolà's letter of introduction Lanapoppi, who doubts Da Ponte's account of receiving a letter from Mazzolà, terms his appointment 'a true miracle'. See Lanapoppi, *Realtà e leggenda*, p. 106 and pp. 116–17.

Salieri managed the matter *Memorie*, pp. 146–7.

109　**searched out the sources** *Ibid.*, p. 148. Da Ponte's account of the encounter with Varesi is from pp. 148–9.

was particularly fond of singing Kelly, *Reminiscences*, p. 133. Kelly was a good mimic, and based his Gaforio in Paisiello's opera *Il re Teodoro* on Varesi, to great public amusement and acclaim.

110　**Poor Italy, what poor stuff!** *Memorie*, pp. 148–9.

My dialogue felt dry *Memorie*, p. 149.

in the finale Da Ponte's heartfelt lament on the trials of writing an operatic finale are from *Memorie*, pp. 149–50, and a verse letter to the Abbé Casti written in 1786, and published in Da Ponte's *Saggi Poetici*; also in *Lettere*, p. 94.

111　**the midwives of Pindus** Pindus was the mountain range that included Mount Parnassus, in classical mythology the home of the Muses.

112   **A blaze of beauty** Kelly, *Reminiscences*, p. 113.

The Burgtheater The theatre was demolished in the late nineteenth century to make way for an extension of the Spanish Riding School. The renovations to the building made by Jean Nicolas Jadot in 1748 rank with his best work – likewise his beautiful University building, which can still be seen in Vienna at the eastern end of Bäckerstrasse. For details of the exterior and changing interior design of the Burgtheater, see Heartz, 'Nicolas Jadot', pp. 1–31.

too small and uncomfortable One of the grumpiest detractors was Johann Friedel, who wrote in 1794: 'the interior disposition does not betray the presence of a great court . . . the loges are small and poorly decorated, and illuminated still worse . . . one must go early to get a place given the niggardly space of the hall.' *Ibid.* p. 17.

113   *jolie figure voluptueuse* Diary entries for 24 April 1783 and 9 May 1783. Part of Zinzendorf's diary is reproduced in Link, *National Court Theatre*, pp. 204– 398. This is the same Count Zinzendorf who noted in Gorizia, on his way back to Vienna from being Governor of Trieste, that Count Torriani was 'an animal'. He was president of the court chamber of audit from 1781 until 1792, when he became a councillor of state.

to play a part Operas were cobbled together bit by bit, without the help of what today would be called a producer or director. The role of the court poet in this respect seems to be similar to that of the dramaturge in present-day continental European opera houses.

We have a certain Abate da Ponte Letter to Leopold Mozart, 7 May 1783, Spaethling, *Letters/Life*, p. 350.

114   **trying to block his path** Much has been made of the image of a jealous Salieri trying to scupper Mozart's career. The story that Salieri poisoned the younger composer had its first literary outing in a verse playlet by Pushkin in the 1820s, and reached its apotheosis in Peter Shaffer's *Amadeus*, yet there is no evidence for this. Indeed, Salieri as composer to the opera and, after 1788, as kapellmeister held an unassailable position (especially as Joseph II preferred his conservative style to that of Mozart's music), and enjoyed wide public renown. The two composers appear to have been on fairly cordial terms – though there is no denying that the letters of both Wolfgang and Leopold Mozart are full of accusations of cabals surrounding Salieri. See Gay, *Mozart*, p. 89.

the first time a German singer See Mozart's letter to his father of 21 June 1783; Anderson, *Letters*, p. 852.

a fine sturdy boy Letter to Leopold Mozart, 18 June 1783; see *ibid.*, p. 851. Raimund Leopold was named for his grandfather and Baron Raimund Wetzlar, who stood godfather. He died on 19 August while in the care of a wet nurse with whom the Mozarts had left him in order to make a visit to Salzburg.

Mad.^me **Lange was here** Letter to Leopold Mozart, 2 July 1783; see Spaethling, *Letters/Life*, p. 357.

[The opera] was a complete failure *Ibid.*, p. 357. Count Zinzendorf, in his diary entry for 30 June, agrees that Anfossi's music was not impressive, and admires Aloysia Lange's bravura arias. According to Mozart, Salieri tricked the other German singer in the cast, the tenor Valentin Adamberger, into dropping an aria Mozart had composed for him.

Chapter Seven

116   **600 gulden** According to the Burgtheater account books; see Link, *National Court Theatre*, p. 409. Not, at this stage, 1,200 gulden as is mistakenly given by some biographers.

     Nancy Storace's 3,240 gulden Storace's exact salary for the 1783–84 season was 3,247 gulden and 44 kreuzer; it was even higher the following year. See Link, *National Court Theatre*, p. 409.

     takings from the third performance Mozart points out that it was custom for a librettist to receive this payment, and estimates the sum of fee together with takings to be 400–500 gulden (see letter of 7 May 1783; Anderson, *Letters*, p. 847). Composers enjoyed a similar arrangement, and singers and some musicians were also given the opportunity to supplement their income by benefit performances. Some (like Kelly) received additional monies in the form of housing allowances and other expenses.

     he had moved Da Ponte does not mention the move, but later in his memoirs writes that when he again met Casanova (who moved to Vienna in 1784) he was living on the Graben, one of the most fashionable streets in town. He does refer to lodging at the tailor's again, but this is in the context of a retrospective anecdote about Joseph II. See *Memorie*, pp. 166ff; p. 233.

     Girolamo Da Ponte died Girolamo died in Ceneda, of a lung infection.

117   **fret about his father's approval** Da Ponte's attitude to his father is evident in the letter he wrote to Michael Colombo while at his lowest ebb in Venice, imploring Colombo not to let his father know of his situation, as well as the verse letter written to his father in 1788 pleadingly justifying his misfortunes in Vienna (see *Lettere*, p. 57 and p. 101). His collected poems, *Saggi Poetici*, contain other tender verses to his family.

     a son of feather and fashion A phrase used to describe contemporary English fops, quoted in Charles Beecher Hogan, *The London Stage 1776–1800: A Critical Introduction* (Southern Illinois University Press, 1968), p. ccvii.

118   **very peculiar, rather dandyish** Kelly, *Reminiscences*, pp. 130–1. The OED defines 'coxcomb' as: 'a foolish, conceited, showy person, vain of his accomplishments, appearance, or dress; a fop; a superficial pretender to knowledge or accomplishments'.

     bowing, smirking, smart abbé In 'The Progress of Error' Cowper's abbé, 'always primed with *politesse*', dazzles and dupes gullible tourists with his sophistication.

     softened anti-Jewish laws Joseph II's patent still failed to provide freedom of public worship for Jews, though it did open the ghettoes and allow Jews the privilege of bearing arms for their country (this was at the time considered an honour rather than a task of dubious worth, as it accorded full status as a citizen). See Sagarra, *Social History of Germany*, p. 162.

a hurried visit from the Pope Pope Pius VI travelled uninvited to Vienna in the hope of persuading the Emperor to reverse his policies. Joseph skilfully manipulated protocol so that, without it appearing as an affront, he made sure the Pope was so busy with sightseeing and ceremony that there was little time for negotiations; he also made use of an eye condition he was suffering from to excuse his presence, and to ensure that any talks that did take place had to happen in the dark. More heavy-handedly, he closed three Viennese monasteries during the Pope's visit – and made no concessions at all. See Braunbehrens, *Mozart in Vienna*, pp. 176–8.

119 **almost as a race apart** An idea suggested by the historian W. H. Bruford, cited in Steptoe, *Mozart–Da Ponte Operas*, p. 15, to whose discussion on class in Vienna I am indebted.

People of different ranks From his *View of Society*; quoted in Steptoe, *Mozart–Da Ponte Operas*, p. 16.

there exists a certain realm Quoted in Outram, *The Enlightenment*, p. 21.

120 **over seventy coffee-houses** For Viennese coffee-house life see Pezzl, *Sketches*, reproduced in Robbins Landon, *Mozart and Vienna*, p. 82 and p. 154.

fashionable to learn English See Pezzl, *Sketches*, reproduced in Robbins Landon, *Mozart and Vienna*, pp. 159–60. Round hats and other English fashions may be seen in prints from the time.

A slovenly, heavy gait Carlo Gozzi also mentions a specific English gait, some decades earlier. One Signor Gratarol enters a room 'walking more like an Englishman than a Venetian'; and later comes 'swaggering into my tiny workroom with the swaying gait which is called "English style"'. See Gozzi, *Useless Memoirs*, p. 238 and p. 259.

mode à l'anglaise See Robbins Landon, *Mozart and Vienna*, pp. 45–6.

121 **very much in the classical mould** This is hardly surprising for an Italian who did not speak German, as *Sturm und Drang* and Romanticism were largely German and English movements. Italian Romanticism occurred later (from around 1816 onwards) and was short-lived. But Da Ponte's detachment from what was in essence a movement (similar to that of the 'angry young men' of the 1950s) with a widespread social correlate (there were Werther tea-sets and even perfumes on sale) is significant in that it helps position how he saw himself at the time, gives a clue to his politics, and is perhaps the beginnings of what would become an increasing distance from the changes of his times.

mutilating or stretching *Memorie*, p. 151.

122 **two men arrived in Vienna** Mention of Casti in a letter from Zaguri to Casanova, dated 11 May 1784, indicates that he arrived in Vienna in late April or early May; Paisello arrived from Russia on May 6–7. See *Memoirs*, p. 114n.

Giambattista Casti. See Einstein, *Mozart*, pp. 440–1. FitzLyon, *Lorenzo Da Ponte*, pp. 103–6; Lanapoppi, *Realtà e leggenda*, pp. 120–4.

123 **a shameless libertine** Vèze, *Mémoires de Casanova*, X, p. 201.

great learning, sound judgement Quoted in FitzLyon, *Lorenzo Da Ponte*, p. 105.

Metastasio's recently relinquished lyre He would achieve his ambition in 1790, under the new Emperor, Leopold.

running to twelve performances *Barbiere* went on to become the most popular single opera in the history of the Burgtheater in the eighteenth century, with some sixty performances. See Robbins Landon, *Golden Years*, p. 157.

two of the greatest geniuses See Kelly, *Reminiscences*, p. 132.

no talk of anyone but Casti *Memorie*, p. 151.

124   **put to sleep** *Ibid.*, p. 151.

monkey anticks Kelly describes this enviable soirée in *Reminiscences*, pp. 131–3.

not lacking in purity of language *Memorie*, p. 152.

The opera had its premiere Kelly's and Da Ponte's comments are taken from their memoirs, and Zinzendorf's from his diary entry for 23 August.

125   **would make one shudder** See *Memorie*, pp. 154–5 for the reactions to *Il ricco d'un giorno*.

how the maestro In parts of the opera, the partnership appears to have worked rather well, as in a remarkable passage from '*Dopo pranza addormentata*', where the heroine Lauretta describes a nightmare in which a horde of ugly black devils lay about Mascherone with cudgels, whacking his bones. Rolling Italian *r*s, exploding *t*s and cracking *ch*s ('*Brutta, brutta, nera, nera*' and '*la braccia / Cricche cracche*') combine with orchestral *sforzati* and changes in dynamic, in a bravura syllabic staccato that was a characteristic of buffo style. Da Ponte was brutally honest about the shortcomings of his libretto, though he attributed the failure of the opera as a whole as much to the music as the book, writing that Salieri had come back from Paris 'with his ears full of Gluck, of *Lais*, of *Danaids* – of shrill screaming music. He was writing in an entirely French style, and the beautiful melodies and popular songs whereof he was once so fertile he had drowned in the Seine'. See *Memorie*, p. 154.

stealing from everywhere '*Musique de Salieri vole de partout*'. Diary entry from 6 December 1784, in Link, *National Court Theatre*, p. 237.

some trifling point Da Ponte of Casanova, though it could quite as easily be the other way around. See *Memorie*, p. 233.

126   **nominated him to a literary academy**. See *Memoirs*, p. 120n.

After the applause Quoted in FitzLyon, *Lorenzo Da Ponte*, p. 109.

than the bread I eat Don Giovanni's lines about women from the beginning of Act II: '*Sai ch'elle per me / Son necessarie più del pan che mangio, / Più dell'aria che spiro!*'

Vienna abounds with beautiful women Nathaniel Wraxall in *Memoirs of the Courts of Berlin, Warsaw and Vienna*, quoted, together with Kelly's reference to serving maids' handsome feet, in Steptoe, *Mozart–Da Ponte Operas*, p. 23.

their fine complexions See Kelly, *Reminiscences*, p. 140.

127   **some nifty detective work** The existence of Felice Da Ponte is revealed in a paper entitled 'Felice Da Ponte, Il figlio naturale che il liberettista di Mozart ebbe a Vienna' by Giampaolo Zagonel, published in *Il Flaminio*, 8, 1995, pp. 51ff.

strange and cruel misadventure Da Ponte tells the story in *Memorie*, pp. 156–8.

128   **lisp that had always hissed** Kelly mentions Da Ponte's 'strong lisp and broad Venetian dialect', *Reminiscences*, p. 131.

malice of my persecutors See *Memorie*, p. 154; also verse letter to Pietro Zaguri of 1785 in *Lettere*, p. 82.

129   **Excesses, intrigues, frauds** Pezzl, in Robbins Landon, *Mozart and Vienna*, p. 62.

130   **various rumours** Letter of 13 October 1791, to Maria Anna von Genzinger; in Robbins Landon (ed.), *Notebooks of Joseph Haydn*, p. 120.

Nancy Storace's brother Stephen Nancy appears to have pronounced her surname in the Italian manner (it is sometimes written 'Storaci' or 'Storachi' in contemporary English publications), while her brother Stephen appears to have favoured an English pronunciation (which is as he is known today). Kelly writes that the 't' was a later insertion to their original name of Sorace, to avoid indelicate double entendre in English, an anecdote also related in Joseph Haslewood's 1790 publication *The Secret History of the Green Room*, but on which subsequent commentators cast doubt. See Jane Girdham, *English Opera in Late Eighteenth-Century London: Stephen Storace at Drury Lane* (Clarendon Press, 1997), pp. 4–9.

Zinzendorf could not restrain himself The count mentions Nancy's desirable physical attributes on four separate occasions in the course of a few weeks on first seeing her perform in 1783. It is he who writes that she has the 'naïveté and petulance of a child' (diary entry for 1 July 1783). See Link, *National Court Theatre*, pp. 204–7.

the Spanish Ambassador's wife If this refers to the wife of Ambassador De Llano, Link points out, he arrived in Vienna some time after Martín, so his wife could not have been on intimate terms with Joseph (see *ibid.*, p. 278). Lanapoppi objects that Martín arrived in Vienna only after Storace's opera had been produced (see Lanapoppi, *Realtà e leggenda*, p. 133). Madame De Llano (if it was she to whom Da Ponte refers) may well have recommended Martín through a letter of introduction. This confusion notwithstanding, the formation of factions around the composers is in line with current behaviour at the Burgtheater, and Da Ponte's recollection of the situation is revealing of his perception of the forces ranged against him, whatever mistakes he might make with the chronology. That the conniving surrounding the two composers did not happen concurrently does not mean it did not exist.

various connivings See *Memorie*, p. 156 for Da Ponte's account of the machinations following the composers' arrival in Vienna.

131   **sweet melodies** *Ibid.*, p. 184.

his was a soul of melody Kelly, *Reminiscences*, p. 108.

'Serious' . . . need not necessarily mean 'solemn' Andrew Steptoe makes this point in *Mozart–Da Ponte Operas*, p. 107.

Bertati's script See Einstein, *Mozart*, pp. 442–3.

132   **absence of copyright laws** Most of Da Ponte's libretti were adaptations of straight plays or other works for opera.

Both playwrights had ripped the masks off For the rivalry between Gozzi and Goldoni, and for their influence on Da Ponte, see Robert Oresko,

'Culture in the Age of Baroque and Rococo', in Holmes, *History of Italy*, pp. 163–4; Steptoe, *Mozart–Da Ponte Operas*, pp. 99–109.

from motives of complaisance Goldoni, writing in his memoirs, quoted in Steptoe, *Mozart–Da Ponte Operas*, p. 105.

133   **worked closely with both Nancy Storace and Benucci** See Sheila Hodges, 'Lorenzo Da Ponte's First Susanna', in *Atti del Convegno Lorenzo Da Ponte*, p. 359.

Da Ponte, your friend Casti Reported in *Memorie*, p. 159. We have perhaps to allow for a little retrospective sharpening of wit.

***Il burbero di buon cuore* was a conquest** The opera remained in the repertoire for many years, and was performed throughout Italy, though apart from Zinzendorf's opinion that Storace sang well and Benucci performed perfectly, we have no other response to the evening than Da Ponte's own, and his recollection of the Emperor's aside, in *Memorie*, p. 159.

What can I do for the *signor poeta*? Da Ponte reports this conversation, his decision to resign, and subsequent visit to the Emperor, in *ibid.*, pp. 159–60.

134   **most intimate and long-standing** See Beales, *Joseph II*, I, p. 322.

support from court composer Salieri The composer had, in the interim, enjoyed possibly one of his greatest successes in *La grotto di Trofinio*, with a rather weak libretto by Casti, which premiered on 12 October 1785.

created new spirit *Memorie*, p. 161.

finished the opera he was busy with Rosenberg had instructed him to work on an opera to open just a few weeks after *Burbero* – *Il finto cieco*, an adaptation of Legrand's *L'Aveugle clairvoyant* for the composer Giuseppe Gazzaniga. Da Ponte calls Gazzaniga a composer in 'a style no longer in vogue', and says he dashed off the libretto in a few days, while the composer (distracted by a love affair) dug out scenes from old operas to save time, creating 'a pudding'. The libretto is unremarkable, except for the way in which servants backchat their masters and conventional social hierarchies are barely observed. See *ibid.*, p. 163, and Hodges, *Lorenzo Da Ponte*, pp. 65–6.

Chapter Eight

135   **as touchy as gunpowder** Kelly's description of Mozart, in *Reminiscences*, p. 140.

the ache of the loss of a mother Mozart's mother, Anna Maria, had died in Paris in 1778, when she was escorting him on a concert tour. Leopold, who had insisted that Wolfgang go to Paris, and that his Anna Maria accompany him, undeservedly turned on his son with bitter recriminations, blaming Anna Maria's death on his neglect and irresponsible behaviour, and implying that this would soon cause his father's death, too. See Gay, *Mozart*, p. 37.

136   **a subtle and complex conflict** *Ibid.*, Chapter Two and *passim*, outlines the Mozarts' difficulties with each other, the contest between father and son and

the 'worries and hatreds' that marred Leopold's dealings with Wolfgang.

a circle of ennobled Jewish converts Some of the leading members of Vienna's aristocratic intelligentsia, including the Auersberg, Kaunitz and Arnstein families, were of Jewish origin, many descendants of the *Hoffuden* ('Court Jews'), who had been granted special privileges in the past as suppliers or bankers to the imperial family. Mozart was also friendly with the Arnsteins, and played in concerts at their house. See Sagarra, *Social History of Germany*, pp. 156ff.

playing the guitar See Braunbehrens, *Mozart in Vienna*, p. 184.

137   **I should say that** Letter to Leopold Mozart, 13 October 1781; Anderson (ed.), *Letters*, pp. 772–3.

easy, harmonious and almost singing This, and Da Ponte's opinions on the role of the librettist that follow, are taken from an early draft of his memoirs, published in 1819 as *An Extract from the Life of Lorenzo da Ponte* (printed by J. Gray, 1819), written in response to seeing a review of *Don Giovanni* in the *Edinburgh Magazine* that did not mention his name. The italics and capitalization are his. The extracts are taken from pp. 17–18. Da Ponte lightly echoes Mozart's 'phoenix' reference in describing a perfect comic opera as a *rara avis*.

138   **to show here what I can really do** From the letter to his father of 7 May 1783; see Anderson (ed.), *Letters*, p. 847.

Da Ponte was not forthcoming In any event, Mozart was away from Vienna from the beginning of August until the end of November 1783.

139   *L'oca del Cairo* **(The Goose of Cairo) and then on** *Lo sposo deluso* Varesco wrote 'The Goose', but the librettist of *Lo sposo deluso* is unknown. Some commentators speculate that Da Ponte was the author, but this seems unlikely given his extreme busyness at the time, and the fact that he was already having such difficulty with his debut opera for Salieri. Neither Mozart nor Da Ponte mention the latter as poet for *Lo sposo deluso*. A draft score of *L'oca del Cairo* survives, and fragments of *Lo sposo deluso*.

far more complex characters Einstein, *Mozart*, pp. 440–2, makes this point about the impact of *Teodoro* on Mozart.

his frequent response Mozart's father put his indisposition down to rheumatic fever (letter of 14 September 1784) – but the composer frequently reacted to emotional stress with illness, and Einstein argues that this was a violent reaction to the new perspectives *Teodoro* opened to him. See *ibid.*, p. 440.

La villanella rapita The score was by Francesco Bianchi, who in this and his subsequent opera *Il disertore francese* created a stir with his innovative combination of the serious and the comic.

La finta giardiniera Ibid., pp. 428–31.

In an *opera seria* Letter to his father, 16 June 1781; see Anderson (ed.), *Letters*, p. 746.

140   **the whole story** Letter to his father, 7 May 1783 (his italics); *ibid.*, p. 847.

pinnacle of Mozart's performing career See Steptoe, 'Mozart and Poverty', p. 196.

living in lavish style See Gay, *Mozart*, p. 80. Gay also makes the point about vanity and status anxiety. When Leopold left on 25 April, it was the last time

Wolfgang would see his him. He died in 1787.

developing enemies in common Not only Salieri. Count Rosenberg (from whom Da Ponte complained of so much antagonism) was described in a musical journal of 1793: '. . . the avowed enemy of the Germans, who will hear nothing that is not Italian'. *Berlinische Musikalische Zeitung*, p. 141, quoted in Robbins Landon, *Golden Years*, p. 243, n13 to Chapter IX.

'Davidde Penitente' Mozart adapted the cantata from his earlier Mass in C minor. The evidence that Da Ponte was involved in the process is, as Robbins Landon puts it, 'scanty but based on an unimpeachable source, the Abbé Stadler [a close friend of Mozart's, who completed and re-orchestrated some of his works]', and is now generally accepted. See *ibid.*, pp. 127–8.

for Nancy Storace See Zagonel, *Bibliografia*, p. 12. Storace had been briefly and unhappily married to the violinist John Fischer, who had beaten her, and whom the Emperor had as much as banished from Vienna some time before Nancy announced her pregnancy (some say to further his own cause in her affections). Mozart, too, has been romantically linked with her. Einstein has described an earlier aria Mozart wrote for Storace ('*Ch'io mi scordi di te*', K. 505) as 'a declaration of love in music' (Einstein, *Mozart*, p. 85).

more likely to be related to pregnancy See Girdham, *English Opera*, p. 13–15.

141 **Mozart suggested to the theatre poet** Da Ponte tells us in his memoirs that this was the case, and though factual elements of the memoirs are often to be faulted there seems little reason to doubt that a man otherwise so eager to claim credit for himself would untruthfully hand it to another. Mozart's letters covering this period are lost. See *Memorie*, p. 163.

I hear that Reproduced in Deutsch, *Mozart*, p. 235.

Le Mariage de Figaro **was notorious** I am indebted to Braunbehrens, *Mozart in Vienna*, pp. 209–15 for the discussion of the relationship between the Beaumarchais and Da Ponte texts, and the light he throws on Joseph II's policy.

jus primae noctis Till points out that this *droit de seigneur* was obsolete, and most likely a social myth, although it did characterize the ills of feudalism, and that the Count goes beyond it in that he wants Susanna to remain a paid mistress well beyond her wedding night. See Nicholas Till, *Mozart and the Enlightenment* (Faber and Faber, 1992), p. 148.

142 **No Count, you won't have her** *The Marriage of Figaro*, Act V, scene iii, in Beaumarchais, *The Figaro Trilogy*, trans. David Coward (Oxford University Press, 2003), p. 192; used by permission of Oxford University Press.

It is the heart that ennobles a man Letter to his father, 20 June 1781; see Anderson (ed.), *Letters*, p. 74–6.

that godless arch-rascal Voltaire Letter to his father, 3 July 1778; see *ibid.*, p. 559.

Cela est detestable 'This is atrocious, this will never be played!'; quoted in Robbins Landon, *Golden Years*, p. 158.

143 **less a device of suppression** See Yates, *Theatre in Vienna*, p. 10.

approved for publication Braunbehrens, *Mozart in Vienna*, p. 211.

afforded the young men personal dignity See Steptoe, *Mozart–Da Ponte Operas*, pp. 80–6.

144   **to work on the opera in secret** Many have disputed Da Ponte's version of events, most specifically that *Figaro* was completed in six weeks (see below). Leopold Mozart, in a letter to his daughter of 3 November 1785, mentions that Mozart is working on 'a new opera', and in another of 11 November writes that Wolfgang is 'up to his eyes in work at his opera *Figaro*'. Michael Kelly writes that Salieri, Mozart and Righini were all vying for the same empty slot in the Burgtheater program, which *Figaro* later filled (initially scheduled for late April). Based on this evidence, I posit that Da Ponte's version of events in the *Memorie* is largely true: that he and Mozart worked on *Figaro* in October and November (or November and December) of 1785, in relative secrecy (Michael Kelly appears to have stumbled in on Mozart as he completed a duet; see below), and that they found their 'favourable moment' to present it to the Emperor in the wake of Da Ponte's early-January success with *Burbero*, which coincided with the news that a spring slot was available in the program. Da Ponte gets the general shape of events correct, but writing some forty years later gets the timing wrong – he appears to imply that he and Mozart began work only after the success of *Burbero*.

living near the Stephansplatz The Mozarts had moved to the house at 846 Grosser Schulstrasse at the end of September 1784; it seems most likely that Da Ponte had rooms on the Graben (which is where he mentions he was living when he ran into Casanova, who arrived in Vienna in 1784), but that his accommodation was not at all sumptuous (in his 1785 verse letter to Zaguri, he melodramatically describes it as 'poor hovel'). Probably he had forfeited space and comfort in order to move back from the unfashionable suburbs to an address in the city that better befitted his new position – or he might simply have been soliciting Zaguri's pity for his plight (which much of the rest of the letter goes on to do).

For the next six weeks Controversy surrounds Da Ponte's claim in his memoirs that *Figaro* was written in six weeks (elsewhere he says eight weeks). For years this was doubted, but Robbins Landon argues convincingly that this was indeed the case – citing, amongst other evidence, the recent discovery of the second part of the Mozart autograph of *Figaro* in a Silesian monastery that shows that the score was initially laid out in a kind of musical shorthand; and references to his having written the finale to Act II during two nights and a day. Other Mozart scholars agree, including Ludwig Finscher, editor of the definitive *Neue Mozart Ausgabe* edition of *Figaro*. (See Robbins Landon, *Golden Years*, pp. 156–7.) Such speedy composition was not at all unusual. Steptoe draws parallels with Haydn's prolific working life, and Dittersdorf's composing one Italian and three German operas during an eighteen-month sojourn in Vienna in 1785–7. Our present-day attitudes to creativity are, he points out, very much a product of the tortuous soul-searching of nineteenth-century composers. (See Steptoe, *Mozart–Da Ponte Operas*, p. 69.) The desirability of *Figaro* being seen as a sequel to Paisiello's successful *Barbiere*, and the necessity of working fast in the absence of a commission, also argue in favour of Da Ponte's version of events.

Neither has left posterity details An occasional tantalizing glimpse exists elsewhere. Michael Kelly recalls calling on Mozart just as he had finished the duet sung by Count Almaviva and Susanna, '*Crudel perchè finora . . .*', and that they sat down immediately to sing it – which would indicate that in this part at least the verse existed intact prior to the music. See Kelly, *Reminiscences*, p. 141.

145   *Quì cangiar vuol metro* From Da Ponte's verse letter to Casti, written in 1786, *Lettere*, p. 94.

Anna Gottlieb as Barbarina She would later play the first Pamina in *The Magic Flute*.

As Da Ponte moulded My reading of *Le nozze di Figaro* is informed by Gay, *Mozart*; Robbins Landon, *Golden Years*; Steptoe *Mozart–Da Ponte Operas*; and Till, *Mozart*, pp. 140–71.

theatrical pragmatism Steptoe points out that in addition to excising Figaro's politically inflammatory speech, Da Ponte also removed much from the original play that would have been quite acceptable by contemporary standards of satire – the point being to make the action more governable by removing elements tangential to the central comedy. See Steptoe, *Mozart–Da Ponte Operas*, pp. 113–14.

147   **personal conflict** See Till, *Mozart*, pp. 145–7.

By equality I do not understand Quoted in *ibid.*, p. 146.

Cherubino's aria A point made by Steptoe, *Mozart–Da Ponte Operas*, p. 108.

the magnificent finale Robbins Landon lists this and a number of other prototypes for *Figaro* in *Golden Years*, pp. 163–4.

148   **other considerations of prudence** Prefaces to libretti were rare. The one Da Ponte provided for the original libretto is quoted in full in Einstein, *Mozart*, p. 445.

using the word '*commedia*' See Till, *Mozart*, p. 140.

Before Christmas The sequence of events is deduced from Leopold Mozart's letter of 11 November 1785, and Da Ponte's version in his memoirs. (See note 'For the next six weeks', above.)

Hai già vinto la causa! In Act III, scene iii. A point made by Hodges, *Lorenzo Da Ponte*, p. 59.

'What?' he said *Memorie*, p. 164. The Emperor was wrong on both counts regarding Mozart's experience in writing opera – *Die Entführung* had been a success, and Mozart had written around a dozen operas and shorter operatic pieces before it. Da Ponte characteristically confuses the time-scale and retrospectively puffs his own early perception of Mozart's worth, but it is interesting that he raises the question of objections of morality and taste, rather than political ones. Those were the grounds on which Joseph had objected to the play in his directive to his minister Count Pergen, lending credence to the view that Joseph may well have tacitly approved of an opera that, in the context of the Burgtheater with its aristocratic audience, offered a satire that supported his belief in reform.

149   **a solo for French horns** See Robbins Landon, *Golden Years*, pp. 159–60.

at three o'clock From the *Wiener Zeitung* of 8 February 1786; quoted in

Christopher Raeburn, 'An Evening at Schönbrunn', in the *Music Review*, XVI (1955), p. 94.

150   **two performances that toyed wittily** *Ibid.*, pp. 94ff.

My style of dress *Memorie*, p, 165. Da Ponte goes on to say that he thought the satire a more accurate portrayal of its author, Casti, than of himself.

151   **The first night of the performance** Kelly, *Reminiscences*, p. 131. Kelly misremembers the role as being of a poet, which has led to some confusion and certain commentators conflating his performance with the lampoon in *Prima la musica* – but Kelly did not perform in the opera at Schönbrunn (nor, is it likely, in any of the later public renditions), as Raeburn and others have clearly demonstrated. That the role Kelly refers to is the philosopher in *Demorgogone* was first proposed by Edward Dent, cited in Raeburn, 'An Evening at Schönbrunn', p. 110.

he would write of Kelly In a collection of three of his libretti, published in 1826, Da Ponte dismisses Kelly's memoirs as 'jests and romantic nonsense', 'ridiculous' and 'worthless', writing that his 'crazy book' contains 'not one syllable of truth' about him [Da Ponte]. See Hodges, *Lorenzo Da Ponte*, p. 74.

politically inexpedient fragments Joseph appears initially to have been quite amused by Casti's *Il poema tartaro* when parts began circulating in 1784, but by 1786 he was looking to an alliance with Russia, and was shortly to visit Catherine.

show amity for each other One might see a parallel with twenty-first-century politicians, who form strong friendships across party lines, though they sincerely disagree with each other's beliefs; or conversely, people within the same party, who appear amiable colleagues in public yet are ruthlessly fighting for personal advancement behind the scenes.

152   **cherished it** *Memorie*, p. 161.

one of the Emperor's closest friends On his deathbed, Joseph wrote a moving letter of appreciation to Rosenberg for his loyalty and friendship. See Hodges, *Lorenzo Da Ponte*, p. 72.

competition for the vacant spring slot See Kelly, *Reminiscences*, p. 140. Kelly remembers Salieri's opera as being *La grotta di Trofonio*, but that could not be the case as it had already been staged in October of the previous year, before Mozart was working on *Figaro*. His *Tarare*, which eventually premiered in June 1787, is a more likely candidate.

153   **Francesco Bussani, reported to Rosenberg** Da Ponte recalls that Bussani was 'inspector of costumes and stage properties'. It appears that he did take on the role of '*Sopraintendente del scenario e vestario*' (keeper of costumes and scenery) in 1787. See Robbins Landon, *Golden Years*, p. 243, n13 to Chapter IX.

So, the *signor poeta* *Memorie*, p. 172. Joseph had indeed put a stop to insertion of unrelated ballets into opera when he formed the Italian company. Da Ponte's account of this event is the only one we have, and allowance must be given for his bias and imaginative recollection (as in being able to describe the nature of Casti's smile, when he was not present), though it is quite clear that attempts were being made to upset the opera; and the opening night was indeed postponed from 28 April to 1 May. Leopold Mozart, writing to his daughter on 28 April, still assumes that to be the date for the premiere, and reports that the soprano Josepha Duschek and her husband (then in Vienna) have written to them of the cabals against Wolfgang: 'Salieri and his followers have set heaven and earth in motion yet again to defeat him.'

he once broke a shoe buckle The incident occurred when frustrated with the aging members of the Gewandhaus orchestra in 1789. See Robbins Landon, *Golden Years*, p. 205.

154 **he visited the Emperor** Kelly points out that Joseph II often attended rehearsals (see *Reminiscences*, p. 116); Zinzendorf in his diary also mentions attending Burgtheater rehearsals.

155 **Mozart was on the stage** *Ibid.*, p. 141. I have corrected Kelly's various spellings of 'Benucci'.

In a billet *Handbillet* to Rosenberg of 14 August 1783; see Rudolf Payer von Thurn, *Joseph II als Theaterdirektor*, pp. 34–5.

156 **great vivacity and playful expression** From a review in the *Morning Chronicle* of her performance in Guglielmi's *La serva raggatrice* in 1809, quoted in Steptoe, *Mozart–Da Ponte Operas*, p. 150.

Vienna was comparatively advanced See Steptoe, *Mozart–Da Ponte Operas*, p. 155.

That which is called From Schink's *Dramaturgische Monate*, 1790, quoted in Otto Erich Deutsch, *Mozart: A Documentary Biography* (Simon and Schuster, 1990), p. 356.

out of hate Quoted in Robbins Landon, *Golden Years*, p. 166.

Count Zinzendorf in his box '*Louise dans notre loge, l'opera m'ennuya*'; diary entry for 1 May, in Link, *National Court Theatre*, p. 270.

The *public* . . . Quoted in Deutsch, *Mozart*, p. 278. The review, incidentally, confirms the existence of rival composers and cabals against Mozart: 'The music by Herr Mozart was admired generally by the public at the first performance, and I make an exception only for those whose self-love and pride do not allow them to find anything good except in that which they themselves have composed . . . Some newspaper writers have taken it upon themselves to relate that Mozart's opera was no success at all. It can be imagined what kind of correspondents they are to circulate such lies.'

157 **five numbers had to be repeated** See Robbins Landon, *Golden Years*, p. 163; Deutsch, *Mozart*, p. 272.

a ban on encores Joseph's note to Rosenberg and the poster text; quoted in Deutsch, *Mozart*, p. 275.

Nothing is played Letter to Baron Gottfried von Jacquin, 15 January 1787; see Anderson (ed.) *Letters*, p. 902.

Chapter Nine

158 **the busy theatre poet** In his memoirs, Da Ponte gets the order of the operas incorrect, placing *Demogorgone* after *Una cosa rara*. I follow the order in the

Performance Calendar compiled by Dorothea Link. See Link, *National Court Theatre*, pp. 88–94.

159 **These will serve** See *Memorie*, p. 175. Da Ponte puts Casti's expulsion as much down to his lasciviousness and lewd verse as to what he sees as the Emperor's near worship of Catherine II.

with such celerity See *Ibid.*, p. 178.

Luis Vélez de Guevara Da Ponte mistakenly attributes it to Calderon in his memoirs.

to grumble in little *Ibid.*, p. 179.

160 **The moment the parts were distributed** *Ibid.*, p. 178.

on its opening night The opera opened on 17 November 1786, with further performances on 20 and 24 November. Despite its success, the repertory system at the Burgtheater made it difficult to squeeze in extra performances. The next was on 4 December, then 12 January, after which weekly performances commenced. See Link, *National Court Theatre*, p. 487.

a roar of applause *Memorie*, p. 180.

A pedestrian passing An anonymous writer in the *Wiener Theater Almanach* for 1794 records his astonishment at hearing a choral rendition of '*Paca, caro mio sposo*' by the 'unfortunate wretches' interred in the military prison, as he passed by. Quoted in Peter Branscombe, 'The Land of the Piano: Music, Theatre and Performance in Vienna around 1800', in Ritchie Robertson and Edward Timms (eds.), *Theatre and Performance in Austria from Mozart to Jelinek*, Austrian Studies IV (Edinburgh University Press, 1993), pp. 10–11.

Count Zinzendorf was thoroughly charmed Diary entries for 17 November, 20 November, 24 November and 4 December. He later (January 17) considered the duet dangerous to youth, who would not have the experience to control the emotions it aroused; and he thought the plot 'lacked common sense'. (Reproduced in Link, *National Court Theatre*, pp. 282–4.) An English translation of the duet runs:

Lilla:	Peace, my dear spouse.
Lubino:	Peace, my dear love.
Lilla:	You won't be jealous any more?
Lubino:	No, I won't be, my heart.
Lilla:	Will you always love me . . .
Lubino:	. . . well.
Lilla:	You will always be my . . .
Lubino:	. . . lover.
Lilla:	I am your only . . .
Lubino:	. . . hope
Lilla:	You shall remain . . .
Lubino:	. . . constant.
Lilla:	Come here among my laces.
Lubino:	Pull them tight, my dear prize
(both):	My soul you are, I shall die in your bosom.

Goodbye torments,
Goodbye fears,
joy and happiness,
fly over to me.

Love is not
always the cause
Only of worries,
Only of deceptions.

[*Una cosa rara*] **was the piece** Pezzl, 'Skizze', reproduced in Robbins Landon, *Mozart and Vienna*, p. 137.

162   **The ladies in particular** *Memorie*, pp. 181–2.

163   **with great ingenuity** Kelly, *Reminiscences*, p. 131. Zinzendorf thought the music '*jolie*', but was confused by the subject matter (diary entry for 27 December 1786).

  a coach-and-four Kelly describes their departure in *ibid.*, pp. 150–1. Leopold Mozart met them as they passed through Salzburg, by which time they had teamed up with Lord Bernard in his landau, and wrote: 'They had two carriages, each with four post-horses. A servant rode in advance as courier to arrange for the changing of eight horses. Goodness what luggage they had! This journey must have cost them a fortune!' (Letter to his daughter, 1 March 1787; see Anderson (ed.), *Letters*, p. 906.)

  had been prevailed upon by Nancy See Girdham, *English Opera*, pp. 13–14.

  to get the matter out of the way *Memorie*, p. 177.

  write operas for Mozart, Martín, Salieri *Ibid.*, p. 184. Da Ponte always referred to Martín as Martini, and to his dying day used the spelling 'Mozzart'. These have been corrected in quotations.

164   **The opportunity was offered me** *Ibid.*, p. 184.

  In his version of events Da Ponte's claim to have written all three operas simultaneously is sometimes viewed with doubt or disbelief, yet *L'arbore di Diana* and *Don Giovanni* opened within weeks of each other – one in Vienna, the other in Prague – in October 1787, and though *Axur* did not premiere until 8 January 1788, it is evident that what began as a simple translation of the Beaumarchais libretto (thus a lighter workload and so manageable in conjunction with working on other libretti) soon developed into a more complex adaptation. It is conceivable that Da Ponte began work on this simultaneously with the other operas after *Tarare* was completed (June 1787), but set it to one side as the task became more complicated. Mozart arrived in Vienna from Prague, apparently with a contract for a new opera, in mid-February 1787, and left for Prague again, apparently with *Don Giovanni* ready to perform, on 1 October 1787, the same day that *L'arbore di Diana* opened at the Burgtheater. In his thematic catalogue no other work follows the A-major violin sonata he enters on 24 August, indicating that he must have been working on *Don Giovanni*. See Hermann Abert, *Mozart's Don Giovanni*, (Eulenberg Books, 1976), p. 9.

  I shall write *Memorie*, p. 184.

  a bottle of *tokai* Da Ponte's 'tockai' is usually translated as Tokay, at the time an immensely expensive sweet wine that Pezzl points out was drunk mainly by women, was good for weak nerves and stomach cramps, and was served 'hardly anywhere except at court or great houses' (Pezzl, 'Skizze von Wien', in Robbins Landon, *Golden Years*, p. 165). Perhaps Da Ponte was flaunting his wealth and extravagant tastes (Spanish snuff was also considered the best), though he may also have been referring to *tocai*, a slightly effervescent white wine from the region between Ceneda and Gorizia, which he would surely have known.

165 **His young Calliope** Da Ponte gives his muse her nickname, interestingly naming her not after the muse of lyric poetry or tragedy, but of heroic epics.
Tarare **took Gluck's reforms** No composer would go quite this far, until Wagner more than half a century later.
certain policies of my august protector *Memorie*, p. 186.

166 **appearing in a radiant cloud** Da Ponte had not lost his sound, pragmatic theatrical touch. Opera no longer subscribed to the elaborate spectacles of yore, but a modest *gloire*, or cloud machine was fairly standard equipment, as in the 'small Cupid Carr with Clouds' and 'small working Clouds of Adonis' mentioned as operating at the Pantheon Theatre in London. See Judith Milhous, Gabriella Dideriken and Robert D. Hume, *Italian Opera in Late Eighteenth-Century London*, II (Clarendon Press, 2001), pp. 351–2.
Quanto è possente amor! This is pointed out by Hodges, *Lorenzo Da Ponte*, p. 83.
a miserable, botched-up piece Quoted in *ibid.*, p. 82.
quelle belle cose *Memorie*, p. 186.
Mozart received similar criticism See letter to Baron Gottfried von Jacquin, of 15 October 1787; Anderson (ed.), *Letters*, p. 911.

167 **Times had changed** Link, *National Court Theatre*, pp. 303–4, n182 and n183 discuss the change.
No opera in the world Letter to Baron Gottfried von Jacquin, of 15 October 1787; Anderson (ed.), *Letters*, p. 911.
fifty-nine performances See Steptoe, *Mozart–Da Ponte Operas*, p. 48.
Wolfgang and Constanze Mozart left Vienna A letter from Mozart to his brother-in-law Baron von Berchtold zu Sonnenburg (reproduced in Anderson (ed.), *Letters*, no. 549), dated Vienna, 29 September 1787, states that the Mozarts were leaving the following Monday (1 October). As the original opening date for *Don Giovanni* was set for 14 October, and even though Da Ponte would briefly join Mozart to work on the opera in Prague, this argues strongly for the case that the opera was in good enough shape by the time Mozart left Vienna for rehearsals to begin, and for the speed with which he and Da Ponte could work. It is quite possible, though, that (as was often the case) he carried the score in his head, and wrote it down at the last moment.
catastrophic slump in invitations See Steptoe, 'Mozart and Poverty', p. 198. The decline did not stop. Steptoe points out that not a single appearance of Mozart as a soloist is recorded between 1788 and 1790, and that his attempts to mount a series of concerts in 1789 failed miserably.
a humbler house They moved to no. 224 in the High Street of the suburb

of Landstrasse. This was a dramatic move indeed. It may be remembered that their rent in Schulerstrasse had been 480 gulden. See Dimond, *Mozart Diary*, pp. 179–80; and Anderson (ed.), *Letters*, p. 908 n5.

168 **After God . . . comes Papa** I am indebted to Peter Gay's analysis of Mozart's relationship with his father. See Gay, *Mozart*, p. 22; and also pp. 22–5 and pp. 83–5.

Distress about debt As a number of scholars have recently shown, the idea that Mozart died destitute must be carefully re-examined. His lack of money was more the result of bad management and a spendthrift nature than a low income; his begging letters an attempt to avoid debt and loss of honour through paying off one creditor by borrowing from another. In 1787 he earned in excess of 3,300 gulden, and even in his leanest years – 1788 to 1790 – never earned less than 1,400 gulden. See Gay, *Mozart*, pp. 78–9; and Andrew Steptoe, 'Mozart and Poverty: a re-examination of the evidence', in the *Musical Times*, LXII (1981).

very dirty with narrow streets Quoted in Robbins Landon, *Golden Years*, p. 200.

retain[ed] some marks Quoted in Steptoe, *Mozart–Da Ponte Operas*, p. 117.

a ragged and half-ruined Piozzi, *Observations and Reflections*, pp. 382–5.

the stage personnel Letter to Baron Jacquin, 15 October 1787. The premiere of *Don Giovanni* was twice postponed.

the old story of Don Juan For the origins of the myth and the background to Da Ponte's *Don Giovanni* see Hermann Abert's benchmark essay, written for the sixth German edition of Otto Jahn's *Life of Mozart* (Cooper Square Publishers, 1970), and republished in a translation by Peter Gellhorn as *Don Giovanni*, pp. 26ff; also Einstein, *Mozart*, pp. 443ff; and Steptoe, *Mozart–Da Ponte Operas*, pp. 114–19.

169 **was played every night** Quoted in Abert, *Don Giovanni*, p. 33.

this bad Spanish play From a passage in his memoirs; quoted in Einstein, *Mozart*, p. 450n.

170 **cautious about using the coarse tale** See Steptoe, *Mozart–Da Ponte Operas*, p. 116.

transfer to Vienna Mozart's letters from Prague suggest that he did not originally expect the opera to go to Vienna, until 4 November 1787, five days after *Don Giovanni* finally opened in Prague, when he writes to Baron Jacquin: 'But perhaps my opera will be performed in Vienna after all! I hope so.' Anderson (ed.), *Letters*, p. 913.

notoriously scatological letters Most notably the so-called Bäsle-Briefe to his cousin Maria Anna Thekla Mozart in 1777, full of such phrases as 'I shit on your nose' and 'Now I wish you a good night, shit in your bed until it creaks.'

jests of a nature Reproduced in Deutsch, *Mozart*, p 503.

everyday turn of mind In her memoirs, printed in 1844, quoted in Einstein, *Mozart*, p. 105.

171 **it was a subject** *Memorie*, p. 184.

172 **more consciously engaged** Da Ponte's deliberate support of Josephian policies in *L'arbore di Diana* bears this out.

becomes a stirring triumphal march See Robbins Landon, *Golden Years*, p. 170.

followed Bertati's libretto For the relationship between the Da Ponte and Bertati libretti, see especially Abert, *Don Giovanni*, pp. 37ff; also Einstein, *Mozart*, pp. 452–5; and Steptoe, *Mozart–Da Ponte Operas*, pp. 118–20.

173 **into a close rendition** Anthony Burgess makes a similar point about '*Là ci darem la mano*' in his introduction to the Cassell edition of *Don Giovanni*; and the comparison of the two versions of the 'Catalogue Song' is drawn from Einstein, *Mozart*, pp. 452–4.

Là ci darem la mano From Act I, scene ix.

174 **A comparison of the two** Given in Einstein, *Mozart*, pp. 452–3.

Mozart originally wanted Fitzlyon, *Lorenzo Da Ponte*, p. 142.

175 **whose works both men knew** Da Ponte had already adapted *A Comedy of Errors* for Stephen Storace; Mozart refers in letters to the ghost scene in *Hamlet* when he was composing *Idomeneo*, and productions of Shakespeare plays were staged at the Burgtheater throughout the 1780s.

Da Ponte labelled his See Steptoe, *Mozart–Da Ponte Operas*, p. 198. Much is often made of Da Ponte's label, as if it were something new, but as Steptoe points out, the term *dramma giocoso* was often used by Italian poets to describe work with no pretensions to tragedy at all, such as *Il barbiere di Siviglia*. Goldoni frequently used the term.

mere philanderer Critical opinion is divided. See Steptoe, *Mozart–Da Ponte Operas*, pp. 201–2 for his chameleon-like character and its musical correlates; and Abert, *Don Giovanni*, p. 49 for the Don as elemental force: '[T]he main point of Don Giovanni's nature is not his ability to seduce this or that woman who happens to cross his path, even if there were "a thousand and three", but in the elemental, sensual urge to live and love which he has the uncontrolled energy to satisfy. The more he reveals himself the more dangerous, but also the greater, he becomes.'

elements of a Romantic hero The manuscript score (now in Paris) omits the final sestet, and has all the characters ending on a cadential 'Ah!'; and the libretto for the Vienna version also omits the scene (see Robbins Landon, *Golden Years*, p. 171; Einstein, *Mozart*, p. 457). Performances without this finale became the norm in Vienna (and in most cities other than Dresden) in the early 1790s and throughout the Romantic era, often with additions that gave even more of a Romantic turn to the opera. Goethe, whose hero Faust has a rather more ambiguous relationship with the Devil, wrote to Schiller in 1797: 'The hopes you had for opera you might have seen fulfilled to high degree quite recently in *Don Giovanni*; however, this work stands entirely on its own, and Mozart's death has destroyed any prospect of its being repeated.' Quoted in Abert, *Don Giovanni*, p. 22.

176 **does not . . . have his own aria** See *ibid.*, p. 42. Don Giovanni's musical adaptability is discussed in Steptoe, *Mozart–Da Ponte Operas*, pp. 201–2, and in Erik Smith's entry on *Don Giovanni* in Amanda Holden (ed.), *The New Penguin Opera Guide* (Penguin Books, 2001).

add colours to the chameleon Spoken by Richard III in an earlier incarnation, as the Duke of Gloucester in *Henry VI Part Three*, III. ii. 191.

arriving on 8 October The arrival of 'Herr Abbee Laurenz da Ponte' is reported in the *Prager Oberpostamtszeitung* of 9 October. See Deutsch, *Mozart*, p. 299.

I found on my arrival Letter to Baron Gottfried von Jacquin, 15 October 1787; Anderson (ed.), *Letters*, p. 911.

could speak to each other Abert, *Don Giovanni*, p. 10.

musical friends the Duscheks Franz Xaver Dushcek was a renowned pianist, and his wife Josepha a soprano.

177 **Professor August Meissner** Augustus Gottlieb Meissner left notes and related his reminiscences of the period to his grandson Alfred, who published them in 1870 as *Rococo-Bilder*. Filtered through time and a second person, they need to be viewed cautiously – there is no proof, for example, that Casanova was in Prague at the same time as Da Ponte was, before 25 October (though as Dux was just a day's journey away, it is highly probable that he was); and Da Ponte was back in Vienna when Mozart, at the last minute, composed the overture to *Don Giovanni* (which Meissner relates occurred at the afternoon party). But although the two events Meissner describes might be a conflation of a number of visits, and allowing for a little gloss in recollection and narration, what emerges through the foliage of possibly spurious anecdote gives us a sudden clear glimpse of the characters of Da Ponte and Casanova – one that tallies with other sources – and a scent of the atmosphere at such a party. Passages from the *Rococo-Bilder* dealing with the party at Bertramka are reproduced in translation in Hodges, *Lorenzo Da Ponte*, pp. 86ff, and Paul Nettl, *The Other Casanova* (Da Capo Press, 1970), pp. 220ff.

178 **the Prague company** Details of the Prague singers from Abert, *Don Giovanni*, pp. 15–17.

Bondini sings Quoted in Deutsch, *Mozart*, p. 281.

179 **the leading female role** A point made by Steptoe, who notes that when it came to *Figaro* it would seem that Susanna had the edge over the Countess as a part – Nancy Storace as leading soprano played the first Susanna in Vienna, and Luisa Laschi played the Countess. After Storaci left, Laschi became prima donna – and when *Don Giovanni* transferred to Vienna, she played Zerlina, rather than either of the heavier female roles. Steptoe also offers substantial musical evidence for Zerlina as the leading role. See Steptoe, *Mozart–Da Ponte Operas*, pp. 150–1 and pp. 200–1.

in the Gazzaniga/Bertati *Don Giovanni* See *ibid.*, p. 154. n35.

most beautiful but utterly stupid Quoted in Abert, *Don Giovanni*, p. 15.

[His voice] range Quoted in *ibid.*, p. 15.

did not allow singers We know this from his work on *Idomeneo*. See Abert, *Don Giovanni*, p. 10.

the trombones in particular The use of trombones (previously known as sackbuts) was innovative; they had fallen from fashion since Handel, though Gluck had used them in *Alceste*. In England in 1784, Burney had to scour the country to find either instruments or players for the great Handel commemoration in Westminster Abbey, eventually finding six German musicians who could play the instrument in the King's military band.

180   *friseurs* **and housemaids** Mozart gives an account of the ball in a letter to his father of 5 December 1781; Anderson (ed.), *Letters*, p. 781.
goings-on in rehearsals *Ibid.*, pp. 10–11.

181   **fiery letter** *Memorie*, p. 187. Archduke Franz married Princess Elizabeth of Württemberg. The wedding had just been advanced from Easter 1788 to 6 January 1788, hence the urgency. *Axur* was first staged on 8 January.
Casanova stepped into the breach Casanova was in Prague from at least 25 October, when he wrote to Count Max Lamberg. He conducted negotiations with a publisher, but the presence of the fragment of *Don Giovanni* discovered by Paul Nettl and Bernhard Marr in the Bohemia Casanova Archives in the 1930s indicates he had some contact with opera rehearsals, though it has never been established for certain just how this fragment came into being. See Deutsch, *Mozart*, p. 301; and Nettl, *Other Casanova*, pp. 233ff.
before the final rehearsal Some say the overture was finished only just before the first performance, but Constanze Mozart's recollection and Mozart's catalogue entry point to its being finished on the night of 27/28 October. Meissner gives an amusing story of how Mozart was tricked into a room with a harpsichord in it and locked there during a party at the Duscheks to complete the overture, as Bondini was growing worried that it would never be finished. See Abert, *Don Giovanni*, pp. 13–14.
Herr Mozard [sic] conducted Quoted in Deutsch, *Mozart*, p. 303.
was welcomed joyously Quoted in *ibid.*, p. 304.

182   **loud applause** Letter to Baron Jacquin of 4 November 1787; Anderson (ed.), *Letters*, p. 922.
Evviva **Da Ponte** Da Ponte mentions the letter in his memoirs, but a copy does not exist (see *Memorie*, p. 160).

Chapter Ten

183   **the unhappiest mortal alive** See Derek Beales, 'Was Joseph II an Enlightened Despot?', in Ritchie Robertson and Edward Timms (eds.), *The Austrian Enlightenment and its Aftermath*, Austrian Studies II (Edinburgh University Press, 1993), p. 1 for Joseph's statements of his condition; also, Beales, *Joseph II*, I, pp. 314–15.

184   **had trodden over peasants** See Till, *Mozart*, p. 165 and p. 190 for Joseph's unpopularity and about-face.
The best among people Quoted in *ibid.*, p. 165. The pamphlet was written by the playwright and satirist Josef Richter.

185   **not nearly the amount** Gluck's salary was 2, gulden. The difference is to be expected, given his fame and status in comparison with Mozart's at the time. Da Ponte's official annual salary for all his arduous duties as theatre poet was still 600 gulden.
Rosenberg's apparent displeasure That Rosenberg initially argued against programming the opera can be deduced from his correspondence with Joseph during the rehearsal period. See Robbins Landon, *Golden Years*, p. 173.

186   **a busy correspondence** See *ibid.*, p. 173; and Deutsch, *Mozart*, p. 315.
The opera did not please! *Memorie*, p. 188.
the music learned Cited in Deutsch, *Mozart*, p. 314.

187   **The opera is divine** *Memorie*, p. 188. Da Ponte implies that the Emperor made these remarks around the time of the premiere. That could not have been the case, although given their similarity to the opinions of Mozart's music Joseph had expressed privately in his letter to Rosenberg, his comment does have an air of authenticity; and Mozart's notion that frequent repetition of the opera might win over Viennese audiences is borne out by the performance program.
Vienna's literary world See *Lettere*, p. 107 n2.

188   **Three buffo singers** In a *Handbillet* to Rosenberg in 1783; reproduced in Payer von Thurn, *Joseph II*, pp. 33–4.
closed the old Kärntnertortheater See Link, *National Court Theatre*, pp. 2–3.
in order to consolidate In the spring of 1788 Salieri was appointed first kapellmeister of the Hofkapelle in addition to his role as composer to the opera – as much a decision for reasons of economy on Joseph's part as it was an honour for Salieri. The appointment could well indicate that the Emperor already had plans to dissolve the opera company and was creating a new role for the master composer. Ignaz Umlauf, former kapellmeister to the *Singspiel* company, which was dissolved that spring, was appointed second kapellmeister under Salieri.
an 80,000-gulden deficit For the events leading up to Joseph's decision to disband the company, see his correspondence with Rosenberg between 3 May 1788 and 2 August 1788; in Payer von Thurn, *Joseph II*, pp. 74–82.

189   **[M]y hope [is] scattered** Letter to his father, 1788; *Lettere*, p. 101.
I am losing my work '*E ch'io perdo uffizio, e titolo / Di poeta imperiale / E per ultimo capitolo / La mia paga mensuale.*' His elevation of himself to imperial poet rather than mere theatre poet is perhaps for reasons of rhyme, though most likely in an attempt to add to his lustre in his father's eyes.
appears to have been in Vienna He refers to Paolo in the letter to his father, and also in his memoirs, as being in Vienna at the time he was writing *Don Giovanni*.
a somewhat violent disposition *Memorie*, p. 192.
her '*laide figure*' In a billet to Rosenberg of 26 July 1788; in Payer von Thurn, *Joseph II*, pp. 80–1.

190   **Da Ponte's scheme** See Link, *National Court Theatre*, p. 326 n212 and p. 327 n213; and *Memorie*, pp. 189ff. Some commentators doubt Da Ponte's version of events, but given that Joseph reversed his decision, that the Italian opera continued very much along the lines Da Ponte describes (though there is no evidence of subscriptions to single seats), that no royal subsidy is recorded for the opera for the rest of Joseph's reign and that Da Ponte's salary was indeed doubled as he maintains (1791–2 Account book, Consignation no. 167, see Link, p. 327 and p. 3), and Zinzendorf's diary entry (see below), it would appear that these doubts are unfounded.
Da Ponte requested an audience *Memorie*, pp. 190–1. Casti's lines are from *Prima la musica e poi le parole*.

192 **Count Zinzendorf records** See Link, *National Court Theatre*, p. 326.
At last the business Quoted in Hodges, *Lorenzo Da Ponte*, p. 97.
The performers [at the Mendicanti] Burney, *Present State of Music*, p. 114.
La Ferrarese's voice did not always please. In London, William Parke, who played in the orchestra during her first season, thought 'she had a sweet voice, and sang with taste, but she was not calculated to shine as a prima donna'; and opera connoisseur Lord Mount Edgcumbe, though he had had La Ferrarese 'much extolled' to him, found her 'a very moderate performer' (but he was heavily prejudiced at the time in favour of her rival Brigida Banti). See Steptoe, *Mozart–Da Ponte Operas*, p. 103.
The son of the Roman Consul 1 November 1783, quoted in Otto Michtner, *Das alte Burgtheater als Opernbühne* (Böhlaus, 1970), p. 418 n70.

193 **In addition to** 15 October 1788, quoted in Michtner, *Burgtheater*, pp. 272–3.
see, hear and marvel 25 October 1788, quoted in Michtner, *Burgtheater*, p. 273.
though a vulgar woman *Memorie*, p. 192.
with their teeth From the verse letter to his father, Vienna 1788, *Lettere*, p. 102.

194 **L'ape was a musical pastiche** See Hodges, *Lorenzo Da Ponte*, pp. 98–9.
had slowly been rehabilitated Da Ponte recalls that in the period leading up to *L'ape* Salieri was 'more than a friend, a brother' to him. See *Memorie*, p. 193.
two new arias They were '*Un moto di gioia*' (K.579), replacing '*Venite, inginocchiatevi*' in Act II; and the rondo '*Al desio di chi t'adora*' in Act IV.

195 **The little aria** Letter to Constanze ?19 August 1789; Anderson (ed.), *Letters*, pp. 933–4. Some weeks earlier, writing of another singer, Mozart had opined that she was 'far better than Ferraresi, which, I admit, is not saying much' (letter to Constanze of 16 April 1789; *ibid.*, p. 922).

Chapter Eleven

196 **[The news] excited** From a Foreign Office report dated 29 July 1789; quoted in Steptoe, *Mozart–Da Ponte Operas*, p. 29.
In France, a light Quoted in Steptoe, *Mozart–Da Ponte Operas*, p. 30.

197 **one never speaks openly** Reproduced in Robbins Landon, *Mozart and Vienna*, p. 186.
list of the differences Reproduced in *ibid.*, p. 189.
Mozart seemed unmindful He does not once mention revolution in France in his letters.
originally begun work An incomplete autograph score by Salieri, from 1789, is held in the Österreichischen Nationalbibliothek in Vienna. The reason for Salieri's abandoning the project is not documented. The feud over *L'ape* and the souring of the relationship between the opera's poet and its composer may well have been reason for stopping work on *Così*, but in view of the evidence it does seem quite likely that the Emperor intervened to give the project to Mozart.

198 **an astonishing 200 ducats** Mozart mentions the amount in a letter to Michael Puchberg in December 1789 – though he was trying to borrow money off Puchberg at the time, on the strength of his future fee. The theatre account books for this period are lost, so the amount cannot be verified. Niemetshcek is quoted in Deutsch, *Mozart*, p. 508. Niemetschek and Vincent Novello joined other nineteenth-century commentators in an attack of prudishness, condemning the libretto on moral grounds, and either making excuses for the composer's accepting it, or condemning him for demeaning his art.

the Emperor also suggested See Einstein, *Mozart*, p. 458; and Robbins Landon, *Golden Years*, p. 174.

Da Ponte (rarely for him) The only opera he claims originality for is *L'arbore di Diana*. Curiously, he barely mentions *Così* in his memoirs, apart from a fleeting reference to it as one of the operas he wrote for La Ferrarese, but no other direct source has been discovered. The various possible thematic sources of *Così fan tutte* – such as the wager myth (in Boccaccio and others) and the myth of Pocris in Ovid and Ariosto are discussed in detail in Andrew Steptoe, 'The Sources of *Così fan tutte*: a Reappraisal' in *Music & Letters*, Vol. LXII (1981), pp. 281ff.

Gozzi's *Le droghe d'amore* The influences of Castí and Gozzi, as well as Cervantes and others, on the shaping of *Così* are argued in some detail by Steptoe, *ibid.*, and in *Mozart–Da Ponte Operas*, pp. 134ff.

200 **[D]earest little wife!** Letter to Constanze, August 1789; Spaethling, *Letters/ Life*, p. 414. Mozart's emphasis. The name of N.N. is deleted by a later hand, probably Constanze's.

a modern attitude See Steptoe, *Mozart–Da Ponte Operas*, p. 88.

201 **My heart was not** *Memorie*, p. 217.

madness, anguish, remorse In Act II scene vii Fiordiligi sings: '*Io ardo, e l'ardor mio non è più effetto / Di un amor virtuoso; è smania, affano / Rimorso, pentimento / Leggerezza, perfidia e tradimento!*'

202 **to the Fair Sex** Part of the preamble to the *canzonetta* that Giuseppe Coletti published in his newspaper in Trieste in celebration of the supposed success of *Il ricco d'un giorno* in 1784. (See p. 126.)

a miserable thing Quoted in Deutsch, *Mozart*, p. 394.

critics arguing for centuries As a taster, for Edward Dent in *Mozart's Operas: A Critical Study* (Oxford University Press, 1966) it is 'the most exquisite work of art among Mozart's operas', while in *Opera as Drama* (Vintage, 1956), Joseph Kerman finds it 'unsatisfactory' and 'problematic'. See Gay, *Mozart*, p. 125; Edward J. Dent, *Mozart's Operas*, p. 190; Joseph Kerman, *Opera as Drama*, p. 109.

iridescent, like a glorious soap-bubble Einstein, *Mozart*, p. 462.

203 **exploring possibilities in arias** Steptoe notes the unusually large number of arias composed in late 1789 for singers who appeared in *Così*, and mentions A. Tyson's observation that the ensembles of Act I were almost all written before the solo numbers, suggesting consultation with the singers over their arias. See Steptoe, *Mozart–Da Ponte Operas*, p. 209.

Mozart replaced a superb '*Rivolgete a lui lo sguardo*' (K.584) was replaced by '*Non siate ritrosi*' (No. 15). See Einstein, *Mozart*, p. 460.

204   **I invite you** Letter to Michael Puchberg, December 1789; Anderson (ed.), *Letters*, p. 934.

       We are having our first Letter to Michael Puchberg, 20 January 1790; *ibid.*, p. 935.

       The music by Mozart Reproduced in Link, *National Court Theatre*, p. 350.

       impressed by the monarch's dignity See Beales, 'Was Joseph II an Enlightened Despot?', p. 1.

       My dear Count Rosenberg Reproduced in Payer von Thurn, *Joseph II*, pp. 84–5.

205   **Although he did not** Casanova, *Story of My Life*, pp. 196–7.

       I could have wept From *Briefe zur Beförderung der Humanität*, quoted in Steptoe, *Mozart–Da Ponte Operas*, p. 30.

       the poet composed a *canzone* See Lanapoppi, *Realtà e leggenda*, p. 214.

206   **three new operas** They were *Nina o sia la pazza per amore* for Paisiello, with extra arias by Weig (premiere 13 April 1790); *La quacquere spiritosa* for Guglielmi (13 August); and *La caffettiera bizzarra*, for Weigl (15 September). In the first two Da Ponte's role was more tweaker and adapter than librettist. The third was very loosely based on Goldoni's *La locandiera*. See Zagonel, *Bibliografia*, pp. 21–2; and Michtner, *Burgtheater*, pp. 309–10.

       such an 'Unding' From his autobiography; quoted in Michtner, *Burgtheater*, p. 310.

       Marquis Marzio del Gallo See *Memorie*, pp. 196–8.

207   **librettist had failed them** The errant librettist was Abbé Gian Vincenzo Serafini.

       the most prestigious patron See Link, *National Court Theatre*, p. 203.

208   *Di gemme e di stele* Quoted in *Memorie*, p. 195, where Da Ponte gives a full account of the event.

209   **At the Burgtheater** Da Ponte recalls the events of 1790–1 in his *Memorie* (pp. 198–203), but with considerable personal bias. Even the petitions he penned at the time are contradictory in their accusations – yet other sources, such as the leaflet entitled *Anti-Da Ponte*, clearly also have an axe to grind. What is indisputable is the vehemence of the infighting, and its result. Otto Michtner's article '*Der Fall Abbé Da Ponte*' in *Mitteilungen des Oesterreichisches Staatsarchiv*, Vol. XIX (1966), pp. 170ff, helped comb out the tangle, and reproduces reams of documentation. See also Lanapoppi, *Realtà e leggenda*, pp. 213ff; and Hodges, *Lorenzo Da Ponte*, pp. 106ff.

       Da Ponte identified This he did in a series of memoranda written later in 1791. He lists a full seven points of complaint against Salieri. See Michtner, '*Der Fall*', pp. 177ff; Hodges, *Lorenzo Da Ponte*, pp. 107–8.

       Casti was back See Einstein, *Mozart*, p. 441.

       two outside singers See Lanapoppi, *Realtà e leggenda*, pp. 217–19.

210   **private interest, personal malice** The petition is held in the Vienna State Archives, and reprinted in *Lettere*, p. 109.

       empty theatres, enormous losses *Ibid.*, p. 110.

       the number of my enemies *Memorie*, p. 199.

211   **To the devil** *Ibid..*, pp. 198–9.

       [By granting this request] Quoted in Lanapoppi, *Realtà e leggenda*, p. 219.

cosy *ménage à trois* Luigi appears resigned, if not amenable to the third person in his marriage. While in Venice, he discovered his father's financial affairs were not in good order, and wrote to Da Ponte asking him to persuade La Ferrarese to economize and to follow up the sale of some paintings. See Hodges, *Lorenzo Da Ponte*, p. 112.

212 **nefarious conspiracies** These and similar claims were made in his 1788 verse letter to his father. See *Lettere*, p. 101.

My destiny does not depend Verse letter to Leopold II, February 1791; *ibid.*, p. 114.

213 **The entire city** Michtner, '*Der Fall Abbé Da Ponte*', p. 181.

an imaginary court case Partially quoted in Deutsch, *Mozart*, pp. 397–8.

replaced Count Rosenberg See Link, *National Court Theatre*, p. 4.

oratorio entitled *Il Davide* The score is now lost, but appears to have been a pastiche by various composers. See *ibid.*, p. 165.

most shows given as benefits The fact that academies (benefit performances), were given for Da Ponte after his dismissal may either have been part of the financial arrangements because his contract had been severed; or the Burgtheater may have been honouring part of the deal he had made when taking over the running of the theatre. See Link, *National Court Theatre*, p. 19n.

214 **seriously considering the idea** In a letter of 1–2 March 1787, shortly after Leopold Mozart had met the Storace party on their way back to London, he wrote to his daughter that Wolfgang was seriously considering going to England, but that he, Leopold, thought he had dissuaded him, for the time being at least. Mozart's interest in English lessons in the late 1780s, and a line in a letter of 4 November 1787 stating that he was unable to accept the proposal that he stay on in Prague and write another opera, are often given to substantiate the view that he had plans to leave for London.

La clemenza di Tito Composed as part of the celebrations for Leopold's coronation as King of Bohemia – an *opera seria* at Marie Luisa's instigation, though she conceded to the people of Prague their choice of composer. *Die Zauberflöte* represented a complete step away from court, to a suburban theatre.

full of a thousand *Memorie*, p. 202.

The Italian court poet Quoted in Hodges, *Lorenzo Da Ponte*, p. 112.

twenty-four hours to leave See Michtner, '*Der Fall Abbé Da Ponte*', p. 175.

[M]y presence [in Vienna] *Memorie*, pp. 202–3.

two peremptory police injunctions Although the injunctions no longer exist, they are referred to as attachments to one of Da Ponte's written protests in a bundle entitled *Cose dell' Abbate da Ponte* in the Vienna State Archive; reproduced in Michtner, '*Der Fall Abbé Da Ponte*', pp. 203–5.

215 **He carries within him** Zaguri writes of Da Ponte's '*versi San Servolici*', a reference to the Venetian insane asylum on the island of San Servolo – hence 'insane' verses. The remainder of the quote is from his letter of 1 June 1791 to Casanova; in Molmenti (ed.), *Carteggi Casanoviani*, II, pp. 140–1. The letter is in Italian, but Zaguri writes the final sentence of the passage quoted in French, as '*Il y a des choses qui ne piquent point a force d'être extremes.*'

Chapter Twelve

219 **one of the most terrible** *Memorie*, p. 203. For details of Da Ponte's time in
Brühl and Trieste, and his efforts to gain clemency from Leopold II, see
Michtner, '*Der Fall Abbé Da Ponte*', pp. 170–209; and Hodges, *Lorenzo Da
Ponte*, pp. 114–29. Michtner reproduces many of the relevant documents,
including Da Ponte's memoranda to Stieber, from which a picture of his last
days in Vienna can be constructed.

    every feature of his face Major Stieber writing to Leopold II in mid-May;
reproduced in Michtner, '*Der Fall Abbé Da Ponte*', p. 197.

220 **his own report** *Ibid.*, pp. 197–8.

    from the capital The account of Da Ponte's arrest is taken from *Memorie*,
p. 204. See also Michtner, '*Der Fall Abbé Da Ponte*', p. 176.

221 **act for [him]** Letter to Giacomo Casanova, 18 June 1791; in *Lettere*,
p. 121.

    Lorenzo was a 'madman' Zaguri reports this to Casanova in a letter of 14
January 1792. See Molmenti, *Carteggi Casanoviani*, II, p. 168.

    his wicked uncle See Zagonel, '*Felice Da Ponte*', in *Il Flaminio*, VIII, 1995,
pp. 51ff.

    the usual refuge Letter to Casanova, 13 July 1791; in Molmenti (ed.),
Carteggi Casanoviani, II, p. 149.

222 **pained and astonished** Pittoni describes the incident to Casanova, writing
from Padua some weeks later on 6 September 1791. See *ibid.*, p. 233.

    summoned to an audience Pittoni's letter to Casanova confirms that Da
Ponte was summoned to an audience which lasted an hour and a half at
eleven a.m. on the day following the opera. The contents of the interview are
reported in the *Memoirs*, and though they may be embroidered are borne out
by the subsequent sacking of many of the Burgtheater staff, and by an early
review of the *Memorie* in *Antologia*, no. 88, April 1828, in which the critic
notes, 'Everything I have ever heard recounted of different conversations
held by Leopold gives [Da Ponte's] narration in my eyes the strictest air of
truth.' See Hodges, *Lorenzo Da Ponte*, p. 119.

223 **Madame Lamotte's** The Countess de Lamotte was involved in the
notorious Diamond Necklace Affair, a swindle in which a prostitute posed
as the Queen in order to extract payment for some extraordinarily valuable
jewellery. She was tried and imprisoned, but later escaped to England from
where she penned scurrilous pamphlets against Marie Antoinette that were
hugely popular in France.

    given to Bertati Initially, Da Ponte's post had been filled on a temporary
basis by his friend Caterino Mazzolà, who returned to Dresden when Bertati
took over, some time in mid-1791.

    On 20 July, Da Ponte wrote to Stieber *Lettere*, pp. 124ff. Da Ponte's very
sound suggestions for the running of the Burgtheater are reproduced in
Michtner, '*Der Fall Abbé Da Ponte*', pp. 199ff. Lucchesi did not take
Thorwart's place.

224 **filled her naturally romantic head** *Memorie*, p. 216.

    Da Ponte hit on a plan Da Ponte's correspondence with Manolesso and the

Inquisitors is reproduced in *Lettere*, pp. 127–32. The plan is unravelled in the editor's footnotes and in Hodges, *Lorenzo Da Ponte*, pp. 123–5.

225 **Pilate's words** Da Ponte slightly misquotes '*Innocens ego sum a sanguine iusti huius*' (Matthew, xxvii, 24).

If it is true See Molmenti (ed.), *Carteggi Casanoviani*, II, p. 159.

published a sonnet *Sonetto sull'Ingratitudine dell'Uomo* appeared in *L'Osservatore Triestino* on 8 October. See Zagonel (ed.), *Bibliografia*, p. 25.

Il Mezenzio See Francesca Bonanni, '*Una tragedia di Da Ponte*: Mezenzio, re d'Etruria' in *Atti del Convegno Lorenzo Da Ponte* pp. 175ff; Zagonel (ed.), *Bibliografia*, p. 26; *Lettere*, p. 134.

226 **My cries of despair** Given in *Memorie*, pp. 221–2.

Del Bene wouldn't allow In a letter of 28 March 1792, quoted in Hodges, *Lorenzo Da Ponte*, p. 127.

as he will be remaining Quoted in Michtner, '*Der Fall Abbé Da Ponte*', p. 177.

generous but firm Da Ponte writes in his memoirs that Franz gave him permission to remain in Vienna at his own discretion, and to publish notice of his innocence in all newspapers of the Austrian states – but no such notice appeared. See *Memorie*, p. 224.

la bella inglesina According to Hodges, *Da Ponte*, p. 129. Zagonel refers to her as '*La Grahal* [sic] *bella*' in a letter to Casanova of 14 February 1794; see Molmenti (ed.), *Carteggi Casanoviani*, II, p. 260. The history of the Grahl family is carefully reconstructed by Arthur Livingston in his annotations to Da Ponte's memoirs, reproduced in the Abbott translation. See *Memoirs*, p. 194. Da Ponte gives a perhaps romanticized account of his meeting with Ann Grahl in *Memorie*, pp. 217–19.

228 **independence of Englishwomen** By, among others, Professor Lichtenberg, visiting London in the 1770s. See Richard S. Lambert, *The Fortunate Traveller* (Andrew Melrose, 1950), p. 101.

early to endure Quoted in Dominique Godineau's essay 'The Woman'; in Vovelle (ed.), *Enlightenment Portraits*, p. 402, which has been useful to me in its views on marriage in the Enlightenment.

after social ceremonies *Memorie*, p. 227. His words are: '*dopo le sociali cerimonie e formalità, mi fu consegnata da' suoi genitori*'. '*Consegnata*' can also mean 'handed over' – much in the sense that Matilda, the lady in the gondola, was 'handed over' by her parents in a formal ceremony. Livingston discusses various possibilities for the ceremony in a long note in the Abbott translation of the memoirs.

229 **Apropos Da Ponte** Letter to Casanova, 16 November 1793; Molmenti (ed.), *Carteggi Casanoviani*, II, p. 246. By this stage Casanova knew more than Zaguri did about the affair. Zaguri and Da Ponte had stopped writing to each other after the latter's betrayal of Luigi Del Bene. Casanova wrote to the chief of police Pittoni enquiring about the marriage, and Pittoni replied on 15 April 1794 with the curious misinformation: 'Da Ponte did not marry a Jewess. He left Trieste with the self-styled [or so-called] daughter of an English merchant named Krahl'; *ibid.*, p. 246n. Some commentators say that what Savordello witnessed was a Protestant ceremony, and that the couple

were married according to Anglican rites. A Protestant clergyman willing to perform the ceremony may well have been found in Trieste, but would surely have had qualms about even a Roman Catholic breaking his sacred vows, if not fears of the consequences of abetting such a union for his position.

How the devil Letter to Casanova, 19 March 1794; Molmenti (ed.), *Carteggi Casanoviani*, II, p. 266.

had pointedly . . . to remind Casanova See letter of 24 September 1792; *Lettere*, p. 140.

flee Rome and all Italy See Livingston in *Memoirs*, p. 210.

230 **dazed by the vivacity** *Memorie*, p. 230.

231 **sale of his coach** Casanova asked to travel a small part of the way with them, which necessitated selling the two-seater calash, and buying a larger coach. This vehicle proved unsafe – the party had an accident, after which repairs seemed pointless, and Da Ponte sold the coach at a loss. Travellers, especially those crossing the Channel, frequently bought a vehicle at the beginning of a journey and sold it again at the end, sometimes even realizing a profit – not only did it make travelling more comfortable, but ultimately cheaper than using a public diligence. Da Ponte would, no doubt, have sold his calash once he and Nancy had reached the coast, but Casanova's intervention as second-hand coach salesman made the rest of the journey inconvenient as well as expensive.

Prince of Orange coffee-house See Casanova, *Story of My Life*, p. 357.

did not want competition See letter to Casanova of 24 September 1792; *Lettere*, p. 140. From the same letter it would appear that Da Ponte was still passing Nancy off as his sister-in-law in Dresden, probably so as not to offend the pious Father Huber.

robbed just outside Dux At Oberleutendorf, now Livitnow; see Livingston's note in *Memoirs*, p. 220.

the wind grew stronger Letter to Maria Anna von Genzinger, 8 January 1791; in Robbins Landon, *Notebooks of Joseph Haydn*, p. 111.

232 **The moment one sets foot** From his diary; translated by Margaret L. Mare and W. H. Quarrell as *Lichtenberg's Visits to England* (Benjamin Blom, 1969), p. 115.

a crabby J. H. Campe See Lambert, *Fortunate Traveller*, p. 105.

the high road becomes See Christian Goede, *A Foreigner's Opinion of England* (C. Taylor, 1821), p. 13.

on Silver Street See Hodges, *Lorenzo Da Ponte*, p. 131.

the English disease These impressions of Haydn's are recounted in his letters of 20 December 1791 and 14 January 1792, and in a notebook entry for 5 December 1791. See Robbins Landon, *Haydn Letters*, pp. 124ff and p. 278. The 'English disease' or 'English humour' was widely seen as a national characteristic – some attributing this to 'satiety', others to the beer. Even in places of entertainment (noted one Monsieur Grosley), 'the joy which they seem in search of at these places does not beam through their countenances; they look as grave at Vauxhall [pleasure gardens] as at the Bank, at church or a private club.' (See André Parreaux, *Daily Life in the Reign of George III* (George

Allan, 1966), pp. 182–3). English drinking habits were notorious, frequently mentioned by Haydn, Lichtenberg, Goede and many other travellers.

232 **knew hardly any English** By his own admission. See *Memorie*, p. 249.

a profession currently practised Letter to Casanova, 2 April 1793; *Lettere*, p. 153.

'Improvement' was the word See Parreaux, *Daily Life*, p. 192.

So strange, so varied From *An Extract from the Life of Lorenzo Da Ponte* (printed by J. Gray, 1819), p. 32.

So much of London See Bernier, *The World in 1800*, pp. 89–91; Burton, *The Georgians at Home*, pp. 97ff; Parreaux, *Daily Life*, pp. 79ff.

'she-dog' *Ibid.*, p. 196.

234 **Oxford Street alone** Archenholz, quoted in *ibid.*, p. 92.

the spacious streets Goede, *Foreigner's Opinion*, p. 18.

thousand twinkling lights *Ibid.*, p. 91.

Imagine a street Letter to Ernst Baldinger, 10 January 1775. See Mare and Quarrell (trans.), *Lichtenberg's Visits to England*, pp. 63–4.

235 **16 Sherrard Street** See Hodges, *Lorenzo Da Ponte*, p. 131. Details of housing conditions derived from M. Dorothy George, *London Life in the XVIIIth Century* (Kegan Paul, 1925), pp. 80–96; Parreaux, *Daily Life*, pp. 100–103; also Haydn's letters and notebooks.

The rent for such a room George cites rent for an artisan in a poorer part of town, earlier in the century, being three shillings and sixpence, and for a single lodger in Holborn in 1795, five shillings – though prices did rise substantially that year (George, *London Life*, pp. 92–3). In December 1794, John Aspinwall (the great-grandfather of Franklin Delano Roosevelt) paid six shillings a week for a first-floor bedroom in Aldgate (see Aileen Sutherland Collins, *Travels in Britain 1794–1795: The Diary of John Aspinwall* (Parsons Press, 1994), p. 54).

236 *putana borsa* The reference to Nancy's purse translates vulgarly. Both this and Da Ponte's bewailing of his financial predicament are in his first letter to Casanova from London, on 13 January 1793. See *Lettere*, p. 144.

He who in the present Quoted in Petty, *Italian Opera*, p. 4.

post of librettist See letter to Casanova of 13 January 1793; *Lettere*, p. 144. This and a letter of 1 March outline Da Ponte's attempts to gain employment through Kelly and Storace.

Carlo Francesco Badini See *Lettere*, p. 145n.

[a master] of satire See *Memorie*, p. 238.

237 **Lorenzo unleashed his energies** Da Ponte recounts his attempts to get money in his correspondence with Casanova, especially a long letter of 10 May 1793. See *Lettere*, pp. 155ff.

238 **adapted his Trieste play** Da Ponte mentions Madame Mara and the commission in his letter to Casanova of 19 January. In his memoirs he gives the amount of the fee (paid on delivery, some months later). The libretto was supposedly set to music by another friend of Pozzi's, Giacomo Ferrari, though no performance has ever been recorded.

arrived in Brussels Da Ponte's experiences in the Low Countries can be reconstructed from his intensive correspondence with Casanova at the time.

See *Lettere*, pp. 161–84; and *Memorie*, pp. 238–45.

Audaces fortuna juvat Letter of 18 July 1793; *Lettere*, p. 161.

239   **[W]e lived [there]** *Memorie*, pp. 240–1.

As far as Letter to Casanova, 17 November 1793; *Lettere*, pp. 182–3. Casanova's suggestion has to be inferred, but is fairly clear from the response it generated. Horns were the traditional symbol of the cuckold.

240   **'Opera' Taylor** See Hodges, *Lorenzo Da Ponte*, p. 135.

Chapter Thirteen

241   **The character of Mr Taylor** John Ebers, *Seven Years of the King's Theatre* (W. H. Ainsworth, 1828), p. 3. Other references to Taylor's character from pp. 3–18.

that miserable cur In his 1793 notebook; reproduced in Robbins Landon, *Notebooks of Joseph Haydn*, p. 297.

[l]eft to himself *Memorie*, p. 248.

Machiavellian scheming For the full story of the politics and turmoil surrounding the building and licensing of the new King's Theatre, see Curtis Price, Judith Milhous and Robert D. Hume, *Italian Opera in Late Eighteenth-Century London*, I (Clarendon Press, 1995), pp. 540ff.

242   **the press erupted** Various reactions from *The Times*, the *Morning Chronicle*, and the *London Chronicle* are given in Price et al., *Italian Opera*, I, pp. 562ff. There was some criticism, too, especially regarding the low ceilings of the fifth tier of boxes, cramped in along the sides of the theatre for extra capacity, and barely allowing even the shortest person to stand upright; and the central auditorium candelabra – magnificent with near one hundred wax candles, sparks from which put the ladies to flight.

the rendezvous of all From the *Morning Chronicle*, 9 January 1797; quoted in William C. Smith, *The Italian Opera and Contemporary Ballet in London 1789–1820* (Society for Theatre Research, 1955), p. 41.

243   **paraded themselves in Fops' Alley** See Daniel Nalbach, *The King's Theatre 1704–1867* (Society for Theatre Research, 1972), p. 88; and Petty, *Italian Opera*, pp. 56–7.

The Prince of Wales *The Times*, 28 January 1793; quoted in Petty, *Italian Opera*, p. 288.

The Duchess of Gordon's box From *The Times*, 17 January 1788; quoted in *ibid.*, p. 54.

not nearly as raucous Petty quotes a number of startled reactions by English opera-goers on tour in Italy at audience behaviour they encountered. See *ibid.*, p. 55.

The English are not too fond Letter to Luigia Polzelli, 22 May 1792; reproduced in Robbins Landon, *Notebooks of Joseph Haydn*, p. 136.

What a jabbering Fanny Burney, *Evelina*, p. 92. Real-life equivalents of Mr Branghton clearly existed. In the 1780s, a young clergyman in the pit, 'being somewhat disordered by the bottle, chose to amuse himself by imitations of *Italian singing*' and caused such a riot in the audience as to alarm the ladies, and bring to a near faint one Mrs Morse, 'to whom Sir John Dick offered his best consolation'. From an unidentified cutting in *King's Theatre Cuttings Book: A collection of cuttings from newspapers relating to the King's and Haymarket Theatres, 1757–1829*, II, held in the British Library.

244 **The absurdity of managing** Quoted in Petty, *Italian Opera*, p. 77.

this *exotic monster* From an anti-opera passage in the *Oracle*, 8 January 1790; quoted in *ibid.*, p. 69. Samuel Johnson famously called opera 'an exotick and irrational entertainment', but it is less well known that he went on to say that opera 'has always been combated and always has prevailed', an acknowledgement perhaps of the power of its association with the elite; see Dizikes, *Opera in America*, pp. 43–4.

The general populace The upper classes did of course also frequent the theatres at Covent Garden and Drury Lane for theatre and ballad opera, but the King's Theatre remained expensive and exclusive. Whereas the pit (stalls) at the former theatres was one of the cheapest parts of the house (classier folk occupying the boxes and lower gallery), at the opera it was one of the most fashionable and pricey areas – something that causes Fanny Burney's Branghtons some confusion on what is clearly their first visit.

standards were slipping Hogan, in *The London Stage*, p. ccxiv, notes a number of contemporary complaints at declining standards of dress in the pit, most notably the wearing of enormous hats and bonnets, which obscured a view of the ballet. (Interestingly, not being able to see the opera does not seem a ground for complaint.)

the cheapest tickets See Dizikes, *Opera in America*, p. 44.

The Italian opera would instantly Quoted in Petty, *Italian Opera*, p. 41.

He was modestly paid Alfred Loewenberg, in 'Lorenzo Da Ponte in London', in the *Music Review*, Vol. IV (1943), p. 174, quotes an anonymous pamphlet entitled *Veritas* which gives Da Ponte's annual salary as £250 (60 guineas of which, Da Ponte says in his memoirs, he had to forfeit in his first year as it had already been paid in advance to the sacked Badini). To this was added – as it had been in Vienna – 'the prerequisite of opera books, estimated at £500 per annum'. This may be compared with fees paid to the leader of the orchestra Federici (£350) and the ballet master Noverre (£600). The star singers Banti and Morichelli received £1,400 each, though Milhous disputes this amount for Banti's first season (see Milhous et al., *Italian Opera*, II, p. 211.)

245 **tinkering with other men's libretti** The season opened on 11 January with Cimarosa's *Il matrimonio segreto*, libretto by Bertati. Da Ponte was probably not involved, but on this and a number of other published London libretti, his name is given as 'Poete'. This is misleading and is probably merely an attempt to establish his new position. His first season at the King's Theatre was as follows:

> *I contadini bizzarri*; composer Sarti; librettist Tommaso Grandi ('Signor N.') with additions and alterations by Da Ponte, premiere on 1 February.
>
> *Il capriccio drammatico*; Cimarosa; Diodati with additions and alterations

by Da Ponte, in a double bill with:

Il Don Giovanni [*Don Giovanni Tenorio*], Gazzaniga and Sarti, Federici and Guglielmi; Bertati with additions and alterations by Da Ponte, premiere on 1 March.

La bella pescatrice, Guglielmi; Zini with additions and alterations by Da Ponte, premiere on 18 March.

La Semiramide, Bianchi; Moretti, based on Voltaire, with additions and alterations by Da Ponte, premiere on 26 April.

Il burbero di buon cuore, Martín y Soler, with additional material from Trento, Ferrari, Pozzi and Haydn; Da Ponte, based on his original Vienna libretto, premiere on 17 May.

La serva padrona, Paisiello; Federico with a sonnet by Da Ponte, benefit for Banti on 29 May.

La frascatana, originally Paisiello; considerable amendments and additions by Da Ponte, benefit for Morichelli on 5 June.

La vittoria, cantata by Paisiello; Da Ponte, performed in honour of Lord Howe's victory of the 'Glorious First of June' on 23 June.

See Loewenberg, 'Lorenzo Da Ponte in London', pp. 175ff.

in bestial preference *Memorie*, p. 245. Nancy Storace had also championed Mozart in London. She first sang a Mozart aria in 1789 when, newly arrived from Vienna, she included '*Crudel perchè finora*' from *Figaro* into Gazzaniga's opera *La vendemmia*. A performance of *La villanella rapita* in 1790, again with Storace as lead singer, had included four Mozart pieces, though his name was not mentioned in the published libretto (and misprinted as 'Hogart' in some newspaper reviews). English versions of Mozart arias were also occasionally given as part of other operas at Drury Lane. See Alfred Loewenberg, 'Some stray notes on Mozart', in *Music and Letters*, Vol. XXIV (1943), pp. 164–5. Loewenberg makes the point that the 'Catalogue Song' in the London *Don Giovanni Tenorio* was the Da Ponte–Mozart one and not that of Bertati–Gazzaniga. See Loewenberg, 'Lorenzo Da Ponte in London', p. 176.

practicable hell *Morning Chronicle*, 3 March 1794; quoted in Smith, *Italian Opera*, p. 29, who also mentions hi-jinks at the funeral procession.

special venom See Petty, *Italian Opera*, pp. 80–1.

The Italian gentry *Morning Chronicle*, 3 March 1794; quoted in *ibid*., p. 28.

246 **to take a hatchet** See Petty, *Italian Opera*, pp. 40–1.

an asp, a fury Da Ponte's views on Banti and Morichelli are given in *Memorie*, p. 246.

conversing *mezza voce* From a contemporary newspaper report, quoted in Smith, *Italian Opera*, p. 56.

ecstasy to listen to Quoted in Collins (ed.), *Travels in Britain*, p. 156n.

Her natural powers Earl Mount Edgcumbe, *Musical Reminiscences* (fourth edition), (John Andrews, 1834) p. 79. When she died, Banti bequeathed her larynx to the University of Bologna.

247 **tiny and very ugly** Quoted in Hodges, *Lorenzo Da Ponte*, p. 140.

An anonymous pamphlet Quoted in Milhous et al., *Italian Opera*, II, p. 212.

her secret young Adonises *Memorie*, p. 259.

most Saturday-night performances This is verified by performance records; see Milhous et al., *Italian Opera*, II, p. 226. Michael Kelly pointed out the enormous difference in attendance and prestige between Saturdays and Tuesdays, noting that the same opera with the same singers might take £500 at the doors on a Saturday, and just £60 on a Tuesday, 'such is the power of fashion'; see Kelly, *Reminiscences*, p. 251.

the more bitter *Memorie*, p. 246.

Gaetano Andreozzi had Related in Kelly, *Reminiscences*, p. 71.

idols of the public *Memorie*, p. 246.

God help you See *Memorie*, p. 248. For details of the debuts, see Loewenberg, in 'Lorenzo Da Ponte in London', pp. 177–8.

248　**gave exquisite delight** See Petty, *Italian Opera*, p. 300; and Smith, *Italian Opera*, p. 29.

groundshift in London opera See Milhous et al., *Italian Opera*, II, pp. 210ff. Banti earned at least £1, for her first season, though some sources put her fee at £1,400 or £1,500 (*ibid.*, p. 211).

was but poorly supported See Mount Edgcumbe, *Musical Reminiscences*, pp. 80–1. One possible reason for the dearth of good singers was recruitment difficulties as a result of the revolutionary wars with France, which affected travel by sea and slowed communications. The theatre had tried, but failed, to attract better male singers. As a result only one *opera seria* was staged that season. See Milhous et al., *Italian Opera*, II, pp. 209–11.

No opera ever had See Mount Edgcumbe, *Musical Reminiscences*, p. 80.

Lord Howe's victory Lord Howe, commander of the British fleet, had captured six ships in a significant victory over the French on 1 June 1794. Haydn notes that the whole city was illuminated three nights in a row, and that in a stifling hot June, celebrations got out of hand. People fired off guns in the street and windows were broken. Haydn remarked a popular toast at the time was to quote the first two words of the third psalm: 'Lord! How' [are they increased that trouble me!] See Robbins Landon, *Notebooks of Joseph Haydn*, p. 287 and p. 300.

with as perfect articulation . . . From the ever-admiring *Morning Chronicle*, 4 June 1794; quoted in Smith, *Italian Opera*, p. 30. Less ardent observers noted that however many times she sang the anthem, she never appeared to know more than the first verse, and even then had often to be prompted.

debut in Martín y Soler's Not *La scuola di maritati* as Da Ponte mistakenly states. He confuses the chronology at this point in his memoirs. See Loewenberg, 'Lorenzo Da Ponte in London', pp. 179–81.

249　**a duet by Haydn** *Ibid.*, p. 178; and Hodges, *Lorenzo Da Ponte*, p. 142.

at Da Ponte's instigation An unidentified newspaper cutting in the *King's Theatre Cuttings Book* (Vol. II) maintains that Martín was brought to London by his friendship with Nancy Storace. All three (Da Ponte, Kelly and Storace) probably were of influence in attracting him to the King's Theatre.

remaining in Sherrard Street Deduced from the fact that in a letter of 25 August 1795, Da Ponte does not inform Casanova of any change of address, having told him in an earlier letter (9 November 1793) to write to 16 Sherrard Street. In the same letter Da Ponte writes that Martín's nine-month stay had cost him forty guineas, part of which might be explained by rent on his room that the Da Pontes as roomkeepers might otherwise have earned. Martín's complaint was that his stay with the Da Pontes had cost too much, which still argues the same point.

a precondition of his appointment Da Ponte points this out in his letter to Casanova of 25 August 1795, and given that Martín had more success with him as librettist than with any other, there seems no reason to doubt the case.

La scuola di maritati Also known as *La moglie corretta*, *Gli sposi in contrasto*, and today most commonly as *La capricciosa corretta*. See Loewenberg, 'Lorenzo Da Ponte in London', p. 180.

did wonders Review in *The Times*, 29 January 1795; quoted in Smith, *Italian Opera*, p. 33.

many pieces *Morning Chronicle*, 28 January 1795 and 2 February 1795; quoted in Petty, *Italian Opera*, p. 299 and p. 300.

a first-night Italian cabal Mentioned by Da Ponte in *Memorie*, p. 250. Michael Kelly suffered similar opposition from an Italian claque jealous of foreigners' encroachment on their turf, when he stepped in to replace the castrato Neri in a performance of *Semiramide* the following month. The *Morning Chronicle* of 9 February reports:

> A little miscreant Italian cabal, who have endeavoured to derange the performances of this Theatre, attempted to hiss Mr Kelly, who had generously come from Drury Lane Theatre, that the serious Opera might not be interrupted. The liberal feelings of the English subscribers overpowered the noise, and Mr Kelly received the applause which his spirit deserved.

Quoted in Milhous et al., *Italian Opera*, II, p. 227.

250 **Nancy was pregnant again** In his letter to Casanova of 25 August 1795, Da Ponte asks his friend permission to name their second-born after him, but no further mention of the child is made. Nancy next gave birth three years later. She appears also to have lost a child soon after they came to London, before Louisa was born.

was written on an Isle of Ice *Memorie*, p. 251. Da Ponte relates the events around the break-up in *Memorie*, pp. 250–1, and in his 25 August letter to Casanova.

a lot of old stuff In his 1795 notebook; in Robbins Landon, *Notebooks of Joseph Haydn*, p. 301.

the last mainpiece Apart from the two Martin operas in the 1794–95 season, Da Ponte no doubt also wrote the words for an intermezzo by Martín, entitled *Le nozze de contadini spagnuoli*, performed on 28 May, the second night of *L'isola del piacere* (the composer's benefit performance). Da Ponte also provided the original poetry for 'Six Italian Canzonetts', composed for a private commission by Martín, and translated into English in 1795. See Loewenberg, 'Lorenzo Da Ponte in London', pp. 180–1.

251 **The following three seasons** Da Ponte's new contributions to the opera in the 1796–98 seasons were:

> *La bella Arsene*, composed by Monsigny with additional material by Mazzinghi; libretto 'improved by Laurence Da Ponte'; premiere on

12 December 1795 (start of the 1796 season).

Ifegenia in Tauride, Gluck; libretto by Guillard, translated by Da Ponte; 7 April 1796.

Antigona, Francesco Bianchi; libretto attributed to Da Ponte; 24 May 1796.

Il tesoro, Mazzinghi; Da Ponte; 14 June 1796.

Zemira e Azore, Grétry; original libretto by Marmontel, translated by Da Ponte; 23 July 1796.

Il consiglio imprudente, Bianchi; Da Ponte based on a comedy by Goldoni; 20 December 1796.

Evelina, Sacchini; Guillard's libretto translated by Da Ponte; 10 January 1797.

A cantata, with music by Bianchi; part of a gala event to celebrate the victory of Admiral Jervis off Cape St Vincent (an adaptation of the cantata Da Ponte had originally written for the royal wedding of the Prince of Wales and Caroline of Brunswick); 11 March 1797.

L'arbore di Diana, Martín y Soler; Da Ponte; 18 April 1787.

Nina, or *Love has turned her Head*, Paisiello; adaptation of libretto attributed to Da Ponte; 27 April 1797.

Merope, Bianchi; Da Ponte; 10 June 1797.

La scuola de maritati, Martín y Soler; Da Ponte; 23 January 1798.

Cinna, Bianchi; 'the greatest part' of the poetry by Da Ponte; 20 February 1798.

La Cifra, Salieri; Da Ponte; 10 March 1798.

See Loewenberg, 'Lorenzo Da Ponte in London', pp. 181–5.

very ably translated From an unidentified clipping; quoted in Petty, *Italian Opera*, p. 313.

stale, flat and unprofitable *Monthly Mirror*, quoting *Hamlet* in June 1797; in *ibid.*, p. 316.

as this lady's figure *Monthly Mirror*, April 1797; quoted in Smith, *Italian Opera*, pp. 43–4.

he will give us *Morning Chronicle*, 28 November 1796; quoted in *ibid.*, p. 42.

strain on his meagre income Da Ponte wrote to Casanova on 25 August 1795 that cabals at the theatre had caused his income to be reduced. This does not appear to have applied to his annual salary (still £250 for 1795–6, according to Smith, *Italian Opera*, p. 36), but might well have been a deduction in other benefits, such as from book sales, which would then add additional weight to his decision to publish libretti himself.

252   **a 90 per cent soar** See Burton, *The Georgians at Home*, p. 206.

eight fine Cream-Coloured Horses From the diary of J. Woodforde; quoted in *ibid.*, p. 206.

debut as a publisher See Zagonel (ed.), *Bibliografia*, p. 39.

Nancy also began Wives commonly contributed to the family income, often, where appropriate, in some work connected to their husband's. See George, *London Life*, p. 168.

one of the most beautiful The description comes from what was evidently a press release (printed in varying forms in the *Oracle*, the *St James's Chronicle* and the *Star* in 1791) for the first opening of the concert-room/coffee-room (see note below). Quoted in Price et al., *Italian Opera*, I, p. 567.

for some years been inoperative The coffee-room served as a concert room on non-opera nights. When it was first built in 1791, Taylor's cavalier manner in demanding extra money from box-subscribers to fund its lighting led to a revolt, which kept it closed for coffee (though still functioning as a concert hall) from 1791/2 until 1797, when it would appear that it was again in use for refreshment on opera nights. See Milhous et al., *Italian Opera*, II, p. 207 and pp. 237–8; and for a report of the re-opening, Smith, *Italian Opera*, pp. 40–1.

The paintings and decorations From an unidentified newspaper clipping, dated 8 January 1797; in the *King's Theatre Cuttings Book* (Vol. II).

253 **This Coffee Room** From the *Morning Chronicle*, 9 January 1797; quoted in Smith, *Italian Opera*, p. 41. 'Puppies in pantaloons' from an unidentified newspaper clipping in the *King's Theatre Cuttings Book* (Vol. II).

Fanny Burney's Mrs Harrel From Fanny Burney's *Cecilia*; quoted in Hogan, *The London Stage*, p. cli.

heave-ho of carriages Newspaper advertisements for operas during the period frequently contained the plea: 'The Nobility are earnestly entreated to give directions to their servants to set down and take up at the Theatre with the horses' heads towards Pall Mall. The Doors in Market Lane for chairs only.' See the *King's Theatre Cuttings Book* (Vol. II).

several parties kept up Unidentified cutting for 24 July 1797; see *ibid*.

Lorenzo had estimated In his letter to Casanova of 25 August 1795; see *Lettere*, p. 185.

on various matters *Memorie*, p. 255.

bill of exchange A bill of exchange was a promissory note for a specific sum to be paid without interest on a specific date sometime in the future.

254 **the dear little infants** *Monthly Mirror*, June 1797; quoted in Smith, *Italian Opera*, p. 41.

a very smooth young man Da Ponte relates the incident in *Memorie*, pp. 256–7.

a sum approaching See *Memorie*, pp. 257ff. For some time commentators thought Da Ponte's tales of his embroilment in Taylor's chaotic financial affairs was a wild exaggeration, but, as Milhous points out, most of what Da Ponte has to say about his involvement is extensively documented in lawsuits of the time. See Milhous et al., *Italian Opera*, II, pp. 248–9.

left to himself *Memorie*, p. 260. The observation could equally apply to Lorenzo himself.

255 **I a poet** *Ibid.*, p. 256.

Chapter Fourteen

256 **I heard someone cry** *Memorie*, pp. 261–64.

257 **(once again widowed)** Orsola Pasqua died in 1790.

258   **local assistant police commissioner** See Hodges, *Lorenzo Da Ponte*, p. 155.

    Venice shocked him See Norwich, *Paradise of Cities*, pp. 1–17.

    As I turned my eyes *Memorie*, pp. 269–75.

259   **left Venice before dawn** Da Ponte gives as his reason for not returning to Ceneda that there was conflict imminent near by between Austrian and French forces (see *Memorie*, pp. 283–4), but as Hodges points out, there were no troops in the area at the time (see Hodges, *Lorenzo Da Ponte*, p. 155).

    his Ceneda family His father Gaspare died in 1806.

260   **renowned dramatist Vittorio Alfieri** Da Ponte recounts a meeting in London with Alfieri in his introduction to the American edition of *Il Mezenzio*, but Hodges suggest that this meeting must have been in Florence, as Alfieri and Da Ponte were not in London simultaneously (see *ibid.*, p. 156).

261   **also young Felice** Felice's story is unravelled by Giampaolo Zagonel in 'Felice Da Ponte, *Il figlio naturale che il librettista di Mozart ebbe a Vienna*', *Il Flaminio*, 8, 1995, pp. 51ff. Apart from the tangential reference to 'a lad of the same age who was with me', Da Ponte never once mentions Felice in his memoirs, though names him in two letters to Paolo, one on 29 November 1798 and the other on 18 February 1800. The documents uncovered by Zagonel, and reproduced in his *Il Flaminio* article, include the statement Felice (said to be twelve or thirteen years old) made to the head of police on his arrest in December 1797, which begins with the words: 'My name is Felice Da Ponte, son of Lorenzo and Annetta. My father is located in London, where he is a poet with a stipend: my mother stays with a lady in Vienna, actually a small country home in that area. My uncle Agostino Da Ponte, my father's brother, took me with him from Vienna where I was born, taking me from my mother's arms five years ago by promising her he would take me to my father in England. He took me to Italy, and kept me at his side, bringing me to Lodi, to Milan, to Mantua, and then even to this city [Venice]'.

    splutters and snores *Memorie*, p. 293.

262   **a number of bucks** Goede, *Foreigner's Opinion*, pp. 115–16.

    Younger men discarded wigs For the changes in fashion see James Laver, *Costume and Fashion*, (Thames & Hudson, 1969), pp. 148–53.

263   **gaudy and inane phraseology** In his 'Advertisement' to the first (1798) edition of *Lyrical Ballads*, and elaborated in his preface to subsequent editions in 1800 and 1802.

    His successor as See Loewenberg, 'Lorenzo Da Ponte in London', p. 185.

    The abysmal failure On the failure of Allegranti and Damiani, see Hodges, *Lorenzo Da Ponte*, p. 158.

    morning of his fiftieth birthday Chronology in this part of Da Ponte's memoirs is particularly confused, and at one point he appears to set the date of his arrest on his fiftieth birthday (10 March 1799), though later he writes he had never been jailed 'in all the fifty-two years of my life'. Records in Ian Maxted's revised *The London Book Trades 1775–1800* (available via www.devon.gov.uk) show his bankruptcy and subsequent Certificate of Conformity to have occurred in February and May of 1800 respectively. Hodges places his 10 March arrest in 1800, but it is arguable that Da Ponte's order of events (arrests preceding declaration of bankruptcy) offers a more feasible chronology. This confusion has led some to doubt the veracity of Da Ponte's statements of the extraordinary way Taylor ran the King's Theatre by means of juggling bills of exchange (and other more nefarious dealings), but as Milhous et al. point out, Da Ponte's claims are supported by reference to lawsuits of the time. See Milhous et al., *Italian Opera*, II, pp. 248–9.

264 **member for Leominster** See Nalbach, *King's Theatre*, p. 95, citing Sheppard's *Survey of London*. Milhous et al. have 1798.

not in her hands *Memorie*, p. 301.

moving his press See Zagonel (ed.), *Bibliografia*, pp. 39ff; and Ian Maxted, *The London Book Trades 1775–1800* (via www.devon.gov.uk).

Corri and Dussek Domenico Corri and Jan Ladislav Dussek. See entries in *ibid.*; and Hodges, *Lorenzo Da Ponte*, pp. 159–60. In his memoirs Da Ponte transfers his mishaps with Corri and Dussek to 1803 (by which time Corri had already been declared bankrupt, and freed, and Dussek had fled the country). Da Ponte clearly had dealings with Corri after Corri's bankruptcy in 1800, as he rented shop space from him, so it is not unlikely that Corri also contributed to his financial problems in 1803/4.

If it had not been Letter to Paolo Da Ponte, 18 February 1800; *Lettere*, p. 193.

265 **without property, without employment** *Memorie*, p. 301.

266 **fashionable lounging places** *The Picture of London for 1802*, p. 27.

Lord Douglas and Lady Devonshire *Memorie*, p. 305.

thought Da Ponte a genius See Hodges, *Lorenzo Da Ponte*, p. 162.

267 **too filthy** *Memorie*, p. 315.

Michael Kelly began to publish opera music Kelly set up shop in 1802, but went bankrupt in 1811. Da Ponte moved to 28 Haymarket in 1803, renting from Corri (according to the *Memorie*) first 'part of his shop, which was a very large one, and, in the end, the whole building'. See Maxted, *London Book Trades*; Smith, *Italian Opera*, p. 63; and *Memorie*, p. 309.

Nor had he entirely lost Da Ponte's final contributions to opera in London were:

> *Angelina*, composed by Salieri; libretto by Defranceschi with 'many alterations' by Da Ponte; 29 December 1801.
>
> *Mitridate*, Nasolini; Sografi's original libretto amended by Da Ponte; 23 February 1802.
>
> *Armida*, Bianchi; Da Ponte; 1 June 1802.
>
> *La grotta di Calipso*, Winter; Da Ponte; 31 May 1803.
>
> *Il trionfo dell'amor fraterno*, Winter; Da Ponte; 22 March 1804.
>
> *Il ratto di Proserpina*, Winter; Da Ponte; 31 May 1804.
>
> [Also possibly *Zaira*, Winter; Da Ponte; 19 January 1805.]

See Loewenberg, 'Lorenzo Da Ponte in London', pp. 187–8.

If a modern Italian Opera *The Times*, 2 June 1802; quoted in Smith, *Italian Opera*, p. 66.

268 **her voice sweet**. See Mount Edgcumbe, *Musical Reminiscences*, pp. 90ff.

his last three operas See Loewenberg, 'Lorenzo Da Ponte in London', pp. 187–8. Loewenberg points out that the libretto for one later opera by Winter (produced in January 1805) was on one occasion in 1811 attributed to him, but there is no further evidence for this.

she soars above *The Times*, 6 February 1804; quoted in Smith, *Italian Opera*, p. 73.

grand triumph Kelly, *Reminiscences*, p. 251.

beginning to lose See Nalbach, *King's Theatre*, pp. 94–5.

269   **a hand of ice** *Memorie*, p. 325.

Chapter Fifteen

273   **the 'uphill' passage** See Collins (ed.), *Travels in Britain*, p. 156.

Columbia **made the crossing** Da Ponte's differing journey times are given in various early versions of his reminiscences. True details of the voyage and of the *Columbia* and its captain were tracked down by Arthur Livingston, and are given in his annotations to the English edition of Da Ponte's memoirs (see *Memoirs*, pp. 337–8). The account here is based on Livingston's findings, on the *Memorie*, and on the *Compendium of the Life of Lorenzo Da Ponte*, which the poet published in New York in 1807 (which differs in some details from the version in the *Memorie*).

a curious collection The prices as assigned by customs officials are given by Livingston in his English edition of *Memoirs*, pp. 337–8.

hid on board In the *Memorie* Da Ponte gives his departure date as 5 April, while records show it to have been two days later.

a right name Quoted in Marcus Rediker, *Between the Devil and the Deep Blue Sea* (Cambridge University Press, 1987), p. 31.

274   *New American Practical Navigator* This enabled navigators to calculate Greenwich time (and thus establish longitude and latitude) simply by using a sextant and the tables of *The Nautical Almanac*. It became known as 'the seaman's Bible'. See Collins (ed.), *Travels in Britain*, p. 156.

the foremost ship See Aspinwell's diary entries reproduced in *ibid.*, p. 49 (punctuation modernized).

Felt seasick this morning For the experiences of bad weather see *ibid.*, pp. 44ff; also Rediker, *Deep Blue Sea*, p. 161; and Philip Edwards, *The Story of the Voyage* (Cambridge University Press, 1994), p. 182.

275   **like the vilest sailors** *Memorie*, p. 331. Da Ponte quite possibly exaggerates, though he shows unreserved venom for Hayden in both *Memorie* and *Compendium of the life of Lorenzo Da Ponte* (I. Riley, 1807).

they drank and gambled Da Ponte is silent about this in his memoirs, though in the *Compendium* includes the curious line (following an account of early losses of money in America): 'A glass of wine, given to me with affected compassion by a needy sharper on board the fatal Nantucket vessel, cost me three hundred [dollars] more.' This would appear to apply to gambling aboard the *Columbia* (which is how Livingston reads it). Da Ponte does mention (in the *Compendium*, p. 17) that Nancy was obliged to 'pay several dollars in duties upon some books and a box of violin strings' (which, as Livingston discovered, were the only items admitted through customs free of duty). 'Mr. Richard Edwards' paid the $32.31 due on the violin, carpet and tea-urn.

I feel as if Letter of 15 June 1794; quoted in Henry F. May, *The Enlightenment in America* (Oxford University Press, 1976), p. 220.

276   **I well knew** From *Compendium*, pp. 13–15.

At Philadelphia In *The Rambler in North America* (1835); quoted in Philip Stevick, *Imagining Philadelphia* (University of Pennsylvania Press, 1996), pp. 22–3.

277   **something which shows** *permanency* In his diary for 1834; quoted in *ibid.*, p. 155.

a general air of sombreness Lieutenant Colonel A. M. Maxwell, in *A Run through the United States* (1841); quoted in *ibid.*, p. 147.

house of Captain Collet See Livingston's annotation to *Memoirs*, p. 327, p. 340.

Nancy had moved Da Ponte's account is contradictory regarding Nancy. At one point he writes that she was on the eve of departure to rejoin him in London when he arrived; at another that the family were worried that he had been aboard the *Jupiter* (he calls it, the *Jove*) when it was sunk by an iceberg in April (concern that indicates they must have known he was coming). The fact that, by his own admission, he did not know their address or even that they were in New York argues that his arrival was a surprise. Letters were expensive to send, and would have taken a good two months to cross the Atlantic. Da Ponte's departure from London was so hasty that there would have been little point in his sending any notice of his arrival.

Bones of me Quoted in Lambert, *Fortunate Traveller*, p. 154. Lambert provides further details of stagecoach travel on pp. 152–4.

The soil is all clay Quoted in Bernier, *World in 1800*, p. 149 (spelling modernized).

278   **the people of New York** Irving, writing in collaboration with his brother William and James Kirk Paulding in *Salmagundi; or The Whim-Whams and Opinions of Launcelot Langstaff, Esq. & Others*, brought out in twenty paperbound numbers between 24 January 1807 and 25 January 1808; quoted in Edwin G. Burrows and Mike Wallace, *Gotham: A History of New York City to 1898* (Oxford University Press, 2000), p. 420.

There is no need *Memorie*, p. 333.

apparently her savings Da Ponte is quite clear in his memoirs, and even more so in the *Compendium*, that this is entirely Nancy's money, and so has nothing to do with profits from the book sales in London. In the *Compendium* he writes that the sum comprised not only money from her London savings, but also from work she had already been doing in America, as well as remittances from Louisa in London.

earned just $500 The various salaries and costs are given in Bernier, *World in 1800*, p. 128, p. 141, pp. 176–7, and p. 209.

population having more than doubled See Ric Burns and James Sanders, *New York* (Alfred A. Knopf, 2003), p. 43.

first impressions of activity The quotations are from François Marie

Perrin du Lac, 1801; John Lambert, 1807; Theodore Dwight, 1833; and John Bernard, 1797. All reproduced in Bayrd Still's compilation of writing on the city, *Mirror for Gotham*. The subsequent description of New York is based on that of Lambert and of Bernard.

279 **John Jacob Astor** German-born Astor began buying real estate in 1800. By the time of his death in 1848 he was worth $25 million; the second-richest man in America was then worth $10 million. See Burns and Sanders, *New York*, p. 51.

one of the most rucketing In a letter to his sister, 29 August 1847; quoted in Burns and Sanders, *New York*, p. 61.

a frantic love Quoted in Burns and Sanders, *New York*, p. 51.

280 **to avoid yellow fever** See Burrows and Wallace, *Gotham*, pp. 358–9. Some 27, residents fled New York in 1805, most to Greenwich Village, though this was to be the last outbreak for fourteen years. Da Ponte names his partner in the *Memorie*, p. 334.

Sometimes deceived *Compendium*, pp. 17–19.

as far as the Italian language *Memorie*, p. 336.

only 438 Italians See Howard Marroro, 'Italians in New York During the First Half of the Nineteenth Century', in *New York History*, XVI (July 1940), p. 317. Marroro also cites the *Evening Post* advertisements.

281 **from its united sweetness** From a discourse Da Ponte delivered in English in New York in February 1821, published in Italian as *Sull' Italia. Discorso Apologetico di Lorenzo Da Ponte in Riposta alla Lettera dell' Avvocato Carlo Phillips, al Re D'Inghilterra*; reported in John W. Francis, *Old New York: Reminiscences of the Past Sixty Years* (Charles Roe, 1858) (pub. 1858), p. 262.

in December 1806 In the *Memorie*, Da Ponte dates his first meeting with Moore as the beginning of December 1807, but this cannot be correct as Moore was undoubtedly present at Da Ponte's birthday celebrations on 10 March 1807 (his presence is recorded in the *Conversazione* published in 1807; see below). In the *Compendium*, Da Ponte implies that he was visiting and teaching in New York before the family finally moved in early 1807, so the encounter with Moore must rather have been in December 1806.

He had been counting *Memorie*, p. 337–8.

282 **the best-known verse** A point made by Burrows and Wallace in *Gotham*, p. 463. They argue that Moore's poem was influential in the transmutation of St Nicholas into Santa Claus, and the development of the cosy, domestic American Christmas.

group of young gentleman See *Memorie*, p. 338. A fourth member of the group was one E. Pendleton, whom Livingston suggests is Edmund Pendleton II of Virginia.

education of their daughters See Burrows and Wallace, *Gotham*, pp. 376–7.

American involvement *Ibid.*, pp. 410–12.

283 *Agli Stati Uniti d'America* Da Ponte posted his poem back to Paolo, who published it in London in 1808 – the last evidence we have that Paolo was alive. See Zagonel (ed.), *Bibliografia*, p. 51.

The Picture of New-York. See Burrows and Wallace, *Gotham*, p. 385.

A new spirit See Nelson Frederick Adkins, *Fitz-Greene Halleck: An Early Knickerbocker Wit and Poet* (Yale University Press, 1930), pp. 1–44; and the introduction to Bruce I. Granger's and Martha Hartzog's edition of Washington Irving's *Salmagundi* on Irving, *Salmagundi*, and the literary clubs.

284 **home on Partition Street** On moving back to New York, the Da Pontes lived first at 29 Partition Street (later Fulton Street), later moving to somewhere on the Bowery (1808–9), then to 247 Duane Street. See Livingston's annotations to *Memoirs*, p. 396.

Advertisements for their Manhattan Academy See Hodges, *Lorenzo Da Ponte*, p. 175. The reference to visits of inspection by Rev. Magee is one of many similar, and comes from the *New York Spectator* for 19 November 1825.

takes the glory See 'Memorie de Lorenzo Da Ponte', in *Antologia*, p. 80.

285 **the hours passed** In a letter to Da Ponte, quoted in his memoirs; see Russo, *Da Ponte*, p. 123. Recalled in Samuel Ward's obituary article in the *New-York Mirror*, 29 September 1838.

how the schoolgirls Brander Matthews, recording his mother's recollections in *These Many Years: Recollections of a New Yorker* (Charles Scribner's Sons, 1917), p. 33.

day and evening assemblies *Memorie*, p. 340.

There is no doubt Hodges, *Lorenzo Da Ponte*, p. 176.

286 **neither as tender** *Memorie*, p. 343.

John Grahl had moved Da Ponte's and the Grahls' time in Sunbury was extensively researched by Arthur Livingston early last century. Information about the Grahls and others in Sunbury is derived here from Livingston's footnotes to the English edition of the *Memoirs*, together with an old typed copy of an extended version of those notes held at the Northumberland Historical Society in Sunbury (filed anonymously, but clearly by Livingston), and from George G. Struble, 'Lorenzo Da Ponte Our Neglected Genius', *Northumberland County Historical Society: Proceedings*, XVI (1968)

287 **not at all, at Sunbury** *Memorie*, pp. 352–3.

One arrives at *Memorie*, pp. 347–8.

almost all amiable *Ibid.*, p. 348.

On Peter Grahl's advice Peter Grahl is surely the 'Dr. G—' Da Ponte refers to in his memoirs. He was considered one of the leading physicians in the region. See Struble, 'Lorenzo Da Ponte', p. 76.

house beside the river Livingston notes that the house was on Water Street, officially known as Broadway since 1808, later Front Street. See *Memoirs*, p. 353n.

288 **college for young gentlemen** A copy of the proposal, in Da Ponte's hand, is held in the library of Penn State University in Pennsylvania.

nightly *conversaziones*, country dances *Memorie*, p. 348.

a drinker, gambler, schemer *Ibid.*, p. 356.

289 **the finest edifice** *Ibid.*, p. 357.

a good figure Quoted in Hodges, *Lorenzo Da Ponte* p. 180n; and Struble, *Lorenzo Da Ponte*, p. 85.

290 **boarded in Chestnut Street** See Livingston in *Memoirs*, p. 367n.

making off with stoves Stoves, rather than open hearths for heating, and a pianoforte (mentioned a few lines earlier as part of the Da Pontes' household furniture) were at the time considered blatant signals of wealth. See Burrows and Wallace, *Gotham*, p. 464.

court case that followed Wads of frantically written depositions are held in the library of Penn State University in Pennsylvania, as well as a printed broadside, littered with exclamation marks, in which Da Ponte protests his treatment.

291   **Nancy herself intervened** In a letter of 26 April 1817; a copy is held in the library of Penn State University.

292   **a curious, sorrowful poem** See Struble, 'Lorenzo Da Ponte', p. 85.

wrote urgently to Nathaniel Moore Letter of 26 September 1818; in *Lettere*, p. 207.

not twice but twelve times Da Ponte to Nathaniel Moore, 2 October 1818; *ibid.*, p. 212.

Would to God Letter of 2 October 1818; *ibid.*, p. 212.

293   **to the cultivation** *Memorie*, p. 371.

Chapter Sixteen

294   **Like Washington Irving's** The parallel between Rip Van Winkle's experience and the changing cityscape of New York is drawn by Burns and Sanders in *New York*, p. 61. For Manhattan's new grid see Burns and Sanders in *New York*, pp. 52–5; and Burrows and Wallace, *Gotham*, pp. 420–2 and 447–8.

Steamboats now ferried passengers The world's first practicable steamboat had been built by a New Yorker (transplanted from Philadelphia), Robert Fulton, in 1807. It looked like 'a backwoods sawmill mounted on a scow and set on fire', but by Da Ponte's return less-frightening steam-ferries were crossing the Hudson.

295   **a miraculous enterprise** *Memorie*, p. 394.

poems he wrote Da Ponte attached two tender poems to his daughters to the second edition of his translation of Byron's *The Prophecy of Dante*, which he published in 1822, and wrote a series of poems on Nancy's death.

small house on Chapel Street The Da Pontes lived at 54 Chapel Street, with a separate classroom, probably, at 17 Jay Street. See Livingston's note in *Memoirs*, p. 396.

to deprive [Joseph] Letter to William Harris, 2 November 1819; in *Lettere*, p. 216 (with misspellings not present in the original). The Reverend Mr Harris had succeeded Bishop Moore as president. In the letter Da Ponte mentions Livingston (probably John R. Livingston, as Da Ponte later taught his daughters) and Clement Moore as willing to help out with credit – though this contravened a college regulation. Some way around the impasse was found, as Joseph took up his place in the autumn.

296   **landlord of five** See Burrows and Wallace, *Gotham*, p. 484.

keep alive a true feeling See Marroro, 'Italians in New York', p. 318.

a swarm of exiles *Memorie*, p. 381.

a defrocked priest See Hodges, *Lorenzo Da Ponte*, pp. 183–4.

297 **truly a good man** See 'Memorie di Lorenzo Da Ponte', in *Antologia*, p. 80.

a *canzone* It is now lost. See Zagonel (ed.), *Bibliografia*, p. 51.

298 **which he delivered** Da Ponte writes that he had the *Discorso* 'translated into English' (probably by a family member), though it is clear he also delivered the oration in English – Dr Francis remembers it as such, and a large audience would hardly have listened 'with delighted attention' to a discourse they could not understand. Da Ponte's facility with English is not known. His handwriting in the letter he sent to William Harris in 1819 appears stilted, as if laboriously copied out, yet earlier letters to Charles Hall in 1818 and 1819, also in English, are as fluently scripted as those in Italian. None contains any serious errors. A letter in 1832 to Robert Hall contains only two errors (an incorrect preposition and 'hair' for 'heir'), and would seem to indicate Da Ponte's near fluent control of the language. In his annotation to the incident where Da Ponte meets Clement Moore, Arthur Livingston notes that Da Ponte spoke English fluently, 'but with a trace of defect in his speech – if with a foreign accent', though Livingston does not provide a source for this and his research into Da Ponte, though exacting, is sometimes embellished. In any event, it would appear that Da Ponte's years in London and then in America had led to his having a better command of English than his time in Vienna ever improved his ability in 'the language that would frighten St Francis'.

one of the most numerous Cited in G. C. D. Odell, *Annals of the New York Stage*, II, (Columbia University Press, 1927) 1927, pp. 602–3.

the earnestness and animation Francis, *Old New York*, p. 262.

move to Greenwich Street It will be remembered that Nancy's real name was Ann. Livingston places the boarding house at 343 Greenwich Street, though it later appears to have moved to number 208, where it was still flourishing in 1840, run after Nancy's death by her daughter-in-law Cornelia Durant-Da Ponte. Burrows and Wallace in *Gotham*, p. 456, point out that, in the 1820s, Greenwich Street was one of 'the choicest addresses in town'.

299 **to her sister Eliza** See Adkins, *Fitz-Greene Halleck*, p. 142. The poem 'From the Italian' is to be found in the 1869 edition of *The Poetical Writings of Fitz-Greene Halleck*. Halleck also wrote a poem entitled 'The Dinner Party', which describes a gathering at the home of John R. Livingston, where 'The wine and the wit sparkled bright / 'Twas a frolic of soul and of reason' – verses that paint a delightful picture of just the sort of supper Da Ponte himself might have attended, though on this occasion he is not a guest.

Giacomo Ombrosi See *Lettere*, p. 224 n6; and *Memorie*, p. 389.

300 **I did not hesitate** *Ibid*., p. 389.

back in business Da Ponte writes that they at first traded from home, though in 1830 he opened a proper book store at 336 Broadway. See Henry Edward Krehbiel, *Chapters of Opera* (Henry Holt, 1909), p. 34.

I am old Letter to Girolamo Perucchini, 4 April 1822; see *Lettere*, p. 226.

301 **at Mrs Green's** A receipt for Italian tuition in class at Mrs Green's boarding school is held among the Da Pontiana at the Butler Library at Columbia University; Matthews in *These Many Years* (p. 32) mentions his mother's recollection of Italian lessons under Da Ponte at Miss McClenahan's; Mrs

Okill is mentioned in a pupil's translation of 'Memorie de Lorenzo Da Ponte', in *Antologia*. It would appear that Da Ponte taught at around eight different schools in the 1820s.

rule which [Da Ponte] From a letter written by a student, cited in the second edition of the *Memorie*; quoted in Hodges, *Lonenzo Da Ponte*, p. 197.

In April 1825 See *Lettere*, p. 234; also Olga Ragusa, 'Lorenzo Da Ponte at Columbia College', in *Atti del Convegno Lorenzo Da Ponte*, pp. 275ff.

Critique on certain passages Da Ponte's critique was published over three issues; the journal unfortunately lasted only a year. See Zagonel (ed.), *Bibliografia*, p. 57.

Professor of Italian Language The minutes of the Standing Committee that considered Da Ponte's request (held in the Butler Library at Columbia University) state Professor of Language, though 'Language' is scored out and replaced by 'Literature' in a different hand, with a different coloured ink (brown rather than black, later written over in black again). Da Ponte's own letter to William Harris, president of the college, on 11 November states quite clearly that Columbia has done him the honour of appointing him Professor of Italian *Language*, and he goes on to propose that he also simultaneously teaches literature. It may thus safely be taken that the initial appointment was for a teacher of language rather than literature.

twenty-three young men See letter to William Harris, 11 November 1825; in *Lettere*, p. 238.

302   **a shepherd without sheep** *Sum pastor sine ovibus . . . sacerdos sine templo / professor sine exemplo*. Given in full in *Memorie*, p. 416.

It seems to me Quoted in *ibid.*, p. 462; and in a slightly different version by Samuel Ward (who may well have had access to the original letter) in his *Sketch of the Life of Lorenzo Da Ponte*, (1838); quoted in Russo, *Da Ponte*, p. 123.

trippingly rhymed verse letter Letter to his sisters, probably 1825–6; see *Lettere*, pp. 245ff.

303   **The Garcias** See Vera Brodsky Lawrence, *Strong on Music*, I (University of Chicago Press, 1987), pp. xliv ff; Dizikes, *Opera in America*, pp. 3–12; Krehbiel, *Chapters of Opera*, pp. 25–30; Martin L. Sokol, *The New York City Opera* (Macmillan, 1981), pp. 20–4.

past a magnificent prime Many commentators say Garcia was past his best as a singer, but Krehbiel (*Chapters of Opera*, p. 26) points out that from 1823 to 1825 Garcia's salary in London increased from £260 to £1,250.

through the dust See Dizikes, *Opera in America*, p. 3.

I love the Andalusian frenzy *Ibid.*, p. 4.

the finest singer According to 'a most competent judge', most likely Dominic Lynch (see below) writing in the *American* in 1825; quoted in Lawrence, *Strong on Music*, p. xlv.

304   **first taste of Italian opera** Until 1825 New York's experience of opera had been of ballad operas, mangled English-language versions of European operas, and performances by a French company on tour from New Orleans.

Garcia's company had been lured Some commentators have it that Da

Ponte also had a hand in bringing Garcia to New York, but as Krehbiel (*Chapters of Opera*, p. 29) points out, Garcia made his debut in London three years after Da Ponte had left, and the two men did not know each other. In his memoirs, Da Ponte makes no such claim, and greets the news of Garcia's arrival with delight and surprise.

the greatest swell See Lawrence, *Strong on Music*, p. xlv.

A man was nobody Scoville, writing under the pen-name of Walter Barrett in the first volume of his *Old Merchants of New York* (1860); quoted in Lawrence, *Strong on Music*, p. xlv.

His voice, though not powerful See Julia Ward Howe, *Reminiscences*, p. 24.

highest and most costly entertainments *New York American*, 7 November 1825; quoted in Lawrence, *Strong on Music*, p. xliv.

[t]hey had not crossed Francis, *Old New York*, pp. 259–60.

305 **The story spread** Krehbiel, a meticulous researcher of Da Ponte's time in New York, writing (just) within living memory, considers this story to have the 'color of verity' (*Chapters of Opera*, p. 29).

Mrs Meigs's cook Deduced from information in *Memorie*, pp. 406–7, and a letter from William C. Bryant to Frances Bryant, 2 August 1826; in Thomas G. Voss (ed.), *The Letters of William Cullen Bryant* (Fordham University Press, 1975), pp. 209 and 210n. The former pupil's recollection of Aunt Sally's cuisine is quoted (without detailed attribution) in FitzLyon, *Da Ponte*, p. 263.

signing himself 'Musœus' See Lawrence, *Strong on Music*, p. xlvi.

306 **joined by 'Cinderella'** Also in the *American*, on 28 November, the day before the premiere; see *ibid.*, p. xlvii.

theatre-loving Knickerbockers In 1809, Irving published *A History of New York, from the Beginning of the World to the End of the Dutch Dynasty*, an account that mixed fact and fiction, purportedly written by one Dietrich Knickerbocker. The volume gave New York its nickname of 'Gotham', and it wasn't long before the oldest colonial families started calling themselves Knickerbockers.

jostled for place See Dizikes, *Opera in America*, p. 8.

307 **twenty-four-piece orchestra** *Ibid.*, p. 6.

one of the most full *New-York Spectator*, 30 November 1825. Other critical reaction is taken from the *American*, the *Evening Post* and the *Albion* for the same date.

Da Ponte was surely there It is inconceivable that Da Ponte would not have attended, though in his memoirs he mentions only a fifth performance of *Il barbiere*, to which he takes a group of students who have expressed scepticism about opera.

308 **'truly astonishing' singing** Dominick Lynch's letter and Henry Anderson's comments in the *New York Review and Athenaeum Magazine*; reproduced in Lawrence, *Strong on Music*, pp. xlix–l.

One Signora Bartoline Advertisement in the *American*, 30 November 1825.

309 **not much at home** Quoted in Nettl, *Other Casanova*, pp. 265–6.

William Cullen Bryant wrote Letter to Frances F. Bryant, 29 July 1826; in Voss (ed.), *Letters of William Cullen Bryant*, pp. 208–9.
Everything pleased *Memorie*, p. 405.

310   **nine months** See Dizikes, *Opera in America*, p. 11.

311   **Ballad opera and pastiche** See Krehbiel, *Chapters of Opera*, pp. 4ff; and Sokol, *New York City Opera*, p. 16–19.

too dull to keep us awake In an essay 'On Italian Opera', in *Westminster Magazine*, X (1782); quoted in Petty, *Italian Opera*, p. 70.

not only [was] there no sleeping *Memorie*, p. 412.

It's an insult See Dizikes, *Opera in America*, p. 9.

recitative is an affront Hone's diary entry is quoted in Krehbiel, *Chapters of Opera*, pp. 23–4.

312   **no harmonious influence Samuel** Ward, *Sketch of the Life of Lorenzo Da Ponte* (reprinted from the *New-York Mirror*, 29 September 1838), p. 18.

313   **It has sometimes been objected** Thomas Hastings, *Dissertation on Musical Taste* (Mason Bros, 1853), p. 235. Hastings is best known for his hymn 'Rock of Ages'.

opera in America became a battleground My views on opera in the New World have been much influenced by Dizikes's analysis in the opening chapters of *Opera in America*.

Chapter Seventeen

315   **the family also came** The Da Ponte household was at 342 Broadway, with the shop at no. 336. See Livingston's note to *Memoirs*, p. 396; and Krehbiel, *Chapters of Opera*, p. 34.

at cock's crow *Memorie*, p. 463.

316   **a Turk must do** Letter to Domenico Rossetti, 26 July 1828; in *Lettere*, p. 276.

as early as 1823 See Hodges, *Lorenzo Da Ponte*, pp. 206ff.

317   **acquired US citizenship** *Ibid.*, p. 211.

eligible . . . for nearly a decade A Naturalization Act, passed shortly before Da Ponte arrived in America, had increased the period of residence required for citizenship from five to fourteen years; nevertheless, Da Ponte had been eligible for citizenship since 1819. See Bernier, *World in 1800*, p. 161.

hiring the Bowery Theatre See Hodges, *Lorenzo Da Ponte*, p. 207.

318   **not made for the stage** *Memorie*, p. 458.

without even saying goodbye Lorenzo seems never to have become reconciled with Agostino, though in a letter of 30 September 1832, clearly in reply to a conciliatory one from Staffler and Giulia, he writes: 'I should indeed have been glad to have seen you and Giulia before you left, but what is done is done and cannot be undone.' See *Lettere*, p. 471.

You could not imagine Letter to Michele Colombo of 9 June 1832; *ibid.*, p. 468.

319   **in a collection of sonnets** *Versi composti da Lorenzo Da Ponte per la Morte*

D'Anna Celestina Ernestina, sua virtuosissima e adorata consorte was published in New York in 1832.

kind, candid, sincere From Sonnet IX; *ibid.*

wife, friend, companion From Sonnet III; *ibid.*

not only robbed me Letter to Gulian Verplanck, 18 March 1832; *Lettere*, p. 463.

wrote within forty-eight hours A copy of the letter is held in the library of Penn State University in Pennsylvania.

his surviving children moved See Livingston's notes to *Memoirs*, p. 396 and pp. 410–11; also Hodges, *Lorenzo Da Ponte*, p. 212. Cornelia continued to run the boarding house until Lorenzo L. Da Ponte's death in 1840, after which she moved to New Orleans (where her father lived).

his grandson Lorenzo III Lorenzo L. and Cornelia would have four children, though only one survived infancy: Lorenzo III (1827–36); John Durant (1829–94); Angelo Grahl (1836–7); Algernon Sydney (1839–40). Lorenzo L. Da Ponte died in 1840, after which the family moved to New Orleans. Fanny and Henry Anderson had six children: Henry C. (1832–9); Elbert Ellery (1833–1903); Fannie (1836–42); Arthur E. (who lived for two months in 1838); Edward H. (1840–86); Walden A. (1842–3). Fanny died while on a visit to Paris in 1844.

320   **Whenever the words** Ward, *Sketch of the Life*, p. 19.

     a head of Roman beauty *Ibid.*, p. 12.

     a good and well-regulated company Da Ponte's advice is taken from letters to Giacomo Montresor from 1 August 1831 through to 14 January 1832; *Lettere*, pp. 444–59. Much of it is reproduced in his pamphlet *Storia incredible, ma vera*, published in two parts in 1833 and translated into English as *A History of the Italian Opera Company, Imported into America by Giacomo Montresor*.

321   **must waste their sweetness** Entry for 1 August 1832; see Allan Nevins (ed.), *The Diary of Philip Hone 1828–1851*, I (Kraus Reprint, 1969) p. 71.

322   **Rossini's *La Cenerentola*.** Other operas in the repertoire included Rossini's *L'Italiana in Algieri*, Bellini's *Il Pirata*, and *Elisa e Claudio* by Saverio Mercadante.

     A lead soprano For details of the opening season, see Krehbiel, *Chapters of Opera*, pp. 17–19; and Dizikes, *Opera in America*, pp. 74–5.

     the worn and dirty finery Da Ponte in *Storia incredible, ma vera*; quoted in *ibid.*, p. 74.

     Da Ponte was devasted He tells the story, with many a sarcastic aside, in *Storia incredible, ma vera*; quoted in Dizikes, *Opera in America*, p. 74.

     thousands of copies of libretti See Hodges, *Lorenzo Da Ponte*, p. 215.

     The nightingale, mourning From an original and translation held in the Butler Library at Columbia University.

323   *Der Amerika-Müde* See Nettl, *Other Casanova*, pp. 271–3.

324   **to erect upon the land** From a copy of the shareholders' agreement held at the New-York Historical Society.

     first purpose-built opera house It was arguably the first building in the United States designed exclusively for opera. The New Orleans impresario John Davis had built the Orleans Theatre in New Orleans for his French opera company in 1819, but that staged melodrama and sometimes other theatre as well.

Minutes of the association See entries for 8 January 1833 and 1 March 1833; in the Minutes Book held at the New-York Historical Society.

325   **edged out of** Some commentators follow Krehbiel (*Chapters of Opera*, pp. 20–1), who wrote in 1909 that Da Ponte and Rivafonili jointly ran the first season of the new opera house, but Krehbiel offers no evidence of this and would appear to be mistaken. Da Ponte's notices in the press before the opening night quite clearly state that the 'new director' has become his enemy 'for no other reason . . . than because I sustained the rights of Montresor' (*Evening Post*, 16 November 1833), and the minutes and accounts of the Board of Trustees refer only to Rivafonili taking over, making no mention of Da Ponte.

the generous American public See the *New-York Evening Post* for 16 November 1833.

this venerable individual See the *American* for 16 November 1833.

one of the most beautiful From a description reproduced in the *Albion* of 16 November 1833. See also the *Evening Post*, 16 and 19 November 1833, and the *American*, 16, 19 and 21 November 1833. See also Dizikes, *Opera in America*, p. 77.

a style of magnificence Entry for 19 November 1833; Nevins (ed.), *Diary of Philip Hone*, I, pp. 103–4.

consequent straining of necks *American*, 19 November 1833.

326   **To those Americans** Da Ponte, *Frottola per far ridere* (Joseph Desnoues, 1835), pp. 21–3.

327   **final volume of memoirs** Da Ponte mentions this twice, in a letter to Giovanni Perucchini of 24 January 1837, and again to Joseph Staffler on 11 April 1838. If the indignant, accusatory and often self-pitying tone of his final letters carried over into the memoirs, it is possible that his family suppressed them.

ardent promoter According to Samuel Ward in his lengthy obituary in the *New-York Mirror*, 19 September 1838.

I believe that my heart From *Storia incredibile, ma vera*; quoted in Hodges, *Lorenzo Da Ponte*, p. 223.

328   **Dr John W. Francis** See Francis, *Old New York*, p. 264. This is the same Dr Francis who had so admired Da Ponte's skills of oration some years earlier. He was at the time also attending Edgar Allen Poe.

It was one of those afternoons Taken from Ward's obituary in the *New-York Mirror*, 19 September 1838. A slightly different wording is given in his *Sketch of the Life* (p. 20).

The funeral took place *Ibid.*; the *Evening Post*, 21 August 1838; and an eyewitness account by H. T. Tuckerman; quoted in Russo, *Da Ponte*, pp. 137–8.

Obituaries spoke of *Evening Post*, 20 August 1838; *American*, 20 August 1838; *Albion*, 18 August 1838.

329   **moved to Queens** Krehbiel made great efforts to discover Da Ponte's grave in the old Catholic cemetery in 1887, but no trace of a headstone nor any

record of its location remained. Remains disinterred from the cemetery were reburied in the Calvary Cemetery in Queens, where a monument to Da Ponte was erected in 1987.

Appendix I

See Smith, *Italian Opera*; and Milhous et al., *Italian Opera*.

322   **a fellow that yelled** See Robbins Landon, *Notebooks of Joseph Haydn*, pp. 294–5.

Bibliography

A Note on Da Ponte's Memorie

The first three volumes of Da Ponte's *Memorie* were published in New York in 1823; a second, revised and expanded edition appeared in three parts from 1829 to 1830. The first unabridged edition to be published in Italy was brought out in the *Classici Italiani* series Da Ponte so admired, in 1915–16. In 1929, Elisabeth Abbott translated the full text of the *Memorie*, published with annotations by the indefatigable scholar of Da Ponte's American period, Arthur Livingston. This remains the standard English translation (although L. A. Sheppard brought out an abridged translation in England in the same year as Abbott).

Page references in the endnotes are to the *Classici Italiani* edition.

Selected Works of Lorenzo Da Ponte

Discorso Apologetico / Apologetical Discourse on Italy, printed by J. Gray, 1821

An Extract from the Life of Lorenzo Da Ponte, printed by J. Gray, 1819

Frottola per far ridere, printed by Joseph Desnoues, 1835

A History of the Italian Opera Company, Imported to America by Giacomo Montresor, published by the author in two parts, 1833

Lorenzo Da Ponte, Le Memorie (ed. Serafino Paggi), *Classici Italiani*, Istituto Editoriale Italiano, 1916

Memoirs, Lorenzo Da Ponte (trans. Elisabeth Abbott; ed. and annotations Arthur Livingston; preface Charles Rosen), reprinted by the New York Review of Books, 2

Saggi Poetici, Vols I and II, printed by Sordi and Muti; Vol. I only, printed by L. Da Ponte, 1801

Storia Americana, printed by Joseph Desnoues, 1835

Storia Compendiosa della vita Lorenzo Da Ponte / Compendium of the Life of Lorenzo Da Ponte, I. Riley, 1807

Storia incredible, ma vera, published in two parts printed by John Turney / Joseph Desnoues, 1833

Versi composti da Lorenzo Da Ponte per la morte d'Anna Celestina Ernestina, sua virtuosissima e adorate consorte, printed by J. H. Turney, 1832

Manuscripts and Primary Biographical Sources

Bankrupts and Insolvent Debtors, 1710–1869, available at http://www.national archives.gov.uk/catalogue/leaflets/ri2223.htm

King's Theatre Cuttings Book: A collection of cuttings from newspapers relating to the King's and Haymarket Theatres, 1757–1829, British Library, Th.Cts. 41, 42, 43

Lettere (see Zagonel, below)

Letters and documents from the Da Ponte exhibition, held in the Penn State University Libraries

Letters and documents from the New-York Historical Society collection (Verplanck Papers; Minutes of the Board of Trustees of the Italian Opera Association; Papers of the Italian Opera Association (BV Italian Opera); Villiers-Hatton Collection; Documents on Da Ponte's Italian Library)

Letters and documents from the Rare Book and Manuscript Library, Butler Library, Columbia University (General Manuscripts: Da Ponte)

Lorenzo Da Ponte: A Vision of Italy from Columbia College, Columbia University exhibition leaflet, 1991

'Memorie de Lorenzo Da Ponte', from *Antologia*, No. 88, April 1828; also in an English translation by Da Ponte's pupils, printed by Gray and Bunce, 1829

Sketch of the Life of Lorenzo Da Ponte [by Samuel Ward], reprinted from the *New York Mirror*, 29 September 1838

Secondary Sources

Abert, Hermann, *Mozart's Don Giovanni*, Eulenburg Books, 1976

Aderman, Ralph M. et al. (ed.), *Washington Irving, Letters*, Vol. II, Twayne Publishers, 1979

Adkins, Nelson Frederick, *Fitz-Greene Halleck: An Early Knickerbocker Wit and Poet*, Yale University Press, 1930

Anderson, Emily (ed.), *The Letters of Mozart and his Family*, Macmillan, 1989

Anonymous, *A new Moral System of Geography containing An Account of the Different Nations Ancient & Modern*, G. Riley, 1792

Aspinwall, John, *Diary*, see Collins, Aileen

Atti del Convegno Lorenzo Da Ponte [Papers from Columbia University conference of 28–30 March 1988], Ministero per i Beni Culturale e Ambientali, 1988

Barbier, Patrick, *The World of the Castrati*, Souvenir Press, 1998

Baretti, Giuseppe, *An Account of the Manners and Customs of Italy*, T. Davies, 1768

Beales, Derek, *Joseph II*, Vol. I, Cambridge University Press, 1987

— 'Was Joseph II an Enlightened Despot', in *The Austrian Enlightenment and its Aftermath*, ed. Robertson, Ritchie, and Timms, Edward, Austrian Studies II, Edinburgh University Press, 1993

Beaumarchais, Pierre Augustin Caron de, *The Figaro Trilogy*, trans. David Coward, Oxford University Press, 2003

Beckford, William, *The Travel Diaries of William Beckford of Fonthill*, Houghton Mifflin, 1928

Bernier, Olivier, *The World in 1800*, John Wiley & Sons, 2

Black, Jeremy, *The British Abroad: The Grand Tour in the Eighteenth Century*, Sutton Publishing, 2003

Blanning, T. C. W. (ed.), *The Eighteenth Century*, Oxford University Press, 2

Boccardi, Virgilio, *L'Ambiente Teatrale Della Venezia Musicale Del '700*, Filippi Editore, 1998

Brandes, Frances (ed.), *Jewish Itineraries: Venice and Environs*, Marsilio, 1997

Branscombe, Peter, 'The Land of the Piano: Music, Theatre and Performance in Vienna around 1800', in *Theatre and Performance in Austria from Mozart to Jelinek*, ed. Robertson, Ritchie, and Timms, Edward, Austrian Studies IV, Edinburgh University Press, 1993

Braunbehrens, Volkmar, (trans. Timothy Bell), *Mozart in Vienna 1781–1791*, Grove Weidenfeld, 1990

Brogan, Hugh, *The Penguin History of the USA*, Penguin Books, 2001

Bryant, William Cullen, *see* Voss, Thomas G.

Burford, E. J., *Wits, Wenchers and Wantons*, Robert Hale, 1986

Burgess, Anthony, (introduction), *W. A. Mozart: Don Giovanni, Idomeneo*, Cassell, 1970

Burke, Peter, *Popular Culture in Early Modern Europe*, Temple Smith, 1978

Burney, Charles, *Memoirs of the Life and Writings of the Abate Metastasio*, Vol. III, Da Capo Press, 1973

Burney, Charles, *The Present State of Music in France and Italy*, T. Becket and Co., 1773; published as *An Eighteenth-century Musical Tour in France and Italy*, (ed. Percy Scholes), Oxford University Press, 1959

Burney, Frances (Fanny), *Evelina*, Oxford University Press, 1968

Burns, Ric, and Sanders, James, *New York*, Alfred A. Knopf, 2003

Burrows, Donald, and Dunhill, Rosemary, *Music and Theatre in Handel's World*, Oxford University Press, 2002

Burrows, Edwin G., and Wallace, Mike, *Gotham, A History of New York City to 1898*, Oxford University Press, 2

Burton, Elizabeth, *The Georgians at Home*, Arrow Books, 1973

Casanova, Giacomo, *The Story of My Life*, Penguin Books, 2

— *see also* Molmenti; Vèze

Christiansen, Rupert, *Prima Donna*, Pimlico, 1995

Collins, Aileen Sutherland (ed.), *Travels in Britain 1794–1795: The Diary of John Aspinwall*, Parsons Press, 1994

Cusin, Silvio G., and Zorattini, Pier Cesare Ioly, *Jewish Itineraries: Friuli, Venezia Giulia*, Marsilio, 1998

Dent, Edward J., *Mozart's Operas: A Critical Study*, Oxford University Press, 1966

Deutsch, Otto Erich, *Mozart: A Documentary Biography*, Simon & Schuster, 1990

Dietrich, Margret, *Das Burgtheater und sein Publikum*, Der Österreichischen Akademie der Wissenschaften, 1976

Dimond, Peter, *A Mozart Diary: A Chronological Reconstruction of the Composer's Life, 1761–1791*, Greenwood Press, 1997

Di Robilant, Andrea, *A Venetian Affair*, Fourth Estate, 2004

Dizikes, John, *Opera in America*, Yale University Press, 1993

Ebers, John, *Seven Years of the King's Theatre*, W. H. Ainsworth, 1828

Edwards, Philip, *The Story of the Voyage*, Cambridge University Press, 1994

Einstein, Alfred, *Mozart, His Character, His Work*, Grafton Books, 1969

Ellis, Markman, *The Coffee House*, Weidenfeld & Nicolson, 2004

Evans, Hilary, *The Oldest Profession*, David and Charles, 1979

Fiske, Roger, *English Theatre Music in the Eighteenth Century*, Oxford University Press, 1986

FitzLyon, April, *Lorenzo Da Ponte: A Biography of Mozart's Librettist*, John Calder, 1982

Foreman, Amanda, *Georgiana, Duchess of Devonshire*, HarperCollins, 1998

Fortis, Umberto, *The Ghetto on the Lagoon*, Storti Edizioni, 2001

Francis, John W., *Old New York: Reminiscences of the Past Sixty Years*, Charles Roe, 1858

Gay, Peter, *Mozart*, Phoenix, 2003

George, M. Dorothy, *London Life in the XVIIIth Century*, Kegan Paul, 1925

Girdham, Jane, *English Opera in Late Eighteenth-Century London: Stephen Storace at Drury Lane*, Clarendon Press, 1997

Godwin, Parke, *A Biography of William Cullen Bryant*, D. Appleton and Company, 1883

Goede, Christian, *A Foreigner's Opinion of England*, C. Taylor, 1821

Goethe, Johann Wolfgang, *Italian Journey* (trans. W. H. Auden and Elizabeth Mayer), Penguin Books, 1970

Gozzi, Carlo, *Useless Memoirs*, (trans. John Addington Symonds), Oxford University Press, 1962

Halleck, Fitz-Greene, *Poetical Writings*, (reprint of 1869 edition), AMS Press, 1969

Hamm, Charles, *Music in the New World*, Norton, 1983

Hastings, Thomas, *Dissertation on Musical Taste*, Mason Bros, 1853

Haydn, Joseph, *see* Robbins Landon

Heartz, Daniel, 'Nicolas Jadot and the Building of the Burgtheater', in the *Musical Quarterly*, Vol. LXVIII, no. 1, January 1982

Hemphill, C. Dallett, *Bowing to Necessities: A History of Manners in America, 1620–1860*, Oxford University Press, 1999

Hodges, Sheila, *Lorenzo Da Ponte: The Life and Times of Mozart's Librettist*, University of Wisconsin Press, 2002

Hogan, Charles Beecher, *The London Stage 1776–1800: A Critical Introduction*, Southern Illinois University Press, 1968

Holden, Amanda (ed.), *The New Penguin Opera Guide*, Penguin Books, 2001

Holmes, George (ed.), *The Oxford Illustrated History of Italy*, Oxford University Press, 1997

Hone, Philip, *see* Nevins

Hornblow, Arthur, *A History of the Theatre in America from its Beginnings to the Present Time*, J. B. Lippincott, 1919

Howe, Julia Ward, *Reminiscences, 1819–1899*, Negro Universities Press, 1969

Irving, Washington, *Letters of Jonathan Oldstyle, Gent. / Salmagundi*, Twayne Publishers, 1977

—, *see also* Aderman

Israel, Jonathan I., *European Jewry in the Age of Mercantilism, 1550–1750*, Clarendon Press, 1985

Jahn, Otto, *Life of Mozart*, Cooper Square Publishers, 1970

Kelly, Michael, *Reminiscences / Solo Recital*, Folio Society (reprint), 1972

Kerman, Joseph, *Opera as Drama*, Vintage, 1956

Krehbiel, Henry Edward, *Chapters of Opera*, Henry Holt, 1909

Lambert, Richard S., *The Fortunate Traveller*, Andrew Melrose, 1950

Lanapoppi, Aleramo, *Lorenzo Da Ponte, Realtà e leggenda nella vita del librettista di Mozart*, Marsilio, 1992

Laver, James, *Costume and Fashion*, Thames & Hudson, 1969

Lawrence, Vera Brodsky, *Strong on Music*, Vol. I, University of Chicago Press, 1987

Lichtenberg, G. C., *see* Mare

Link, Dorothea, *The National Court Theatre in Mozart's Vienna*, Clarendon Press, 1998

Loewenberg, Alfred, 'Lorenzo Da Ponte in London', in the *Music Review*, Vol. IV, 1943

— 'Some stray notes on Mozart', in *Music and Letters*, Vol. XXIV, 1943

McCalman, Iain, *The Seven Ordeals of Count Cagliostro*, Arrow Books, 2003

Mare, Margaret L., and Quarrell, W. H., (trans.), *Lichtenberg's Visits to England*, Benjamin Blom, 1969

Marroro, Howard, 'Italians in New York During the First Half of the Nineteenth Century', in *New York History*, Vol. XVI, July 1940

Matthews, Brander, *These Many Years: Recollections of a New Yorker*, Charles Scribner's Sons, 1917

Maxted, Ian, *The London Book Trades 1775–1800: A Checklist of Members*

— *The London Book Trades 1775–1800: A Topographical Guide*, both at http://www.devon.gov.uk/etched?_IXP_=1&_IXR=100154#0

May, Henry F., *The Enlightenment in America*, Oxford University Press, 1976

Michtner, Otto, *Das alte Burgtheater als Opernbühne*, Böhlaus, 1970

— 'Der Fall Abbé Da Ponte' in *Mitteilungen des Österreichisches Staatsarchivs*, Vol. XIX, 1966

Milano, Attilio, *Storia degli ebrei in Italia*, Giulio Einaudi, 1963

Milhous, Judith; Dideriksen, Gabriella; Hume, Robert D., *Italian Opera in Late Eighteenth-Century London*, Vol. II, Clarendon Press, 2001 (*see also* Price)

Molmenti, Pompeo (ed.), *Carteggi Casanoviani*, Vols I and II, Remo Sandron, 1917

Monnier, Philippe, *Venice in the Eighteenth Century*, Chatto & Windus, 1910

Mount Edgcumbe Earl of, *Musical Reminiscences*, (fourth edition), John Andrews, 1834

Müller, Ulrich, and Panagl, Oswald, *Don Giovanni in New York*, Ursula Müller-Speiser, 1991

Murphy, Emmett, *Great Bordellos of the World*, Quartet Books, 1983

Nalbach, Daniel, *The King's Theatre 1704–1867*, Society for Theatre Research, 1972

Nettl, Paul, *The Other Casanova*, Da Capo Press, 1970

Nevins, Allan (ed.), *The Diary of Philip Hone 1828–1851*, Kraus Reprint, 1969

Norwich, John Julius, *A History of Venice*, Penguin Books, 2003

— *Paradise of Cities*, Penguin Books, 2003

Odell, G. C. D., *Annals of the New York Stage*, Vol. II, Columbia University Press, 1927

Ottenberg, June C., *Opera Odyssey: Toward a History of Opera in Nineteenth-Century America*, Greenwood Press, 1994

Outram, Dorinda, *The Enlightenment*, Cambridge University Press, 1995

Parreaux, André, *Daily Life in England in the Reign of George III*, George Allen, 1966

Payer von Thurn, Rudolf, *Joseph II als Theaterdirektor*, Leopold Heidrich, 1920

Petty, Frederick C., *Italian Opera in London 1760–1800*, UMI Research Press, 1980

Pezzl, Johann, *see* Robbins Landon

Piozzi, Hester Lynch, *Observations and Reflections*, (ed. Herbert Barrows), Ann Arbor, 1967

Price, Curtis; Milhous, Judith; Hume, Robert D., *Italian Opera in Late Eighteenth-Century London*, Vol. I, Clarendon Press, 1995 (*see also* Milhous)

Raeburn, Christopher, 'An Evening at Schönbrunn', in the *Music Review*, Vol. XVI, 1955

— 'Figaro in Wien', *Österreichische Musikzeitschrift*, July/August 1957

Raeburn, Michael, *The Chronicle of Opera*, Thames & Hudson, 1998

Ravid, Benjamin, *Studies on the Jews of Venice 1382–1797*, Ashgate Variorum, 2003

Rediker, Marcus, *Between the Devil and the Deep Blue Sea*, Cambridge University Press, 1987

Robbins Landon, H. C., *The Collected Correspondence and London Notebooks of Joseph Haydn*, Barrie and Rockliff, 1959

— *Mozart and Vienna: including selections from Johann Pezzl's 'Sketch of Vienna' (1786–90)*, Thames & Hudson, 1991

— *Mozart: The Golden Years, 1781–91*, Thames & Hudson, 1989

Rorato, Giampiero, *La cucina di Carlo Goldoni*, Stamperia di Venezia, 1993

Roberts, Nickie, *Whores in History*, Grafton, 1992

Robinson, Michael F., *Opera Before Mozart*, Hutchinson, 1978

Roth, Cecil, *The History of the Jews of Italy*, Jewish Publication Society of America, 1946

Russo, Joseph Louis, *Lorenzo Da Ponte, Poet and Adventurer*, Columbia University Press, 1922

Sagarra, Eda, *A Social History of Germany 1648–1914*, Methuen, 1977

Smith, William C. (compiler), *The Italian Opera and Contemporary Ballet in London 1789–1820*, Society for Theatre Research, 1955

Smollett, Tobias, *Travels Through France and Italy*, Oxford University Press, 1979

Sokol, Martin L., *The New York City Opera*, Macmillan, 1981

Spaethling, Robert, *Mozart's Letters, Mozart's Life*, Faber and Faber, 2

Spence, Joseph, *Letters from the Grand Tour*, Queen's University Press, 1975

Steinbach, Marion, *Juden in Venedig 1516–1797*, P. Lang, 1992

Steptoe, Andrew, *The Mozart–Da Ponte Operas*, Clarendon Press, 2001

— 'Mozart and Poverty: a re-examination of the evidence', in the *Musical Times*, Vol. CXXV, no. 1694, April 1984

— 'Mozart, Mesmer and *Così fan tutte*', in *Music & Letters*, Vol. LXVII, no. 3, July 1986

— 'The Sources of *Così fan tutte*: a Reappraisal', in *Music & Letters*, Vol. LXII, 1981

Stevick, Philip, *Imagining Philadelphia*, University of Pennsylvania Press, 1996

Still, Bayrd, *Mirror for Gotham*, Fordham University Press, 1994

Struble, George, 'Lorenzo Da Ponte Our Neglected Genius', *Northumberland County Historical Society: Proceedings*, Vol. XVI, 1948

Till, Nicholas, *Mozart and the Enlightenment*, Faber and Faber, 1992

Toffoli, Aldo, 'Lorenzo Da Ponte e Ceneda', in *Atti del Convegno Lorenzo Da Ponte*, Ministero per i Beni Culturale e Ambientali, 1988

Townson, Robert, *Travels in Hungary in the Year 1793*, G. G. and J. Robinson, 1797

Vaussard, Maurice, *Daily Life in Eighteenth Century Italy*, Allen & Unwin, 1962

Vèze, Raoul, (ed.), *Mémoires de J. Casanova de Seingalt*, La Sirène, 1924–35

Villanova, Girolamo, *Serravalle nella storia e nell'arte*, Piave, 1977

Volpi, E. Cav., *Storia intime di Venezia Repubblica*, Filippi Editore (reprint of 1893 edition), 1984

Voss, Thomas G. (ed.), *The Letters of William Cullen Bryant*, Fordham University Press, 1975

Vovelle, Michel (ed.), *Enlightenment Portraits*, University of Chicago Press, 1997

Wolf, Edwin, *Philadelphia: Portrait of an American City*, Stackpole Books, 1975

Woodfield, Ian, *Opera and Drama in Eighteenth-Century London*, Cambridge University Press, 2001

Woodman, Thomas, *Politeness and Poetry in the Age of Pope*, Fairleigh Dickinson University Press, 1989

Yates, W. E., *Theatre in Vienna: A Critical History 1776–1995*, Cambridge University Press, 1996

Zagonel, Giampaolo, '*Felice Da Ponte, Il figlio naturale che il liberettista di Mozart ebbe a Vienna*', in *Il Flaminio*, Vol. VIII, 1995

— *Lorenza Da Ponte, Bibliografia*, (ed.), Dario De Bastiane Editore, 1999

— *Lorenzo Da Ponte, Lettere, epistole in versi, decicatorie e lettere dei fratelli*, (ed.), Dario De Bastiani Editore, 1995

Zobel, Konrad, and Warner, Frederick E., 'The Old Burgtheater: A Structural History, 1741–1888', in *Theatre Studies*, Vol. XIX, 1972/3.

Index

A NOTE ON THE TYPE

The text of this book is set in Bembo. This type
was first used in 1495 by the Venetian printer Aldus
Manutius for Cardinal Bembo's *De Aetna*, and was
cut for Manutius by Francesco Griffo. It was one
of the types used by Claude Garamond (1480–1561)
as a model for his Romain de L'Université, and so it
was the forerunner of what became standard
European type for the following two centuries. Its
modern form follows the original types and was
designed for Monotype in 1929.